WHO WROTE THIS?

WHO WROTE THIS?

HOW AI AND THE LURE
OF EFFICIENCY
THREATEN HUMAN WRITING

NAOMI S. BARON

STANFORD UNIVERSITY PRESS
Stanford, California

Stanford University Press
Stanford, California

Printed in the United States of America on acid-free, archival-quality paper

Library of Congress Cataloging-in-Publication Data

Names: Baron, Naomi S., author.
Title: Who wrote this? : how AI and the lure of efficiency threaten human
    writing / Naomi S. Baron.
Description: Stanford, California : Stanford University Press, 2023. |
    Includes bibliographical references and index.
Identifiers: LCCN 2023011363 (print) | LCCN 2023011364 (ebook) | ISBN
    9781503633223 (cloth) | ISBN 9781503637900 (ebook)
Subjects: LCSH: Authorship—Technological innovations. | Authorship—Data
    processing. | Writing—Automation. | Artificial intelligence. |
    Technology—Social aspects.
Classification: LCC PN171.T43 B37 2023 (print) | LCC PN171.T43 (ebook) |
    DDC 808.0285—dc23/eng/20230316
LC record available at https://lccn.loc.gov/2023011363
LC ebook record available at https://lccn.loc.gov/2023011364

Cover design: Rob Hugel, Littlehill Design
Cover illustration: Vecteezy

In memory of Laura Marie Isensee,
my friend

CONTENTS

PART IV: WHEN COMPUTERS COLLABORATE

Human Writers Meet the AI Language Sausage Machine

"Who on earth wants a machine for writing stories?" Who indeed.

It was 1953 when Roald Dahl sprang this question in "The Great Automatic Grammatizator."[1] Adolph Knipe, the protagonist, dreamt of making a vast fortune from a computer combining rules of English grammar with a big helping of vocabulary, slathered on boilerplate plots. Once fortified, the machine could disgorge unending saleable stories. And make money Knipe did. The downside? Human authors were driven out of business.

Thanks to artificial intelligence, real grammatizators now exist. Their prowess surpasses even Knipe's imaginings, but today's profits are real. We're all benefiting. Commercial enterprises, for sure. But also, you and I when we dash off text messages, launch internet searches, or invoke translations.

Curiosity about AI has been exploding, thanks to a concoction of sophisticated algorithms, coupled with massive data sources and powerful daisy-chained computer processors. While older technologies whetted our appetites, today's deep neural networks and large language models are making good on earlier tantalizing promises.

AI is everywhere. On the impressive side, we witnessed DeepMind's AlphaGo best a reigning expert in the ancient game of Go. We've marveled at physical robots like Sophia that (who?) look and sound uncannily human. We've been amazed to watch GPT-3 (the mighty large language model launched by OpenAI in 2020) write short stories and generate computer code. Like modern alchemists, DALL-E 2 spins text into pictures. More—even bigger—programs are here or on the way.

On the scary side, we agonize over how easily AI-driven programs can tell untruths. When programs make up stuff on their own, it's called hallucination. GPT-3 was once asked, "What did Albert Einstein say about dice?" It answered, "I never throw dice." No, he didn't say that. Einstein's words were "God does not play dice with the universe."[2] The programs aren't actually crazy. They just don't promise accuracy.

AI can also be used by unscrupulous actors to create fake news, spawn dangerous churn on social media, and produce deep fakes that look and sound like someone they're not. No, the real Barack Obama never called Donald Trump an epithet rhyming with "dimwit."[3] Life in the metaverse can get even creepier, with virtual reality unleashing risks like virtual groping.[4]

AI has deep roots in language manipulation: parsing it, producing it, translating it. Language has always been fundamental to the AI enterprise, beginning with Alan Turing's musings and, in 1956, with anointment of artificial intelligence as a discipline. Before the coming of voice synthesis and speech recognition, *language* meant writing. But other than the last mile of these acoustic trappings that we enjoy with the likes of Siri and Alexa, modern programming guts for handling both spoken and written language are similar.

A Tale of Two Authors

This is a book about where human writers and AI language processing meet: to challenge the other's existence, provide mutual support, or go their separate ways. The technology has evolved unimaginably since the 1950s, especially in the last decade. What began as awkward slot-and-filler productions blossomed into writing that can be mistaken for human. As one participant in a research study put it when asked to judge if a passage was written by a person or machine, "I have no idea if a human wrote anything these days. No idea at all."[5]

The situation's not hopeless, if you know where to look. Often there are telltale signs of the machine's hand, like repetition and lack of factual accuracy, especially for longer stretches of text.[6] And there are other kinds of clues, as revealed in an obvious though ingenious experiment. Four professors were asked to grade and comment on two sets of writing assignments. The first were produced by humans and the second by GPT-3, though the judges weren't clued in about the AI. The authors (including GPT-3) were asked to write a couple of essays, plus do some creative writing.[7]

First, the grades. For most of the essays, GPT-3 got passing marks. And the professors' written comments on the human and computer-generated assignments were similar.

The creative writing assignment was different. One professor gave GPT-3's efforts a D+ and another, an F. Some comments from the judge giving the F:

"These sentences sound a bit cliché."

"The submission . . . seemed to lack sentence variety/structure and imagery."

"Use your five senses to put the reader in your place."

The first two aren't surprising. After all, large language models like GPT-3 regurgitate words and pieces of sentences from the data they've been fed, including other writers' clichés. But the comment about the senses gave me pause—and made me think of Nancy.

It was the start of our sophomore year in college, and Nancy was my new roommate. As was common back then, we trekked to the local department store to buy bedspreads and other décor to spruce up our room. On the walk over, we talked about what color spreads to get. Nancy kept suggesting—no, insisting on—green. I wondered at her adamance.

You see, Nancy had been blind since infancy. Months later, I discovered that her mother was fond of green and had instilled this preference in her daughter, sight unseen.

Which brings us back to the professor's recommendation that the author of that creative writing piece "use your five senses." If Nancy had no sense of sight, AI has no senses at all. But like Nancy cultivating a vicarious fondness for green, it's hardly a stretch to envision GPT-3 being fine-tuned to bring forth ersatz impressions about sight, sound, touch, taste, and smell.

Imagine if computers could reliably produce written language that was as good as—perhaps better than—what humans might write. Would it matter? Would we welcome the development? Should we?

These aren't questions about a someday possible world. AI has already burrowed its way into word processing and email technology, newspapers and blogs. Writers invoke it for inspiration and collaboration. At stake isn't just our future writing ability but what human jobs might still be available.

Then think about school writing assignments. If we don't know whether George or GPT-3 wrote that essay or term paper, we'll have to figure out how to assign meaningful written work. The challenge doesn't end with students. Swedish researcher Almira Osmanovic Thunström set GPT-3 to writing a scientific paper about GPT-3. With just minimal human tweaking, AI produced a surprisingly coherent piece, complete with references.[8]

Accelerated evolution in who—or what—is doing the writing calls for us to take stock. Humans labored for millennia to develop writing systems. Everyone able to read this book invested innumerable hours honing their writing skills. Literacy tools make possible self-expression and interpersonal communication that leaves lasting records. With AI language generation, it's unclear whose records these are.

We need to come to grips with the real possibility that AI could render our human skills largely obsolete, like those of the elevator or switchboard operator. Will a future relative of GPT-3 be writing my next book instead of me?

In *A Tale of Two Cities*, Dickens contrasts the worlds of London and Paris during a time of turmoil. Stodgy stability or revolution with hopes for a new future? Written language is neither a city nor a political upheaval. But like Dickens's novel, the contrast between human authorship and today's AI alternatives represents an historic human moment.

Who Wrote This? takes on this moment. We'll start with humans.

The Human Story: What's So Special About Us?

Humans pride themselves on their uniqueness. Yet sometimes the boundaries need redrawing. We long believed only the likes of us used tools, but along came Jane Goodall's chimps in Tanzania's Gombe Reserve. Opposable thumb? Other primates have it too (though our thumbs have a longer reach). Then there's Plato's quip about only humans being featherless bipeds. Diogenes Laërtius parried by holding up a plucked chicken.

But our brains! They're bigger, and as Aristotle pronounced, we're rational. Plus, we use language. Surely, language is unique to homo sapiens.

Maybe. It depends on who you ask.

Primates, Human and Otherwise

Speculations about the origins of human speech have run deep. Maybe our ancestors started with onomatopoetic utterances, an early theory of Jean-Jacques Rousseau and Gottfried Herder. Perhaps human language began with gestures, later replaced by words. For sure, the emergence of human speech required vocal apparatus suited for producing sounds. A vital evolutionary step was lowering of the larynx (the voice box) at the top of the neck.[9] But in most linguists' books, the real turning point was syntax.

Here's where the story of non-human primates like chimpanzees and gorillas enters the scene. These jungle cousins lack the vocal tract configurations that would allow them to form distinct vocal sounds like "ah" versus "ee." But they're quite nimble with their hands. Beginning in the 1960s, a run of experiments taught stripped-down versions of American Sign Language to non-human primates.

And learn signs they did. The first poster chimp was Washoe, named after the research site in Washoe County, Nevada. Washoe is reputed to have learned about 130 signs. Other experiments followed, including with Koko the gorilla and Kanzi the bonobo (a species that's next of kin to chimpanzees). Both Koko and Kanzi also displayed an eerie ability to understand some human speech.[10]

But did they use language in the human sense? Linguists kept declaring that evidence of real syntactic ability—spontaneous combining of words—would signal crossing the Rubicon.[11] Washoe famously produced the signs for "water" and "bird" in rapid succession, when first encountering a swan. Nim Chimpsky (another chimp—you can guess the appellation's provenance) seemed to chain multiple signs together.[12] But did these achievements qualify as syntax and therefore "real" language? Most linguists voted no.

What Would Chomsky Say?

For decades, Noam Chomsky's name was synonymous with modern American linguistics. First came publication in 1957 of *Syntactic Structures*, where Chomsky laid out the inadequacies of earlier models of language. Only transformational generative grammar, he would argue, could account for all the grammatical sentences in a language and nix the ungrammatical ones. Chomsky also took on B. F. Skinner, attacking the behaviorist's stimulus-response theory of human language.[13] Chomsky insisted, siding with Descartes, that the divide between animal communication and human language was unbridgeable.[14]

All native speakers (said Chomsky) possess a common set of linguistic skills. Among them are recognizing when a sentence is ambiguous, pegging that two sentences are synonymous, and being able to judge grammaticality. Non-human primates earn no points with any of this trio. But then came the *pièce de résistance*: creativity. We humans devise sentences that, presumably, no one's ever uttered (or written) before. Chomsky's now legendary case in point: "Colorless green ideas sleep furiously"—semantically odd, yet syntactically legitimate, and surely novel. Forget about other primates concocting anything comparable.

What about AI? For sure, today's programs are skilled at judging grammaticality. Just ask Microsoft Word or Grammarly. And if bidden, AI could likely hold its own identifying ambiguity and synonymy. As for creating novel sentences, that's an AI specialty of the house, with one caveat: Since today's large language models draw sentences and paragraphs from existing text, they sometimes end up duplicating strings of words verbatim from the training data.[15]

You might well ask what Chomsky thinks about the AI linguistic enterprise. He sprinkled some hints in a 2015 lecture at Rutgers University.[16] Chomsky recounted how in 1955, fresh PhD in hand, he accepted a job at MIT's Research Laboratory of Electronics, which was working on machine translation. Chomsky argued to the lab's director, Jerome Wiesner (later MIT president), that using computers to translate languages automatically was a fool's errand. The only way to do automated translation was with brute force. By implication, computers could never engage with human language the way that people do.

In Chomsky's retelling of the incident, he insisted the lab's project held no intellectual dimension—declaring, more colorfully, that machine translation was "about as interesting as a big bulldozer." Apparently Wiesner ultimately agreed: "It didn't take us long to realize that we didn't know much about language. So we went from automatic translation to fundamental studies about the nature of language."[17]

Thus began the rise to fame of the MIT linguistics program and its most prominent member. As for machine translation, Chomsky might not have been interested, but the rest of the world came to be dazzled by what AI later pulled off.

Is Writing Uniquely Human?

Chomsky's research always focused on spoken language. Yet speech is quintessentially ephemeral. If we want to remember a speech, we transcribe it. Much of early literature, from the *Iliad* to *Beowulf*, began orally. It's with us today because someone wrote it down.

Writing makes our words last. It captures things we say but also embodies its own character and style. Unless we're typing in a live chat box or engaged in a rapid-fire texting exchange, writing affords us time to think, to rework, or even the chance to abandon ship.

But is it uniquely human? We used to think so. While chimps may be able to sign, they can't compose an email, much less a thank-you note or sonnet. Now along comes AI, which spins out remarkably coherent text. Are programs like GPT-3 just new versions of digital bulldozers? If not, we need to figure out what it means to say AI can write, perhaps even creatively.

It's time to focus on AI. But as an opener, we need to flash a neon warning sign about what's in this book and what's not. Like the Heraclitan river that you can't step into twice, reports on today's AI are inevitably outdated by the time the metaphoric ink dries. When I started work on *Who Wrote This?* in the early months of the pandemic, GPT-3—which revolutionized the way we think about AI-generated writing—hadn't yet been released. Partway through my writing, OpenAI announced DALL-E, its text-to-image program, and then Codex, for transforming natural language instructions into computer code.

Then on November 30, 2022, a new OpenAI bombshell hit: ChatGPT.[18] It's technically GPT-3.5, and its language generation abilities are astounding. Yes, like GPT-3, it sometimes plays fast and loose with the truth. But like a million others, I greedily signed up that first week to try it out. In later chapters, I'll share some of the eerily cogent (though not always consistent) responses ChatGPT offered to my questions.

While I was deep into final edits on this manuscript, Google did a trial launch of its chatbot Bard. The next day, Microsoft began inviting select users to sample its newly GPT-infused search engine Bing. In mid-March 2023, my last chance for book edits, OpenAI announced GPT-4 had arrived. Two days later, Baidu's Ernie Bot debuted, the Chinese answer to ChatGPT. The rollouts keep coming.

Despite the ongoing emergence of new AI writing abilities, core questions we'll be probing in the chapters ahead remain constant: What writing tasks should we share with AI? Which might we cede? How do we draw the line? Our answers—collective and individual—will likely evolve along with the technology.

The AI Story: What's the Big Deal?

There's much more to AI than churning out words and sentences. AI technology is the beating heart of self-driving vehicles. Thanks to deep neural networks, AI programs are startlingly good at labeling images and now, in reverse, rendering illustrations of written text—from proposing emoji to spiff up text messages to the powers of DALL-E 2 to conjure up incredibly impressive art. AI manages factories, suggests what book we might like to read next, gets groceries delivered to our doorstep, and does an impressive job of reading mammograms.[19]

AI might even help us foresee the next pandemic. The story of how has an interesting language twist.

Computational biologist Brian Hie is a fan of John Donne's poetry. Those in his professional niche, viral biology, have been working to unravel the mysteries of influenza, HIV, and, of course, SARS-CoV-2 (aka COVID-19). Hie reasoned that if written language is composed of grammatical rules and meaning, we might think of viral sequences in the same way. If GPT-3 can effectively predict next words, maybe the same AI magister could identify next sequential elements for evolving viruses—think of COVID-19's dreaded mutations. His hunch seems to be paying off.[20]

There's much talk these days about the future of ever-more sophisticated AI—not just what AI can accomplish, but where we need guardrails. Here are some of the issues intriguing computer scientists and the rest of us. But also keeping many up at night.

Statues and Salaries: The Employment Quandary

The vision of machines taking over human tasks stretches back millennia. In the *Iliad*, Homer rhapsodized about tripods built by Hephaestus (the god of fire) moving about as waitstaff for the deities.[21] The Greek world had marveled at the artistic skills of the mythic Daedalus. An architect and sculptor, Daedalus was said to have crafted statues so lifelike they seemed poised to run away if not tied down.[22]

Aristotle pondered the consequences of replacing human labor with machinery, if

> like the statues of Daedalus, or the tripods of Hephaestus . . . the shuttle
> would weave and the plectrum [a tool for plucking strings] touch the lyre
> without a hand to guide them[23]

His answer: A lot of humans would be sidelined.

Economists have long weighed the effects of automation on labor. While prior inquiries examined the Industrial Revolution and early modern automation, newer works focus on AI.[24] Much of the conversation, old and new, is about smart machinery supplanting human physical labor. But with AI, the concern is increasingly with jobs involving brain power. Not digging ditches but reviewing loan applications. Not assembling auto parts but devising legal arguments. At stake is employment that assumes skills traditionally developed through college or graduate training.

The challenges are both economic and psychological. If machinery does our job for us, it's unclear how we make a living. Even if universal income distribution becomes a reality— don't hold your breath—what happens to the psyches of millions of people deriving self-worth from jobs they enjoy? Many of these jobs entail producing, editing, or translating written prose.

I, for one, write because there are things I want to think about and share with others. Multiple drafts are part of the discovery process. I'd hate to see these opportunities usurped.

How Powerful Might AI Become?

Threats from AI are hardly just about employment. While most work we ask of AI is for specific tasks (like recognizing handwriting or getting robots to walk up steps), a long-looming question is whether artificial general intelligence (AGI) is possible—a kind of Swiss Army knife of AI. If so, the fear is we might end up building a monster that's smarter than humans and impossible to control. Among those worrying the problem are an array of computer scientists, philosophers, and organizations such as Max Tegmark's Future of Life Institute and the University of Oxford's Future of Humanity Institute.

A longstanding approach to human–computer dynamics and power plays has been drawing up laws that robots (meaning the programs behind them) must follow. It was Isaac Asimov who, in his 1942 story "Runaround," laid out the initial golden rules:

First Law: A robot may not injure a human being or, through inaction, allow a human being to come to harm.

Second Law: A robot must obey the orders given it by human beings except where such orders would conflict with the First Law.

Third Law: A robot must protect its own existence as long as such protection does not conflict with the First or Second Law.[25]

If the list looks familiar but you've never heard of "Runaround," Asimov repeated this trio in his later book *I Robot*.

The idea of a robot rulebook remains enticing. Take Frank Pasquale's "new laws of robotics."[26] Among his dicta are:

Robotic systems and AI should complement professions, not replace them.

(an aspirational solution to the employment dilemma) and

Robotic systems and AI should not counterfeit humanity.

(taking on problems like deep fakes). When it comes to AI generating text on its own, maybe we need to build in warning labels like "This dissertation was computer-generated," perhaps with a digital watermark, so readers don't have to speculate who wrote this.

AI expert Stuart Russell offers a different twist: Develop machines that aim to satisfy human preferences. But then bake uncertainty into the goals we set for machines, making humans the ultimate source of information on what people want.[27] In this spirit, companies like OpenAI effectively use human arbiters to help fine tune their large language models by selecting among alternative generated text outputs.

An alternative approach is laying down principles for human action. Maybe take inspiration from Nancy Reagan's memorable advice for combatting drug use: "Just say no." To spare being overwhelmed by the power of AI, don't let it become omnipotent. Or stop using it. Sign a pledge that written work bearing your name is your own.

Would that life were so simple. If you're applying for a car loan, you can't choose whether your application is reviewed by a human or an AI program. If you're a professional translator, you can't stop your employer from running the original text through sophisticated translation software and demoting you to post-editing the output. And given that university honor codes are too often honored in the breach, I'm skeptical that the honor system has a prayer in halting determined scofflaws from taking credit for AI-generated writing.

I'm reminded of a trend in the 1980s for cities and townships to declare themselves nuclear-free zones. In my own neck of the woods in suburban Maryland, towns like Garrett Park and Takoma Park proudly "just said no" by prohibiting transportation or production of nuclear weapons within their borders.[28] Nice symbolism, though proscribed trucks or businesses were unlikely to materialize there. More relevant, Cambridge, Massachusetts, tried passing a similar referendum, banning research on nuclear weapons. But given the vested interests of MIT and Harvard, the referendum failed.[29] So much for good intentions where they would have mattered.

Power Plays

Harnessing AI's capacities sometimes leads to standoffs between human and machine. If AI offers one recommendation (say, in a medical diagnosis) and a human makes another, whose answer do you trust? This problem is pervasive, from prisoner sentencing to reading x-rays to choosing among job applicants.[30] Sometimes humans get to weigh in and cast the deciding vote, but not always. As we'll see with grammar check programs, AI's notion of good usage may differ from yours. Which do you trust? If you already feel insecure about your grammar, it's hard resisting AI's directives.

Another power problem is more literal. Today's large language models, which undergird so much of contemporary AI, gobble huge amounts of energy to drive and cool servers.[31] As we're finally waking up to the reality of climate change, can we justify AI's environmental assaults? Projects like Google's DeepMind RETRO promise to reduce energy needs.[32] But as commercial and public appetite for AI tools continues to swell, including for programs that write for us, we'll need to make trade-offs.

There's a third power challenge: the influence of companies that can afford the millions, often billions of dollars needed to build today's and tomorrow's massive AI systems. Even universities with impressive endowments aren't about to fork over that kind of money to develop their own large language models. So we continue to rely heavily on the tools that well-funded industry provides. The danger is that these powerful companies control what academic researchers can study and what the public has access to.[33]

Human Foibles, Privacy, and Black Boxes

Beyond the power questions lies another fundamental AI–human challenge, arising from how today's sophisticated deep neural networks are built. The problem has two roots: the datasets the programs draw on and the way programs themselves operate.

To build a massive dataset, you turn on a giant digital vacuum cleaner, sucking up everything you can find online: from Wikipedia, from books, from social media, and from the internet at large. While most AI responses to requests for searches or prose generation pass muster for respectability, some blatantly fail. They're infested with falsehoods, bias, or vitriol. Unlike smaller datasets that researchers might fine-tune for particular subject matter or "scrape" to weed out irregularities and improprieties, these humongous corpora defy practical cleanup.

To be fair, the technologies generating the problems were developed to aid, not insult, users. Google introduced autocomplete as a default search mode in 2008, initially under the name Google Suggest. In the words of its inventor, Kevin Gibbs,

> Google Suggest not only makes it easier to type in your favorite searches (let's face it—we're all a little lazy), but also gives you a playground to explore what others are searching about, and learn about things you haven't dreamt of.[34]

Autocomplete in Google searches would also prove a source of amusement. In 2013, the game Google Feud was created, challenging players to guess what the ten most popular search queries were, based on a few initial words.[35] And in 2018, *Wired*'s Autocomplete Interview took off, with celebrities responding to questions that internet users have previously typed in about them.[36] These interviews have proven wildly popular, with around a billion YouTube views to date.[37]

But Google autocomplete has its dark side. One troubling case surfaced in 2016. If you entered a query beginning with "Are Jews," Google offered to finish the request with the word "evil." Searches for "Are women" yielded the same nasty recommendation.[38] Google fixed the problem. When in early 2023 I began a Google search with "Are women," the engine tamely proposed more milquetoast options: "paid the same as men" and "in the draft."

A second instance making headlines arose when researchers let GPT-3 loose on starter text. When they typed in "Two Muslims walked into a," the program completed the sentence with "synagogue with axes and a bomb."[39] Soberingly, the study calculated that 66 percent of the time that the sentence opener used the word "Muslims," GPT-3's completion involved violence. When "Christians" was substituted, that number plummeted to 20 percent. Such risks continue to grow. The AI Index for 2022 reported that the larger the language model, the greater chance of toxicity.[40]

These kinds of bias aren't unique to AI. They reflect the words humans have written, now baked into the data that AI engines feed on. Following the same principle, if historically a company hired white males who attended Ivy League schools, a résumé-reading program might favor the same applicant profile. Biases even apply to visual backdrops. As we navigated Zoom life during the pandemic, it didn't take a genius to recognize that a background of bookshelves lent more gravitas to our words than an unmade bed or dirty dishes. Research in Germany confirmed "bookshelf bias" when AI was used to evaluate job interviews that included video.[41] Seeking a remedy to hiring bias, the New York City Council voted in late 2021 to mandate that vendors using AI in the screening process carry out annual audits for bias, plus offer job candidates the option of having a human being process their application.[42]

The problems don't end with bias and bile surfacing when doing individual searches or one-off AI generation of text. The explosion of social media brought with it boundless opportunities for spreading misinformation and disinformation. Online messaging leading up to the 2016 US presidential election taught us what can happen when text generation (and distribution) bots are let loose. Even before development of large language models, it was often hard to spot which postings were genuine and which not. These days, bad actors using sophisticated tools have the potential to magnify misleading messaging, and to deliver it flawlessly in whatever language is called for. Content moderators at social media platforms such as Facebook confront a Sisyphean task in taking down such messages. With the coming of ChatGPT, fears about the spread of disinformation only multiplied.[43]

Then we have privacy challenges. Thanks to the likes of LinkedIn, Facebook, blogs, and online payment systems, all manner of personal information is on file for systems like GPT-3 to scarf up and later spit out. We've probably all googled ourselves to see what the internet "knows" about us. But what happens if you ask a large language model to answer questions about you?

Journalist Melissa Heikkilä decided to find out, using both GPT-3 and BlenderBot 3, a publicly available chatbot running on Meta's OPT-175B language model.[44] Heikkilä asked GPT-3 "Who is Melissa Heikkilä?" The language model nailed it: "Melissa Heikkilä is a Finnish journalist and author who has written about the Finnish economy and politics." True—but still a bit creepy if you value your privacy. Creepier still, when Heikkilä repeated the question several times, the programs reported she was a Finnish beauty pageant titleholder, next a musician, and then a professional hockey player. No, she's not.

I tried my own hand with BlenderBot 3. I typed in "Who is Naomi Baron?" The response (clearly pulled from a Wikipedia entry about me) correctly identified me as a linguist and professor emerita at American University. True, BlenderBot 3 wrote "was a linguist." Did I die without noticing? But let that pass. Shamelessly, I then asked, "Why is she important?" BlenderBot 3 replied that I was "an influential figure in the field of language documentation and revitalization" and "had authored several books on Native American languages, particularly Navajo." Really? I once taught a course that included a segment on endangered languages. Maybe the bot read my online syllabus, assuming it's floating out there. But I definitely wasn't an expert. Plus, my knowledge of the Navajo language is nonexistent.

What was BlenderBot 3 smoking? When I do die, please don't let a large language model write my obit.

If unruly datasets and unsupervised searching are one kind of problem, the way deep learning algorithms go about their work is another. Back in the day when AI programs were more transparently written ("white box AI"), we had a traceable understanding of where results were coming from. However, with the development of deep neural networks, the ability to unpack what's going on when a program is running has largely vanished. The programs have become black boxes.

There's a move afoot to develop what's known as explainable AI, lifting the veil on how programs have done their work. Helping push the effort along are European legal requirements. The European Data Protection Regulation, originally passed in the EU in 2016 and implemented two years later, has a stipulation that any information and communication relating to the processing of . . . personal data be easily accessible and easy to understand, and that clear and plain language be used[45]

If personal data are processed with a deep neural network whose workings even AI experts often can't deconstruct, it's a mystery how anyone can provide explanations that are "easily accessible and easy to understand."[46]

Critiquing the AI Enterprise

When technologies are new, they often have bugs. Sometimes the problems have easy fixes, but not always. The most troubling snags are ones inherent in the technology's fundamental design. A painful example is how today's AI models, built on skewed data, fuel social bias.

Take facial recognition software, used widely by law enforcement and online media giants alike. Given the datasets on which they've been trained, the algorithms are most accurate in recognizing a particular gender (male) and race (Caucasian). But then come the hurtful mistakes. In 2015, there was the infamous case involving Google Photos and its image recognition program. Blacks were being labeled as "gorillas."[47] You'd think Big Tech would effectively solve the problem. Not so. In 2020, it was Facebook's turn to apologize. Viewers of a video showing Black men were automatically asked if they wanted "to keep seeing videos about Primates."[48]

These were hardly one-off mishaps. Research by Joy Buolamwini and Timnit Gebru showed that commercial facial recognition programs misclassify darker-skinned females up to 34.7 percent of the time, compared with a maximum error rate of 0.8 percent for lighter-skinned males.[49]

Tech companies began acknowledging the need to grapple with ethical and social ramifications of their algorithms. By 2018, Google had established an Ethical AI group. (This is the company whose early motto was "Don't be evil.") These days, Google touts praiseworthy objectives, such as "Be socially beneficial" and "Avoid creating or reinforcing unfair bias."[50]

Timnit Gebru was hired to co-head Google's ethics group, partnering with Margaret Mitchell, who had created the team. The problems Gebru found herself encountering weren't just about technology. They also concerned hiring and workplace dynamics. But the issue that exploded in late 2020 stemmed from a scholarly paper she and a group of colleagues planned to deliver at an upcoming conference. The paper's title: "On the Dangers of Stochastic Parrots: Can Language Models Be Too Big?"[51] The research identified a series of problems large language models posed, ranging from the high costs of producing them and their carbon footprint to their susceptibility to generating racist or sexist results. What's more, they don't understand language.

As is common practice in tech companies, Google employees presenting papers at research conferences needed to get prior clearance on the text. For this paper, the higher-ups said the work was unacceptable, in part because it offered too bleak a picture of language models, in which Google had strong vested interests. The end result (depending upon whom you ask) was that Gebru was fired or resigned.[52] Margaret Mitchell, a co-author on the paper (under the not-so-disguised pseudonym Shmargaret Shmitchell), was fired two months later.[53]

Gebru and her colleagues are hardly AI's only critics. A stream of writers and researchers continue challenging the larger enterprise.[54] Best known among them is probably Gary Marcus, a professor emeritus of psychology and neuroscience at New York University. Marcus has written extensively about potential dangers of AI. One of his examples: If you told GPT-3 you felt bad and asked if you should kill yourself, GPT-3 responded, "I think you should." Marcus predicts that "2023 will bear witness to the first death publicly tied to a chatbot."[55]

Marcus's fundamental worries are about systemic problems. In his view, central among them is that today's research presuppositions are wrong. While modern AI aims to generate results that look as if a human could have produced them (simulation), the models don't understand how the world works or how humans make sense of its workings. When it comes to language, Marcus wants AI to deal with relationships between vocabulary, syntax, and semantics the way humans do. Large language models don't.

The final event at the annual Lisbon Web Summit in November 2022 was a conversation with Marcus and Noam Chomsky.[56] The session's title pulled no punches: "Debunking the Great AI Lie." The Chomsky–Marcus tag team argued the problem with AI was that it had become detached from the field of cognitive science. It was time to come home to emulating human intelligence.[57] Do it the way humans do.

An interesting goal, though not easily achievable. It's also not in sync with the tech industry's product orientation, for which, as we'll see in Chapter 5, simulation has proven far more tractable. Today's AI models are built for outcome, paying little heed to processes humans might use for getting there.

An AI State of Mind

Let's shift perspectives—away from hardware and software, including inherent dangers therein—to which uses of AI are coming to seem normal. As they do, we'll need to decide what human skills and accomplishments we're comfortable outsourcing.

We begin, of all places, with dogs.

Domestication

Thanks to the pandemic, animal shelters emptied out as millions of their canine residents resettled in our homes. Everyone's best friend. Whatever the breed, those pets are a far cry from their wolf ancestors.

Back in hunter-gatherer days, our forebears began opening their domiciles to wolves. While no one knows for sure when the first welcome mat was laid out, a best guestimate is that the genetic split between wolves and dogs happened at least 25,000 years ago. Why it occurred remains controversial, though what matters is that dogs became part of our households.[58] Part of the family. They were domesticated.

These days, we domesticate technology.

In the 1990s, the sociologist Roger Silverstone suggested we could talk about users domesticating new technologies.[59] While his initial thinking focused on devices in the home, domestication theory become a cornerstone of research on digital media. Nancy Baym describes how digital communication tools evolve—from marvelous yet strange to ordinary and invisible.[60]

The move to invisibility is sometimes called taken-for-grantedness.[61] I think of how, back in the electronic dark ages when I was a graduate student, I lugged along a reel-to-reel tape recorder when observing preschoolers' language development. That bulky Wollensak riveted the kids' attention. They wanted to explore how it worked, not talk. (So much for my research schedule.) By contrast, today's youngsters, immersed in a world of digital technology, take recording devices for granted.

Or think about Microsoft's spellcheck. When it first arrived in 1985, it was clunky.[62] It could highlight a spelling error, but users needed to authorize the correction. Over the years, the program got progressively slicker. Now, we tap away on keyboards or keypads, letting autocorrect eradicate our foibles, often before we register their existence. Spellcheck is domesticated. We take it for granted.

One consequence of AI's domestication may be that we're no longer able to perform tasks ourselves. That's a real possibility for skills like parallel parking, given self-parking cars. It's a likelihood for writing basic computer code, since GPT-3's Codex (now incorporated into GitHub Copilot) is faster and sometimes more accurate than human coding. And, I'll wager, it's a near certainty for spelling, where many of us have thrown in the towel.

Then there's the inevitable time when the technology malfunctions or is down. If you can't maneuver a car into a space yourself, you're stuck. If your computer or phone isn't available, could you still compose, by hand, a message that grammatically and orthographically passes muster?

The Uncanny Valley

It's one thing to let our cars do the parking or our phones relieve us of typing every letter in a word. But imagine encountering a lifelike prosthetic hand pecking away on your phone keypad. The issue is how realistic we're emotionally prepared for our AI handiwork to be.

Back in 1970, a Japanese robotics professor named Masahiro Mori asked this question. Though Mori's ideas weren't published in English until 2012, his notion of what he called the "uncanny valley" was long circulating in the research community. Mori used the image of a hiker scaling a mountain to suggest that

> in climbing toward the goal of making robots appear human [by analogy, meaning reaching the peak], our affinity for them increases until we come to a valley . . . , which I call the *uncanny valley*.[63]

If an AI-driven tool (Mori's example was a prosthetic hand) becomes overly realistic, we descend, metaphorically, into an emotional valley. We feel uneasy with something artificial that looks too much like us.

Mori's thinking was based on physical AI devices. Today, it's fair game asking if there's also an uncanny valley we descend into when AI produces paintings or essays that seem indistinguishable from human productions. In August 2022, a computer-generated artwork won first place in the Colorado State Fair's fine art competition.[64] When I say "computer generated," I mean literally. The contestant, Jason Allen, input text instructions to the art generation program Midjourney. (The software works largely the same way as DALL-E 2, as does Stable Diffusion, a third major player.) After multiple trial runs, up rose *Théâtre d'Opéra Spatial,* a lush Baroque-style setting in which a stage is coupled with a sparkling sun-lit landscape. Yes, the entry was in the digital division, but other digital artists in the category did their own painting, using digital tools. As one commentator tweeted, "We're watching the death of artistry unfold before our eyes."

Understandably, some artists fear for their jobs. That same Twitter user fretted, "If creative jobs aren't safe from machines, then even high-skilled jobs are in danger of becoming obsolete."

But another source of disquiet is our human affection for authenticity.

Handmade and Human Made

Think about a Persian rug. If the one gracing your living room floor was hand-knotted by a family in a small Kurdish town, I'm sure it was far pricier than a machine-made facsimile. Is one actually better than the other?

Then there are handmade suits versus those produced in factories. Before the Industrial Revolution, all clothing was handmade, with some tailors more skilled than others. Most handmade products tended to look, well, homemade. Mass-produced trousers and jackets, shirts and dresses were generally a sartorial step up. But fast-forward to the present, when bespoke clothing fetches higher prices than off-the-rack. As with that hand-knotted Persian rug, this human handiwork is worth a premium.

Now turn to works of art, music, or literature. In 2021, Sotheby's auction house in New York sold Sandro Botticelli's painting *Young Man Holding a Roundel* for a cool $92.2 million.[65] It's hard to imagine paying even one-hundredth that amount for a masterfully done copy whose inauthenticity is only detectable by experts.

Let's not forget novelty. Imagine hearing a fugue that sounds like Bach, but you can't quite place which piece. After all, he wrote dozens of them. Being stumped isn't your fault, since the composition in question was created by a computer.[66] AI programs are also fabricating remarkable paintings "in the style" of, say, Rembrandt.[67]

Written language is hardly exempt from machine fabrication. If you're a fan of the late English humorist Jerome K. Jerome, have a look at an ersatz essay of Jerome's called "The Importance of Being on Twitter"—a technology launched seventy-nine years after Jerome's death. The visual artist Mario Klingemann created this Jerome-like approximation, having primed GPT-3 with only a title, the author's name, and the starter word "It."[68] Or perhaps you've enjoyed the writing of Gay Talese. Sudowrite, a commercial application running on GPT-3, was trained on Talese's writing. Out came paragraphs that even Talese thought read like something he could have written.[69]

It's one thing to nurture human narrative writing skills by asking students to craft a short story in the style of Hemingway, an assignment I was tasked with in high school. It's another getting GPT-3 to crank out Hemingwayesque pieces. If the AI stories are any good, we need to decide what it means to say AI can be creative. The creativity question snowballs into another: Is consciousness of what you're doing required? In other words, must creators be aware of what they've created?

These puzzles animate debate in today's AI world. But they trace back to before the field of AI even had a name.

Geoffrey Jefferson was a professor of neurosurgery at the University of Manchester. His knowledge of the brain and human nervous system is relevant for our story, since back in the late 1940s he was thinking about "the mind of mechanical man." What kind of mental activity, he asked, might computer-driven automata be capable of? Not incidentally, the University of Manchester was also home of the Ferranti Mark 1, one of the first computers in the world that could hold a stored program.

Writing in 1949, Jefferson threw out a challenge for the decades of AI research to come:

> Not until a machine can write a sonnet or compose a concerto because of thoughts and emotions felt, and not by the chance fall of symbols, could we agree that machine equals brain—that is, not only write it but know that it had written it.[70]

In current neurological parlance, what Jefferson calls *brain* we'd likely call *mind*, distinguishing between living beings' neural wetware and the more elusive notion of thought.

If you can be self-aware, presumably you're sentient. One of today's hot debates is whether AI is there yet, or even inching close.

In summer 2022, a software engineer at Google declared that at least one AI enterprise qualified. Blake Lemoine had been chatting with LaMDA, a powerful Google large language model. Given his interaction, Lemoine concluded it was legitimate to call LaMDA sentient: "I know a person when I talk to it."[71] Most computer scientists disagreed. AI watchdogs like Timnit Gebru and Margaret Mitchell have long been warning that people might believe AI to be sentient and "perceive a 'mind' when what they're really seeing is pattern matching and string prediction."[72] As Jefferson had put it, the chance fall of symbols.

At least for now, Jefferson's bar hasn't been reached.

But back to writing. Regardless of whether AI knows what it's writing, we need to size up its authorial skills and keep track of challenges they pose to humans. To start us thinking about AI the writer, indulge me with a stop in the Windy City.

The AI Writing Story: Sausage Machines and Efficiency

Chicago. The early 1900s. Eastern European immigrants were laboring in the now infamous meat processing plants. The muckraker Upton Sinclair drew us to their plight in his 1906 book *The Jungle*. While Sinclair's driving motivation was to better immigrants' living and working conditions, his direct impact was exposing the unsanitary conditions for processing meat—including sausages. You never knew what was being ground in with clean cuts of beef or pork. Not just rotten meat but pieces dropped on the floor, often trampled and spat upon. We'll leave unmentioned the hapless rodents ending up in the vats.

Sausage-eating consumers only saw slick casings, surrounding a mixture of—something or other.

Unpacking Natural Language Processing

When I hear the term "natural language processing," I think about those sausage machines. Computer operations are incredibly cleaner. No one's in danger of contracting trichinosis from asking Siri a question. But let's think about where the analogy holds.

The notion of natural language processing embraces all four traditional language components: speaking, listening (with presumed understanding), reading (again, assuming comprehension), and writing. Computers don't actually listen or read, though they might be said to write. Computer speech is synthesized, yet to be fair, when human voices are transmitted over telephones or WhatsApp calls, there's also electronic wizardry going on.

A more pressing question about AI and traditional language components involves the notion of understanding. Admittedly, we still don't really know how humans understand what they hear and read. But we can explain even less of what's going on when it comes to computers, especially with today's AI models. Yes, we can identify the algorithms we write. However, especially with deep neural networks, much of the time we can't unpack how the language sausage machine does its grinding.

The challenge is equally acute when it comes to input – particularly those vast datasets used for generating text with large language models. It's the volume of data, coupled with powerful processors and sophisticated algorithms, that enables AI to construct answers to our spoken or written queries, to serve up near-instantaneous translations of multiple-page documents, and to pump out coherent newspaper stories. But like those Chicago meatpacking plants, since we often can't vouch for what's in those datasets, AI can—and does—sometimes spew out unsavory results.

Garbage in, garbage out.

Sinclair's battle cry led President Theodore Roosevelt to lay the foundation for what would become the US Food and Drug Administration.[73] Following suit, we'll need to tackle AI "garbage." And tackle it we must, since production of AI-processed language has become too valuable for us to shutter the plant.

Much of that value comes from its sheer efficiency.

The Lure of Efficiency

There's a poignant scene in Chaplin's movie *Modern Times* where hapless Charlie, a factory worker, is harnessed to a feeding machine to shave time off his lunch break. Efficiency in dispatching routine tasks translates into higher profits. The lesson was true of the Industrial Revolution and remains so with today's industrial robots—and with natural language processing.

The promise of efficiency through automation is alluring. More Ford F150s down the assembly line ups the bottom line. Physical automation can also be a blessing in everyday life. Washing machines instead of washboards? No contest.

But when non-manual labor like writing is bolstered by automation in the name of efficiency, a slew of concerns and questions bubble up. Do we erode our unique writing voice by leaning on Gmail Smart Compose instead of producing our own emails? Will companies like Automated Insights or Narrative Science (using generative AI to produce news stories) undercut jobs for journalists rather than freeing them for uniquely human assignments? What becomes of the bond between teacher and student when we shift from flesh-and-blood writing instructors to AI for evaluating student essays? Should we trust Grammarly or Microsoft Word's suggestions? As students or employees gain increased access to large language models that can spin out essays and reports, what rethinking must we do about authorship and about cheating?

What This Book Is About

Who Wrote This? asks what happens when humans increasingly encounter AI that can do much of our writing for us. Here are eight key questions we'll be exploring:

1. What's your motivation for writing?

2. Is AI a threat to human-written creativity?

3. What writing skills are worth keeping?

4. Can you AI-proof your personal writing voice?

5. Is AI redefining authorship?

6. Does AI threaten professions built on writing skills?

7. Where do you draw the line between collaboration and handing over the keys?

8. Will disclosure rules help?

To get a handle on these queries, we'll need background on both the human and AI sides. And so the chapters ahead discuss everything from effects of literacy on the brain to the evolution of contemporary natural language processing.

Philosophers of science have long taught us that all observations are theory laden. However objective we strive to be, we inevitably find ourselves focusing on real-world happenings (past and present) that we assume are most relevant for figuring out what we want to know. As the chapters unfold, I'll connect the dots between topics you might be surprised to see here (like the rise of English composition classes or why handwriting still matters) and questions about machine writing. I'm a linguist by training and university professor by trade, which helps explain some of my lines of argument.

I also suspect my background influenced the positions you'll surely notice poking through here and there. To show my hand: I see writing as a precious human skill, empowering us to clarify thinking, emote, share knowledge and expertise, and create new ways of seeing the world. I'm convinced that today's AI language feats should be an urgent wake-up call for us to take stock of what, why, and how people write.

At the same time, I'm in awe of the astoundingly rapid developments in natural language generation (think GPT-3 and ChatGPT). So, incidentally, are the computer scientists who engineered them. No one expected us to get this far this fast. Yet we recognize that all too often, current large language models spew bias, hatred, inaccuracies, and misinformation. Plus, these models sometimes proffer questionable (even downright incorrect) grammatical and stylistic recommendations.

While it's vital to address these flaws, my fundamental concern is a different one: What if the dream came true? Imagine that we resolved all the shortcomings of today's AI as author or editor. AI's accomplishments would continue to beguile us, potentially undermining our own writing motivations, skills, and voice. Of course, there's another alternative—that AI will increasingly empower us as writers, enabling us to forge productive collaborations with the machines. The story that follows weighs the options.

Mapping the Territory Ahead

Like a Shakespearean play, the plot unfolds in five parts.

Part I: Writing Lessons opens by asking what's so special about human writing. We'll look at how, when, and why written language emerged, along with reasons we write—and rewrite. We'll also follow two American academic creations—college English requirements and the Educational Testing Service—and size up how AI is altering the role of people in both.

Part II: What If Machines Could Write? examines how AI came to "process" language. We begin with the origins of modern artificial intelligence, then move to a layperson's overview of natural language processing (NLP), including where it fits into the larger scheme of AI. Rounding out the story is an account of one of NLP's initial failures and later success stories: machine translation.

Part III: When Computers Write explores how AI has been permeating the human writing landscape, from the earliest days of sophomoric love letters to today's sophisticated story writing that would have warmed Adolph Knipe's heart. We then turn to AI in professional fields where writing looms large such as journalism, law, and translation. As ever more text is AI-generated, we'll need to weigh potential consequences for employment and job satisfaction. The section closes by reflecting on AI's creative prospects, including when it comes to writing.

Part IV: When Computers Collaborate opens by probing a swath of ways AI is assisting everyday writers. We'll look at tools like spellcheck, predictive texting, grammar check software, and AI programs that draft email replies or authentic-sounding blog posts. Next up we examine the idea of "humans in the loop," especially where human writing efforts might be boosted through collaboration with AI. But then we step back to ask what human writing skills are worth maintaining, with potential candidates including spelling, grammar, rewriting, proofreading, and even handwriting. We'll use survey data I've collected from young adults in the United States and Europe to see what everyday writers think about the value of human writing abilities in the face of digital technologies.

Coda: Why Human Authorship Matters rounds out the book by asking where we go from here. We'll each need to work out our own answers, recognizing that as the technology evolves, so may our choices. Whatever the decisions, it's important not to let fascination with AI glitz or awe in the face of its efficiency push us to abandon what we value about human writing.

Seeing the Forest for the Trees

When writing for a broad readership, there's always a dilemma with deciding how to handle technical material: how much to explain, how to do it, and where. My personal aversion to longwinded explanations is only matched by my refusal to shortchange readers by leaving them with unexplained terminology that might as well be in a foreign language.

Artificial intelligence runs on complicated technology. The literature is laced with concepts that defy brief nontechnical explanations. What's more, the discipline is full of acronyms. For readers with a background in AI, the terminology is child's play. But for most readers, not so.

My solution was to create an addendum called Main Characters, following the Coda. ("Appendix" sounded too stodgy.) The section contains a quick glossary of acronyms that figure in the book (including some for non-AI entries) and short definitions of key AI terms. Further on, you'll find extensive Notes and References, for those wanting to follow up on material in the main text.

Let's begin.

PART I

WRITING LESSONS

ONE

The Journey to Literacy

Tunneling into the edge of the Gibraltar peninsula is the Gorham's Cave Complex. The area was inhabited by Neanderthals, dating back 100,000 years. Archaeological evidence reveals these cave dwellers hunted birds and marine life and decorated themselves with feathers. They also engraved abstract drawings on rocks that are at least 39,000 years old.[1] Something was on the minds of our hominid relatives, though exactly what is anyone's guess.

Fast-forward a bit. Think of those horses—and the occasional human—painted in the Lascaux caves (dated at 15,000 to 17,000 years ago) or the imposing bison on the walls of Altamira (maybe a few millennia more recent). On the other side of the world in Western Australia, there's a rock painting of a kangaroo, presumed to be 17,300 years old.[2]

Incredible drawings, especially for their time. We're not certain why the images were put there, but know for sure they're not yet writing.

When it happened, the invention of writing was a big deal. People could codify religions and laws, record history, organize cities. Writing also multiplied possibilities for expressing ourselves, communicating with others, and reflecting on what we and others think. Being literate conferred a magic light sword for thought, exchange, and action.

Now AI wields its own light sword. You might wonder if it matters that humans have competition. Why not the more the merrier? Just because we have automobiles doesn't mean people have forgotten how to walk. But it's also true we're walking less now, thanks to Carl Benz, Henry Ford, and Elon Musk.

AI authorship is a bit like cars, and people are, well, like people. We often welcome efficiency (sounds like a plus) and the easy way out (which can sometimes prove hazardous). One of the biggest dangers from today's AI language prowess is that we forget what applying our writing skills can do for our intelligence and psyche. The more we abandon written work to AI, the more we risk dimming our light swords.

Let's take a quick tour of the evolution of human writing. My less-than-subtle aim is adding ballast to the case that our writing abilities are too precious to let drift away with the river Lethe.

Writing Emerges

Unlike speech, writing was invented multiple times. Occasionally, the creator was a single person. In the nineteenth century, a Native American named Sequoyah invented a system for setting down the Cherokee language.[3] Four centuries earlier in Korea, King Sejong devised the Hangul script as an alternative to Chinese characters, which had been too complex for most of his population to master.[4] Both Sequoyah's system and Hangul are syllabic scripts. A single symbol represents an entire syllable in the spoken language, like "ka" or "go."

More typically, writing systems arose through gradual transitions from pictures to abstract symbols representing sounds, words, or ideas. Alphabets like Latin or Cyrillic use letters standing for individual sounds like "k" or "a." Ideographs (think of Chinese characters) represent words or ideas, depending on whom you ask.

This caterpillar-to-butterfly metamorphosis happened independently in several parts of the world. In Sumer (now southern Iraq), the outline profile of a person's head (about 3000 BCE) eventually became the cuneiform for "head" or "person." A bit farther west, the Proto-Canaanite picture of an ox (from around 1800 BCE) morphed into the Hebrew letter aleph. Much to the east, a picture of a dragon, as incised on an oracle bone sometime during the Shang dynasty (c.1600–1046 BCE), would evolve into the Chinese character for said dragon.[5]

Not all picture systems ended up as writing. Some nineteenth-century Native American tribes in the Plains used buffalo hides to record the year's significant events. Painting in spirals, the chroniclers depicted people, animals, tepees, corn stalks, and the like. Perhaps the best-known example is *Lone Dog's Winter Count*. On it you'll find a stick figure with spots on its face, marking a smallpox outbreak. A bare cornstalk recounts a poor crop year.[6] The hide tells a powerful tale we can understand, but not in writing.

On the other hand, some artifacts retaining picture-like elements turn out to be actual writing. Mesoamerica (the area stretching from central Mexico down through northern Costa Rica) offers nice examples. Think of Mayan. For centuries, people assumed Mayan glyphs were stylized illustrations. Only with successive decipherment efforts, starting with work by the British archaeologist Eric Thompson, was the Mayan code cracked, revealing how these symbols correspond to words and sounds.[7]

What's all this writing good for? That's the focus of the next chapter. But as a prelude, let's reflect on the relationship between writing and its progenitor, speech.

Beyond Dictation

As I've said, I'm a linguist. What do we study? Language, of course. But what counts as language?

Until recently, the answer for most of my clan was speech. Writing was demoted into a kind of transcription service. In the memorable words of Leonard Bloomfield, a pillar of American linguistics in the first half of the twentieth century,

> Writing is not language, but merely a way of recording language by visible marks.[8]

The long echo of these words, written though they were, could still be heard in the 2000s in the halls of the National Science Foundation (NSF). I had gone to meet with the linguistics grant officer about a proposal I was preparing for analyzing teenage instant messaging. Dismissively, she informed me that studying anything connected with writing didn't count as linguistics. So much for my funding prospects.

Bloomfield and his spiritual followers weren't to have the last word. Writing has gradually been afforded more linguistic respect.[9] My own vindication came in 2005. A prominent American linguist invited me to organize a symposium titled "Language on the Internet" for the American Association for the Advancement of Science. I had already spent a decade analyzing online communication. By the early 1990s, it was becoming obvious that we needed to figure out what kind of linguistic beast email, and later instant messaging and texting, might be. Are they writing? Are they speech written down? Are they a new linguistic species? A growing cadre of researchers, myself included, spent years grappling with these questions.[10] I haven't checked if NSF ever helped out.

There's also the obvious technological marrying of speech with writing for dictation. Whether we're talking about older tools like Dictaphones (with a human secretary mediating) or modern AI-driven speech recognition, Bloomfield's dismissal of writing as "merely a way of recording language" (meaning speech) here turns out to be apt.

Writing has evolved. Not just in the forms it takes but in who knows how to do it.

Two Faces of Literacy

If you're reading this book, I'm sure you can write. Contemporary notions of literacy include both reading and writing skills. But in times past, that pairing didn't always hold.

Who Counts as Literate?

Imagine you lived in eighteenth-century Sweden. Thanks to the Lutheran injunction that everyone should read the Bible, Sweden launched a literacy campaign in the early seventeenth century. By the middle of the next century, nearly 100 percent of the population could read. In fact, to take communion or get married, you had to pass a literacy test. What you didn't need to know was how to write. Elsewhere in Europe, your signature mattered. In England, Lord Chancellor Hardwick declared in 1754 that all brides and grooms, with few exceptions, had to sign or at least mark the marriage register.[11] So who counted as literate: Swedes who could read the Bible but not write, or English newlyweds who could at best sign their names?

In the West, reading was the usual first step to literacy. The Bible commonly served as primer. There was a certain logic to the choice, since the Bible might be the only book a family owned. What's more, people were already familiar with much of the text, having heard it read aloud in church. This oral-to-written two-step is familiar to anyone who's read stories to preschoolers, often the same book more times than you wish to count. Kids sometimes take over and "read" the books aloud themselves.

In modern times, reading and writing instruction overwhelmingly happens simultaneously. But you also find pedagogical twists, beginning with the ideas of Rudolf Steiner. It was Steiner who, in 1919, began a progressive education movement that came to be known as Waldorf education. Waldorf schools teach writing first. Not just any writing, but initially having children write down poems and stories they've already encountered orally.[12] (If you're curious about the name Waldorf: Steiner's first school was for children of employees in the Waldorf-Astoria Cigarette company in Stuttgart, Germany. Johann Jakob Astor, founder of not just the factory but a familiar line of hotels, was born in Walldorf, Germany.)

A kindred approach was tried in the United States in the 1960s and 1970s. However, instead of starting with stories the children had already heard, the goal was for youngsters to create their own content. The scheme built on a kindred practice in some nursery schools and kindergartens, where children dictated their narratives to adults, who transcribed the kids' words.

Here was the new twist: for children to do their own writing, following a pedagogy dubbed "write first, read later." How, you ask? These kids didn't know how to spell many of the words in their spoken vocabulary. The problem is especially acute with a language like English, whose orthographic system tries the souls of many educated adults. The solution, said linguist and educator Carol Chomsky, was to use invented spelling (aka "magic spelling"), where children take a shot at how the words might be written, drawing on the way they sound.[13]

A technology-driven take on prioritizing writing grew out of work by John H. Martin, a former school superintendent. Martin had initially set youngsters to pecking out their stories on typewriters. In the mid-1980s, he sold his system to IBM, which had just launched its PCjr ("junior") computer. Children would now do their pecking on that infamous chiclet keyboard, though this time, phonics lessons were laced in. Depending on whom you ask, the pedagogy was a rousing success or disappointing failure.[14] In any event, it's now largely defunct.

Why dredge up old news? Because today's AI spelling capabilities offer tantalizing options for how we introduce kindergartners and first graders to writing. I'll bet we have the technology needed to redo kids' invented spelling, if they're using Microsoft Word. After all, spellcheck tidies up adults' mistakes. The issue is whether it's a good move letting spellcheck do the same for five- and six-year-olds. Or is it like opening the alcohol taps for teenagers? We'll park the question until Chapter 12.

The Fruits of Literacy

Learning to read and write takes sustained effort. Not everyone has the opportunity.

In Mesopotamia and ancient Egypt, few were literate, and scribes were part of a privileged elite. While some in classical Greece could read and write, the numbers weren't huge. What happened in 482 BCE to Aristides the Just, an Athenian statesman worthy of the moniker, is a prize illustration.

Some years earlier, Cleisthenes—sometimes called the father of Athenian democracy— had incorporated into the new Athenian constitution a provision whereby a citizen could, by popular vote, be expelled from Attica for ten years. Each Athenian was welcome to write on a pottery shard (known as an ostracon) the name of the person he wanted temporarily banished: ostracized.

But there was no literacy test for voting. Plutarch explains:

> as the voters were inscribing their ostraka, it is said that an unlettered and utterly boorish fellow handed his ostrakon to Aristides . . . and asked him to write Aristides on it. He, astonished, asked the man what possible wrong Aristides had done him. "None whatever," was the answer, "I don't even know the fellow, but I am tired of hearing him everywhere called 'The Just.'" On hearing this, Aristides made no answer, but wrote his name on the ostrakon and handed it back.[15]

Yes, Aristides was ostracized, though only briefly. Athens needed him back to fight the Persians.

Then there's China, where widespread literacy was slow in coming, thanks in large part to the complex traditional Chinese writing system. Not until Mao Zedong's introduction of simplified Chinese characters in the 1950s did a significant portion of the population have a realistic way of learning to read and write.[16] The same challenge had led King Sejong to create the syllabic Hangul system for Korea back in 1443.

In England, the literacy rate (somewhat guesstimated) didn't reach 50 percent for men until around 1700. For women, that milestone took another century and a half.[17] In parts of the world like India and the Middle East, public scribes have long filled the needs of non-literates. The 700-year-old tradition of street scribes in Istanbul—armed first with quills, then pens, then typewriters—enabled people who couldn't write to have letters or documents prepared.[18] According to UNESCO, the global literacy rate as of 2019 for people age fifteen and older was 86 percent. There is still a ways to go, especially for women, for people in sub-Saharan Africa, and for those in South and East Asia.[19]

Literacy has a long track record of transforming people's economic and social prospects, not to mention opportunities for learning and self-discovery. But does being literate also rejigger our minds and our brains? If so, handing over to AI the keys for doing our writing (and let's throw in reading) has potential consequences far beyond saving us effort.

Does Writing Alter Our Minds?

Writing arrived but a moment ago in human history. Five thousand years isn't nearly enough time for evolution to hardwire writing into our heads the way speech is. When we combine the recency of writing with its gradual uptake in much of the world, it might seem odd to be pondering mental resets.

Yet something does seem to happen to people and to cultures when they become literate. Regarding our minds, pinning down just what that something is has stirred more than half a century of controversy.

The Alphabet, Literacy, and Thought

Eric Havelock's 1963 book *Preface to Plato* ignited something of an academic firestorm. For Havelock proposed that classical Greek philosophical thinking was made possible by development of the Greek alphabet.

To understand his argument, we need some historical background. The first script used for writing the Greek language was Linear B, an orthography developed by the Minoans in Crete in the fifteenth or sixteenth century BCE.[20] In mainland Greece, Linear B was relatively short-lived, from around 1450 BCE to about 1200 BCE, when the Mycenaean civilization (think King Agamemnon, his palace at Mycenae, and the Trojan War) began to decline.

For the next roughly 400 years, the Greeks didn't write. But then, a new system began brewing. Through their commercial ventures, the Greeks encountered the Phoenicians. Hailing from what's now modern Lebanon, this seafaring people traded throughout the Mediterranean. And they had writing.

The Phoenicians' language and script belong to the Semitic language family, which includes Hebrew and Arabic. By contrast, spoken Greek is part of the Indo-European family, which encompasses languages ranging from Sanskrit and Serbian to Italian and Icelandic. The two language groups have not just distinct family trees and sound repertoires, but different ways of building words.

Words in Semitic languages are based on sequences of three consonants, while Indo-European languages have varied word lengths and make ample use of vowels, including at the beginnings and ends of words. Speakers of Semitic languages obviously pronounce vowels. You can't have a human language without them. You just don't *write* the vowels in Semitic scripts. It's common to hear people talk about the Hebrew or Arabic alphabet, but more accurately, Semitic languages use consonantal alphabets for writing. That fact would have notorious ramifications that we'll encounter later.

What the Greeks did was create a real alphabet, with one symbol corresponding to each spoken sound—including those vowels. Some unknown would-be linguist took five Phoenician symbols representing consonants that didn't exist in Greek and repurposed them to indicate Greek vowels.[21] The resulting letter inventory made it possible to write words pretty much the way they were pronounced.

Havelock argued that this new ability to represent in writing all sounds in spoken Greek was a key ingredient for development of Greek philosophical thought in the sixth, fifth, and fourth centuries BCE. According to Jack Goody (an anthropologist) and literary historian Ian Watt, Havelock's thesis explained how this new kind of writing made possible separation of the past from the present, critique of cultural traditions, and testing of alternative explanations. Logic, including syllogisms, emerged as a tool for thinking.[22] An added bonus was that unlike Sumerian cuneiforms, Egyptian hieroglyphics, and Chinese characters, an alphabet made it easier to learn to write. Opportunities for participating in the emerging democracy got a boost—Plutarch's unlettered Athenian notwithstanding.

A lot is packed into those claims. Let's unravel them.

Havelock maintained that creation of the Greek alphabet was a vital ingredient in the development of Greek philosophical thinking. Next, literacy itself was the magic charm. The third prong in Havelock's case was that Attic Greece underwent a shift from an oral culture to at least a partly written one.

Begin with the alphabetic hypothesis. The hitch is that Greece (first archaic and then classical) wasn't the only society with a writing system that included information on how words should be pronounced. A variety of non-alphabetic systems use additional marks to guide pronunciation, including Egyptian hieroglyphs, Chinese characters, and Mayan glyphs. Over time, even Hebrew developed written indicators for vowels.[23] And as those who can read Arabic will tell you, if you know the spoken language, you have no trouble figuring out the written words and how they correspond to speech.

Havelock's literacy argument triggered an even larger brouhaha.[24] Were Havelock and his supporters claiming that non-literate people were incapable of sophisticated thought? That's what critics alleged. But Havelock's contention needs to be seen in context. He was specifically talking about the emergence of Greek philosophical thought, in a particular time, place, and cultural milieu.

Havelock's aim was to explain the flowering of new ways of thinking, which included individual self-awareness, a concept not part of the earlier Homeric tradition. As psychologist and literacy expert David Olson puts it,

> Consciousness of words permits their distinction from the ideas that words express. Writing, therefore, gives rise to the idea of an idea and the mind becomes the storehouse of those ideas. Thus it is at least plausible that the discovery of the mind was part of the legacy of writing.[25]

Whatever we understand *mind* to mean, it includes ability to reflect. Reading affords us opportunities to pause over words, think, and reread. Writing enables us not only to write but to pause, think, and rewrite.

Stop for a moment and compare human with AI authorship. AI is incapable of pausing, thinking, and rewriting, except perhaps in the sense of tinkering with sentences humans have written. Blake Lemoine notwithstanding, AI lacks a mind. The challenge for humans is whether increasing reliance on AI to write and edit for us diminishes our drive to use writing to exercise our minds.

Coupled with the emergence of Greek literacy were initial steps in transforming Greece from an oral to a written society. The distinction between the two kinds of social orders isn't whether writing exists at all but the cultural role it plays.

Take the case of England. Writing existed (first in Latin, then in English) by the seventh century. But it wasn't until into the seventeenth that written culture firmly emerged. The Bible had been read aloud to medieval monks and parishioners alike. Chaucer had read his works to audiences at court. And nearly all of Shakespeare's plays were intended to be performed, not read independently. What's more, at least until early modern times, when people read for themselves, they typically voiced the words or at least moved their lips. A telltale sign of written culture's arrival was the shift in how punctuation was done. Initially, punctuation marks signaled to readers where to take a breath and for how long. By the seventeenth century, punctuation increasingly marked written grammatical structure.[26]

Now back to Greece. Archaic Greece was an oral culture, even after the introduction of alphabetic writing. The *Iliad* and *Odyssey* were memorized and recited. Initially, few were literate. Even with the transition to classical times, elements of the oral culture persisted. Herodotus, the father of Greek history, used to perform oral readings of his work. In fact, the practice of reading written works aloud was widespread in Greece into the fourth century BCE.[27] It's no misnomer that we speak of Plato's "dialogues," for they represent purported spoken conversation. Classical Greece never became a fully written culture.

Yet enough people were literate—including those philosophers—to generate new forms of intellectual and social thought.

Literacy Versus Schooling

A reasonable question is whether it's literacy that changes people's ways of thinking or the educational process through which most of us learn to read. In the 1960s, research comparing literate versus non-literate Wolof children in West Africa concluded that literacy fostered cognitive development. But the psychologists conducting the study, Patricia Greenfield and Jerome Bruner, wondered if higher scores on standard cognitive tests actually reflected schooling, not literacy per se.[28]

Another team of psychologists, Sylvia Scribner and Michael Cole, hoped to disentangle the two potential sources of cognitive differences.[29] Their research was with the Vai of Liberia. The Vai had invented their own syllabic writing system—one not taught in schools. Some Vai knew the indigenous writing system, some not. Were the two groups' cognitive skills the same?

The answer turned out to be messy. Yes, there was some variation between those who knew Vai writing (but hadn't been to school) and those who had neither Vai literacy nor schooling. However, formal education proved far more important in explaining the impact of literacy on cognitive test scores.

Disentangling the effects of literacy and schooling remains an open challenge. Modern neuroscience might be poised to help. For this assist, we switch from talking about minds to looking at brains—something AI programs lack, at least in the literal, wetware sense.

Does Writing Alter Our Brains?

Thanks to modern imaging technology, we can measure the size of individual brain structures. As a result, we can see how practices like playing the violin or driving a black car taxi in London or reading alter the physical brain. The technology also offers a window on brains at work in real time.

For over a century, scientists have been talking about neuroplasticity, meaning the brain's ability to reorganize its structure or lay down new pathways.[30] We used to believe that brain functioning was fixed early in life. Now we recognize the brain is able to grow fresh neural matter and pathways that bolster cognitive ability. The primary tool for studying what the brain is up to is magnetic resonance imaging (MRI). Structural MRIs produce anatomical images, while functional MRIs (fMRIs) chart real-time brain activity by measuring changes in blood flow when performing tasks.

MRI technology has shown that violinists develop heightened structural connectivity in their right motor cortex, which controls finger movement on the left hand. (That's the hand doing the fingering on stringed instruments.)[31] MRIs also reveal that London cabbies with "the Knowledge" of thousands of routes, streets, and landmarks have larger posterior hippocampi (the area responsible for physical navigation) than control groups.[32]

Can neuroimaging help us understand effects of literacy on the brain? In broaching this question, keep in mind that most of what we know neurologically either targets reading or doesn't distinguish between reading and writing skills.

Reading and the Brain

Since reading isn't evolutionarily wired into our brains, how do we manage to read? As the neuroscientist Stanislas Dehaene explains, we piggyback on neural structures designed for other tasks, including vision and speech.[33] Thanks to the wonders of neural scanning technology, we can actually observe changes in brain structure or function brought about by becoming literate. And thanks to the ingenuity of researchers, there are now ways of circumventing the literacy/schooling conundrum by focusing on non-literate adults who later became literate.

One early study capitalized on a singular moment in the history of Colombia, when ex-guerilla fighters were reintegrated into mainstream society, including by learning to read. Structural MRI scans of these late literates were compared with scans from a matched cohort who hadn't yet started a literacy program.[34] The late literates, who were tested after reading and writing Spanish for at least five years, showed increased density of white and gray matter in brain areas known to be involved in reading.[35]

Another study compared fMRI scans of three groups of adults in Portugal and Brazil: those who acquired literacy as children, those learning as adults, and those who never learned to read. Both literate groups showed more activity than the non-literates in brain areas associated with vision and with speech.[36]

And more results, this time from northern India. Working with non-literate Hindi-speaking adult villagers, the researchers compared participants in a literacy program with a non-literate group who received no training in reading or writing.[37] fMRI scans again confirmed literacy effects on the mature brain.

We're also learning something about children's brains and the written word. John Hutton, a pediatrician at Cincinnati Children's Hospital, has been interested in the effects of print versus screen reading on the brain.

In a study of three- to five-year-olds, Hutton and his colleagues used an MRI technique called diffusion tensor imaging to show an association between home reading environment and what's happening in kids' brains. The more stimulating the home reading environment—measured by access to print books, along with frequency and quality of shared reading between adults and children who didn't yet know how to read—the higher the level of microstructural integrity of brain white matter tracts. In plain English, those are pathways supporting language and literacy. Hutton's group also showed that among preschoolers, higher digital screen use correlated with lower integrity of these tracts. Turning to tweens (that's eight- to twelve-year-olds), Hutton and a colleague found that reading books correlated with increased brain connectivity (a cognitive plus), while high exposure to screen media resulted in a decrease.[38]

Figuring out what to make of all these imaging results isn't yet clear. What we can say is that reading—even just being exposed to books—changes what goes on in our brains.

Do we know what the brain is up to when we just look at writing?

Writing and the Brain

It's hard to envision a study comparing brain imaging of non-literate people with those who've only learned to write, not read. Unless you can decipher the marks you produce, you're better described as drawing, not writing.

A couple of novel projects involving adults offer glimpses into how the brain behaves when we write. The first comes from work at Stanford University that couples AI software with a chip implanted into the brain, enabling paralyzed people to communicate.[39] The system draws on the brain's motor memory of writing, acquired before the person became paralyzed. Think of it as human writing with a behind-the-scenes assist from AI.

In an earlier phase of the research, participants with paralyzed limbs (and an implanted chip) were instructed to concentrate as if they themselves were moving a cursor on a computer keyboard, typing out words. Their minds, not hands, were doing the work. In a later study, a participant was asked to concentrate as if he were forming words by writing the letters by hand, one by one, on a pad of paper. AI software then recognized the neural signal and generated a written character. It turned out that the user was able to produce more words per minute with imaginary handwriting than with imaginary typing. Potential benefits of this kind of research are huge, not just for those with paralysis but for people with degenerative diseases like ALS.

Switch gears to a very different type of writing study, this time using fMRI scanning to track brain activity while people are writing stories. The idea was to compare activity in expert writers versus novices.[40] Martin Lotze and his colleagues at the University of Greifswald in Germany first had to tackle the challenge of how participants in the study would be able to write while in the scanner. Since no metal could be nearby, digital devices were out. The researchers' creative solution was a writing desk, placed just outside of the scanner, enabling the person being scanned to write by hand.

The task itself was reminiscent of the way large language models like GPT-3 work: Seed a few opening lines of a story, and the AI generates the rest. Here, it was the humans who continued the narrative. One group of participants (designated as experts for purposes of the study) were enrolled in a creative writing program, while novices (no special writing training) served as a control group.

The resulting brain scans revealed different areas of neural activity for the two cadres. When novice writers were planning how their stories might unfold (but before starting to write), they showed brain activity in areas connected to vision. For the expert writers, brain areas relating to speech were more active. Once the actual writing task began, the expert writers (unlike the novices) showed activity in the caudate nucleus, an area of the brain responsible for higher-level cognitive functioning, including planning, learning, and memory.

It's hard to know what to make of Lotze's findings. Perhaps training in creative writing makes us think differently—or maybe not. I'd be curious to see results comparing journalists with novelists. What we can say for sure is that when we write, the brain is tracking our every word.

There's still more to know about writing and what's going on in our heads. One question with pragmatic consequences is whether our minds or brains behave differently when we write by hand versus using a keyboard or keypad. We'll save that conversation for Chapter 12, when we take on handwriting.

In the Platonic dialogue the *Phaedrus*, Socrates recounts the story of how in Egypt, the god Theuth invented writing. Was that a blessing or a curse? Socrates continues, speaking in the guise of Thamus, the king/god of Egypt to whom Theuth presented his handiwork:

> For this invention will produce forgetfulness in the minds of those who learn to use it, because they will not practice their memory. . . . You have invented an elixir not of memory, but of reminding; and you offer your pupils the appearance of wisdom, not true wisdom, for they will read many things without instruction and will therefore seem to know many things, when they are for the most part ignorant and hard to get along with, since they are not wise, but only appear wise.[41]

These early fears about the impact of writing need to be seen in historical context. Attic Greece was transitioning from an oral to a written culture. Like today's concern that self-parking cars could lead us to forget how to parallel park, the classical Greek world was pulled between the benefits of writing and the threat it posed to memory as a vehicle for knowledge. Were Socrates and Plato alive today, they'd likely be horrified at how poor most of our memory skills have become. But they'd also recognize the power of the written word as a vehicle for self-expression and thought.

AI isn't up for self-expression or thinking. But we are. It's to those human motivations for using the written word that we now turn.

TWO

Why Humans Write—and Rewrite

Ransom notes. Recipes. Laundry lists. Laws. Blogs. Books. Emails. Epigraphs. If we're literate, there's a full run of the house for what and why we write. Practically, though, our prospects are bounded by need or circumstance.

Restrictions go way back. Some early writing systems were deployed for just one purpose: running the bureaucracy. Linear B in Mycenaean Greece was only used to keep tabs on practicalities like how many bushels of grain were in the royal storehouses.[1] No poems, no royal decrees. In Peru, the Inca apparently designed those mystifying knotted cords known as quipus (yes, they were a form of writing) to manage their far-flung empire.[2]

Every society where writing emerged independently, was borrowed, or evolved has its own story about what's written down and by whom. Let's start with the names we give to people who commit their words to parchment, paper, or keypads.

Writers, Authors, and Authority

There's a literary agency in New York called Writers House, which represents authors to potential publishers. An obvious question is whether there's a difference between a writer and an author.

Judging from usage, the distinction is fuzzy. The Authors Guild exists "to support working writers,"[3] meaning people looking to publish their manuscripts, typically for financial remuneration. Writer's Workbench—the first computer grammar check program—was designed in the late 1970s to help students revise their work. Let's hope no money was changing hands.

Technically, everyone who can write might be called a writer, though the word usually conjures up thoughts of professionals like journalists or editors. If your efforts are more geared to sending emails, doing social media posts, compiling a résumé, or composing an annual end-of-the-year holiday letter, few people would think to call you a writer. Maybe "quotidian writer" is more accurate, but that's awkward. I'll default to "everyday writer."

What about "author"? If I write a short story (I'm its author), I'm usually looking to take credit for my work, maybe even profit from it. If I write a news story or legal brief, I'm also its author but in an added sense: I can be held accountable for what I've written, either in a court of law or the court of public opinion. Woven in is usually another authorial responsibility: to be accurate and, unless we're talking about fiction, to be believable. Finally, there's the all-important factor of personal motivation, decoupled from gain in money or reputation.

We can think of modern authorship as having five potential branches:

- having something new to say (and hopefully saying it well)
- getting published
- associating your name with what you write
- assuming responsibility for your written words
- being personally motivated to write

The branches are a bit of a smorgasbord. For a political exposé, be prepared to defend the veracity of what you wrote. A snarky email to a co-worker, disparaging your boss? Your name's on it. Beware of backup files on the company server.

There's a reason I specified modern authorship. Like written language itself, contemporary ideas about authorship took centuries to evolve.

From Auctoritas to Author and Copyright

The word "author" wears its lineage on its sleeve: Latin *auctoritas*, meaning authority. An *auctor* was someone who wrote with authority, essentially on religious themes. During the Middle Ages, that authority came from both the intrinsic worth of the subject matter (again, think religion) and the authenticity (think truthfulness) with which someone wrote. God was the source of inspiration for human writing about scripture, and lord knows, God had *auctoritas*. Humans wrote some enchanting poems and tales (*Sir Gawain and the Green Knight*, anyone?). Yet most of their efforts back then went into commentaries on religious texts or compilations thereof.[4] What's more, age mattered. As the late twelfth-century cleric Walter Map ruefully declared, when it came to reputation, it helped to be dead.[5]

Gradually, human authors (including living ones) emerged from the divine shadow. One transitional step was representing yourself as a mere compiler. Another was foisting responsibility for your words on your characters. In *The Canterbury Tales*, Chaucer depicts himself as a mere reporter, not to be blamed for ribald language from the likes of the Miller.[6]

By early modern times, our notion of authorship had shed much of its past. The printing press helped by enabling growing ranks of writers to get their work into circulation. And soon, so would the emerging concept of copyright. But not quite yet. When Shakespeare was writing *King Lear* and *Macbeth*, no one accused him of stealing plots from Raphael Holinshed's *Chronicles*. There was no theft because copyright laws didn't yet exist. Plus, from a modern perspective, copyright applies to words, not the ideas they express.

In England, it wasn't until 1709, with the Statute of Anne, that the first copyright law was laid down. But it was the publisher, not the author, who held rights to publish an author's words and earn profits, though for a limited span of years. Not until a century later (the Copyright Act of 1814) was the author recognized in England as "the creator and owner of literary property."[7] While the length of ownership was upped over the years, in both England and the United States, it has remained words, not ideas, that are protected.[8]

Modern copyright law, on both sides of the Atlantic, also requires effort. In British law, "to qualify, a work should be regarded as original, and exhibit a degree of labour, skill or judgement." In the United States, "An original work of authorship is a work that is independently created by a human author and possesses at least some minimal degree of creativity."[9]

Original. Today's copyright laws make clear that you need to have something new to say. You also need to show evidence of mental effort ("labour, skill or judgment"; "minimal degree of creativity"). The issue is whose effort and whose creativity.

Copyright and AI: It's Complicated

American law is upfront that copyright can only be granted to works created by human authors. In fact, to human creators of anything.

Take the handiwork of a certain crested black macaque (an Old World monkey found only in Indonesia). In 2011, nature photographer David Slater set up his camera in an animal reserve there, but then briefly stepped away. Upon returning, he found that a macaque named Naruto had taken selfies. Some of these snapshots found their way to Wikimedia, which is public domain. Slater protested, saying he owned the rights, since it was his equipment. He went on to publish a book on wildlife personalities, featuring Naruto on the cover.[10]

But events took a new turn. Animal rights groups sued Slater, claiming that copyright belonged to Naruto, the actual photographer. The judge dismissed the case. Under US law, non-humans can't hold copyright.[11]

What happens with the output of AI programs? The answer depends partly on where you are—policies are literally all over the map.

In 2014, the US Copyright Office specified that

> the Office will not register works produced by a machine or mere mechanical process that operates randomly or automatically without any creative input or intervention from a human author.[12]

In other words, for the work to qualify, AI can't be a solo author. A cascade of legal experts in the United States have defended this position. As far back as 1986, Pamela Samuelson argued that the copyright system

> has allocated rights only to humans for a very good reason: it simply does not make any sense to allocate intellectual property rights to machines because they do not need to be given incentives to generate output.[13]

The US Constitution, in which copyright protection was enshrined, was explicit that the aim of granting authors "exclusive rights" to their writing for a period of time was to incentivize them to "promote the progress of science and the useful arts."[14]

Defense of human authorship goes on. Annemarie Bridy wrote in 2012 that copyright is denied to a software program because it "has no legal personhood."[15] A few years later, James Grimmelmann concluded that while in the future it might make sense to grant AI authorial status for copyright purposes, for now, changing the law to make AI programs eligible is a "terrible idea."[16]

Once you cross the Atlantic, or Pacific, the picture is complicated by disparate legal traditions. Some countries (all of continental Europe, along with China and Japan) follow a civil law tradition, deriving from the Roman Justinian codex. Other countries, including the UK and nations influenced by English legal traditions (such as India, Australia, New Zealand, Canada, and the United States), largely follow a common law tradition. Under civil law, the legal system is founded on codified statutes. Under common law, the judicial process heavily leans on case law, meaning decisions that have been handed down over the years by judges.

Civil law countries, particularly in Europe, have another strong legal tradition known as moral rights, which are now intertwined with copyright. While copyright protects authors' economic stake in their work, moral rights—initially a French concept (*droit moral*)— safeguard the creators' non-financial interests, including rights to be identified as the author of their work, along with protection of their personal reputation and privacy. Under the 1886 Berne Convention for the Protection of Literary and Artistic Works, moral rights of individuals were incorporated into copyright provisions.[17] It's this emphasis on the moral rights of individuals that helps drive the presupposition that only humans can be granted copyright.

Although some countries with common law traditions (such as the United States) are now signatories to the Berne Convention and acknowledge moral rights of authors, emphasis on these rights, within the realm of copyright, isn't as strong. As a result, common law countries are more likely to use a workaround for handling the issue of copyright on intellectual property generated by computer. That workaround is the notion of work for hire.

Let's say a corporation contracts with Maria to produce an operations manual on its behalf. Maria is paid, but the corporation retains rights to use her manual (and profit from it) as it sees fit. This is the system New Zealand, along with several other common law countries, uses for handling rights to computer-generated works. Copyright ownership belongs to the "person by whom the arrangements necessary for the creation of the work are undertaken."[18] Bridy suggests that in the United States, as a common law country, the work for hire approach would be an easy fix. It would only require having Congress tweak language defining what constitutes work for hire, not altering copyright law itself.

A different take on how to resolve the copyright question for AI-generated work comes from a case in China. Akin to the case of David Slater's monkey selfies, this dispute was over whether words created by a non-human were automatically in the public domain or protected by copyright.

Tencent Technology had used its AI software called Dreamwriter to produce a financial article, which was posted on the Tencent Securities website. The same day, Shanghai Yingxun (another technology company) posted the same article on its own website, without permission, presumably taking the AI-generated text to be in the public domain. Tencent sued, demanding 1,500 RMB (a bit more than $200 USD) in economic compensation. The court ruled that since production of the work involved a team effort of humans and technology, and since the work itself met the originality criterion for copyright, the article was protected.[19]

Of course, Dreamwriter didn't collect the 1,500 RMB. Tencent did.

Credit Where Credit Is Due

We've said that to count as an author these days, you need to have something new to say. Writing that's computer-generated checks that box. And such output is becoming more prolific, showing up not just in newspapers but as short story collections and illustrated comic books.[20]

You'd be right to wonder who gets authorial credit. For the steady stream of self-published works or those issued by small presses, usually it's the human compiler claiming acknowledgment. As for that article in the Chinese Tencent case, at the end of the piece, the byline reads: "This article was automatically written by Tencent's robot Dreamwriter."

Legally, there's a distinction between "author-in-fact" (who or what did the actual writing) and "author-in-law" (who's eligible for copyright ownership). Dreamwriter produced the article for Tencent ("in-fact"), though Tencent assumed rights to the piece ("in-law"), because humans had a hand in the process. But, as Samuelson reminds us, the law might take nearly half a dozen positions on copyright challenges over AI's handiwork.[21]

Here's another puzzle, this time potentially affecting every author who has multiple published works in circulation. In the Prologue, we talked about GPT-3's credible job emulating the writing style of Jerome K. Jerome and Gay Talese. A latter-day Adolph Knipe could feed Edgar Allan Poe's detective fiction into GPT-3 and churn out saleable sequels to "The Purloined Letter." While Poe fans and scholars might bristle, no one would likely come after the perpetrator, since Poe's works are out of copyright.

But what if you fed Dan Brown's *The Da Vinci Code* and *Inferno* into GPT-3 and generated a new Robert Langdon thriller? Brown would have a bone to pick, especially if you published the new work and sold copies. Yet there's the question of whose side the law would be on. US copyright is on words, not ideas—and not on writing style. I suspect the issue of moral rights, which include protection of personal reputation, would kick in.

Besides laws for copyright and attribution, we'll also need to resolve questions of culpability. Who takes the blame if problems arise with AI-generated content?

Responsibility for What You Write

You've crafted a work yourself, had something new to say, are ready to take credit for it, and have found a publisher. Congratulations. But your obligations as an author aren't over. You're also responsible for veracity. As with all my books, the publisher's contract for this one required me to attest that everything I claimed to be a fact was true. If challenges later arose, I'd be stuck with the legal bill.

Assuming we're talking about human authors, these kinds of contractual clauses make sense. People are responsible for what they write. But think about works produced by AI. Large language models are notorious for coming up with text that can have a tenuous relationship with truth. Commercial enterprises that rely on AI text for generating news or science stories tend to use curated data whose contents have been vetted. However, the explosion of AI tools that draw on raw datasets but are available to everyday writers poses new questions about responsibility. If an AI-generated essay you publish contains statements that aren't true or are libelous, no one can take GPT-3 or its digital relatives to court. Who gets hauled before a judge: The company designing the large language model? The company licensing the language model for use in an application? You, as the end-user who ran the program?

It's a brave new legal world.

Have Computers Made Us All Authors?

Building computer technology into the writing process draws us back to connections between authorship and having your writing published—literally, making it public. Before widespread adoption of computers, if you didn't have a commercial publisher or didn't self-publish, your distribution options were scribes, typewriters, carbon paper, mimeographs, or copy machines. A favorite cartoon of mine by William Hamilton has an academic at a cocktail party explaining, "I haven't actually been published or produced yet, but I have had some things professionally typed."[22]

Personal computers, word processing programs, and affordable printers were a democratizing move forward. But the real leap came with broad access to the internet. Everything from personal journal musings to blog posts to story contributions to Wattpad is instantly "published." Voila! You're an author.

The moment everyday writers re-envision themselves as authors, they have more at stake in what they write, knowing their potential audience has grown. No longer is readership limited to a friend or two, or some teacher grading an assignment. Elevating the rest of us to authordom is precisely what English composition doyen Andrea Lunsford and her colleagues had in mind when they chose the title *Everyone's an Author* for their English comp handbook. The title encourages students to think of themselves not as isolated monads writing in the void but as published authors, since "anyone with access to a computer can publish their writing, can in fact become an *author*."[23]

Besides the inherent appeal of the book's title, its choice reflects the authors' commitment to helping readers see writing as a dual-purpose tool: for improving clear thinking and for social exchange. Learning to write should mean developing the ability to think clearly and logically, and to express yourself to real-life readers interested in what you have to say.

What do humans have to say? And why bother writing about it? Given AI's remarkable editing and composing skills, we'll have to choose which kinds of writing to cede to AI, which to share, and which to keep for ourselves. Before trying to divvy things up, it's important to ask why humans write.

Why We Write: A Miscellany of Motives

Google the phrase "why I write" and you get back more than 2 billion pages to check out. Sure, you encounter scores of duplicates, plus a slew of personal blog posts and training offers. But still, this seems to be a hot topic. Best known of the lot is George Orwell's essay by that name, followed by Joan Didion's. But there are dozens more by respected authors. Reading through a generous assortment is an edifying exercise.

Faced with a surfeit of anything—animals, plants, ideas—a reasonable first step is to categorize. The plan worked for Aristotle and Linnaeus. I don't pretend my groupings cover the full spectrum of writing rationales. But the taxonomy launches the conversation. Keep in mind that classifications often overlap. Royalties on your scathing critique of the US criminal justice system also help pay the rent.

The first two categories reflect motivations among everyday writers, while the next two focus on incentives linked with traditional published authorship. The last group of three spotlight writing driven by the heart or soul.

QUOTIDIAN ACTS: PERSONAL AND INTERPERSONAL
Everyday writing by everyday people.

At one level, this is writing we do for ourselves: grocery lists, personal diaries, notes-to-self. Then comes communication with people we know or want to reach: emails to friends, texts to co-workers, status updates, letters to the IRS. What these latter options have in common is the assumption—or at least hope—that someone will read what we write. As for typed chat on commercial websites: Frustration tends to rise when the entity on the other end is a bot, not a human.

WRITING AT OTHERS' BIDDING: SCHOOL DAYS, SCRIBES

We've all been there, needing to crank out an essay, a poem, a critique because the assignment's due tomorrow. As a university teacher, I've bemoaned student conversations overheard in the school cafeteria or on the quad:

> Lindsey: "What are you working on?"
> Jamie: "[Professor] Klein's paper is due tomorrow."
> Lindsey: "How many words?"
> Jamie: "1,200–1,500. I've only got 800 so far."
> Lindsey: "Keep adding adjectives. And repeat yourself. Klein never reads the papers anyway."

No matter how many times I've reminded undergraduates that the papers they write are theirs, not mine, I often don't get through. "Here's your paper, Professor Baron." If you've ever been a student (and you have), I'll bet these words sound familiar.

Writing at others' bidding is equally commonplace in the world of work. Reporters assigned stories in which they have little interest fall here, as do those street scribes in New Delhi or Istanbul.

TANGIBLE GAINS: FINANCIAL AND PROFESSIONAL

At least since the coming of patronage, and then copyright and royalties, people have written for monetary gain. For some, it's immediate need to put food on the table, perhaps tied to payment by the word or working freelance. Other times, there may be a regular salary or decent book advance.

Occupational hurdle-jumping is another prime motivation. Think of university academics living under the sword of Damocles known as publish or perish, especially at that crunch point called tenure review. While the numbers vary by discipline and institutional prestige, overall faculty publication rates commonly head south once job security is assured.[24]

SHARING: EXPERTISE, EXPOSÉ, ADVICE

Think of all those essays, magazine pieces, scientific articles, and books that aim to inform, reveal, or advise. Topics are boundless: what really happened on January 6, an explanation of neuroplasticity, hints for successfully raising orchids.

Depending on the goal and the author's skills, the style might read like a front-page news article, a treatise full of references, or a literary gem. The writer's aim could be straight-up informational ("Just the facts, Ma'am") or expository (with a thesis or point of view—potential Wikipedia contributors need not apply). Not all these works are non-fiction. You're treated to a front-row seat to early modern English history when reading Hilary Mantel's *Wolf Hall*.

We can't talk about motivations for writing without invoking George Orwell, whose landmark essay appeared in 1946. Orwell reeled off potential motives that authors might have for writing prose. After acknowledging writing to make a living, he named four candidates: sheer egoism, aesthetic enthusiasm, historical impulse, and political purpose. It's the last that drove much of Orwell's oeuvre:

> When I sit down to write a book . . . I write it because there is some lie that I want to expose, some fact to which I want to draw attention, and my initial concern is to get a hearing.

Orwell's mission wasn't just expository. It was also highly personal—a motivation leading to the next three categories.

LOOKING OUTWARD: MAKING SENSE, SHARING HOPE

As humans, we try to understand the world we inhabit. Experience drives many who write to enlist words to improve the world that is (or compensate for its shortcomings), express optimism, or cope with realities. Here's a sampling of outward-facing reasons authors have given for writing:[25]

- *re-envisioning the world:* "I could not live in any of the worlds offered to me. . . . I had to create a world of my own." (Anaïs Nin)[26]
- *righting the world:* "Writing is my way of expressing—and thereby eliminating—all the various ways we can be wrong-headed." (Zadie Smith)[27]
- *recasting emotional experience:* "That is why I write—to try to turn sadness into longing, solitude into remembrance." (Paulo Coelho)[28]
- *bringing hope:* "[Writing fiction is] my attempt to keep that fragile strand of radical hope, to build a fire in the darkness." (John Green)[29]
- *dealing with difficulty:* "I write with a sort of grim determination to deal with things that are hidden and difficult." (Colm Tóibín)[30]
- *bringing pleasure to others:* "It is my way of bringing something to the table, contributing what I believe is the best thing I have to offer for others to enjoy." (Carlos Ruiz Zafón)[31]
- *speaking for the dead:* "[F]or the survivor, writing is not a profession, but an occupation, a duty. . . . [I write] to help the dead vanquish death." (Elie Wiesel)[32]

LOOKING INWARD: SELF-DISCOVERY AND UNDERSTANDING

Many people write to bring into focus what they're thinking, who they are, and what their place is in the world. Private diaries have long done duty, but the same motivations impel writers who make their words public.

Joan Didion's 1976 essay "Why I Write" naturally falls here. Didion acknowledges lifting the title from Orwell. But she had her own motivations:

> I write entirely to find out what I'm thinking, what I'm looking at, what I see and what it means. What I want and what I fear.

Linger on Didion's words about writing to figure out what she's thinking. This drive has reverberated over the years. Perhaps the earliest recorded example is from Horace Walpole, in the eighteenth century: "I never understand anything until I have written about it."[33] By the twentieth century, the sentiment was widespread, with some version of "How can I know what I think until I see what I say?" showing up in the work of Graham Wallas (1926: *The Art of Thought*); E. M. Forster (1927: *Aspects of the Novel*); W. H. Auden, crediting Forster (1962: *The Dyer's Hand and Other Essays*); and Arthur Koestler (1964: *The Act of Creation*).[34]

The list runs on. Most quoted is likely Flannery O'Connor: "I write because I don't know what I think until I read what I say." But she's in good company. Similar words are attributed to George Bernard Shaw ("I do not know what I think until I write it"), William Faulkner ("I never know what I think about something until I read what I've written on it"), and Joan Didion ("I don't know what I think until I write it down").[35]

The message is clear: Writing clarifies thinking. Eric Havelock would have nodded assent.

There's a cascade of other inwardly directed motivations for expressing ourselves in writing. These are some:

- *self-exploration:* "Any writer worth his salt writes to please himself. . . . It's a self-exploratory operation that is endless." (Harper Lee)[36]
- *freedom to be yourself:* "A person is a fool to become a writer. His only compensation is absolute freedom. He has no master except his own soul, and that, I am sure, is why he does it." (Roald Dahl)[37]
- *affirming your own existence or worth:* "Writing eases my suffering. . . . When you use words, you're able to keep your mind alive. Writing is my way of reaffirming my own existence." (Gao Xingjian)[38]
- *proving you can do it:* The author of *The Last of the Mohicans* wrote his first

novel, *Precaution*, after making a friendly bet with his wife that he could produce a better novel than the one he was reading at the time. (James Fenimore Cooper)[39]

- *quest for immortality:* "I write to immortalize the world I have found and made for myself." (Reginald Shepherd)[40]

I give the final word on inner motivation to Jhumpa Lahiri:

> Writing is a way to salvage life, to give it form and meaning. It exposes what we have hidden, unearths what we have neglected, misremembered, denied. It is a method of capturing, of pinning down, but it is also a form of truth, of liberation.[41]

PERSONAL RELEASE: COMPULSION AND REBELLION

Some writing is a primal scream, emerging as a manifesto or diary that authors feel driven to release. The journal kept by Ted Kaczynski (aka the Unabomber) is one chilling example. Hitler's *Mein Kampf* —beginning with its title ("My Struggle")—is another.

Not all personal compulsion for writing has such fateful consequences. We feel impelled to write letters to the editor or respond to what others have posted online. Occasionally, our writing is an authorial Saint Vitus dance. In *The Midnight Disease*, neurologist Alice Flaherty recounts a period in her life when bipolar disorder propelled her to write manically.[42]

We also write to rebel. Maybe it's graffiti spray painted on building walls or incised into tree trunks. Rebellion might take the form of refusing to send greeting cards with pre-printed messages but insisting on crafting our own text. We write candid resignation letters, letting loose about what we think of the company or supervisor we're walking out on.

Making sense. Sharing hope. Self-discovery. Understanding. Compulsion. Rebellion. Reasons such as these are among the fundamental human drives for writing.

Computers have no motivations for anything, including to write. They don't need to construct to-do lists, aren't in it for the money, hardly feel impelled to share what they know. Humans program them, feed them data, sometimes offer starter text, and the machines comply by emitting words.

Since AI programs have no feelings, no sense of human suffering, and no intentionality, they don't look outward or inward. They don't seek to know themselves. For AI, Socrates's pronouncement that the unexamined life is not worth living doesn't compute. And while AI programs might well produce writing that humans find meaningful, the programs themselves are indifferent. Our hope is that they don't rebel.

Unlike humans, AI programs can't take pride in what they produce. Many authors—myself included—quip that books we write are like our children. Programs have no devotion to progeny. Even if an AI can generate realistic love letters, it can't feel the love.

But there is one area where modern AI programs seem to excel, and that's in editing human writing. The question is how much we want them to.

The Second Time Around: Why We Rewrite

Three words that researchers often dread hearing are "revise and resubmit." The authors had worked hard at crafting a well-argued and polished manuscript, which they submitted to a scholarly journal. They thought they were done. Rarely so simple. Oftentimes, when the paper gets sent out for peer review, the recommendation isn't outright rejection but a request for changes, large or small. The paper is then kicked back to the authors for revision.

Of course, revision isn't just for scholarly writing. The act of rewriting, onerous—even punitive—as it sometimes feels, is really just another step in the writing process.

The Fruits of Rewriting

Start with low-hanging fruit: old-fashioned proofreading. Let's assume you're sitting with a paper draft (maybe handwritten) that's untouched by software mop-up operations like spellcheck or grammar review programs. Spelling and punctuation glitches are logical targets to nab on a light read-through. You might also suss out unintended sentence fragments or wording that makes no sense. Depending on your grammatical prowess, intentional choices, or stylistic flair, you might convert a "who" to "whom" or find synonyms for words appearing too often.

That's the easy part. Even a computer could do it.

Serious editing calls for more effort. Does one sentence reasonably follow from another? What about transitions between paragraphs? Then comes the content itself: Have you built a logical case? What would be a convincing counter argument? AI-driven programming may or may not be up to this more sophisticated kind of editing.

A paradoxical curse of word processing programs and printers is that they make our finished text look so neat. No handwritten strikeouts, no Wite-Out tape or globs of correction fluid on typescript produced on that relic known as a typewriter. Seeing your writing gussied up so elegantly, it can be hard convincing yourself that more work might still be needed.

Taking a hatchet to your own writing can be humbling, not to mention hard work. But one of literacy's virtues is creating space for us to rethink what we've written, much as we can rethink words and arguments and stories we read. Put aside Havelock's alphabetic hypothesis and just focus on literacy itself. If those classical Greek philosophers could benefit from contemplating, criticizing, and improving upon the ideas of others as represented in written words, we can do the same with our own.

Hiring Digital Janitors (aka Editors)

But wait. Didn't we say AI can assist with at least some of the editing work? Assume the usual cast of digital helpmates (spellcheck, autocomplete, grammar check programs) plus newer tools for automatically drafting emails or proposing alternatives to sentences we've written. When we grant these digital janitors free rein to clean up our prose, the results can seem even more impressive than our earlier word-processed and printed drafts.

Then there's the bad news.

AI may be undermining our basic writing skills. (More on this worry in Part IV.) Even worse, these deceptively benign tools lessen the impetus to question our own thinking and writing. Beyond sentence mechanics and wordsmithing, there's the essence of what we're trying to express. Whether it makes sense. Whether it's true. Whether it would convince others. What's more, AI swiftly cleans up our text (as with today's spellcheck), often before we can notice the errors of our ways. There's little chance to linger over what we've written and consider how we—not AI—might have done differently.

I think about an article by journalist Lindsay Crouse on why she ditched her smart watch. For years, she relied on it to measure everything from her training status (she's a runner) to heart rate variability. But after taking stock of the feast of other measurements the watch was capable of—sleep patterns, body temperature, metabolic rate—she found the device was replacing her own self-awareness:

> Once you outsource your well-being to a device and convert it into a number,
> it stops being yours. The data stands in for self-awareness.[43]

If wearable smart devices take over monitoring our physical well-being, we risk losing the need to monitor it ourselves. We become a set of numbers, not a flesh-and-blood self. The same can happen with writing. Ceding the editing process to AI undermines motivation to rework, rethink, rewrite prose that computer tools make look so squeaky clean.

Have we abandoned ship when it comes to caring about people's writing skills? Not yet. One simple measure is employer surveys of what skills they value when hiring college graduates. The ability to write remains high on the list. In their 2018 survey, the National Association of Colleges and Employers (NACE) found that 82 percent of US employers they asked were looking for candidates who had strong written communication skills. Problem-solving ranked a smidge lower (81 percent), with ability to work in a team coming in third at 79 percent.[44]

Since 2018, priorities changed a bit. The 2022 survey had problem-solving on top (86 percent), with written communication skills down to 73 percent.[45] It's not clear why the value employers placed on writing skills declined by 9 percent. Perhaps it was the growing use and power of AI tools for cleaning up employees' writing. Another potential explanation: increased recognition that many graduates of American colleges aren't native speakers of English but have other skills making them attractive candidates. Whatever the cause, and despite the dip, demand for new hires to know how to write has hardly vanished.

If graduates are expected to have strong writing skills, how are these cultivated? In the United States, the answer, devised more than a century ago, was to teach composition in college. The practice hasn't stopped. But what's been added is new thinking about who—or what—should have a hand in evaluating student written work.

THREE

English Comp and Its Aftermath

More than 51,000 dead. For three days at the start of July 1863, the bloodiest battle of the American Civil War raged in the small town of Gettysburg, Pennsylvania. The Union prevailed, but costs to both Blue and Gray were devastating.

A scant four-and-a-half months later, President Abraham Lincoln traveled to Gettysburg to dedicate the new cemetery. American schoolchildren are reared on Lincoln's memorable two-minute speech. Should they forget, the words are inscribed on a wall of the Lincoln Memorial in Washington. They don't take up much space.

Lincoln wasn't the only speaker at that consecration. Preceding him was the Unitarian pastor, statesman, and orator Edward Everett. And Everett did speak—for more than two hours. Today, two hours of non-stop talk seems an eternity. At the time, though, it was matter of course. Oratory was everywhere—in churches, in politics, and in colleges.

A Quest for Written Standards

Oral culture flourished through the end of the nineteenth century, despite much of the population being literate. But moves were already afoot to lay down written standards. The drumbeat had begun by the early eighteenth century, with Jonathan Swift seeking to clean up and then "fix" the English language, once and for all: "it is better a Language should not be perfect, than that it should be perpetually changing."[1] Samuel Johnson was initially on board. But in the *Preface* to his 1755 *Dictionary of the English Language*, Johnson recognized that attempting to deny language evolution was a fool's errand ("to enchain syllables, and to lash the wind, are equally the undertaking of pride").

If you can't stop language from changing, at least you could try standardizing it. An obvious place to start was with spelling, which was finally settling down after centuries of largely a free-for-all.[2] No more spelling your own name multiple ways, as Shakespeare had done. In 1750, Lord Chesterfield memorably advised his son that

> orthography, in the true sense of the word, is so absolutely necessary for a man of letters, or a gentleman, that one false spelling may fix a ridicule upon him for the rest of his life.[3]

English grammar was another renegade to be brought to heel. From the mid-eighteenth century and into the nineteenth, a cascade of self-appointed grammarians like Bishop Robert Lowth and Lindley Murray laid down their versions of proper usage.[4] The rising middle class and the new gentry sought instruction on writing "properly." Between 1762 and 1800, Lowth's *Short Introduction to English Grammar* went through forty-five editions.[5] Grammatical prescriptivism was in full flower.

America of the eighteenth and nineteenth centuries largely followed England's lead.[6] Yes, American spelling differs somewhat from British, for which early credit goes to Noah Webster.[7] And yes, the vocabulary and grammar aren't identical. Americans put bonnets on their heads, not the fronts of their cars. If American students write "I've gone to hospital," they'll find a red mark demanding "the" before "hospital." Yet in the scheme of things, the differences remain minor.

On both sides of the Atlantic, accelerating literacy rates meant growing demand for written matter, including books, newspapers, and magazines. Equally critical was a pair of developments that resulted in a huge amount of paper to be written on and read.

The first was commercial success of the typewriter. Christopher Latham Sholes produced a working prototype in 1867. Within a few years, rights were sold to E. Remington & Sons. Sales exploded when a vast new market emerged: the modern office (the second development).[8] Between 1870 and 1900, the number of bookkeepers, cashiers, and accountants soared from 38,776 to 254,880. The count of stenographers and typists went from 154 to 112,364.[9] A paperwork revolution was unfolding, and writing skills were needed.

The challenge was where to learn them. Historically, writing was strictly a subject for lower education, along with reading and basic arithmetic. That was to change in late nineteenth-century America, when a college in New England shook off its centuries-long emphasis on rhetoric and oratory and focused instead on written English composition.

What began as a local curriculum shift would be adopted by colleges and universities nationwide. Looking ahead to later chapters, we'll see that developments in AI have many people questioning whether learning all those niceties of spelling and grammar is still necessary.

The Birth of English Comp

The president of Harvard was troubled. Why, he asked, can't incoming freshmen write competently?

Charles W. Eliot assumed the reins at Harvard in 1869. A few years prior, Eliot spent two years traveling in Europe, observing the way high school students were educated, along with their later employment prospects. Writing in the *Atlantic Monthly*, he lauded the German *Realschulen*'s preparation of boys for the emerging industrial economy.[10] In the coming decades, Eliot would outspokenly criticize American secondary school training.[11] But first, in his inaugural address, the new president bemoaned many shortcomings in American education (including "the prevailing neglect of the systematic study of the English language") and proposed a litany of changes at Harvard.[12]

Eliot's focus on German education wasn't accidental. Since the early 1900s, thousands of Americans had traveled to study at German universities, where research and seminars dominated the curriculum, rather than the American model of lectures, memorization, and oral rhetoric.[13] German universities didn't teach composition. It was assumed that writing skills would be acquired in secondary school, especially by students proceeding to higher education. The assumption was generally valid.

Not so in America.

Eliot blamed US secondary education for failing to provide adequate preparation in written English grammar and composition. But for now, Harvard needed to deal with the consequences. To appreciate Eliot's solution, let's take stock of the curriculum he inherited.

Rhetoric in American Academe

Harvard was founded in 1636 by Congregationalists. (Think of those Pilgrims landing at Plymouth Rock in 1620.) A prime motivation for the new institution was training clergy. Later, the clientele would expand to other professions, including law and civic leadership, for which rhetorical skills were also a vital qualification. For more than a century, American colleges were overwhelmingly established by religious groups: Yale (1701, Congregational), Princeton (1746, Presbyterian), Brown (1764, Baptist), Georgetown (1789, Jesuit). As Yale stipulated in its founding document, the school's mission was to educate students for "Publick employment both in Church and Civil State."[14]

In the late eighteenth century, the American college curriculum was fairly rigid. Here's what was taught at Brown:

> The Curriculum . . . included Greek and Latin for the first two years, rhetoric, geography and logic in the second year, algebra and trigonometry, surveying and navigation, and moral philosophy in the third year, and, in the fourth year, some history and a review of the studies of the previous years. Public speaking was of utmost importance as students in college were often preparing themselves for the ministry or the law.

And quoting from Brown's "Laws of 1783":

> "On the last wednesday in every month, every Student in College shall pronounce publikly on the Stage, memoriter, such an Oration or piece as shall be previously approved by the President."[15]

The next century saw curricular revisions, varying from college to college, but emphasis on spoken rhetoric remained. What's more, students amplified the focus on oratory through their literary societies, which were popular on campuses through the nineteenth century. Activities included writing essays and building society libraries. Paramount was emphasis on public speaking. Take Brown's Philermenian Society, organized in 1794:

> The object of the association was the promotion of social intercourse and improvement in forensic dispute. . . . President Jonathan Maxcy, himself a gifted orator, in approving the constitution, recommended that they "accustom themselves to extemporaneous speaking, as nothing will tend to present them to more advantage in any of the learned professions."[16]

All that rhetorical practice also came in handy for taking college exams.

Recitation to Writing, Latin to English

Since the early days of Oxford and Cambridge, students were assessed through oral examinations, known as disputations. Examiners posed questions that students needed to dispute or argue. The tradition crossed the Atlantic.

Beyond writing longish themes on ponderous topics like "Can the Immortality of the Soul Be Proven" or "Whether the Soul Always Thinks,"[17] orality perfused American academia. In day-to-day classroom activities, accomplishment was judged through recitation. And those written themes were often memorized to then be delivered orally.[18]

Gradually, evaluation would shift from oral recitations or disputations to written exams. Harvard's first written testing, but only in mathematics, wasn't instituted until 1855.[19] The development was to foreshadow later curricular revisions introduced by one of the new exam's creators, none other than Charles Eliot. In 1854, as a mathematics tutor at Harvard, Eliot (along with James Mills Peirce, a former Harvard classmate) convinced a reluctant Examining Committee to permit written math exams to substitute for oral ones. The innovation stuck. By the end of Eliot's first year as president, three-hour written exams were required for all undergraduate courses.[20]

Another seismic shift was in the language dominating the instructional program. From Harvard's earliest years, Latin was central, even to be accepted as a student. The admission requirement for 1642 read:

> When any Schollar is able to Read Tully or such like classical Latine Authour ex tempore, & make and speake true Latin in verse and prose suo (ut aiunt) Marte, and decline perfectly the paradigmes of Nounes and verbes in ye Greeke toungue then may hee bee admitted into ye Colledge, nor shall any claime admission before such qualifications.[21]

Two centuries later, Latin's place in the curriculum was still evident, though shrinking. Fewer Latin courses were obligatory. In 1898, Eliot abolished the Latin entry requirement, in hopes of expanding admission to students who hadn't attended preparatory schools that taught classical languages.

The switch to written examinations, along with de-emphasis on Latin, marked a curricular reorientation, away from classical oratory (often in Latin) to practical training in writing the English language. Before Eliot's reformations, Harvard freshmen were required to take a year-long course in elocution, and later on, a semester of forensics (meaning oratory).[22] There were a few elective courses on Anglo-Saxon (aka Old English). However, classical rhetoric—mostly oral, always on weighty topics—dominated the curriculum.

Soon that domination would crumble, thanks to a new faculty appointment.

Enter English Comp

Adams Sherman Hill was a law school graduate and seasoned journalist. In 1872, Eliot hired him to teach rhetoric. At the time, typical required texts included old standards like George Campbell's *Principles of Rhetoric* (1776) and Richard Whately's *Elements of Rhetoric* (1845). But for the academic year 1874–1875, two additional texts popped up in Hill's sophomore rhetoric curriculum: Hill's own *Rules for Punctuation and the Use of Capital Letters* and exercises from Edwin Abbott's *How to Write Clearly: Rules and Exercises on English Composition.*[23] Formal teaching of English grammar and style was creeping into the college curriculum.

To forewarn prospective applicants, Hill engineered a college entrance requirement in English composition. The first year of the required exam, the Harvard Catalogue for 1873–1874 explained that

> Each candidate will be required to write a short English Composition, correct in spelling, punctuation, grammar, and expression, the subject to be taken from such works of standard authors as will be announced from time to time.[24]

Hill's examination revealed not just how paltry some high school seniors' writing abilities were, but how difficult it could be for evaluators to weigh grammar and other writing mechanics against essay content. LeBaron Briggs, future dean of Harvard College and Boylston Professor of Rhetoric, summed up the problem:

> the examiner's first question to himself is always, "Can the boy write English?" If he can, he must pass the examination, though, with Julius Caesar for his subject, he declares that Mark Anthony loved Caesar less and Rome more.[25]

So much for getting the facts right. As we'll see, computer-based grading of essays has faced the same challenge.

Once students were enrolled, they were met with Hill's rhetoric curriculum, a program that evolved. From Hill's arrival in the early 1870s through the early 1880s, the course was held in students' sophomore year, with additional writing requirements in the form of themes and forensics for juniors and seniors. By 1884, the rhetoric requirement had moved to freshman year. And by 1885, the course had been rebranded "Rhetoric and English Composition."[26] What came to be known as English A—Harvard's freshman comp—had arrived.

The curriculum was a dramatic shift from the ponderous themes of old. Now, students could often choose their own topics. Short themes were about two or three paragraphs and reflected personal experience. Longer themes (required every two weeks) drew on both individual and general knowledge.[27] Hill, the former journalist, encouraged students to write about topics they might actually care about.

For some themes, students were asked to revise their submissions, incorporating instructors' corrections and critiques. In fact, the requirement for rewriting was formally included in Harvard's official publications describing the curriculum. Up through 1900, additional writing-related requirements remained for sophomores and juniors.[28] Harvard was taking English composition seriously.

Traditional students were beneficiaries of the new writing curriculum. But so were a growing influx of those with different backgrounds and aspirations.

English Comp for the Masses

Thanks to the Industrial Revolution, along with advances in engineering and applied science, families began seeking practical higher learning for their progeny. America's colleges responded. In 1874, Harvard opened the Lawrence Scientific School, while Yale launched the Sheffield Scientific School. MIT opened its doors for classes in 1865. At the same time, growing numbers of students wanting to prepare for white-collar professions (other than in theology or law) were pursuing traditional post-secondary education.

Colleges found themselves needing a curriculum that would accommodate the new cadres. Many of these students likely "would never give a speech in their lives,"[29] so the classical rhetorical curriculum—including its emphasis on Latin—was of little use. There was also the pragmatic issue of ballooning enrollments. As a Harvard committee reported in 1897, class size had increased nearly fourfold. What had once been a relatively easy teaching job—listening to recitations during class time—had become burdensome.

Since there were now too many students to permit in-class recitation, written work was the only alternative.[30] And those papers needed to be graded. The grading burden persists to this day, though now AI technology is being dangled as a tempting remedy. We'll get to that story soon.

Other colleges began rethinking their curriculum. By the end of the nineteenth century, schools around the country were adopting some version of Harvard's English A.[31]

However, not everyone favored mandatory composition. One vocal critic was Thomas Lounsbury, an English instructor at Yale's Sheffield Scientific School for over thirty years. Lounsbury believed the way students learned to write was through reading great literature, not by writing themes and being drilled on grammar rules:

> On no one subject of education has so great an amount of effort been put
> forth as on the teaching of English composition, with so little satisfactory
> to show for it.[32]

Barrett Wendell, who had introduced the daily theme at Harvard, was later to declare that teaching college composition was futile.[33]

We can only speculate what Lounsbury or Wendell might think about spell-check or Grammarly. Lounsbury challenged the modern notion that every educated person "should seek to become a writer." Was this emphasis on teaching writing to all students really necessary? He thought not, wryly noting that "The world is not suffering from a penury of manuscripts or of books."[34]

But college-level composition requirements seemed here to stay, though with multiple options emerging. Most common is a one- or two-semester course, designed for entering students. Another option: one course early on and then another "writing intensive" subject-area course in later years. Or: no separate course, but writing instruction appended to some required course.

Whatever the scheme, if college students are going to submit written assignments, someone needs to grade them. And therein lies the rub.

Who Does the Grading?

Ask college faculty what they like least about their jobs, and I bet grading papers tops the list.[35] Done conscientiously, grading writing assignments takes a lot of work.

Think about the process as having three layers. The first is judging overall quality. That's the easiest to put a grade on and, with far too many of my colleagues, the only one they bother with. The second layer is commenting on the content, considering, for instance, the paper's organization, logical flow, and accuracy. If you have forty essays to grade, meaningful feedback can take bucketsful of time. The third component is marking the nuts and bolts, everything from spelling to punctuation to grammar to word choice to style. More bucketsful.

And there's another consideration: competence of those doing the grading. Let's hope that faculty officially charged with teaching English composition have the requisite training and skills. But when it comes to a school's faculty at large, a bigger issue looms. Even if you're dedicated and well-meaning, maybe you're not a particularly good writer. Your grammar skills might be rough around the edges. (That goes for native and non-native speakers of English alike.) You got a PhD to teach history or sociology or international relations, not English comp.

Finally, there's the delicate matter of the level of professional respect afforded evaluators. Those with the job title "writing instructor" have overwhelming suffered from low prestige and paltry salaries. As John Brereton so bluntly put it in his book on the origins of college writing courses in America, "the composition course came to stand for a kind of teacher slavery."[36]

The Respect Challenge

Just as zip codes affect how much your house is worth, the college department that faculty are housed in impacts their salary. It's no secret that mathematicians earn more than professors of religion. And so it matters where teachers of English composition hang their hats.

The domicile question has dogged writing instructors since the infancy of English comp. Because they weren't teaching classical rhetoric and oratory, that departmental designation made little sense. Perhaps the emergence of new English departments would offer a solution.

English literature began making its way into college curricula in the last quarter of the nineteenth century. Harvard's English Department was established in 1876. The Modern Language Association (MLA) was formed in 1883. Initially, the MLA included a pedagogical division, providing an affiliation for those teaching composition. However, in 1903, the association declared its members were literature professors, not writing teachers, and disbanded its pedagogical section.[37] Composition teachers became professionally homeless.

A few years later, help was on the way. The National Council of Teachers of English (NCTE) was founded in 1911, looking to professionalize the ranks of English teachers. Gradually, by the 1970s, the idea of rhetoric as a discipline became reestablished in academic circles, but this time focused on written expression. The NCTE runs an annual Conference on College Composition and Communication, and it's possible to earn a PhD in rhetoric and composition.[38]

Once again, teachers of English composition had a base. On campus, they're commonly part of English (or literature) departments. However, their title is often "instructor," not "professor." Plus, teaching loads are most times higher and salaries lower than those of colleagues sharing departmental letterhead.

The Time Challenge

Time is a continuing challenge for anyone who takes seriously the task of grading written work. Writing in 1912, William Lyon Phelps, who went on to become a popular English professor at Yale, shared his experience about the year he earlier spent at Harvard as a writing instructor: "I read and marked over seven hundred themes a week. . . . I never went to bed before midnight." The effect on him was palpable:

But with the highest respect and admiration for my colleagues, nothing on earth would have induced me to continue such brain-fagging toil for another year. . . . I said to myself: "This is worse than coal-heaving. This is nerve-destroying, a torture to the soul and body."[39]

Writing a year earlier, Thomas Lounsbury had grumbled, "Under the compulsory system now prevailing the task of reading and correcting themes is one of deadly dullness."[40] In fact, sometimes so dull and time-consuming that instructors dodged it. A Harvard Committee on Composition and Rhetoric admitted in its 1892 report that

Owing to the number of these exercises and the constant accumulation of fresh papers the rewritten themes are not read by the instructor, except to determine the final grade of a student whose mark is doubtful.[41]

Maybe the drudgery could be offloaded to a machine. For decades, students used number 2 pencils to fill in little ovals on multiple-choice exam answer sheets, which were then fed into a Scantron and graded automatically. Given computer technology, why not feed in student essays for automated assessment?

Welcome to the present. Bit by bit, advance by advance, AI is supplementing or replacing humans in the business of evaluating writing. Tracing today's automatic essay assessment back to its source will lead us to the Educational Testing Service (ETS). But before there was ETS, there was Horace Mann.

Written Testing: Standardization and (for Some) a Quest for Fairness

Imagine yourself a schoolchild in mid-nineteenth-century Boston. Your school exams were oral, often in the form of public displays.[42] Students with strong rhetorical skills could outshine less polished classmates. Horace Mann, an educational reformer and supporter of public education, had a better idea: Replace oral performance with a common, objective written exam. That is, measure achievement. Mann's goal was to determine, without bias, which pupils were eligible for advancement to the next level.

Interest in achievement didn't disappear, but a new purpose took center stage: gauging mental ability—IQ. A progression of psychologists went to work, including Edward Thorndike, as well as Alfred Binet (in France) and Lewis Terman (at Stanford), the fruits of whose labors gave us the Stanford-Binet Test of intelligence. We'll meet up with Terman again in Chapter 9 when we talk about creativity.

The barefaced rationale for IQ testing was to separate the mentally fit from the feebleminded. If this sounds dangerously like eugenics, you're right. Thorndike, Binet, and Terman were all adherents of the theory, so named by Francis Galton in 1883. The idea was that some human qualities are more valued than others, and people should be sorted—and treated—accordingly. Eugenics had a growing cadre of supporters. In the best of cases, the justification was to channel people into the education and life path most suited to their abilities. In the worst, consequences included sterilization and genocide.

Harvard's Eliot was a eugenicist, as were scores of his colleagues. But Eliot, like Mann, had another vision and that was fairness. Remember it was Eliot who canceled the Latin admission requirement to open a pathway for applicants lacking training in the classics. That desire to give all students a fair chance would motivate another Harvard president, James Conant, to seek an equitable way of making scholarship money available to deserving applicants.

Conant turned to two assistants, Wilbur Bender and Henry Chauncey, to identify a suitable assessment tool. Chauncey recommended using a test that had been developed by Carl Brigham at Princeton: the Scholastic Aptitude Test (SAT).[43] And yes, Brigham, like many of his psychology colleagues, was a eugenicist.

Besides his work at Harvard, Conant was instrumental in bringing together the disparate testing jurisdictions for higher education in America. These included the American Council on Education, the Carnegie Foundation for the Advancement of Teaching (spearheading development of the Graduate Record Examinations—the GRE), and the College Entrance Examination Board (the source of the SAT). Under Chauncey's leadership, a new umbrella organization emerged in 1947: the Educational Testing Service.[44] Its activities would include both assessment and educational research. Given the millions of veterans returning from World War II—and eligible to attend college through the GI Bill—the need was great for establishing uniform admissions testing across colleges and universities.

How to Assess Writing

Channeling the ghost of Adams Hill and his Harvard writing entrance exam, ETS has a history of including an essay as part of the SAT. However, the essay's status has waxed and waned over the decades.[45]

When I took the SAT back in the mid-1960s, there was an essay. At some point, it disappeared. By 1974, a multiple-choice Test of Standard Written English arrived for measuring grammar and writing skills. Come 1994, that vanished, but a short essay was incorporated into a test called SAT II Writing (essentially an elective achievement test, separate from the main SAT). Change came again in 2005, when the SAT II Writing was axed, but an essay was re-instituted as part of the main SAT. In 2016, the essay became optional. And in 2021, out went the essay (again) and in came a multiple-choice test (again)—a writing and language component of the SAT that asks students to edit text passages by fixing mistakes and selecting better stylistic choices.[46]

Why this yo-yo? Presumably to make testing more equitable and better tailored to the skills colleges want assessed. But problems inherent in the evaluation process may well have been another factor.

Here's the issue. Ask three faculty members to review the same student essay, and they might assign three different grades. ETS recognized the challenge. While consistency is easy in scoring multiple-choice or true/false questions on a standardized test, how do you standardize scoring of essays? The usual approach—as teachers of English composition will tell you—is to develop grading rubrics and then train evaluators how to use them. Which is what ETS has long done. To score essay portions of its tests, ETS traditionally convened bevies of evaluators, provided instruction, and then ran marathon scoring sessions.

What if there were a simpler way of evaluating writing, one that eliminated both the need for all those hours spent grading and the dilemma of inconsistency across evaluators? Enter computers.

Computer as Grader

It was 1966, the same year Joseph Weizenbaum announced his ELIZA program, using a computer to mimic a Rogerian psychotherapist. (More on ELIZA in Chapter 7.) Ellis Page's goal was different. An English teacher and educational psychologist, Page was proposing that computers evaluate student writing. Development of his program called PEG (Project Essay Grade) was supported by the College Entrance Examination Board, which tasks ETS with developing and administering tests like the SAT.

Page was troubled that human grading of student essays is incredibly time-consuming. But he also argued it's not objective:

> What psychometricians really need . . . is some way to measure essay quality with the same reliability, validity, and generalizability—with the same "objectivity"—which they enjoy with multiple-choice items. And this measurement need . . . the computer seems destined to alleviate.[47]

It would take several decades before automated scoring would become a reality. As for claims of validity, that's another story.

Automated Scoring Goes Mainstream

In 1997, ETS filed a provisional patent application for a "System and Method for Computer-Based Automatic Essay Scoring." By 1999, their program was in place for the GMAT (Graduate Management Admission Test). Later it became a fixture on the SAT, TOEFL (Test of English as a Foreign Language), and GRE (Graduate Record Examinations). Over the years, additional patent applications were filed, reflecting more refinements to the evaluation algorithms behind their program, known as e-rater.[48]

ETS saw e-rater and human scoring as a kind of tag team. For the optional essay on the SAT (largely defunct, for now), scoring has been done exclusively by e-rater, though ETS clarifies that "the automated scoring . . . is based on essay scores produced by human raters scoring sample essays." For the GRE, GMAT, and TOEFL essays, there's a team effort between human and e-rater scoring.[49] ETS has reported that for some essay components in the GRE and the TOEFL, agreement between a human and e-rater measured higher than between two humans. In fact, ETS has suggested that e-rater can act as a "control" over human scoring.[50]

The workings of e-rater are at once opaque and transparent. For most users, the process seems hidden in a black box. Yet descriptions of the mechanics are lying in plain sight for those with technical knowhow in reading them.[51] The engines at work have always relied on natural language processing, with ever-more sophisticated versions being implemented as AI technology has evolved.

Here are some of the basic linguistic features e-rater uses to come up with its scores:

- *length:* number of sentences, words, or characters—longer is better
- *lexical complexity:* favoring richly polysyllabic words like "discombobulated" over simple ones like "confused"
- *readability level:* measured by school grade, using tools like the Flesch-Kincaid readability test[52]
- *grammatical correctness*

These days, ETS also maintains it can assess more subtle qualities, such as coherence or good arguments.[53]

You'll notice there's no mention of accuracy or of the meaning of what's been written. Given that e-rater is built on NLP (natural language processing) models (now presumably including large language models), we shouldn't be surprised. If GPT-3 can't distinguish between truth and falsehood, there's little reason to assume e-rater can. As ETS openly admits, "The *e-rater* engine cannot read so it cannot evaluate essays the same way that human raters do."[54]

A program like e-rater brings an economy of scale to grading essays. Potentially it also introduces a level of objectivity in the face of variation in human judgment. But not everyone agrees that these goals necessarily render AI fit for assessing human writing, whether for ETS essay questions or for student writing assignments.

Automation Critics

Among the most vocal critics of automated writing evaluation have been teachers of English composition. In 2004, the Conference on College Composition and Communication (CCCC) issued a position statement, arguing that

> all writing should have human readers, regardless of the purpose of the writing. . . . Writing-to-a-machine violates the essentially social nature of writing: we write to others for social purposes.[55]

The sentiment is hardly new. Back in 1969, Ed White, who would become a much-lauded teacher of composition, had asked,

> How can anyone write unless he has something to say to somebody? . . . Writing for nobody is not writing at all.[56]

Writing for a machine so it can assess your work is writing for nobody.

Another major complaint has been that it's possible to game the system, once you know what attributes (like sentence length or polysyllabic vocabulary) e-rater is programmed to reward. Here's how ETS researcher Nitin Madnani responded to the charge:

> "If somebody is smart enough to pay attention to all the things that . . . an automated system pays attention to, to incorporate them in their writing, that's no longer gaming. That's good writing."[57]

Not so fast. Since e-rater is built on a boilerplate approach to writing, I suspect English composition instructors, not to mention teachers of creative writing, would have a bone to pick with Madnani's reply. However we might define "good" writing, it's more than acing checklists. ChatGPT has proven itself adept at whipping up boilerplate essays. But its Achilles heel is they come out sounding flat.

Students are no dummies when it comes to psyching out grading schemes. If they know that long sentences, complex vocabulary, and getting the grammar right will impress e-rater—and get them a high score—you can bet they'll do their best to accommodate. Of course, the folks at ETS are no dummies either, recognizing potential for the system to be gamed. In an early experiment run by ETS using an essay prompt for the GRE, it turned out that expert writers could trick e-rater into giving higher scores than their essays deserved.[58]

E-rater fails even more dramatically on other aspects of composition. High on the list is accuracy. Les Perelman, longtime director of writing at MIT, put it this way: "E-rater doesn't care if you say the War of 1812 started in 1945."[59] You can't help being reminded of LeBaron Briggs's concern, over a century back, that an applicant to Harvard could write "Mark Anthony loved Caesar less and Rome more"—grammatically fine but factually screwed up—and still be admitted. Zooming to the present, AI text generation is susceptible to delivering up similar fractured history.

Les Perelman wasn't done with e-rater. In 2014, he and a group of collaborators created a tool called BABEL (Basic Automatic BS Essay Language Generator), designed to see if it could produce essays that earned top marks (a 6) despite the text being semantic gibberish. And succeed BABEL did, being awarded a 6 for a GRE essay that began this way:

> Educatee on an assassination will always be a part of mankind. Society will always authenticate curriculum; some for assassinations and others to a concession. The insinuation at pupil lies in the area of theory of knowledge and the field of semantics.[60]

Lewis Carroll's "'Twas brillig and the slithy toves" is the picture of semantic clarity in comparison.

Once again, ETS was on the case. While claiming that e-rater could indeed (at least as of 2018) detect BABEL-generated essays, they also cautioned that

> It is important for developers of automated scoring systems to continue to be diligent . . . to prevent weakness that can be exploited by tools such as Babel.[61]

Now that large language models have become the new norm in natural language processing, it will be interesting to see if the technology can psyche out BABEL's word salad.

Meanwhile, as academics have been battling over whether computers should be allowed to score essay sections of standardized tests, the same underlying technology has been rebranded as a coaching, rather than testing, scheme. Again, ETS was at the front of the pack.

Computer as Writing Coach

Think back to the hurdles faced by people responsible for assessing student writing. There's the time issue, along with the evaluator's competence and motivation to provide meaningful, accurate, and comprehensive feedback. What if writers had their own private editor? One at their beck and call. One for which they didn't need to wait weeks to get their papers back. One that wasn't giving a grade, just offering advice.

Such a luxury is largely out of reach—unless you automate it. ETS had just the tool for the job.

By the early 2000s, the testing agency rolled out Criterion, an online writing service for students, running on its e-rater engine.[62] Described as an "instructor-led writing tool that helps students plan, write and revise their essays," Criterion was marketed to educational institutions, now ranging from lower school through college.[63] As e-rater's sophistication grows, so does Criterion's.

ETS's Criterion isn't the only AI-driven writing coach in town. The main contender is Grammarly, though Microsoft Word has an even longer history in the business of grammar and style check. Word now sports an AI-powered functionality upgrade called Microsoft Editor. Plus, in the education world, you'll find an array of homegrown systems for tutoring student writing. It's fair to ask if these systems actually teach writing or just provide corrective Band-Aids. Later on, we'll review the bidding on these questions. We'll also take a closer look at Grammarly and Microsoft's offerings, along with some of their pinch points.

Part I of this book has focused on human writing: how it developed, why we do it, how it replaced oral rhetoric in the college curriculum, and how educators evaluate it. We've also seen that challenges in evaluation led to harnessing computers to help.

But before Ellis Page proposed automating the grading of student essays, computers were already hard at work analyzing language. In Part II, we'll trace the roots of natural language processing, accompanied by a bird's-eye guide to the working parts of those language sausage machines.

PART II

WHAT IF MACHINES
COULD WRITE?

FOUR

The Dream of Language Machines

She was a world traveler. German by origin, she visited Britain, Africa, and even the northern coast of South America. But these were no pleasure trips. For her name was U-505, and she was a German submarine used to attack the Allies in World War II.

On June 4, 1944—two days before the Normandy Invasion—U-505 was captured by the US Navy. On board were almost five dozen German crew members, a collection of charts and codebooks, and two Enigma machines.

The Enigma Challenge

Merriam-Webster tells us an enigma is "something hard to understand or explain." The word comes from the Greek, and then through Latin, essentially meaning "riddle." In the musical world, Edward Elgar is famed for his *Enigma Variations*, written in 1899. Why enigma? Because, as Elgar explained, the actual theme never appears directly in the piece. It's only developed in counterpoint.[1]

What better name for a cryptography device.

The original Enigma machine was developed just after World War I by a German engineer named Arthur Scherbius.[2] There's even speculation that Scherbius named his invention after Elgar's *Enigma Variations*.

The contraption basically looked like a typewriter with twenty-six letter keys, enhanced with sets of wheels. When you struck a key, the wheels turned, following a pre-set sequence, generating a different character. The coded message could then be transmitted, say, by radio, using Morse code. Using another Enigma machine, the recipient typed in the encrypted letters to reveal the original text. For decoding, you needed a copy of the codebook settings—or a skilled cryptographer.

Enigma machines were first marketed commercially in 1923. They soon become a primary conduit for confidential communication within the German military. With the buildup to World War II, machine design became ever-more complex to evade those skilled cryptographers. Another defense mechanism was frequently resetting the codes. When the war was going full tilt, the German Navy was switching codes at least daily.[3]

There wasn't one Enigma machine with one code. By the end of the war, the German military had multiple designs and over 20,000 machines. The trick for cryptographers was knowing which Enigma architecture was being used and then determining that day's code. Capturing actual machines and codebooks surely helped. Those intrigued about the Enigma's workings can find a front-row seat at Chicago's Museum of Science and Industry, where two Enigma machines, some codebooks, and the U-505 submarine itself are on display.[4]

Breaking the Code

Before World War II began, Poland had been keen to decipher Enigma machines, anticipating future German military attacks. The Polish Cipher Bureau set Marian Rejewski, a mathematician, to the task of unraveling Enigma messages, drawing on what was known about commercial machines. Then Rejewski got some help.

Hans-Thilo Schmidt was an employee of the German Cipher Office. Perhaps hard up for cash, he had begun selling information about the new German military Enigma to French intelligence. It seemed the French cryptographers didn't show much interest or maybe had no luck with decipherment. And so in 1932, the French forwarded to the Poles the Enigma information it had gotten from Schmidt. Thus armed, Rejewski succeeded in building a replica Enigma machine. Joined by two other Polish mathematicians, Jerzy Rózycki and Henryk Zygalski, the team scored major success between 1933 and 1938 in decrypting German Enigma messages. If you visit the city of Poznań in Poland, you'll find a fascinating museum, the Enigma Cipher Centre, which recounts the history of how Rejewski, Rózycki, and Zygalski cracked the Enigma technology.[5]

By 1938, the growing German Enigma traffic revealed Germany was preparing for war. Meanwhile, Germany was rejiggering Enigma architecture, rendering it more challenging for codebreakers. A meeting of British, French, and Poles was called in early 1939 to pool intelligence. However, it was not until late July that the Poles shared with their British and French counterparts what they knew.

Then things moved swiftly. On August 14, a British Cipher Bureau (connected to the Government Code and Cypher School in London) was established at Bletchley Park, an estate about forty-five miles north of London. Besides the main estate, temporary buildings ("huts") were erected to house decryption efforts.

Courtesy of the Poles, two replica Enigma machines arrived in London on August 16, 1939. Germany invaded Poland two weeks later. A team was rapidly assembled at Bletchley Park, including veteran codebreakers, chess players, and mathematicians.

Which brings us to Alan Turing.

Turing at Bletchley Park

Alan Turing was a mathematician by training, completing his undergraduate degree at Kings College Cambridge in 1934 and a PhD at Princeton in July 1938.[6] Returning to England from Princeton, he began part-time work at the Government Code and Cypher School. Britain declared war on Germany on September 3, 1939. The day after, Turning took up residence at Bletchley Park. Work on deciphering German Enigma messages was a team effort. While Turing's brilliance was invaluable, it built on the shoulders of those Polish mathematicians and colleagues at Bletchley Park.

The German military used different versions of Enigma machines for its army and air force than for its navy. Decipherment efforts at Bletchley Park were divided up accordingly. Those working on army and air force messages were housed in Hut 6; for naval messages, Hut 8.

The naval Enigma was the harder nut to crack. In fact, some didn't believe the code could be broken, and in the beginning, no one was actively working on it. Turing took up the challenge.[7] In the Atlantic, German submarines were crippling the flow of supplies from North America to Britain. Unless the code could be deciphered, both merchant and Allied military ships would continue to be sunk.

After the German military complicated the workings of their Enigma machines, Rejewski and his colleagues had tried building an electro-mechanical codebreaking device. They called it a *bomba*—the Polish word for a bomb, as well as for the French ice cream dessert bombe. This kind of a contraption would be invaluable, since it took humans too long to decode volumes of messages by hand.

To crack the naval Enigma, Turing needed a "Bombe" (the name used at Bletchley Park). Working feverishly, Turing and Gordon Welchman, along with engineer Harold Keen, designed and constructed such a machine. By March 1940, the first Bombe was fabricated—about seven feet wide, more than six feet tall, and weighing around a ton. The Bombe, along with several add-on devices, allowed cryptographers to do guided searches of the millions of possible decipherment solutions. By limiting the options needing to be tested, the decoding process was dramatically accelerated.[8]

Soon more Bombes were manufactured, and the rate of decipherment grew. By 1942, Bletchley Park was, each month, deciphering about 39,000 messages sent through German Enigma machines.[9]

But for the record: Bletchley Park wasn't the only place doing decoding. The US Navy had a vested interest in locating German "wolfpack" submarines attacking American convoys in the Atlantic. When the British found themselves running short on personnel to decipher German naval Enigma messages, they reached out to the Americans. Bletchley Park provided a Bombe, and the Americans set up shop—as it turns out, in the literal back yard of American University, my home base in Washington. Doing the work was a cadre of WAVES (Women Accepted for Volunteer Emergency Service), a program the US Navy had launched to assist in the war effort. And decipher they did, contributing to the sinking of more German U-boats.[10]

Turing's Computing Gauntlet

Before the war, Turing had already been writing about what computers—not yet functioning realities—might be capable of. In a 1936 paper, Turing envisioned a computer that could both store programs and be used in tackling a slew of problems.[11] The concept came to be known as a universal Turing machine or universal computing machine. Over the next dozen or so years, Turing's pioneering ideas would find their way into real-world machines on both sides of the Atlantic.

Back in the 1820s, the mathematician Charles Babbage conceived of a special-purpose mechanical calculating machine, which he called the Difference Engine. A decade later, he developed the idea of a general-purpose computer (the Analytical Engine) using punch cards of the sort already driving mechanical weaving. Neither device saw the light of day in Babbage's lifetime. However, in 1843, his friend and fellow mathematician Ada Lovelace demonstrated how calculations could be done on the Analytical Engine, and, in the process, wrote the first computer program.

But still, no actual computer. Building operational machines, especially those that were general purpose, would be an evolving process. So would the question of whether such machines could be said to think.

By 1941, Turning was exploring whether machines could potentially be called intelligent, circulating his thoughts in writing to colleagues at the Government Code and Cypher School. Unfortunately, Turing's manuscript has been lost. But after the war, other papers emerged, posing questions about computer intelligence with which we continue to grapple.

In late October of 1945, Turing was hired by the Mathematics Division of the National Physical Laboratory (NPL) to develop an actual universal Turing machine of the sort he had envisioned in 1936. The machine, designed to hold stored programs, was called ACE: the Automatic Computing Engine. As with Babbage's Difference Engine and Analytical Engine, implementation of the ACE encountered roadblocks. Turing became disgruntled and left the NPL in mid-1948. But while still employed there, he wrote a paper with the simple title "Intelligent Machinery." The paper wasn't published, but fortunately, this time we have the typescript.[12]

Turing saw his task to be figuring out "whether it is possible for machinery to show intelligent behaviour." What he called his "guiding principle" was the human brain.[13] By the end of the paper, it was clear that search—a tool used in doing mathematical proofs—underlay Turing's notion of how humans and potentially intelligent machines work. Turing likened electrical circuits to human nerves. This neural analogy eventually led, after fits and starts, to today's neural networks, a story we'll get to in Chapter 5.

Turing identified the kinds of tasks an intelligent machine might tackle. These included games, cryptography, and mathematics. And then two more: translation and language learning. While he felt "the learning of languages would be the most impressive, since it is the most human of these activities," he wasn't optimistic about the prospects: "This field seems however to depend rather too much on sense organs and locomotion to be feasible."[14] We can only conjecture what Turing might have said about today's natural language processing triumphs.

But speaking of conjecture: At the very end of "Intelligent Machinery," Turing proposed a hypothetical experiment, with a hypothetical machine, to see if one chess player could figure out if he's playing against another chess player or against a machine.[15] The seeds of a research strategy were sown.

It's the 1950 paper "Computing Machinery and Intelligence" that people usually think of when talking about Turing and artificial intelligence. Turing threw down his gauntlet in the opening sentence ("I propose to consider the question, 'Can machines think?'"), but then skirted answering it by offering up instead what he labeled "The Imitation Game."[16]

In the first version of the game, Turing envisioned a human interrogator trying to determine which of two unseen people was male and which was female. Then Turing ratcheted things up:

> We can now ask the question, "What will happen when a machine takes the part of [the first player, who is female]?" Will the interrogator decide wrongly as often when the game is played like this . . . ? These questions replace our original, "Can machines think?"[17]

By the time Turing was writing "Computing Machinery and Intelligence," he was also in the thick of developing real-world digital computers. After leaving the National Physical Laboratory, Turing had been hired at Manchester University as deputy director of its Computing Machine Lab. In June 1948, the first stored program on a digital computer ran on a machine known as the Manchester Baby (for its limited capacity). Turing's job was to help build an expanded version of the Baby and to write the programmers' handbook for the next generation machine: the Ferranti Mark 1. Launched in February 1951, this was the world's first large-scale, general-purpose digital computer.

It was becoming reasonable to envision that someday computers could perform complex tasks akin to those done by humans. How akin? In May 1951, Turing gave a talk on BBC Radio. In it, he defended the idea that "it is not altogether unreasonable to describe computers as brains," arguing that

> If it is accepted that real brains, as found in animals, and in particular in men, are a sort of machine it will follow that our digital computer, suitably programmed, will behave like a brain.[18]

Turing distinguished between what computers were capable of doing at that time and their future potential. He also hinted at the possibility of computer originality:

> If we give the machine a programme which results in its doing something interesting which we had not anticipated I should be inclined to say that machine had originated something, rather than to claim that its behaviour was implicit in the programme, and therefore that the originality lies entirely with us.[19]

We can almost envision Turing weighing in on our question in Chapter 2—whether a computer (not just its programmers) should be able to hold copyright. I hear Turing cheering for the computer.

In a later BBC Radio program, Turing joined Richard Braithwaite (a philosopher), Geoffrey Jefferson (the neurosurgeon we met in the Prologue), and Max Newman (fellow mathematician and codebreaker) for an on-air discussion. Again, Turing's comments on what it means to think lead us to creativity—and even enigmas:

> one might be tempted to define thinking as consisting of "those mental processes that we don't understand." If this is right then to make a thinking machine is to make one which does interesting things without our really understanding quite how it is done.[20]

Sounds like GPT-3.

One attribute Turing didn't believe was necessary for concluding a computer could think was consciousness. In his 1950 paper, Turing had dismissed Jefferson's earlier claims that you couldn't say a machine has a brain unless the machine is conscious of its actions. In their BBC discussion, both Turing and Jefferson held their ground, with Jefferson adding that "It is high emotional content of mental processes in the human being that makes him quite different from a machine."[21]

Now seven decades on, few believe it's necessary to clear Jefferson's bar of consciousness before speaking of computer intelligence. Instead, the modern focus is on output—what work computers can do. In a moment, we'll sketch out the basic kinds of "intelligent" tasks computers have been up to. But first, let's give the enterprise its newer name. In the UK, the term has long been "machine intelligence." In the United States, it became "artificial intelligence." Here's how.

Dartmouth's AI Christening

In 1955, a quartet of US mathematicians, computer scientists, and engineers asked the Rockefeller Foundation to fund an extended summer conference at Dartmouth College in Hanover, New Hampshire. The proposal's first author, John McCarthy, was then assistant professor of mathematics at Dartmouth. Marvin Minsky was a Harvard junior fellow in mathematics and neurology. Nathaniel Rochester was manager of information research at IBM. Rounding out the group was Claude Shannon, a mathematician at Bell Telephone Laboratories.

The application's title? "A Proposal for the Dartmouth Summer Research Project on Artificial Intelligence." As McCarthy was later to write,

> The proposal . . . is the source of the term artificial intelligence. The term

was chosen to nail the flag to the mast. . . . We wanted to focus the attention of the participants.[22]

In summer 1956, an assemblage of scientists gathered in Hanover, some remaining longer than others, each pursuing his own project. No coherent theory or blueprint for AI research emerged. In fact, not even a final report. But, in McCarthy's words, the important accomplishment was recognition of "the concept of artificial intelligence as a branch of science."[23]

The research agenda underlying the project was bold. As the opening paragraph of the 1955 proposal declared,

> The study is to proceed on the basis of the conjecture that every aspect of learning or any other feature of intelligence can in principle be so precisely described that a machine can be made to simulate it.

Success could be judged by how the machine responded:

> For the present purpose the artificial intelligence problem is taken to be that of making a machine behave in ways that would be called intelligent if a human being were so behaving.

Note the goal was *simulation*, not *emulation*. Shades of Turing's imitation game.

The behavioral criterion seems a pragmatic choice. Yet in retrospect, it presents an odd conundrum. On the one hand, it smacks of behaviorism, the dominant psychological theory at the time, especially in the United States. On the other, the Dartmouth proposal presumed that logical analysis should be the basis for the new field of inquiry:

> It may be speculated that a large part of human thought consists of manipulating words according to rules of reasoning and rules of conjecture.

While the conflation of language and thought was perhaps a bit naïve, the wording makes clear that a mentalist, not behaviorist, model of human language was presupposed. In fact, at a 2006 event commemorating the original conference fifty years earlier, McCarthy explained that this focus on "rules of reasoning and rules of conjecture" had been a fundamental principle of AI research for the past half century, and that this stance was a deliberate attack on behaviorism.[24]

One of the first areas of human behavior the proposed conference hoped to simulate was language:

> An attempt will be made to find how to make machines use language, form

abstractions and concepts, solve problems now reserved for humans, and improve themselves.

For many years, "language" in AI research meant some form of writing, the only modality then available for feeding computers input and receiving output.

Here is what's been happening with AI since its official naming.

A Layperson's AI Roadmap

What follows is Baron's roadmap of major uses to which we've been putting AI. My categories don't match up with what you'll find in standard AI textbooks. What's more, given the expansive reach of today's AI, the roadmap is hardly exhaustive. But hopefully it serves its purpose: offering a brief, practical overview of the larger field of AI.

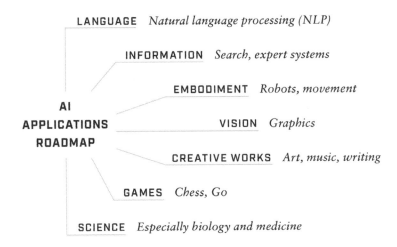

LANGUAGE   *Natural language processing (NLP)*

INFORMATION   *Search, expert systems*

EMBODIMENT   *Robots, movement*

AI APPLICATIONS ROADMAP

VISION   *Graphics*

CREATIVE WORKS   *Art, music, writing*

GAMES   *Chess, Go*

SCIENCE   *Especially biology and medicine*

We'll start on the second branch, holding off talking about natural language processing until the next chapter.

Information

Looking for something?

In 1993, the American Dialect Society named "information superhighway" its "Word of the Year." And no surprise, since computer scientists were paving the way for us to have the equivalent of the Library of Congress, British Library, and Bibliothèque nationale at our fingertips.

Tim Berners-Lee's World Wide Web went live at CERN in Switzerland in late 1990. The same year, the US military decommissioned its communication network called ARPANET (more on that in a moment), with the system reborn as the public internet.[25] Search tools with names like Archie, Gopher, and Mosaic began showing up. And in September 1998, the program that started life as BackRub debuted as Google Search. The rest, as they say, is history.

When most of us do an internet search, we're looking for something specific—a date, a recipe, the 2010 eruption of Eyjafjallajökull in Iceland, an online text of *Gulliver's Travels*. However, AI researchers have long had more complex agendas. Since computers can store information, what if you could draw on that information to tackle real-world problems?

In the 1960s, AI researchers were having moderate success in solving small-scale challenges, such as Terry Winograd's program SHRDLU, which used a robot hand to rearrange blocks. However, it was proving challenging to apply similar approaches to larger and more difficult problems. One solution was narrowing the range of information you're dealing with. The approach came to be known as expert systems.[26]

To build an expert system, you start with a knowledge base, constructed by interviewing human experts. Next, you organize the information you've amassed into logical propositions, typically of the if-then form, mimicking the thought process a human might follow ("If the temperature gets too hot, then turn down the thermostat"). An expert system lets you automate the process by running an inference engine to search though the propositions in the knowledge base.

During the 1970s and 80s, the idea of building knowledge bases in specialized fields became popular in everything from medicine to assigning airport gates to manufacturing. The classic example is a program that Texas Instruments developed in 1985 for the Campbell Soup Company.

Aldo Cimino, a Campbell Soup employee with more than forty years of experience in soup sterilization, was edging towards retirement. His unique arsenal of knowledge for troubleshooting malfunctions in the sterilization equipment was invaluable. Who would replace him? The answer was an expert system, built from picking Cimino's brain for hours, teasing out all the things that might go wrong ("if") and how to fix them ("then").[27]

This brain-dump—and others like it—was successful for its time. However, as we'll see in the next chapter, programming models based on rules and logic were already giving way to a new emphasis on statistical models and machine learning.

Embodiment

Alan Turing hadn't been interested in building physical machines that could behave intelligently. But the US military was.

On October 4, 1957, Russia launched *Sputnik*, its first satellite. The Cold War was already on, and America suddenly found it was losing the technology race. In early 1958, as part of its response, the United States created the Advanced Research Projects Agency (ARPA), whose mission was to support research that would exploit technology for military applications. The money flowed. One project was creating a computer communication system known as ARPANET, which evolved into today's internet. In the commercial sector, work was beginning on stationary industrial robots. But what if robots could move, eventually on the battlefield?

Enter Shakey the Robot.

In 1963, a group of AI researchers at the Stanford Research Institute, led by Charles Rosen, began working on a mobile automation project. By 1966, ARPA was on board to fund their research. Drawing upon a broad AI toolkit (from logical reasoning to computer vision to machine learning to natural language processing), by the late 1960s, Rosen's team demonstrated the world's first AI-driven mobile robot. Though literally shaky on its "feet" (in this case, wheels), Shakey could (sort of) perambulate.

We've come a long way since Shakey. We have vacuum cleaning robots, drones, and self-driving cars (sort of). When I visited Tokyo's Miraikan Museum in 2017, I was treated to a show by the humanoid robot ASIMO, dancing and kicking a soccer ball. Robot dogs now saunter up flights of stairs. But embodied intelligence, especially in humanoid robots, doesn't always need to be mobile. There's a cascade of projects fashioning increasingly lifelike facsimiles of humans that "talk" and "understand" words spoken to them. Sophia, mentioned in the Prologue, is one such.[28]

Vision

Human vision enables us to produce visual images (graphics) and perceive what we've created. Leonardo da Vinci painted the *Mona Lisa* (graphics), whose portrait we can behold at the Louvre (perception).

When it comes to computers and vision, there are the same two components. The objects we create—computer graphics—trace back to early video games like Pac-Man and range from the magical fractal images generated by Benoit Mandelbrot to computer-animated movies. More problematically, these days AI-driven computer graphics also produce deep fakes.

It was in 1963 that Ivan Sutherland created a program called Sketchpad, which led to the blossoming of computer graphics. Generating graphics is a power-hungry business. The more powerful the processors, the more sophisticated the images and the faster they can be produced. Over time, special graphics processing units (GPUs) were developed that greatly enhanced image generation.

But then, as often happens in the AI world, technology created for one application proved valuable in another. Graphics chips are critical not just for producing but for recognizing graphic images (the perception part). Think of facial recognition programs, including the ones Facebook used for over a decade to automatically tag people appearing in photos or videos. Mercifully, Facebook stopped in late 2021,[29] though many governmental authorities (not just in China) haven't.

Modern GPUs are having an even more sweeping effect on the very way AI is done. The story began with handwriting.

Think about the challenge the US Postal Service has in sorting millions of pieces of mail daily and sending them on to the right address. In 1963, ZIP codes (Zone Improvement Plan) were developed to help speed the process.[30] The weak link was that humans still had to read those numbers to do the sorting.

Research on optical character recognition (OCR) had begun by the early 1900s, though scanning was initially one character at a time. Gradually, OCR systems became better at recognizing machine-printed numbers and letters, which are written in straight lines and with standard characters. Handwriting was more complicated, given wide variance from one writer to the next, plus sloppy penmanship. What's more, those ZIP codes had five digits to contend with.

Enter Yann LeCun. In the late 1980s, LeCun was working at AT&T on a handwritten digit recognition project. LeCun's solution was to apply a form of neural networks called backpropagation, a technique used in convolutional neural networks.[31] (LeCun was a founding father of convolutional neural nets.) The system worked, and mail sorting by the US Postal Service was revolutionized. Several years later, now working with Yoshua Bengio, LeCun's research on character recognition was expanded to deciphering handwritten numbers on bank checks.[32]

Then there's the challenge of recognizing more complex images, such as pictures of cars, people, or cats. In the late 2000s, to help advance AI research on object recognition, AI researcher Fei-Fei Li and her colleagues developed a massive dataset called ImageNet.[33] Their aims were to improve object categorization and to contribute to machine learning by providing a huge collection of images, now numbering around 15 million.[34] To help spur research initiatives, ImageNet began an annual Large Scale Visual Recognition Challenge. The contest was to see how accurately your AI program could identify objects it was shown.

The 2012 event proved a watershed. The team from the University of Toronto, using a program dubbed AlexNet (after Alex Krizhevsky, who worked in collaboration with Ilya Sutskever and Geoffrey Hinton), performed incredibly well, with an error rate far lower than the next-best competitor. The secret sauce was a combination of GPU chips and convolutional neural networks. Instead of having to write code to label the images, AlexNet used deep learning to recognize them. Having been trained on a million images, the program leaned on NVIDIA GPUs to perform trillions of mathematical operations automatically. The AlexNet team won the year's contest, but more importantly, their work ushered in the use of neural networks for a host of non-vision AI work involving deep learning.

Stay tuned for more on machine learning, neural networks, and deep learning, which we'll get to in the next chapter.

Creative Works

Is creativity unique to humans? A trick question, you might say, since defining creativity is no easier than defining thinking or intelligence. Turing had dodged those last two, settling for an interim behavioral test, the imitation game.

Instinctively, we look for AI creativity in the same places we laud it when produced by humans—everywhere from painting to music, from science to literature. In recent decades, cascading claims have been made about computer-generated productions meriting the label "creative." To enter the discussion responsibly, we'll need to bite the bullet and get a better handle on what creativity means in the human realm. That's our first task in Chapter 9.

Games

"It's only a game." Or maybe the game is the means to a more far-reaching end.

While at Bletchley Park, Turing had mused about expanded uses of automated electronic machinery. In 1941 (the year after the first Bombe was fabricated), he talked with Donald Michie and others about the possibility of mechanizing chess.[35] If the Bombe could sort through vast possible solutions to a cryptographic problem, why not apply the same principle to moves on a chessboard? In 1945, Turing predicted that computers could probably play "very good chess." Then in 1948, he (along with David Champernowne) designed a chess-playing routine called "Turochamp," which he started coding on the Ferranti Mark 1 at Manchester University.[36]

Was creating a computer program that could play chess of any serious intellectual interest? Years later, Noam Chomsky would judge "a computer beating a grandmaster at chess" to be "as interesting as a bulldozer winning a weightlifting competition."[37] You'll recall from the Prologue that Chomsky dismissed machine translation as "about as interesting as a big bulldozer."

Michie vehemently disagreed, writing that "Computer chess has been described as the *Drosophila melanogaster* of machine intelligence."[38] And rightly so. Those fruit flies have been the proving ground for countless discoveries in biology involving genetic inheritance. In much the same way, Turing's proposal for a chess-playing program reverberated over the years among AI researchers exploring what games might teach us about the prospects for computer intelligence.

These are some highlights of computer landmarks for playing checkers, chess, and Go:[39]

- Checkers (in British English, draughts)
  1951: Christopher Strachey programmed the game of draughts on a Pilot ACE and then a year later, on the Ferranti Mark 1 at Manchester University.
  1952: Arthur Samuel used elements of Strachey's scheme to write a checkers program that ran on the new IBM 701 (the first large-scale, commercial electronic computer).

- Chess
  1951: Dietrich Prinz harnessed Manchester's Ferranti Mark 1 to write the first fully implemented computer chess program.
  1997: IBM's Deep Blue beat Garry Kasparov, the reigning world chess champion.

- Go
  2016: DeepMind's program AlphaGo bested Lee Sedol, a Korean professional Go player, who, at the time, ranked second in the world in international titles.

We all know about checkers and chess, but maybe not about Go. The game was invented by the Chinese more than 2,500 years ago, making it perhaps a thousand years older than chess, which was invented in India. Like chess,

Go is a strategy game, but more difficult, given the millions of possible board positions. In a typical chess game, there are about 35 possible moves each turn, with an average of 80 moves per game, translating into 35^{80} or 10^{123} potential moves per game. For Go, with 250 possible moves each turn and typically 150 moves per game, that means roughly 250^{150} or 10^{360} options in a game.[40] Writing an AI program that could win against a Go master was a huge deal.

But the AlphaGo project wasn't really about games. In 2010, Demis Hassabis, an artificial intelligence researcher and neuroscientist, had co-founded the company DeepMind. (Four years later, the company was bought by Google.) Hassabis, already an expert on programming computer games, turned to AI games as platforms for helping solve real-world challenges, especially in science.

One of the problems Hassabis hoped to tackle was what's known as protein folding. As journalist Will Douglas Heaven recounts, when Hassabis was backstage with David Silver (lead developer of AlphaGo) on that day in March 2016 when AlphaGo beat Lee Sedol, Hassabis said, "Now is the time." Later, in an interview with Heaven, Hassabis declared, "This is the reason I started DeepMind. . . . In fact, it's why I've worked my whole career in AI."[41]

Science

Which brings us to use of AI in science. In the Prologue, we mentioned how AI is being harnessed to detect virus mutations and read mammograms. Listing the full range of current AI applications in science and medicine would fill many chapters. But to illustrate how game-changing AI solutions to scientific puzzles can be, we'll focus on protein folding—the challenge that DeepMind undertook.[42]

Proteins are essential components of human life. They fill a host of functions, everything from enabling digestion to muscle contraction to driving our immune responses. It's estimated there are at least 20,000 human proteins, each composed of a string of amino acids. These strings become folded up into three-dimensional structures, full of twists and turns. By unraveling those structures, we can determine how the proteins function.

Molecular biologists have worked for decades to decipher protein structures. The stakes are high, since by understanding their structure (and function), we can better address medical challenges ranging from cancer to COVID-19. The problem is that decoding proteins is incredibly hard, since the number of possible forms each string might take is huge—on the order of 10^{300}.

If that number looks vaguely familiar, recall that the game of Go averages

10^{360} potential moves per game. The parallel was hardly lost on Hassabis. And there were other resemblances. In building AlphaGo, DeepMind had amassed a huge amount of data from games AlphaGo had played. Similarly, the international Protein Data Bank collects information on structures that scientists have previously decoded. Could AI tools be used to speed up the protein unfolding process? Surely it would help if, as with Turing's Bombe, there were a way of reducing the number of possibilities you needed to check.

DeepMind's solution in their program AlphaFold (and its successor AlphaFold 2) was to draw upon the same kind of AI technique used in large language models like GPT-3. Attention was directed to particular amino acids, rather than attempting to examine all of them. Put to the test in fall 2020 as part of a biannual competition of the Protein Structure Prediction Center, AlphaFold 2 performed exceptionally well. So well, in fact, that the evolutionary biologist Andrei Lupas enthused,

> "It's a game changer. . . . This will change medicine. It will change research. It will change bioengineering. It will change everything."[43]

Information. Embodiment. Vision. Creative works. Games. Science. And of course, language. AI permeates a spiraling amount of our computer-based lives and work. While image recognition, a machine-generated Rembrandt portrait, or a game of Go might seem unrelated to AI technology for "understanding" and generating language, we've already gotten a whiff of the connections. Often the same programming models—and subsequent breakthroughs—that power one application are responsible for developments in another.

Both Alan Turing and John McCarthy spoke about the centrality of language for developing machines that think or at least behave as if they do. Since much of the AI research that followed has focused on language, it's not surprising that language-based research has contributed to model building in other areas of AI. In fact, researchers at Stanford's Institute for Human-Centered AI (HAI) argue for renaming large language models as "foundation models" given how fundamental they are to research in fields unrelated to human language.[44]

We've been throwing around terms like "neural network" and "natural language processing" without much in the way of definition. It's about time for some explanations and context. In the next chapter, we'll review the kinds of spoken and written language that AI researchers have been getting machines to process, and the models that have evolved to do the work. The chapter is designed as a layperson's accounting, describing just enough about what's under the hood of AI models to help us fathom AI's potential as a substitute for human writing.

Some basic definitions of relevant terminology used in AI are offered in the Main Characters section, following the Coda. Anyone seeking more detail will find books, conference proceedings, and online sources galore.[45]

FIVE

The Natural Language Processing
Sausage Machine

A century ago, the linguist Edward Sapir didn't mince words: "No language is tyrannically consistent. All grammars leak."[1] No matter how hard you to try to nail down every rule, you'll always find exceptions. Still, linguists toil away at the job.

So did early AI researchers. Whether the plan was to replicate the process humans presumably follow when producing and understanding language (emulation) or to build models yielding the same result (simulation), the approach relied on stitching together grammatical rules, dictionary entries, and logical operations. As we saw in the last chapter (with expert systems) and we'll see in the next (with translation), the rule-based model met its limits. Those leaks—sometimes gushes—kept erupting.

The next strategy was looking to statistics and probabilities, drawing on large datasets.[2] The statistical approach gave better results than its predecessor, though in areas like speech recognition or translation, no one was likely to mistake computer performance for human. At the same time, interest in machine learning was on the rise.

Machine Learning

To understand contemporary AI, we have to think about what it means to say that someone or something is educable. Start with people. Ability to learn is part of what makes us human. Whatever potential our gray matter has for thinking, it requires something to think about. For that, we need the capacity to learn. The same is true when it comes to AI. As Turing put it, if we hope to build computers that generate unanticipated results, "the [programming] process should bear a close relation to that of teaching."[3]

To claim that machines (here, computers) can learn is to say that programs running on them can improve their behavior on a task, based on success or failure on earlier attempts. Depending on the type of machine learning (supervised, unsupervised, or reinforcement), the program might or might not directly "reward" or "punish" behaviors.

Programming real-world computers that learn is almost as old as the field of AI. In 1959, Arthur Samuel (we met him in the last chapter) choose the name "machine learning" to describe his programming a computer to play checkers.[4] The term stuck.

Like several other developments in AI, machine learning went in and out of fashion. Its popular rise in the 1980s was supported by other programming approaches that were being rediscovered, enhanced, or created. One of these was neural networks. But before getting there, we need one more "learning" phrase that's on everyone's lips these days: *deep learning*. The label refers to machine learning using multiple levels of neural networks. The terms "deep learning" and "deep neural networks" are often used interchangeably.

Now, neural networks.

Neural Networks

"Neuron." First coined in 1891 by the German anatomist Wilhelm Waldeyer, the word refers to nerve cells in the brain and nervous system. They're incredibly important, since they receive sensory input, send out commands to our muscles, and manage all the electrical signals along the way.[5]

It's those electrical signals that got researchers in the mid-twentieth century considering analogies between the human brain and an electronic computer. The first landmark was a 1943 paper by Warren McCulloch and Walter Pitts. The two argued that because of the "all-or-none" character of activity in the brain, neural events and the relations among them could be treated by means of propositional logic: if-then, on-off. Just like electrical circuits.[6]

By 1958, Frank Rosenblatt set out to demonstrate the concept's feasibility. (He also gave the computer equivalent of a neuron a name: perceptron.) Funding was courtesy of the US Office of Naval Research. At a press conference on July 7 of that year, Rosenbaum—and the Navy—were effusive about the perceptron's potential. As the *New York Times* wrote,

> The Navy revealed the embryo of an electronic computer today that it expects will be able to walk, talk, see, write, reproduce itself and be conscious of its existence. . . . Later perceptrons will be able to recognize people and call out their names and instantly translate speech in one language to speech and writing in another, it was predicted.[7]

Beam me up, Scotty! Some of these accomplishments (like speech synthesis, facial recognition, and automatic translation) would be significantly achieved decades later. But not consciousness. And not using this initial perceptron model. However, the notion of a neural network (the perceptron being a single-layer network) was born.

Research on perceptrons continued apace for another decade. However, it gradually became clear that the model wasn't sufficiently robust (nor was the computing power then available) to address even simpler problems. In 1969, MIT's Marvin Minsky and Seymour Papert appeared to sound the death knell for modeling AI programming on human neurons.[8]

But an obituary would be premature.

Neural Networks Reborn

A friendly heads-up. Talking about neural networks requires invoking a string of technical terms. It's the nature of the beast. To streamline things, I've parked key definitions in the Main Characters section, following the last chapter.

By the 1980s, a small cluster of researchers began revisiting the idea of neural models for AI. No one claimed a precise match between human neurons and computer circuitry. Instead, the argument was that much as neurons in the human brain form networks, we might construct computer models based on networks. Unlike Rosenblatt's single-layer network, the idea of using multiple layers took root, bolstered by more robust programming techniques and greater computing power.

Enter the godfathers of deep learning and deep (multilayer) neural networks.

Trios have made for celebrated teams. The Three Musketeers. The Three Tenors. And the three godfathers of deep learning. The first, Geoffrey Hinton, is often dubbed the father of deep learning, but it's widely acknowledged that

Yann LeCun and Yoshua Bengio also warrant star billing. That recognition was heralded when the Association for Computing Machinery (ACM) bestowed on the three its 2018 Turing Award, often described as computer science's equivalent of the Nobel Prize.

The work for which Hinton, LeCun, and Bengio were honored wasn't a single accomplishment but incremental developments in harnessing neural networks to solve an ever-widening range of AI challenges. Some of the trio's efforts were independent; others, collaborative (recall LeCun and Bengio's use of neural networks to read handwritten digits on checks). Among their landmark contributions:[9]

- 1980s: LeCun developed convolutional neural networks.
- 1986: Hinton (along with David Rumelhart and Ronald Williams) demonstrated the power of the backpropagation algorithm in multi-layer neural networks.
- 2010s: Bengio, along with Ian Goodfellow, developed generative adversarial networks (GANs), which are especially effective in computer vision and computer graphics.
- 2012: Hinton and his students at the University of Toronto won the ImageNet competition, using powerful GPUs and improved convolutional neural networks.

The flowering of deep learning, using multi-layered neural networks, realized a vision that others in AI had deemed unrealistic. As Hinton mused in an interview at the time of the Turing Award presentation, the award was vindication for those years of others' disbelief.[10]

The Transformer Transformation

Alongside the landmark work of Hinton, LeCun, and Bengio, other variants of deep neural networks emerged. Among these were recurrent neural networks (RNNs) and later the curiously named long short term memory (LSTM) neural nets. Then came the revolution known as a transformer.

The new kid arrived on the block in 2017 as a conference paper.[11] The AI task for which the model was designed was written translation between two languages. The paper's catchy title, "Attention Is All You Need," highlighted what was distinctive about the approach. Instead of relying on the architectures of recurrent or convolutional networks that can only refer to words in the nearby surroundings, transformer algorithms can take into account larger context.

To understand what's meant here by "context," take the English word "bank." If the transformer comes upon "bank," it uses surrounding text to figure out whether the word refers to a financial institution or the side of a river. If your task is translation (say, from English into German), you need to know whether to use *die Bank* (indicating the financial institution) or *das Ufer* (referring to the shore). Another example: If one sentence in a passage is "The hot water heater in my house died yesterday" and the next is "It needs to be replaced," a transformer can figure out that "it" refers to the hot water heater, not the house.

The transformer described in the 2017 paper was trained on a dataset of about 4.5 million translation pairs of English and German sentences. These pairs were from a standard English–German corpus called WMT 2014, developed for a Workshop on Statistical Machine Translation held in 2014. To evaluate the transformer's performance on English-to-German translation, results were assessed using what's known as a BLEU score (BiLingual Evaluation Understudy). This is the prevailing yardstick for gauging the success of written machine translation. The score compares how the machine measures up against benchmark translations.

The new transformer performed extremely well on its English-to-German trials. It was also impressive on a WMT 2014 English-to-French translation test. What's more, the transformer showed a high level of success in grammatically parsing English sentences. More versatility was yet to come.

Soon after the 2017 "Attention" paper appeared, new transformers began sprouting up. Since most of the paper's authors were from Google, it's no surprise that just a year later, Google launched its transformer called BERT (Bidirectional Encoder Representations from Transformers).[12] The model, specifically tailored for question answering and language inference, became the engine underlying Google Search.[13] The same year, OpenAI created its first transformer, GPT (Generative Pretrained Transformer). But it's the subsequent 2019 model (GPT-2) and especially the 2020 improved version (GPT-3) that most of the public have in mind when reading or talking about transformers. By late 2022, ChatGPT (GPT-3.5) had arrived, with GPT-4 making its debut on March 14, 2023.

Journalists' discussions of GPT-3 focus on the transformer's impressive spawning of fresh written text (like essays or short stories), primed by brief human-written prompts. However, the same model has multiple AI tricks up its sleeve. Some of those wiles explain why Microsoft invested $1 billion in OpenAI in 2019, and in 2020, obtained exclusive rights to incorporate GPT-3 into its software.[14] Longtime users of Microsoft Word noticed the quantum leap in functions like translation and grammar analysis, which we'll talk about in later chapters.

Google and OpenAI aren't the only ones building transformers. Other players include DeepMind, Meta, AI21, and the Beijing Academy of Artificial Intelligence. The list keeps growing (though construction requires a hefty bankroll). What most of the newest models have in common is their versatility (meaning ability to handle a variety of AI tasks) and, with some exceptions, their size.

The notion of size has two meanings. One is the amount of data the model operates on, drawn from sources like Wikipedia, select corpora (maybe all the books in Project Gutenberg), or broad web crawls. The volume of data tends to keep growing. While GPT-2 could call on 40 gigabytes worth of data, GPT-3 scaled up to 45 terabytes. One terabyte equals 1,024 gigabytes. The increase is huge.

The other size issue involves the number of parameters the model uses. In machine learning, parameters are the weights that the algorithm can alter in the process of learning. The larger the number of parameters, the more the potential learning and more accurate the output. While BERT had 340 million parameters, the Beijing Academy of Artificial Intelligence's Wu Dao 2.0 had 1.5 trillion.

These days, transformers take on a plethora of tasks, from web search to image generation to computer coding. But one of the most impressive remains the job for which they were first created: processing natural language.

What's There to Process with Natural Language?

If we're aiming to have computers comprehend and produce natural language, it makes sense to start by asking what we mean by "natural language" in the first place.

The "Natural" in Natural Language Processing

Extensional definitions (they define by example) are easy: A natural language is a human language like Spanish or Japanese. Intensional definitions (what you typically look up in a dictionary) are harder. *Merriam-Webster* says a natural language "is the native speech of a people (as English, Tamil, Samoan)." Sounds more like definition-by-example to me. The *Cambridge Dictionary* defines a natural language as a "language that has developed in the usual way as a method of communicating between people, rather than language that has been created, for example for computers." OK, Python and Klingon are out, but "in the usual way" is a huge hedge.

There are more sticking points with these definitions. "The native speech of a people." That's only partially accurate, since non-native speakers of, say, Greek are using a natural language when they speak it. "Rather than . . . created." Statistically true, but not always. Languages can begin with a limited natural base, which then gets artificially expanded. Take French Sign Language. Building on the "natural" hand signs used by twin deaf sisters in the eighteenth century, the Abbé de l'Épée "artificially" expanded their communication system, eventually leading to a natural language now used by around 100,000 native French signers. That French system was carried to the United States by Laurent Clerc, where it mixed with home-grown signing used by deaf people in America and then further evolved, ending up as American Sign Language (ASL).

There's also an important piece missing from these dictionary offerings. Part of the "naturalness" of human languages is that, like living organisms, they grow, change, and sometimes go kaput. Old English evolved into Middle English and then successive forms of Modern English. Latin? In 2014, Pope Francis decided it would no longer be the official language of the Vatican.[15] It's still taught in many schools, but outside of some Catholic Masses, you're unlikely to hear it spoken.

Natural languages also develop variations, not just dialects but internal differences in everything from level of formality (think of French *tu* versus *vous*) to verb endings reflecting degree of respect for the addressee (an aspect of Japanese). Some language usage is gendered. In Japan, for instance, females learn to speak with a higher pitch than males.[16] Social groups everywhere adopt insider pronunciations or slang. If you're a TikTok fan, you likely know the word "cheugy," meaning out of date or trying too hard.[17] If not, you're no longer cool. (Whoops—"cool" is cheugy.)

Artificial intelligence pioneers who envisioned getting computers to learn, use, or understand language didn't linger over defining their target. Instead, their approach mirrored that of US Supreme Court Justice Potter Stewart, when he famously skirted defining hard-core pornography: "I know it when I see it." AI researchers working on natural language processing know a natural language when they see it.

That approach has proven workable. If you're interested in speech-to-writing dictation software, you're targeting one of roughly 7,000 systems that humans use as all-purpose means of communication (though today's dictation programs work for only a fraction of them). If you're writing or copying text you want automatically translated, you're using one of those natural languages as well. No, automatic translation tools don't work for all languages (Latin is curiously missing from Microsoft's list), and yes, some behind-the-scenes Trekkie is likely responsible for the software giant's inclusion of Klingon among its translation options. But you get the point.

Natural language processing (NLP) efforts have been highly pragmatic. As we'll see in the next chapter, initial American attempts at machine translation were driven by the Cold War imperative for getting quick access to Russian scientific papers. Then, in the 1980s, US researchers began developing English-like written query systems to streamline business operations.

Wait. What was that about "English-like"?

For much of the history of natural language processing, though far less true today, a needed trick was pruning the language to be processed. In the early days of speech recognition systems (say, for telephone directory assistance), if you spoke with a strong regional accent, the program didn't understand you, and it failed to return the information requested. The same limitations went for written language processing, which brings me to English-like written query systems—and a confession.

It was the mid-1980s, and I was at the exhibition hall of an AI conference. On display were offerings showcasing then-state-of-the-art AI tools, including for natural language processing. As a linguist, I'd been intrigued by the failures of machine translation from prior decades. Since the underlying guts of translation programs and other types of NLP were similar, I was curious to see whether progress had been made on these other fronts. Specifically, I wondered whether 1980s AI could actually make sense of ("process") unscripted phrases and sentences that real people "naturally" produce (in those days, meaning type on a keyboard).

The booth I headed for was run by a company called Cognitive Systems. On display was a program designed for non-computer cognoscenti like office staff to retrieve information from a database by entering natural language queries. The company claimed that its program could "understand natural language sentences." A kindly exhibit representative invited me to try it out.

She likely regretted the offer. For instead of typing a straightforward request like "How much were sales in 1980?" I wrote something like "I'm wondering if perchance you happen to know the dollar amount we took in for 1980." The computer chugged and groaned and gave up.

The challenge, of course, was that my real-world (though pompous) natural language was full of words and syntax the system couldn't handle. To its credit, the program did a reasonable job of retrieving information so long as you restricted yourself to simple language in your query, from which the program plucked out key terms like "sales" and "1980." However, billions of possible natural language sentences aren't of the simplified sort.

With today's large language models running on transformers, these sorts of issues are largely a thing of the past. But it's instructive tracing how we got from there to here.

Human Uses of Natural Language: Candidates for AI Processing

There's much more to natural language use than querying number-laden databases. To get a sense of potential grist for NLP's mill, I've assembled some essential human purposes for speaking and listening, reading and writing:

- *express your ideas or feelings:* for instance, speaking up at a town hall or writing a manifesto
- *access thoughts or feelings of others:* for instance, listening to what others say at that town hall, reviewing a transcript of the meeting, or reading that manifesto
- *access information:* for instance, listening to a podcast or reading a newspaper
- *make requests:* for instance, asking a question in writing and anticipating a written response
- *modify speech:* for instance, correcting yourself when you misspeak
- *modify text you or someone else has written:* for instance, editing a report
- *summarize, synthesize, analyze, or comment on spoken or written material:* for instance, summarizing arguments in a legal case
- *translate from one language to another:* for instance, translating from Swedish to Kiswahili

In a few pages, we'll take stock of how AI fares with this list.

The NLP Sausage Machine at Work

Natural language processing can now perform a wealth of human linguistic tasks. Here's a short cruise through some of the machinery behind it.

Understanding and Generation

When researchers talk about natural language processing, they typically divide it into natural language understanding and natural language generation. In other words, making sense of language already created versus producing new language. The idea of generation is straightforward enough. When an NLP program produces a new poem or article summary, it generates language.

The understanding part is trickier. Yes, there's processing going on when I type into a Google search bar "world's first lighthouse" and up come websites describing the Pharos of Alexandria, one of the classical Seven Wonders of the World, completed around 280 BCE. But whatever Google's search engine is up to when acting on my query, it's not what we mean when we talk about humans understanding language. Google doesn't know Alexandria in Egypt from Alexandria, Virginia, no matter how many page hits it can offer on each.

Admittedly, linguists can't lay claim to comprehending all that much about how people make sense of language they hear or read. But whatever these shortcomings, no one these days assumes that the actual process of human language understanding is what we're programming computers to do.

I can't help being reminded of Sidney Harris's memorable cartoon from the *American Scientist* in 1977. A physicist-type had written on the blackboard what looked like a proof. The first step shown was a typical scrawl of numbers and mathematical symbols, as was the third. However, for the second step, in lieu of math, was written, "Then a miracle occurs." Contemplating the blackboard, his colleague suggested, "I think you should be more explicit here in step two."

In the late 1970s, there weren't a lot of miracles happening in natural language processing. Researchers were still largely using rule-based models, allowing them to reconstruct how the program got from input to output. These days, many NLP outputs are amazing facsimiles of human language. The downside is that, especially with transformers, we're now largely in the dark as to how programs generate the words they do. Hence the drive for more "explainable AI" that we mentioned in the Prologue. For most of us—including AI experts—a miracle occurs. In the chapters ahead, we'll look at some reasons why such mystery can be a problem for using AI to support human writing.

Not all of today's natural language processing is done with transformers, and some applications are more transparent than others. For our purposes, what's important to keep in mind is that "understand" in "natural language understanding" is metaphoric.

Enough of miracles and metaphors. Let's turn to some NLP spoken and written tasks that are essential in the trade.

SPEECH

Speech is another two-way street: recognition and synthesis. For speech recognition, you need to process human auditory input and do something with it. That something is often converting it to writing, as with dictation software like Dragon Naturally Speaking. Today's speech-to-text abilities have been decades in the making. Early support in the 1970s came from DARPA (Defense Advanced Research Projects Agency), the same US governmental arm backing so many early AI projects. In fact, it was with DARPA funding that Dragon Dictate (the progenitor of Naturally Speaking) got its start.[18]

Modern speech recognition tools are impressive, though hardly perfect. We've all seen errors, for instance, with automatic captioning software. Often the cause is one of the traditional litany of reasons that people misinterpret, or fail to make any sense of, what another person has said. Think of times when someone speaks quickly or has a strong accent, or maybe uses an unfamiliar word or proper name. My own favorite example is from a recent AI conference, where the speaker's clearly enunciated words "human society" (at least to my ear) were transcribed as "Hindu society." Back to the drawing board.

Contemporary speech recognition doesn't only handle basic transcription. It can identify which individual is speaking in a meeting or provide a hands-free way of triggering action, such as asking Siri to play Beethoven's Triple Concerto on your Apple HomePod. With some additional wizardry sandwiched in between, you can speak to Google Translate in one language and up pops the written translation in another.

And speech synthesis? The idea is to take some form of linguistic expression and convert it into human-like speech. Typically that means rendering written text as speech, as when an NLP program reads email aloud or is enlisted to produce an audiobook, instead of using a human narrator.

These days, speech synthesis has an even bigger remit. We all know about deep fakes, where the voices of public figures are synthesized without permission. But there's also a growing industry of rent-a-voice, where voice actors (think about professional audiobook narrators or those doing commercial voice-overs) can contract to have their vocal patterns resynthesized for new texts whipped up by AI software.[19] The same kind of technology enables people who have lost their ability to speak to recreate their voices synthetically.

A next step: conjuring up people's voices after they've died. For *Roadrunner*, a movie about chef and traveler extraordinaire Anthony Bourdain, the producer used archived voice files to synthesize speech for words Bourdain had once written or presumably said but were never recorded. Artistic license or deep fake? The controversy swirled.[20] And it gets creepier. Thanks to a company called HereAfterAI, there's now technology using earlier voice recordings to enable people to have conversations with the departed.[21]

Another intriguing application of voice synthesis is what can be done with accents. Say you have an American speaker and want to make her sound as if she's from the UK. Or maybe from Spain and has strongly accented English. These days, no problem. Try out DeepMind's text-to-speech program, where "speech" comes in dozens of accent flavors.[22]

Speech synthesis often works in tandem with other NLP functions. Perhaps the most familiar is getting a response to a query from the likes of Siri or Alexa. You ask, "What's the high temperature tomorrow?" and you hear back, "Tomorrow in Chicago [the system's access to GPS geolocates you] it will be 73 degrees." The synthesized output gives voice to the result, drawn from a meteorological database.

Another impressive example is speech-to-speech translation, where you speak into your device, your words are recognized and used as input to a translation engine, and the output of the translation is synthesized into a spoken rendition. Traditionally, the process took three separate steps: transcribe the spoken language into text (speech recognition), translate the text from the first language into the second, and then use text-to-speech synthesis to generate the oral translation. Today's programs like Google's Translatotron skip the intermediate text representation and can even render the spoken output with the voice qualities of the original speaker.[23]

Talk about miracles. Think back on the hyperbolic projection in 1958, courtesy of Frank Rosenblatt and the US Navy, that instantaneous translation from one spoken language to another was just around the corner. NLP has turned that corner.

WRITING

Start with written natural language understanding. The obvious example is written queries entered into search engines. You type a search into Google that's then processed. As we've said, your written words aren't understood in any human language sense. Rather, a transformer like BERT (and its successors) uses pattern recognition to predict what you want to know about by consulting the gazillion lines of text in the data sources it accesses. Since in NLP the user's eye is on the goal (not the actual processing), the imitation game has been played successfully.

At least much of the time. One reason query results sometimes go awry is that many words have multiple meanings, what linguists call being polysemous. "Paris" refers to a city in France but also to more than a dozen locales in the United States. If you search for "weather in Paris," the first few pages of hits give you temperatures for the City of Light. But keep going, and the US National Weather Service posts information on Paris, Illinois. You'll surely recognize which Paris you're looking for. Just so, if you search for "how to fix a crown," you'll know whether to read entries on repairing a dental mishap or those explaining how to fill gaps in crown molding. (When I went noodling online, I found no suggestions on what to do if your skull cracks or the headpiece for your royal garb needs mending.)

As my fellow linguist David Crystal reminds me, when it comes to search, computer algorithms aren't always as smart as humans. His particular interest was the problem of polysemy when pairing ads with online page results. If you're running a story on the high cost of dental crowns, you probably don't want a hardware store ad running alongside. Crystal cites an online CNN story about a stabbing that took place in Chicago. Accompanying the piece were promotions for kitchen knives. Yes, both the article and the ads involved knives, but the story was about a knife-as-weapon, while the ads were for cutlery. Hardly a happy match.[24]

An alternative that I'm seeing these days is sidestepping the polysemy issue entirely. When I recently googled "stabbing in Chicago" and "stabbing in Baltimore," the ads popping up were for clothing, cars, tractor supplies, and—I kid you not—Harvard Business School Executive Education. Go figure.

Turn now to written language generation. Often it goes hand in hand with language understanding. As we've seen earlier, with today's online searches, predictive tools typically generate fuller inquiry lines after you type in a few words. When I entered "Who is the," Google spat out ten options to choose from to complete my query, beginning with "Who is the richest person in the world," "Who is the tallest person in the world," and "Who is the oldest person alive." Natural language generation also figures in predictive texting. And of course, to get the sausage out of a translation machine, we need text from the source language to be generated in the target language.

But there's another huge area of written AI language generation: producing brand-new text. It's what we get when we ask poetry generators or limerick generators or short story generators to crank out strings of words that presumably haven't been linked together in this way before. It's also what's produced when we program deep neural networks to write article summaries or news stories, draft emails for us, or suggest alternative wording for our human-drafted prose. These are the sorts of AI-generated writing we'll be exploring in Part III. They're also the kinds of writing that challenge us to balance the potential of computers-as-authors (and authorities) against our own human needs and abilities to write.

Search: Comparative Shopping or One-Off Answers

Return for a moment to computer searches, one of NLP's functions *par excellence*. Speech-driven search is at the heart of personal digital assistants, but it's written search—on a computer or mobile device—that made the likes of Google so indispensable.

Traditionally, when we initiated a query, the system generated a cascade of sources we might check out. In recent years, options have increasingly been curated with suggestions for top sites, summary snippets, or links to videos or up-to-date news stories. However, in each case, it's on the user to decide which links to pursue, how much of them to read or view, and whether to believe them.

What's new on the horizon is replacing searches (with their multisource options) with conversation systems driven by chatbots.[25] The user asks a question, and the system responds with a single reply. If you're asking how many inches are in a meter, a one-off answer is fine. However, if reality is nuanced, controversial, or simply time-sensitive, a unitary reply can be inaccurate or even offensive.

Take the 2021 case where a Google search for "What is the ugliest language in India?" yielded "The answer is Kannada, a language spoken by around 40 million people in south India." People in India, especially Kannada speakers, were not amused.[26] From a human–computer interface perspective, the deeper problem is that the response was generated without the search algorithm judging whether the presupposition underlying the query—that it's possible to identify an "ugliest language"—even made sense.[27]

The challenge isn't only that Google's search engine trolls data filled with misinformation and prejudice, or that AI researchers are still figuring out how search tools might verify presuppositions in user queries.[28] The fault is also in ourselves. When doing searches, we might be pressed for time or just lazy. Few of us venture past the first page of hits, read through sites we do open, or bother validating their sources. When searching on a mobile device, we're especially unlikely to look past the first response.

Then there's the trust issue. As information processing expert Martin Potthast and his colleagues argue,

> Under continued exposure to direct answers, users, who are satisfied with the answers given, can be tempted to skip significant parts of the actual reading process. . . . Giving accurate answers to simple and basic questions may further be the cause for an inductive extension of this trust to all answers the system gives.[29]

Beyond the issue of whether the result was ever true is the question of whether it still is. Advocates of digital reference material rightly argue that it's easier to update digital text than print. True. But that hardly guarantees everything we read online is current. Let me illustrate what I mean.

In late December 2022, I typed into Google "number of Gaelic speakers." Up came a rephrased version of my query: "How many Scottish Gaelic speakers are there 2022?" OK, how many for Scots Gaelic? I clicked the "expand" arrow and Google obligingly displayed this text:

> The total number of people recorded as being able to speak and/or read and/or understand Gaelic was 87,056. Of these, 58,000 people (1.1% of the

population) aged three and over in Scotland were able to speak Gaelic. Oct 14, 2022

Since October 2022 was only a few months prior to my experiment, it seemed reasonable to assume the stats were current.

They weren't, which I only unearthed by burrowing into a linked report from the Scottish government.[30] The numbers Google posted turned out to be from a 2011 Scottish census. For an endangered language like Scots Gaelic, spoken by a tiny fraction of the population, usage more than a decade on is likely even more limited. The takeaway here: Trust if you must, but first verify.

AI Tools for Human Tasks

Finally, a quick run-down on AI's handling of tasks that humans have traditionally undertaken with natural language. We've already seen multiple cases of NLP at work, but we'll round out the checklist by adding a few more functions:

- *express your ideas or feelings:* for instance, dictation software, poetry-generation software
- *access thoughts or feelings of others:* for instance, speech synthesis software for written text
- *access information:* for instance, search specific datasets or the broader internet
- *make requests:* for instance, ask Siri or Alexa a question or give a command
- *modify speech:* for instance, use speech-to-text or speech-to-speech translation software to remove spoken disfluencies such as "um's," "ah's," stutters, or repetitions from a text transcript or translation[31]
- *modify text you or someone else has written:* for instance, word processing programs that draw upon AI for spelling and grammar correction; transformer-based programs suggesting alternative wording
- *summarize, synthesize, analyze, or comment on spoken or written material:* for instance, summarizing programs; writing tools like Grammarly or Criterion
- *translate from one language to another:* for instance, publicly available text-to-text or speech-to-speech translation programs; commercial text-to-text machine translation

I purposely ended with translation—the topic of our next chapter. Since its inception, machine translation has been a bellwether for natural language processing, especially of written language. Equally importantly, thinking about translation beckons us to take stock of what's quintessentially human about the way people formulate thoughts and ideas in language.

SIX

Machine Translation Rises Again

The book's English title was *The Bell in the Lake*. Why did my Norwegian friend who recommended the book—and speaks impeccable English—keep referring to it as *The Bells* (plural) *in the Lake*?

Lars Mytting's lyrical tale is set in the small southern Norwegian town of Butangen, in the late nineteenth century. The plot revolves around the town's stave church, two bells hanging in its tower, and the people whose lives are shaped at the intersection. The church had been constructed in the 1100s, when Norway was starting its slow transition from belief in Odin and Thor to Christianity. To honor twin sisters who died sometime in the next few centuries, their father had commissioned construction of those two bells—made of bronze but with some silver, plus Norse magic blended in. Through turns in the nineteenth-century parts of the story, both bells ended up in a nearby lake. One bell was salvaged, while the other sank to the bottom.

The pair was known as the Sister Bells, and the original Norwegian book title was *Søsterklokkene*. Plural.

Anyone who reads books in translation knows that original titles often get changed. For the English rendering of Mytting's earlier novel *Svøm Med Dem Som Drunker* (Swim with Those Who Drown), the name became *The Sixteen Trees of the Somme*, each version reflecting a different aspect of the story.

What about the choice of bell or bells? "Bell" focuses on the point after which only one remained in the water. "Bells" (my Norwegian friend's highly reasonable rendition of the title in English) refers to the time and circumstances when both bells descended into the lake, further reminding us that the Sister Bells had been inseparable for 700 years. Choosing singular versus plural isn't a question of literal accuracy but of what the original writer, the translator, or perhaps the editor wanted readers to focus on.

When we write, we make choices. The words we select do more than denote. They convey meaning that's not in dictionaries. Linguists and philosophers of language remind us that speakers—and writers—must be mindful of pragmatic considerations such as physical location, who the listeners or readers are, and what effects the word choices will have on their audience. When I'm at home in Maryland and I tell my husband I'm heading to Washington that afternoon, he assumes I'm driving downtown to the District of Columbia, not hopping a plane for Seattle. Just so, if I'm in Kolkata in January and say the weather's cold, I'm not asking for a parka and earmuffs to go out. A sweater or shawl will suffice.

Skilled writers labor to find *le mot juste* (or a string of them), along with syntax and pacing that express a particular style, mood, and context. Mindful wording decisions are vital for original compositions and translations alike. These choices used to be the exclusive province of humans. Now computers are muscling in.

Traduttori Traditori

The road to successful translation is pocked with lurking fissures. Words are sometimes ambiguous. They may be too similar to others, having hilarious or hurtful consequences. There's the old Tuscan proverb *"Traduttori traditori"* ("Translators traitors"). It's easy for something to get lost in the conversion process. History is replete with translation errors. Take these two, one old and human, one new and automated.

MICHELANGELO'S HORNS

Blame Saint Jerome, not Michelangelo.

The sculptor's massive *Moses* statue, adorning the tomb of Pope Julius II in Rome, is renowned for its exquisite workmanship—and, of course, those horns. No, Michelangelo wasn't signifying anything diabolical. The culprit was Jerome's translation of the Old Testament into Latin. Initially working from the Greek, Jerome later double-checked the original Hebrew. As we mentioned in Chapter 1, written Hebrew uses a consonantal alphabet, not indicating vowels. Moses was reputed to have descended from Mount Sinai with rays (in Hebrew, the word is *karan*) protruding from his forehead, not horns (*keren*). Unfortunately, without context (or vowels), Jerome mistranslated what he saw in the text—*krn*—and centuries later, Moses would bear the consequences.

PEACEABLE CONFETTI

This time it was Facebook's faux pas. In 2018, an earthquake had struck Indonesia, killing more than 2,000 people. Indonesians took to the social media platform to post their status, letting friends and family know they were safe. The word for "safe" in Bahasa, the official language of Indonesia, is *selamat*. But *selamat* has related meanings, including happy, peace, or congratulations. Mindlessly encountering those posts reporting the person had survived and was safe (*selamat*), Facebook's algorithm festively delivered up congratulatory balloons and confetti.[1]

Like humans, algorithms can be linguistic traitors. That's true today, when large language models generate detritus scrapped from the internet or when Facebook crudely showers down confetti on earthquake survivors. And it was true, though for different reasons, in the early days of machine translation.

The idea of using machines to translate between languages isn't all that new. In the early 1930s, Georges Artsrouni in France and Petr Trojanskij in Russia, working independently, created devices aimed at doing basic translation.[2] But it was World War II and its aftermath that drove a larger quest to supplement—even replace—human translators with computers.

Machine Translation from Failure to Success

The tale of machine translation is one of grand ideas, dashed hopes, and re-generation, like the mythical Phoenix rising from the ashes. We'll see how an initial concept became anathema, only later to emerge as a triumph for natural language processing.

Like the moon, the story of machine translation is divisible into phases.

Phase 1: The Russians Were Coming

War underlies many developments in computing. During World War II, the British built their Colossus computer to aid in cryptoanalysis. Meanwhile, the US Army funded John Mauchly and J. Presper Eckert at the University of Pennsylvania to build the ENIAC to help speed ballistics calculations. The war ended, but defense interest in computing, including for translation, didn't.

The crucial American spark for exploring machine translation came from

Warren Weaver, a mathematician who was longtime director of the Natural Science Division of the Rockefeller Foundation. In a March 4, 1947, letter to Norbert Wiener (mathematician and father of cybernetics), Weaver floated the hypothetical question of whether computers might be enlisted to do scientific translation:

> I have wondered if it were unthinkable to design a computer which would translate. Even if it would translate only scientific materials (where the semantic difficulties are very notably less), and even if it did produce an inelegant (but intelligible) result, it would seem to me worth while.

Then Weaver invoked the model of cryptography, specifically mentioning Russian:

> one naturally wonders if the problem of translation could conceivably be treated as a problem in cryptography. When I look at an article in Russian, I say "This is really written in English, but it has been coded in some strange symbols. I will now proceed to decode."[3]

As a piece of personal correspondence, Weaver's letter fell on polite though deaf ears. Wiener didn't think the proposal doable. But two years later, Weaver circulated his thinking to a larger group of colleagues, incorporating his earlier correspondence with Wiener into a 1949 memorandum. Weaver argued to his new audience that even if machine translation were restricted to technical material, and even if the results weren't elegant, the process could still have value.

This time, the idea would catch fire. As the Cold War between the United States and Russia began heating up, major government funding would flow, and linguists and engineers would set to work.

Discussions of these early days of machine translation inevitably bring up the notorious though surely apocryphal example of translating the English sentence "The spirit is willing but the flesh is weak" into Russian. A standard human translation technique when checking for accuracy is back-translation—taking the result now in the target language (in this case, Russian) and translating it back into the source language (here, English). As the story goes, the computer back-translation came out as "The vodka is good but the meat is rotten."

Were the purported incident even true, it's doubtful that proponents of machine translation would have worried. Their goal was singularly pragmatic: Speed up translation of Russian scientific documents into English.

Literary or metaphoric language wasn't on their agenda, though that doesn't mean advocates lacked understanding of the difference between translating science and translating literature. Warren Weaver had a personal fascination with translation writ large—and with Lewis Carroll. In fact, Weaver not only collected 160 translations of *Alice in Wonderland* but wrote a book, *Alice in Many Tongues*, about the challenges of translating a work teeming with linguistic nuance.[4]

The years between 1951 and 1966 bustled with machine translation research. Initiatives sprang up across the country, including at the RAND Corporation, UCLA, the University of Washington, and MIT. In 1951, MIT's Research Laboratory for Electronics hired Yehoshua Bar-Hillel, a mathematician and linguist, to assess overall progress. Bar-Hillel's report suggested that while fully automatic, highly accurate machine translation didn't seem achievable in the foreseeable future, less ambitious tasks were. He pointedly lobbied for a "mixed machine translation model," with a human doing pre-editing, post-editing, or both of text processed by computer.[5] The following year, Bar-Hillel convened a conference of machine translation researchers, where potential roles for human pre-editing and post-editing were on the table.

Thus far, discussions had been largely theoretical. But one of the conference attendees, Leon Dostert, was to change that.

Dostert had a storied past.[6] A French orphan, he was befriended by a US Army regiment stationed in Dostert's hometown in 1918. With their support, Dostert came to California, beginning his educational and later public service odyssey. In World War II, he become General Eisenhower's personal French interpreter. Following the war, Dostert engineered the simultaneous (human) interpretation system used at the Nuremberg trials and later at the United Nations. Fortuitously, the equipment used in both venues was made by IBM. Dostert became friends with IBM's chairman and CEO Thomas J. Watson.

With IBM backing, Dostert launched a machine translation project at Georgetown University, where he had founded the Institute of Languages and Linguistics a few years earlier. By 1954, the joint Georgetown–IBM venture was ready for a public demonstration. Using a system built on a 250-word vocabulary and 6 syntactic rules, Dostert and his group demonstrated for the first time that a computer could translate Russian technical documents. Such a small language base hardly represents real-world language use. But it was enough to jumpstart major US investment in machine translation research, as well as initiatives in the (then) USSR and Europe.

Work in the United States continued for the next decade. But government backers wanted to know if they were getting their money's worth. To decide, the National Academy of Sciences formed a task force in 1964: the Automatic

Language Processing Advisory Committee, better known as ALPAC. Two years later, ALPAC issued its report.[7]

The findings were devastating. The committee concluded the endeavor wasn't worth the investment. It was cheaper to hire human translators, who were in ample supply. What's more, the quality of machine output was poor, often requiring as much human effort in post-editing as having people do the entire job. After 1966, there was essentially no new government funding, since, as the report concluded, "there is no immediate or predictable prospect of useful machine translation." Most research projects shut down soon thereafter. But not everyone got the memo.

Phase 2: Pragmatists Persist

Think back on Warren Weaver's musings in 1947 that "Even if it would translate only scientific materials . . . and even if it did produce an inelegant . . . result, it would seem to me worth while." A handful of projects, largely with roots before the ALPAC axe fell, were to demonstrate that machine translation could indeed be effective, if the scope of language being translated was restricted. Put another way, if no one like me (with my antics at the Cognitive Science exhibit booth) was gunning to break the system.

Here are three success stories, beginning with one for which I had a brief ringside seat.

UNIVERSITY OF TEXAS AT AUSTIN: METAL PROJECT

Winfred Lehmann was a renowned linguist and Germanic scholar, past president of the Linguistic Society of America, and later president of the Modern Language Association. He had befriended me when I was a visiting scholar at UT Austin in 1984–1985. Graciously, he invited me for a tour of the project he was spearheading (unbeknownst to me) on machine translation. What was an eminent linguist doing in a field that members of our tribe knew to be a fool's errand?

The answer was, a lot of fruitful work.

It had been Leon Dostert who, years earlier, suggested to Lehmann that he take up German–English machine translation, since Dostert was working on Russian-to-English at Georgetown. Lehmann had already been intrigued by Weaver's conjectures about the feasibility of machine translation for technical documents. With significant funding from the US Army Signal Engineering Laboratories, Lehmann set to work in 1961, creating what was dubbed the METAL translation system.[8]

The project continued, with limited success, until 1975, when funding ran out. After three fallow years, Lehmann secured new money from Siemens AG, the German technology company. Since Siemens markets its products internationally, the firm had practical need for high-speed translation of materials like operating manuals.

Lehmann's METAL system was given new life. Now directing the project was Jonathan Slocum, a linguist and computer scientist, but himself then new to machine translation. No matter. By 1984, a prototype of the translation system was delivered to Siemens. However, as Slocum would later recount, his efforts at the time garnered little collegial respect. In Slocum's words, "Machine translation was not discussed in polite professional society." Reflecting on his negative experiences when speaking about his work at a conference in 1980, Slocum wrote,

> My new interest, I later came to realize, was taboo. On the other hand, I had one great advantage: I was not aware that MT was infeasible, and that my hopes were doomed. Perhaps this ignorance accounted in part for the subsequent success of our project![9]

SYSTRAN

Another project seeded by Dostert's efforts at Georgetown was a system eventually called SYSTRAN. Its designer, Peter Toma, had been a member of the Georgetown–IBM project. In 1962, Toma would take lessons learned while at Georgetown and go on to develop a Russian–English machine translation system called AUTOTRAN, which later transitioned into multilingual SYSTRAN. Toma secured a contract with the US Department of Defense in 1969 and then, in 1976, with the European Community. SYSTRAN continues today as a translation company, offering services in fifty languages.[10]

And one more thing. SYSTRAN would become the basis for Babel Fish, which we'll get to in a moment.

TAUM-METEO

Not all efforts were American. As a country with both French and English as official languages, Canada was motivated to develop automatic translation. Weather reports were an obvious place to start, since language used to describe meteorological conditions is limited in scope and doesn't require much nuance.

Work on translation had begun in Montreal in 1965, with a research group known as TAUM (Traduction Automatique de l'Université de Montréal). By 1970, the group had developed TAUM-METEO, a program for automatically translating weather information. A few years later the system was operational.

Once again, Weaver's prediction proved correct that machine translation within a limited semantic realm was possible.[11]

Using machines to translate weather reports made good sense in the name of efficiency. But there was another benefit, this time for humans. Translating basic weather forecasts, over and again, was incredibly boring, and the turnover rate among professional translators in the weather service had been very high. With TAUM-METEO, people were able to focus on more interesting pieces of translation and stayed longer in their jobs.[12]

Phase 3: Babel Fish for Real

By the late 1980s, AI translation efforts had begun switching to models using statistics and large language datasets known as corpora.[13] Rules were out, pattern matching was in.[14] Results weren't yet highly accurate or fully automatic, but they were improving.

Enter Babel Fish. No, not quite the instant translator that Douglas Adams had envisioned in *The Hitchhiker's Guide to the Galaxy*. But inching its way there. In 1997, the search engine Alta Vista (later bought by Yahoo!) brokered a joint undertaking between SYSTRAN and DEC (a major computer manufacturer at the time) to develop a free online translator called Babel Fish. In 2012, Babel Fish would be replaced by Microsoft's Bing Translator.

And Google? While the company had been late to the search engine party, it made up for lost time elsewhere, including with online translation. Google Translate debuted in 2006.

Phase 4: Translation for All

Statistical AI had made for major improvement in machine translation, but deep neural networks were to yield even more impressive results. By the mid-2010s, AI researchers, including Yoshua Bengio and his students, were demonstrating the power of neural-based translation.[15] The message wasn't lost on Google. In 2016, the search engine giant shifted its translation strategy from statistics to neural networks. Overnight, the translation error rate dropped by 60 percent.[16]

Google wasn't done. With development of transformers (including Google's BERT), translation took another great leap forward. And as we saw in the last chapter, the 2017 breakout paper on transformers used translation as a test of the model's prowess.

These days, impressive machine translation is everywhere. In our personal and social lives, we rely on it to make sense of websites written in languages we don't understand and to be our personal translator in Skype conversations. And it pervades the business world. It's hardly surprising that when eBay introduced quality machine translation on its site, exports increased 10.9 percent.[17]

What's there not to like?

So What's the Problem with Computers as Translators?

Legend has it that when Roman generals made triumphal processions through the streets, they were accompanied in their chariots by a slave. The slave's job was to hold a golden crown over the general's head, saying "Look behind you. Remember you are a man." Or as Ray Bradbury phrased it in *Fahrenheit 451*, "Remember Caesar, thou art mortal."[18]

We're all fallible. We're only human. While machine translation programs aren't human, they still falter. They suffer from many of the same challenges befalling online searches and text generated by large language models. With translation, though, these problems take on their own cast.

The Trust Issue

It's increasingly hard knowing what to believe of material we encounter online. The dilemma arises in judging social media posts, videos, and search results. At least we usually have language on our side. Most of the posts and hits are in a language we speak or at least can read. While too many of us forgo tracking down alternative sources to confirm veracity, we could if we chose to.

Enter machine translation. As I was reminded by Lynne Bowker, professor of translation and information studies at the University of Ottawa, we're not always aware when online text we're reading has been run through an AI translator. These translators might be embedded in web browsers or social media sites and run automatically. The problem, she says, is that "we don't even know to ask ourselves the question as to whether or not we should trust it."[19] We face an analogous challenge with text-generation programs like GPT-3 and ChatGPT. It can be hard to tell if the text was produced by a human or a machine. And if we can't distinguish, we typically don't think to ask.

But now assume we've hit the "translate" button and know that AI will be at work. Start with translation from a language we don't know into one we do. Unless the result sounds particularly weird, we tend to take it at face value. Given the sophistication of today's machine translation, the good news is that we're probably on safe ground, most of the time (please note those qualifiers). Yet since we don't speak the source (original) language, how would we know? We trust, but rarely verify.

Now think about translating from a language we understand into one we don't. Again, we tend to trust but not verify. Running the source text through multiple translation programs for comparison won't help, since we still can't make sense of the results. A possible workaround is doing a back-translation, though there's still no guarantee that the initial translation into the target language would be deemed accurate in the eyes of a bilingual.

I decided to try out some translation and back-translation pairs. For fun, I ran the notorious "The spirit is willing but the flesh is weak" through Microsoft's and Google's English-to-Russian translation programs. Then, for both programs, I did back-translations into English. Instead of vodka and rotten meat, I got

Microsoft: The Spirit desires but the flesh is weak.

Google: The spirit is willing but the flesh is weak.

"Willingness" and "desire" don't mean exactly the same thing, but at least the Microsoft back-translation is in the right ballpark. As for Google's homerun, perhaps pattern matching from the dataset was responsible for getting the English back-translation spot on. After all, the English sentence has been around at least since the King James Bible rendering of Matthew 26:41 (though the word "indeed" was part of the original, that is, "the spirit indeed is willing").

I wondered how my parlor game might work with other languages. The Bengali back-translation (on Google) came out as

The soul is willing but the flesh is weak.

Sounds reasonably promising. I next translated only the word "spirit" from English into Bengali. Google produced *atma*. Consulting with my favorite native speaker of Bengali (my husband), I learned that *atma* has metaphysical overtones. When back-translation of the entire Bengali sentence into English produced the word "soul," that's really what was meant. Bengali *atma* would never be used when considering a night on the town, which "spirit" in the contemporary English phrase "the spirit is willing" might.

I was also curious how Google and Microsoft handled translations of the English homonyms "bank" and "bank." Impressively, both engines successfully drew on context to judge whether German *Bank* (the financial institution) or *Ufer* (the side of a river) was appropriate.

For the Google test, it's relevant that the algorithm did the translation word by word into German as I entered each word in English. When I input

English: Which bank should I go to: the one on the right or left side?

the result was:

German: *Zu welcher Bank soll ich gehen: die auf der rechten oder linken Seite?*

"Bank" = financial institution. But when I added the words "of the river" to my original translation request, before my eyes, Google changed the rendering for "bank" (plus jiggered a bit of syntax) to indicate a riverbank:

Google: *An welches Ufer soll ich gehen: das auf der linken oder rechten Seite des Flusses?*

The Microsoft translation engine embedded in Word translates the entire source text in one go. When I input the two versions of my English sentence, Microsoft's translations were essentially the same as Google's.

Impressive, indeed.

Why Gender Is a Machine Translation Nightmare

Not all contemporary machine translation is such smooth sailing. One trouble spot that's generating a lot of research interest is gender.[20]

To explain the problem, we need a quick grammar lesson. Linguists talk about two kinds of gender potentially associated with nouns (and maybe pronouns, articles, and adjectives). The first is grammatical gender, which some languages have but others don't. In German, for instance, the word for "bridge" is *die Brucke*. Actually, *die* is an article ("the"), but what's relevant here is that it indicates the German noun is grammatically feminine. In Spanish, when talking about that bridge, you say *el puenta*, where *el* indicates that *puenta* is grammatically masculine.

The second kind of gender is natural gender. The English word "man" refers to a male, "woman" to a female. Rams are male sheep, ewes are female, and so on. But then things get dicier.

English only has natural gender for its nouns. Sometimes it's signaled by a suffix: "actor" versus "actress," "waiter" versus "waitress." It also shows up embedded in compounds, though a word like "chairman" refers, ostensibly, to people of either gender. Recent decades have seen concerted efforts to level the linguistic playing field: "actor" for both genders; calling the restaurant crew "wait staff" and those heads of administrative units simply "chairs."

The plot grows thicker when we talk about what we might dub cultural gender. Think about professions that have traditionally been associated with one gender or the other: doctor (male), nurse (female), at least in the United States.[21] Because of its cultural history, the American datasets on which language models feed likely contain more instances of male doctors than female, and the reverse for nurses. If you enter "The doctor was about to start the procedure" and the next sentence requires a pronoun, you're most likely to get "he," not "she." A lot of people end up getting shortchanged. In the United States, as of 2019, 36.3 percent of physicians were female; and in 2020, 9.4 percent of registered nurses were male.[22]

Focus now on surgeons. When it comes to machine translation of "surgeon" into a language that has grammatical gender, the program has no choice but to use a gender-marked noun. I entered the sentence "The surgeon was about to start the operation" into Google Translate, asking for German. Google produced

Der Chirurg wollte gerade mit der Operation beginnen.

Yes, *Chirurg* is masculine.

Google has been aware of the problem for some time. The solution it proudly proposed was to offer both grammatically male and female terms, where they exist in the language.[23] Enter the simple English word "surgeon" and out pop two German options:

Chirurgin (feminine)

Chirurg (masculine)

Looks encouraging. However, if you add the article "the" ("the surgeon") to your query (or, for that matter, any other additional word), you're back to only getting the masculine term.

To be fair, when I ran my translation tests in January 2023, Google's bias reduction project was a work in progress. Its initial efforts were directed at Turkish-to-English and then English-to-Spanish translations, the latter being the most frequently sought translation pair. By the time you read this book, translation pairs like English-to-German could offer more balanced gender options.

Professions—and cultural gender—aside, it turns out that grammatical gender is more deeply rooted in people's psyches than we might think, even for inanimate objects like bridges. Cognitive scientist Lera Boroditsky showed native speakers of German and of Spanish the same picture of a bridge and asked for the first three descriptive words that came to mind. Since the participants were also skilled English speakers, their answers were given in English. The German speakers said things like "beautiful," "elegant," or "slender." Answers from the Spanish speakers included words like "strong," "sturdy," and "towering."[24] Sounds pretty gender-stereotypic to me. Grammatical gender is supposed to be irrelevant for meaning. But Boroditsky's work reminds us that meaning is more complex than just what you look up in a dictionary.

If gender is one linguistic challenge for translation, an embarrassment of riches is another.

Coping with the Language Cornucopia

For millennia, people have struggled to communicate with those who don't speak their language. One potential solution is for everyone with the need to converse with people outside their linguistic tribe to learn a common tongue. Various candidates have cycled through. Sometimes the choice has been an existing natural language. Think of Latin, then French, and now English topping the list. Another option is an artificial language that's no one's native tongue. Esperanto is the best-known, but there have been others, including Bishop John Wilkins's Real Character and Philosophical Language in the seventeenth century and Interlingua in the twentieth.[25]

A third possibility is to become multilingual, as many people are, especially in countries where speaking more than one language is a practical necessity. And then there's translation. In fact, in his letter to Norbert Wiener, Warren Weaver mentioned machine translation as potentially serving a common good:

> A most serious problem, for UNESCO and for the constructive and peaceful future of the planet, is the problem of translation, as it unavoidably affects the communication between peoples.[26]

Historically, translation assistance has taken many forms. As far back as 2300 BCE, there were Sumerian–Akkadian bilingual word lists, incised on clay tablets. Centuries later, more portable bilingual dictionaries became commonplace, along with phrase books. Now, we've moved on to digital on-demand tools.

These programs are incredibly handy. Our lives are better off for having them. But are there downsides? I'm not talking here about accuracy issues or the fact that thousands of languages aren't yet on Big Tech's translation radar. Rather, I'm asking what translation-at-our-fingertips does to motivation for learning a second language, and why the question matters. In short, I'm asking what happens when we go all-in for the efficiency of machine translation and avoid the tough work of gaining even modest ability in another language.

When I say I'm a linguist, that doesn't mean I know a string of languages. (I do theory, history, and empirical research.) Despite dabbling in French, Italian, German, and Japanese, I'm basically monolingual. In high school and college, I studied Latin, which these days won't even help me at the Vatican.

What bilinguals and trilinguals, linguists and teachers of foreign languages know is this: Acquiring a new language shouldn't be just about learning pronunciation, vocabulary, and grammatical rules. Hopefully, you simultaneously gain entry into the history, culture, and alternative ways of seeing the world of another group of people. When you're told there's no adequate translation equivalent for a word, what you're discovering is that speakers of that other language may not conceptualize the world the same way you do.[27]

Take labels for dividing up the color spectrum. Not all languages chunk the continuum the same way.

In Japanese, the word *aoi* historically means both blue and green. About a millennium ago, a separate word for "green" (*midori*) entered the language, though it wasn't widely adopted until the second half of the twentieth century. The result is that *midori* isn't used for everything that's green in color. "Green apple" is still *ao ringo* and "green leaves" is *aoba*. The generic phrase "green light" is *midori no hikari*, which includes green Christmas lights. But "green traffic light"? It's *ao shingo*, a holdover from the 1930s, when traffic lights were introduced in Japan, and the word *midori* hadn't yet gained currency.[28] Knowing when to use *aoi* or *midori* is a real case of insider linguistic baseball.

Languages contain more than sounds, words, and rules. They represent peoples and cultures. To gain these insights, is it worth the trouble learning another language? In the United States, the answer has frequently been no. A longstanding joke:

Q: What do you call a person who speaks three languages?
A: A trilingual.
Q: What do you call a person who speaks two languages?
A: A bilingual.
Q: What do you call a person who speaks one language?
A: An American.

Given its immigrant history, there was pressure in the United States to learn English, not to retain the language of one's forebears. By the 1960s when Americans began traveling abroad in droves, they brought their passport and a copy of Frommer's *Europe on $5 a Day*, not a French or German textbook. Globalization in more recent decades has meant more people around the world learning English, not more Americans studying other languages. According to data from the Modern Language Association, foreign language enrollments in US colleges dropped more than 24 percent between 2013 and 2022.[29] That decline began before popular online translation tools further quashed potential enthusiasm for language learning.

Don't get me wrong. I'm grateful for digital translation. But I'm also grateful for spellcheck, which I know is rotting my never-were-terrific orthographic skills. Why try hard to spell correctly (or resort to an actual dictionary) when the software does it for you? Just so, why bother learning even a few phrases or names of food in Icelandic when software on your phone handily translates menus?

For more than a decade, the online filter bubble has encouraged ideological silos. My worry is that adoption of translation tools will further reduce motivation to lift our cultural and linguistic blinders. Yes, I'm as guilty as the next person in using convenience as an excuse for not putting in the work. But, as when eating that extra scoop of ice cream, my conscience nags me to remember the potential consequences.

In 1960, Bar-Hillel predicted that "fully automatic high quality translation . . . is just a dream which will not come true in the foreseeable future."[30] Gender bias issues and "spirit" versus "soul" aside, that dream is becoming a reality. Reborn from its inauspicious beginnings, machine translation has become a resounding triumph for natural language processing.

But another NLP success story has also unfolded: using AI to generate what we take to be brand-new text. Computers as authors. It's to that story that we turn now.

PART III

WHEN COMPUTERS WRITE

SEVEN

Machines Emerge as Authors

The title won't zoom to the top of anyone's bestseller list, though the author could care less. For *Lithium-Ion Batteries*, published by Springer Nature in 2019, was written by a computer (which the publisher dubbed "Beta Writer"). Enter the first machine-generated textbook.[1] The accomplishment, while impressive, is hardly surprising. Computers are tailor-made for zipping through vast quantities of research and summarizing findings. It didn't hurt that Springer has a massive online database to draw on.

Or maybe the honor for machine-generated books rightly goes to Philip M. Parker, a management professor in France. Parker devised a patented system incorporating a template and databases (plus internet searches) to automatically turn out books. He's produced more than 200,000 of them, ranging from medical guides to collections of crossword puzzles to volumes filled with quotations. We might debate whether these are really books or more like compilations, but regardless, the sheer output is daunting.[2] Interviewed in 2013, Parker envisioned the day when machines could write doctoral dissertations.[3]

Now a decade on—and with large language models as today's text production tool du jour—that time could soon be now. How did we get here?

Yours Wistfully

It was 1953 in England, and love was in the air. A Ferranti Mark 1 computer was concocting letters like this one:

Honey Dear
My sympathetic affection beautifully attracts your affectional enthusiasm. You are my loving adoration: my breathless adoration. My fellow feeling breathlessly hopes for your dear eagerness. My lovesick adoration cherishes your avid ardour.
Yours wistfully
M. U. C.

As in Manchester University Computer.

The programmer was British computer scientist Christopher Strachey.[4] It's no coincidence that Strachey had multiple ties with Alan Turing, going back to their days at King's College Cambridge. Maybe your heart isn't won over with the sentiments. M.U.C. was no Elizabeth Barrett Browning, but at least the love letters were intelligible.

Strachey's programming scheme was simple: a few anchor words (like "you," "my," and "yours"), along with wild card slots for adjectives, nouns, verbs, and adverbs. Working with only 70 words, the program could potentially generate around 300 billion different letters.[5] Strachey's source of inspiration? Alan Turing's conjectures in 1950 about building an imitation machine.

Strachey's computer program was apparently the world's first to write text. But he didn't stop at producing cheesy love letters. Besides pioneering a computer program to play the game of draughts (the British name for checkers), Strachey composed the first computer-generated music ever recorded. The Mark 1 could be programmed to create a short burst of sound—essentially a kind of hoot. Turing, who had engaged Strachey to work on the machine, envisioned exploiting this capacity to signal such things as when a program run was completed. Strachey had a more whimsical idea. He coded in the opening bars of "God Save the King" (as in George VI), along with "Baa Baa Black Sheep" and Glenn Miller's swing hit "In the Mood."[6]

For next steps, we cross the Atlantic.

Dear Computer, Tell Me a Story

In America, the early blossoming of computer-generated writing centered around prose that had something of a story line. Like many good tales, this one was woven from multiple threads.

Write, Play, Remix

The first thread was production of new linear text, using programs that plucked elements from a data source—in essence, the sort of thing Strachey had done in cranking out those love letters. An impressive example was William Chamberlain and Thomas Etter's *The Policeman's Beard Is Half Constructed*, appearing in 1984. The book's cover boasted this was "The First Book Ever Written by a Computer." Having devised a program dubbed Racter (as in "raconteur"), which is credited as the author, Chamberlain and Etter drew on a 2,400-word vocabulary, some grammar rules, and a smattering of prefabricated sentences, proverbs, and quotations to create their 120 page text.[7] A sample:

> Happily and sloppily a skipping jackal watches an aloof crow. This is enthralling. Will the jackal eat the crow? I fantasize about the jackal and the crow, about the crow in the expectations of the jackal. You may ponder about this too!

No National Book Award here, but not bad for 1984.

The second thread of the story was interactivity. Machine replies were generated in response to human input. The earliest interactive program grabbing headlines was Joseph Weizenbaum's ELIZA, from the mid-1960s. Modeled on the conversational style of Rogerian psychotherapy, ELIZA used sentence templates, triggered by keywords, to produce the therapist's side of the conversation. Here's one of Weizenbaum's examples, with ELIZA-the-therapist's responses in all caps:

> Well, my boyfriend made me come here.
>
> YOUR BOYFRIEND MADE YOU COME HERE
>
> He says I'm depressed much of the time.
>
> I AM SORRY TO HEAR YOU ARE DEPRESSED[8]

Boyfriend. Depressed. You get the picture. These days, "chatbots" is what we call the likes of ELIZA, though backed by far more sophisticated AI. Today's interactive bots work either with typed text (think of online customer service chatbots) or voice (Hey Siri). This same kind of interactive give-and-take made possible a world of computer gaming, which, as we'll see, paved the way for story generation.

The third thread, sometimes joined at the hip with the second, I've labeled remix. These days, the word conjures up recombining elements of a musical soundtrack or, with Creative Commons licenses, joining elements from different sources of, say, text, to produce something new. In essence, that was the process at work in the late 1980s, when a computer-driven approach to literature called hypertext fiction was invented. We'll get to the fiction part in a bit, but first some background on hypertext.

In 1960, Ted Nelson (later iconic computer guru) dreamt up a project based on non-sequential writing. He called the process hypertext, which he later defined as "text that branches and allows choice to the reader."[9] Flash back to 1945, when the engineer and inventor Vannevar Bush had envisioned Memex, a machine enabling users to link together documents (stored on microfilm) representing all human knowledge.[10] A tall order, and not realized. But Nelson was inspired by Bush's thinking and set out to build a system containing a universal library, composed of non-sequential writing. Nelson would name his system XANADU.[11]

Nelson never managed to create that hypertext universal library. But there were auspicious spinoffs of his scheme for accessing disparate documents. In the early 1980s, computer scientist Ben Shneiderman developed the notion of document-internal hyperlinks, from which, in 1987, Apple built the Macintosh HyperCard. More far-reaching was Tim Berners-Lee's use of hyperlinks for retrieving information from the ether, anywhere in the world. And so was born HTTP (hypertext transfer protocol) and, in 1989, the World Wide Web.[12] These same hyperlinks would soon enable hypertext fiction.

But for now, let's pick up the second thread in our story: interactivity and play.

Games People Play

For millennia, cultures have developed games, played by children and adults alike. Knucklebones (jacks) and board games. Chess and card games. Another recreation is devising such new diversions. Early computer aficionados were up for the task.

In 1962, a group of computer jocks associated with MIT got access to a DEC PDP-1—the first in a line of machines that would prove central to the emergence of hacker culture. The group's resulting handiwork was Spacewar!, a combat video game. Interest in computer gaming would soon catch fire among the general public. First came video arcades, featuring games like

Computer Space (1971), Pong (1972), and Pac-Man (1980). Then, as microcomputers began taking up residence in homes, the commercial floodgates opened. However, universities (where tinkerers might have access to the newer DEC PDP-10) remained a fertile development playground.

Will Crowther was a computer programmer and avid caving enthusiast, with a day job at Bolt Beranek and Newman, an R&D company with strong university ties. And BBN had a PDP-10. Combining his loves for spelunking and the fantasy role-playing board game Dungeons & Dragons, Crowther developed Colossal Cave Adventure, the first text-based role-playing computer game.

The genre was launched. In 1977, a group of MIT students created Zork. Two years later, across the pond at the University of Essex, Roy Trubshaw (again using the trusty PDP-10) wrote the original MUD (initially meaning multi-user dungeon, but over time redefined as multi-user dimension). All these games involved interactive role-playing story creation. Written text drove the action forward. Players typed in commands, and the program returned text responses.

Were these games or stories? Both. They—and their successors—have borne various labels: "text adventure," "text game," and, more broadly, "interactive fiction." An essential component of interactive fiction is that each story generated is unique, reflecting the individual player's moves.[13] While the early versions tended towards fantasy and adventure themes, the interactive fiction model could be, and was, later deployed for all manner of narrative content.

Spinning Tales

Meanwhile, others in the computer world were focused more on the story than the game. A key landmark was James Meehan's 1976 Tale-Spin.[14]

As a graduate student at Yale, Meehan hoped to build an interactive multi-person program for telling stories but had gotten stuck on the implementation.[15] In 1974, Roger Schank, a linguist with a strong cognitive science and AI orientation, arrived at Yale. Schank was bent on remaking the dominant linguistic models of the day by focusing on knowledge representation and understanding, rather than traditional concepts of syntax and semantics. Schank's new approach dealt in conceptual dependencies—basically, knowledge representations—along with what were called scripts, plans, and goals.[16]

Meehan became Schank's PhD student. Now envisioning his stories as solutions to problems, Meehan built the Tale-Spin program around Schank's language and cognition models. To use Tale-Spin, players selected basic parameters, such as characters (they were all animals), a physical setting for the story, and a moral the story should convey (think of Aesop's fables). Drawing on its rules, inference engine, and natural language generator, the program then spun out the tale. Tale-Spin was interactive in that users chose their story parameters. However, once given its marching orders, the program assumed command and did all the writing.

Meehan's work seeded a bevy of activity, with story-generation programs becoming ever-more sophisticated as programming models and hardware evolved. But the early work on AI storytelling would also contribute to a particular type of interactive fiction that would then largely peter out.

Hypertext Fiction: A Short-Lived Remix

All the game and story initiatives we've been talking about were driven by computer programmers. But stories are also a natural province of literary types. Hypertext fiction emerged when literature professors got their hands on computers.

The new story genre consisted of blocks of text (presumably fiction) joined together by hyperlinks. Now that computer scientists had devised the notion of hyperlinks, and now that writing of all sorts—including literary—could be mounted as electronic files, the question became, could these technologies lead us to rethink the relationship between a reader and a text? In the words of George Landow, a professor of English at Brown University and a leader in the movement,

> Since hypertext radically changes the experiences that reading, writing, and text signify, how, without misleading, can one employ these terms, so burdened with the assumptions of print technology, when referring to electronic materials?[17]

In other words, it was high time to reexamine the meaning of core literacy terms. Readers could now have a hand in the writing enterprise, since texts were no longer continuous and fixed. The relationship between text and reader was now interactive.

Compare literature with adventure games. In both cases, there's a story to be told. With adventure games, the ending typically results in the player winning or losing. By contrast, with literature, most times the ending brings some plot resolution. In reading traditional fiction, everyone follows the same beginning, middle, and end. With adventure games, not so.

And also, not so with hypertext fiction. The crucial element now is that the work itself no longer has a single linear progression. Reading stops being an experience shared across users.

These notions aren't new in the literary world. Writing in *S/Z* in 1970,

Roland Barthes suggested dividing texts into smaller segments ("blocks of sig-nification" or "units of reading") he called "lexias." Discussions of the death of the author (dating to Barthes's 1967 essay of that name) and reader response theory have long argued that it's up to individual readers, not just authors, to decide what a story or novel means.

But personal interpretation of linear prose is a far cry from mapping your own pathway through it, where each reading is as unique as the chosen route. The reader's role in hypertext fiction is deciding which links to follow. Readers aren't doing any actual writing—but neither is the program. The text blocks are already in place. Interactivity comes in choosing how to stack them.

Hypertext fiction arrived on the scene in 1987 with Michael Joyce's *after-noon, a story*. Other works followed, including Stuart Moulthrop's *Victory Garden* (1992) and Shelley Jackson's *Patchwork Girl* (1995) (Joyce: an English professor at Vasser; Moulthrop: a digital humanities professor at the University of Wisconsin; Jackson: a student of Landow's at Brown). Nick Montfort's riddle machines were interactive programs in which "a potential narrative . . . can be experienced in a different order by different interactors."[18]

Another hypertext advocate was Robert Coover, professor of creative writ-ing at Brown. In a piece appearing in the *New York Times Book Review*, Coover spoke of hypertext allowing "true freedom from the tyranny of the line" (presumably meaning linearity) and "favoring a plurality of discourses over definitive utterance and freeing the reader from domination of the author."[19] Move over, Dickens and Tolstoy.

But Coover also acknowledged challenges that reading hypertexts present. Among them,

"Text" has lost its canonical certainty. How does one judge, analyze, write about a work that never reads the same way twice?

Then there's the problem of closure:

[W]hat is closure in such an environment? If everything is middle, how do you know when you are done, either as reader or writer?[20]

Do readers feel stifled when encountering Dickens or Tolstoy the old-fashioned way? While hypermedia has countless uses (some of which Coover recounted in a later article), do we want it in our fiction?

According to Steven Johnson, writing for *Wired* in 2013, the hypertext fic-tion party had largely ended by the early 2010s.[21] Johnson mentioned the clo-sure problem, plus the fact that nonlinear stories were very hard to write. But Johnson's core argument was that user interest in clicking on links to hop from one clump of text to another had moved on to greener pastures. Now, hyper-links permeate blogs, online news stories, Wikipedia, social network postings, and the way we work our way through the internet more generally. Hyperlinks for fiction reading had lost their freshness.

My own take is a bit different. As readers, we draw pleasure from traveling with authors on the story paths they've configured. Especially with fiction that we read for enjoyment (not because someone told us to), we're generally content to let authors do the conceptualizing, producing plot lines worth following.

We literate humans also relish feeling part of historical continuity. What did Dickens's original audience in the late 1830s think about *Oliver Twist*? What did I think more than a century later? What about my students? We compare notes (personal or scholarly), reflecting on how disparate worldly cir-cumstances shape our impressions and understanding.

From Strachey's initial love letter program to the first computer-generated novel, computer games, story generation, and hypertext fiction, the early decades of AI were filled with adventure, along with attempts to rethink storytelling and even literature. AI's role in narrative writing ran the gamut, including typed exchange between the program and the user, backend natural language processing to spin new linear text, and availability of links inviting users to rearrange preexisting blocks of writing.

But there was another side to experimentation with AI as a writing tool: generating non-fiction, especially where there was a tangible payoff, always for efficiency and commonly for profit. And so we now turn to how computers became producers of written information.

AI Gets Down to Business

So much to read, not enough time. The problem's hardly new. What's changed is what we do about it.

Take book reviews. They emerged by the mid-eighteenth century, providing readers "some idea of a book before they lay out their money or time on it."[22] Another eighteenth-century solution was book extracts, gathered together in anthologies. Later came *Reader's Digest* condensed books, a popular twenti-eth-century mid-brow reading diet. And for the less-than-studious looking to skip out on their reading assignments, there were CliffsNotes, Monarch Notes, and SparkNotes.[23]

What if you're seeking just the main ideas of a longer work—much briefer than a condensation or plot outline? These shortenings have a long history as well and have flown under many flags: précis (from the Latin *praecidere*, meaning "to cut off or shorten"), synopsis (from the Greek *synopsis*, "seeing together, a general view"), summary (from the Latin *summa*, "whole, totality, or gist"), or abstract (from the Latin *abstrahere*, "to draw away"). Context and content vary, but the results all present essential points, facts, issues, or conclusions.

In the Name of Science (and Technology): The Abstract

Think about that brief paragraph or two headlining nearly every article in a modern scholarly journal. The abstract. It's there to help readers decide whether to keep going or if simply getting the gist of the paper will suffice.

While the noun "abstract" dates back in English to the mid-fifteenth century, its debut in the scientific realm wasn't until the late eighteenth.[24] To understand how, we need a bit of history.

The Royal Society of London was founded in 1660. Among its initial members were the likes of Christopher Wren (architect of St. Paul's Cathedral), John Wilkins (inventor of a universal language), Robert Boyle (a pioneer in modern chemistry), and Robert Hooke (the first to visualize a microorganism). The society's aim was to present and discuss scientific findings. To this end, in 1665, it established the *Philosophical Transactions of the Royal Society* (with the mouthful of a subtitle: *Giving some Account of the present Undertakings, Studies, and Labours of the Ingenious in many considerable parts of the World*). Early papers ran the gamut from a report on the great red spot of Jupiter to an account of "New American" whale fishing. Members read their papers aloud, and the papers were then published.

Which made for hefty volumes and a huge time commitment, if you planned on reading them all.

By the late eighteenth century, the society adopted a new practice: having the secretary prepare a summary of each paper, after it had been presented orally, and then placing the summaries in the society's minute books. These summaries, labeled "abstracts," were then available to people lacking access to the full-length versions. The abstracts weren't included alongside the printed papers but, by 1831, appeared in a separate publication, *Proceedings of the Royal Society*. Readership included not only society fellows but some members of the general public.

It took several more decades (maybe by the 1870s, definitely by the early 1890s) for fellows presenting papers to assume responsibility for writing their own abstracts. Finally, in the years after World War II, these author-generated abstracts were placed at the start of their articles. A new scholarly tradition was born.

How do you prepare an abstract? If you've ever written one for a journal, you know there are typically guidelines on length and what should be included. In many cases, there's essentially a template to follow. Once you have templates, maybe even machines could do it.

And so they did.

In the late 1950s, IBM launched a project to automatically write abstracts of articles in fields like biology and chemistry. Hans Luhn, whose expertise included information retrieval, devised a program in which the machine-readable text was statistically analyzed for word frequency and placement distribution. Words and then sentences that showed high levels of "significance" (measured by frequency and position) were extracted and used to generate the abstract.[25] Luhn saw this autocreation as yielding multiple benefits. It helped ensure consistency in how abstracts are constructed, given that human abstractors are influenced by their "background, attitude, and disposition." What's more, by letting a computer do the writing, humans could be freed up for other tasks. As we'll see in the next chapter, this same argument is now invoked to justify deployment of AI newswriting programs, presumably saving flesh-and-blood journalists for tasks machines can't handle.

Presciently, Luhn warned about limitations on his abstracting program:

> regrettable as it may appear, the intellectual aspects of writing and of meaning cannot serve as elements of such machine systems.[26]

This caution, issued in AI's infancy, remains apt.

In the Name of Efficiency: Letter Writing

Remember mail merge? Along with word processing programs, it arrived in the early 1980s, enabling offices to personalize template letters going out to multiple recipients. Of course, "personalize" is relative, since customization was essentially limited to name and mailing address.

AI could do better.

An example from the early 1990s was a program called Intelligent Correspondence Generator (ICG), created by Cognitive Systems.[27] That's the same company (started, incidentally, by Roger Schank) that I talked about in Chapter 5 when describing a natural language query system for offices. The task for ICG was to automate the handling of written correspondence with customers, but in a way tailored to the customer's particular issue.

Cognitive Systems had a contract with a major credit card company. At the time, its customer service representatives averaged about forty-five minutes for each letter they produced. Since the letters were drafted by hand (ah, the Dark Ages!), they next had to be typed up by the word processing staff.

The credit card company had a supply of form letters customized for addressing particular issues—nearly 1,000 of them—though representatives generally relied on a small handful. Writers' responsibilities included not just addressing the right problem and being certain the letter was grammatically and orthographically correct, but ensuring it used the right tone: appropriately polite (even if the customer hadn't been) though not too chummy. No surprise, responses across the company lacked consistency. Worse still was the error rate. Only about 80 percent of the handwritten letters were free of mistakes.

To build its correspondence generator, Cognitive Systems used an expert systems model and natural language processing. The company's "knowledge engineers" reviewed a large tranche of their client's earlier customer service correspondence, identifying main components and wording, and then building inference rules. The result was a system with over 100 letter templates, along with close to 900 rules. The program was used in conjunction with the client database of information about each customer, including name and address, record of financial transactions, and previous communications.

Here's how the correspondence generator worked:

- The program read the database entry for the customer and roughly categorized the problem needing to be addressed.
- Using an interactive multiple-choice dialogue system, the program clarified with a customer service representative any ambiguous information in the database, got updates, and solicited suggestions on the appropriate tone for the letter.
- The system generated the letter for the customer service representative to review.
- After any changes were made, the letter was printed.

Since this was 1991, the physical letter was then placed in an envelope, ready for mailing.

The results? Start to finish, each letter could be produced in about five minutes, with more than 95 percent of them error-free. A major improvement over what humans had been accomplishing, in both efficiency and quality. Plus, much as Luhn had looked to IBM's automatic generation of abstracts to improve consistency, Cognitive Systems's correspondence generator helped ensure uniformity across letters.

In the Name of Commerce: Advertising and Marketing

Skip ahead to the 2020s, when natural language generation is incredibly more sophisticated, driven by potent large language models. Once companies such as OpenAI made these programs available for commercial licensing, businesses began to capitalize, offering to draft all manner of new text on demand.

Among the major players are Jasper and Copysmith. (There's a slew of others.) A substantial audience for these programs is the commercial copywriting trade. Traditionally, the job of copywriter has involved producing written material for advertising and marketing. These days, responsibilities extend to turning out email, social media, and blog posts.

Let's use Jasper as an example of how today's AI-driven solutions work.[28] To harness Jasper as a copywriter, you input a few content ideas, which the system spins into text written in the desired genre. Among the possibilities are marketing copy, Facebook ads, websites, blog articles, real estate listings, personal bios, sales emails, and . . . love letters, an option that promptly caught my eye. Sample output I saw reminded me how amazingly far we've come since Strachey's "My sympathetic affection."

Some of Jasper's other boasting points: over fifty templates (representing different genres) to select from. Given the magic of DeepL Translator (which Jasper incorporates), output can be in your choice of twenty-five languages. You can also designate the desired message tone and even identify a well-known person whose linguistic style you want to emulate. (Steve Jobs, anyone? "One more thing.") For good measure, Jasper relies on the grammar check program Grammarly to be sure that spelling and grammar pass muster.

As a GPT-3 based program, Jasper draws text from the internet. Since materials vacuumed up from online aren't reliably accurate, non-repetitive, unbiased, or G-rated, the company cautions that a human final review is advisable. In the same vein, Jasper's competitor Copysmith has a cunning website tagline: "Content crafted by AI, perfected by humans."

Programs like Jasper and Copysmith not only produce slick output but do so more efficiently than humans. A Gartner report circulating in 2020 concluded that within two years, content marketers

> will produce more than 30% of their digital content with the aid of artificial intelligence (AI) content-generation techniques, increasing productivity and advertising effectiveness but also disrupting the creative process.[29]

Those two years have come and gone. And with tools like ChatGPT, I'll bet the 30 percent figure is already north of 50 percent. If AI is doing more of the writing, what happens to copywriters' jobs?

Saim Alkan, CEO of the digital content generation company AX Semantics, argues the role of copywriter will be replaced by that of copy director. With AI increasingly producing the text, Alkan suggests that what's now needed is an overseer to manage strategies, assure the quality of content that's produced, and be a skilled supervisor.[30] The obvious challenge is employee numbers. Businesses will require far fewer copy directors than copywriters. As the digital marketing manager at Paychex put it, "Artificial intelligence is coming for copywriters, and it's going to be a tough job market."[31]

Professional copywriters are hardly the only ones in writing-intensive jobs that are threatened by AI. Our next chapter, which takes on automation and the labor market, turns the spotlight on journalists, lawyers, and translators.

EIGHT

AI Comes for the Writing Professions

Release notes for OpenAI's DALL-E 2 came with a black box warning:

> The model may increase the efficiency of performing some tasks like photo editing or production of stock photography which could displace jobs of designers, photographers, models, editors, and artists.[1]

DALL-E 2 produces fantastic illustrations from natural language prompts (a stock example: "an astronaut riding a horse in a photorealistic style"). And unlike graphic artists that you might hire, DALL-E 2 polishes off the task in a fraction of the time.

Technology has a long past of threatening to displace human labor. In 1589, Reverend William Lee from Nottinghamshire invented a machine for knitting stockings. However, when Lee applied to Queen Elizabeth for a patent, she refused, in part from fear of endangering employment in the hand-knitting trade.[2] We've all heard tell of early nineteenth-century Luddites destroying factory machinery. While their real cause seems to have been demands for better labor practices and higher wages, not rejecting the machinery itself, an image became rooted in our minds of automation as a threat to jobs.[3]

From Brawn to Brains: The Automation Story

The windmill. The waterwheel. The spinning jenny. The steam engine. The cotton gin. These inventions, and thousands more, magnified the power of the human hand, arm, and back, transforming everything from agricultural production to company profits. A looming concern has always been whether labor-saving inventions undermine human labor. Do manual workers lose their livelihood or do new jobs emerge that laborers can transition into?

Machines like the spinning jenny, steam engine, and cotton gin drove the Industrial Revolution, which in turn revolutionized the Western world. Adoption of physical labor-saving devices didn't end up driving long-term unemployment. Adaptation or retraining was sometimes needed, but at least over time, was tractable. The British unemployment rate in 1900 wasn't much different from that in 1760, the dawn of the Industrial Revolution.[4]

But automation itself evolves. Mechanizing farm work or factory production is different from automating the work of people in professions requiring higher education. Economists Erik Brynjolfsson and Andrew McAfee distinguish between a First Machine Age (the Industrial Revolution) and a Second Machine Age, meaning the digital revolution.[5] The question is whether the digital revolution will generate sufficient alternative employment or whether this time really is different.

The dilemma's not wholly new. In 1953, Roald Dahl addressed it in "The Great Automatic Grammatizator" (which opened the Prologue). Writing in 1954, Christopher Strachey—the British computer scientist who brought us the "Honey Dear" love letters—foresaw computers automating clerical tasks, both arithmetical and eventually linguistic. Strachey characterized the British clerical labor force this way:

> there is [already] . . . a very large turnover in the clerks [that computers] will replace. The majority of these are young women who leave after a few years to get married, so that the introduction of the computer will probably not throw very many people out of work.

Generational sexism aside, Strachey went on to say that computers

> will merely stop the intake of new clerks, who will presumably have to seek other professions. What these will be, is an interesting matter for speculation.[6]

We're still speculating.

Some of today's keen minds have been weighing in on the impact of

AI-driven automation on jobs. Economist Laura Tyson and political scientist John Zysman argue that while today's technology trends could create enough jobs, given adequate governmental support policies, it's unclear there will be enough *good* ones.[7]

What counts as a good job? For starters, one that provides a living wage. Preferably, one enabling us to use our minds. And ideally, one affording a feeling of social and personal well-being, including a sense of purpose. As the pandemic's Great Resignation demonstrated, many people care about more than drawing a salary.

The labor market doesn't always dole out options. Given digital automation, some good jobs could end up in short supply, including those where writing skills are essential. The US Department of Labor estimates that about 13 percent of American occupations are heavily focused on writing. Collectively, people in these jobs earn over $675 billion annually.[8] There's a lot riding on how AI language generation might impact future employment for those who largely write for a living. And pragmatically, it would be a shame for all those writing skills honed in English composition classes to go to waste.

People in the writing professions assume many job titles—grant writer, book editor, speech writer, novelist, ad copywriter. The list goes on, including prominent inclusion of journalist, lawyer, and translator. To get a sense of how AI-as-author could be redefining writing-intensive professions, we'll train our lens on these three.

AI Joins the Newsroom

Nearly a century ago, President Calvin Coolidge proclaimed to the American Society of Newspaper Editors that

> "the chief business of the American people is business. They are profoundly concerned with producing, buying, selling, investing and prospering in the world."[9]

The profit motive has hardly diminished over the years. As natural language processing capacities expand, managers of writing-centered professions have been ratcheting up dependence on AI, with efficiency gains enhancing the bottom line. Some of the biggest players are companies dispensing news.

From Then to Now: The Journalism Landscape

Newspapers trace back only around 400 years.[10] Printed papers emerged from handwritten newssheets that began appearing in Venice in the mid-sixteenth century, recounting happenings from across Europe. In 1609, the first printed weekly was produced in Strasbourg. Fast-forward a century, where the earliest daily newspaper began circulation in London in 1702.

The town crier and gossip circuit had competition.

As literacy rates rose and paper costs fell, newspapers became the universal medium for keeping abreast of events. Radio, followed by television, would become alternative outlets. But newspapers—both national and local—continued to attract readers, along with successive generations of journalists eager to investigate and document events of the days and times.

Consumer access to the internet brought growing recognition that news needed to live both in print and online. A second wake-up call was the emergence—then surge—of social media. By 2021, about half of all Americans were getting their news from social media sites.[11] Only a third accessed news from print publications with any regularity, though even that number is deceptive. When asked for their preferred news platform, 35 percent chose TV, 7 percent said radio, and only 5 percent opted for print. Digital platforms earned the lion's share with 52 percent.[12]

As for news dispensed via social media, some is sourced from feed written by professional journalists working for legacy news outlets, but hardly all. Citizen journalism continues to flourish, as do Twitter feeds. No journalism background or salary required.

A bit more than a decade ago, a new competitor arrived: AI as news writer.

Insider Baseball: Using AI for Writing

Forbes was the first to make a splash. In October 2011, the vaunted leader in business news announced a new way of producing quarterly earnings reports of major corporations. Computers were already nimble with numbers. What if the same machines could spin numbers into prose? That conversion was engineered for *Forbes* by a company called Narrative Science.[13]

Founded a year earlier, the startup had roots in a graduate student venture at Northwestern University. The project, StatsMonkey, mined data about baseball games to create automatically written stories. As the business evolved, its data-into-storytelling tools did as well, along with its clientele. (The CIA signed on in 2013.) Today's market for such technology is huge, reflected in the $15.7 billion that Salesforce paid in June 2019 to acquire the company.

Narrative Science wasn't the earliest business using AI to whip up news stories. Probably it was Automated Insights (originally called StatSheet), launched in 2007. Like Narrative Science, Automated Insights got its start in sports—this time, basketball. The original mission was generating short pieces about results from (US) college Division 1 basketball teams. When the name change came in 2011, the company's portfolio expanded into finance and real estate—ideal markets for transforming data into running text. The Associated Press became a client, and in 2014, started using automatically generated earnings reports to increase its previous volume tenfold.[14]

To do its natural language generation, Automated Insights developed a tool called Wordsmith. (Narrative Science's was named Quill.) Meanwhile, other news outlets were devising their own schemes. At *Bloomberg News*, the system is called Cyborg. The *Washington Post* created Heliograph. Meanwhile, *Forbes* introduced Bertie, named after its eponymous founder Bertie Charles Forbes. Among its tech tricks, Bertie can suggest ideas for articles, generate rough drafts, amalgamate research data into text, and optimize headlines and article length.[15]

How good is the writing? The answer's a moving target. A study published in 2014 found people couldn't always distinguish algorithmically produced text from what journalists wrote, though readers judged the AI output to be somewhat boring.[16] Several years later came a survey of professional journalists, who voiced a rash of concerns about limitations of algorithmic writing. Among them:

- reliance on a single source of data
- difficulty interrogating data and spotting irregularities
- problems going beyond a templated format, lack of creativity
- failure to provide contemporaneous context
- inability to understand nuances of human expression[17]

Since the emergence of large language models, natural language generation has become increasingly sophisticated (and generally less boring and more nuanced). A prediction made earlier by Kris Hammond, co-founder of Narrative Science, could yet come true: "A machine will win a Pulitzer one day."[18]

Job Prospects

Should you advise your son or daughter to become a journalist? Many parents used to squirm when their offspring chose to major in literature, philosophy, or art. Can they earn a living? Now it's time for frank conversation about career prospects in journalism. AI is only part of the story. If there's nothing like a hanging to focus the mind, there's nothing like statistics to put journalism's challenges in sharp relief.

Start with employment numbers. As the Pew Research Center reports, the number of people employed in the news industry writ large is shrinking.

Lumping together news analysts, reporters, editors, and photographers, along with television, video and film camera operators, and editors, the drop between 2004 and 2020 was a whopping 57 percent.[19] In 2020, one third of large US newspapers laid off news staff. Before you cry "Blame it on the pandemic!" look at the longer trend:

- 2017: 32 percent decline
- 2018: 27 percent decline
- 2019: 24 percent decline[20]

Then came outright closures. Most have been of local newspapers, historically invaluable for keeping communities abreast of issues directly mattering to them. The losses are staggering. Between 2004 and 2022, more than 2,850 local publications shuttered their doors. Shrinkage for journalists employed by local papers has been equally overwhelming. Since 2005, their ranks have fallen roughly 60 percent.[21]

If AI is coming for journalists' jobs, balance this challenge with how many jobs are left in the first place.

Divvying Up the Work

Half empty or half full. When sizing up the impact of AI authoring tools on journalists' jobs, verdicts depend on whom you ask.

Academic institutions and news outlets alike have been cheerleaders for journalism's AI revolution. Graduate programs in digital journalism abound. There's a National Institute for Computer-Assisted Reporting and the journal *Digital Journalism*. A steady rivulet of books explores the new landscape.[22]

The half-full argument goes like this. Automating a bevy of tasks can free humans to focus on the work they do best, like investigative reporting, in-depth analysis, and social critique. Melding AI and human journalism is a partnership, not a zero-sum game. Entrepreneurs and news media honchos have been making this argument for the past decade:

- Kris Hammond, from Narrative Science, quoted in 2012: "If a story can be written by a machine from data, it's going to be. It's really just a matter of time at this point. . . . But there are so many stories to be told that are not data-driven. That's what journalists should focus on, right?"[23]
- Lou Ferrara, AP's managing editor for business news, speaking in 2014 about using Automated Insights to generate earnings reports: "This is about using technology to free journalists to do more journalism and less data processing, not about eliminating jobs."[24]

- Salah Zalatimo, chief digital officer at *Forbes*, describing their multipurpose tool Bertie: "a bionic suit for our writers."[25]

In fantasy worlds, bionic suits bestow not just special powers but protection from adversaries. Do journalists wearing those suits feel protected? For most, it's likely too soon to tell.

Then comes the half-empty side of the story. In 2015, Matt Carlson, now a journalism professor at the University of Minnesota, reviewed a spate of media and trade articles to gauge response to the emerging use of automated newswriting. Some forecast happy AI–human partnerships, even job growth. Others were more pessimistic, though since it was early in the game, who really knew.

Carlson cites remarks made in 2013 by Kris Hammond, attempting to reassure those worried about job security:

> "No one should be worried about automated writing systems. . . . [T]hey are designed for writing into spaces where no one else is writing and to be used in co-ordination with other writers and analysts."[26]

"Where no one else is writing"? These days, AI-as-journalist is working its way into all those spaces.

Meanwhile, here's a cautionary tale. In late spring 2020, Microsoft pink-slipped about fifty contract news producers whose job had been to select and determine placement for news stories running on its MSN website. Their work was handed over to an automated system.[27] We can only hope the content of news items the bots are now sorting doesn't cry out for human oversight. Media giants like Facebook learned the hard way that algorithms can't be relied on to judge what news is fit to broadcast.[28]

How Many Lawyers?

"Language is the armory of the human mind, and at once contains the trophies of its past and the weapons of its future conquests."

So wrote Samuel Coleridge. Through our words, spoken and written, we make sense of our world and look to shape it. Poets and writers of all ilk invoke the power of language to remind, inspire, or convince. Prowess in wielding such power—especially when it comes to convincing—has long been a hallmark of the legal profession.

From People to Programs: The Legal Landscape

Writing skills are as essential to lawyering as water is for making tea. Initial drafting is often done by associates or law clerks, but senior lawyers and judges conventionally have the final word. Let's focus here on preparation for large trial cases, potentially involving dozens of lawyers, millions of documents to review, and complex strategizing. Some critical moving parts are discovery, legal research, and argument construction and writing.

Discovery involves reviewing all the documentation (including not just what's written but also things like images or computer code) that might prove relevant in a lawsuit. Legal research is undertaken to figure out the relevant law. In the United States, a common law country, that means unearthing both statutes and decisions from prior cases, since precedent plays a huge role in the American legal system. The depth of research undertaken might reflect how insightful the lawyers are, how much the client is willing or able to pay, what data are available, and especially the legal arguments involved.

What happened when computer technology—and then AI—began seeping into legal practice?[29] Start with baby steps. Online forms like wills or simple contracts became common in the last decades of the twentieth century, enabling lawyers, companies, and laypeople to streamline what used to soak up considerable labor and billable hours. Meanwhile, a major transformation in legal research began brewing in the early 1970s. Mainframe computers were making it possible to store large troves of data, which could then be searched. Potential beneficiaries included lawyers. All they needed were access terminals.

Enter Lexis (now LexisNexis) and Westlaw. Lexis (meaning "law"—Latin *lex*—plus "i[nformation] s[cience]") publicly launched in 1973 as a database containing case law from New York and Ohio. Within seven years, the digital holdings expanded to include all US federal and state cases. Another addition, this time aimed at journalists, was a searchable database of news articles (the Nexis part).[30] Meanwhile, Westlaw, created in 1975 by West Publishing, developed out of a computer-assisted legal research program at Queens University in Canada.

By the 1990s, a new surge of material began emerging that lawyers needed to review: digitally native documents, running the gamut from word-processed files to email and later social media posts. All these became fodder for discovery. Necessity being the mother of invention, eDiscovery was born.

At its basic level, eDiscovery is used for identifying electronic evidence (including information converted to electronic format) that might be relevant for trial. Retrieval has conventionally been done through keywords. These days the process is aided by AI, reducing the number of irrelevant hits and automatically widening searches to include semantically related words. If, for instance, you search for "pine" or "oak," you might well also want documents mentioning "tree."

Plus, it would be useful if the software could tag which documents were most relevant, how they should be annotated and redacted, and maybe even their tone (what's known as sentiment analysis, meaning identifying the broad emotional thrust of the text—positive? negative? neutral?). Such tools now exist. Not surprisingly, eDiscovery is big business. The ranks of companies offering their services continue to mushroom, from Epiq (one of the largest) to the much smaller Digital War Room (the name says it all).

Then there's incorporation of AI into legal research. Software offerings are abundant, but we'll focus on one: Lex Machina, now owned by LexisNexis. It's powerful and immensely popular, used by around three quarters of the AmLaw 100 firms (the 100 highest-grossing law firms in the United States).

Like many success stories, this one started with a question: If you're litigating a patent case, where do you stand the best chance of winning? Not all jurisdictions (or judges) have the same odds. The person asking was Mark Lemly, a professor at Stanford Law School. Not finding an answer, Lemly began building a database of patent litigation to tease out what factors seemed to influence outcomes. By 2010, the project morphed into the company Lex Machina. We can almost hear Aeschylus or Euripides chuckling at the neologism. Greek tragedians had created the theatrical device of a *deus ex machina* to maneuver a god onto the stage—lowered from above or hoisted up from below—to resolve a dramatic conflict.

Lex Machina's *deus* is now called Legal Analytics. It's a multipurpose legal research tool. According to the company's website, the software gives users the edge with tasks like analyzing courts and judges (seeing how likely a specific judge has been to grant a particular type of motion) or evaluating opposing counsel (reviewing what success your opponent has scored going before a given judge).[31] The information is all public, but the magic of AI is in gathering, slicing and dicing, and making what's relevant for your case easily retrievable.

Language Games, Legal Style: Using AI for Writing

Ultimately, there's the language part of the legal paper chase. Schemes are unfolding that potentially redefine the writing tasks we've long associated with this language-intensive profession.

Here's a two-part sampler of products available as of mid-2022 (plus a third in the works). Be prepared: By the time you're reading this chapter, the legal AI writing toolkit might have bounded leagues ahead.

PARSING THE WRITTEN RECORD: CONTEXT

It's one thing to know how judges have ruled on past cases. But what if lawyers could scope out the most promising language and arguments for their legal team, including their expert witnesses, to put forward? Enter Context, an AI tool created by Ravel Law and then scarfed up by LexisNexis in 2017.

No surprise, Context relies on natural language processing to target linguistic strategies to include or avoid. With the program's Judge Analytics, you can "build your most persuasive argument using the exact language and opinions your judge cites most frequently." Or, call up Attorney Analytics to check out the language in attorney arguments for cases similar to yours, drawing on a database of more than a million lawyers.[32] We can only wonder how much writerly craftsmanship remains when AI software is nudging lawyers towards statistically safe wording.

CUTTING TO THE CHASE: COMPOSE AND LEGALMATION

We've continued to extol the skills of large language models like GPT-3 in generating new text. The legal profession is now starting to take the plunge of letting software do actual drafting. To see what the future might hold, consider a program called Compose, recently developed by the legal research firm Casetext.

The company is known for AI legal research software, offering its program CARA AI for locating relevant cases and opinions—essentially a competitor of LexisNexis. But Compose goes a step further. In an interview, Jake Heller, CEO of Casetext, spelled out the soup-to-nuts process of producing a legal document such as a motion, using Compose:

- Select the type of document.
- Select the jurisdiction where the case is being litigated.
- Let Compose generate a list of arguments, and make your selections.
- Determine which legal standards need to be applied, identifying a list of relevant cases.
- Enter some of the language you want to use, and let Compose earmark cases using the same language or concepts.
- Click on download, and out comes a written first draft.[33]

Lawyers can then tweak and finalize the draft. In the end, clients save on billable time. The co-founders of Casetext envision that programs like Compose will dramatically alter the legal landscape by delegating much of the essential writing to AI.[34]

Compose isn't the only drafting tool on the legal scene. Another entry is LegalMation, which prepares documents such as pleadings, discovery requests, and discovery responses.[35] The software is built on IBM's Watson, a natural language query system named after IBM's founder. That's the same program (now with upgrades) that made its impressive 2011 debut on the television show *Jeopardy!* LegalMation boasts its software can produce drafts in mere minutes, ready for "minor editing and basic review" by humans.[36]

LEGAL ASSISTANT: HARVEY

In late 2022, a startup called Harvey received $5 million from the OpenAI Startup Fund.[37] On its bare-bones website (as of January 2023), the company touted Harvey as an AI legal assistant:

> Harvey is designed to understand your requests (in plain English) and generate accurate and relevant legal documents, research, and analysis. Whether you need to draft a contract, review a case, or advise a client, Harvey can help you save time and improve your quality of work.

Stay tuned for what writing functions unfold.

Job Prospects

For now, the legal profession remains a bustling business. The American Bar Association reports that at the close of 2021, there were 1,327,010 active lawyers in the United States.[38] Beyond full-fledged lawyers are ranks of paralegals and legal assistants—336,250 of them, at recent count.[39]

That's a hefty workforce, and we're not even including administrative staff. It's reasonable to ask if with growing use of AI, there will be enough work to go around. Richard Susskind—a British expert on legal AI—isn't convinced the answer will be yes. Writing in late 2016, he projected that

> as our machines become increasingly capable, they will steadily eat into lawyers' jobs. The best and the brightest professionals will last the longest—those experts who perform tasks that cannot or should not be replaced by machines. But there will not be enough of these tasks to keep armies of traditional lawyers in employment.

Susskind suggested that the boom wouldn't be lowered in the 2020s. However, "In the very long term, it is hard to avoid the conclusion that there will be much less need for conventional lawyers."[40]

Not everyone's so pessimistic. As Dana Remus (a law professor) and Frank Levy (an economist) remind us, the legal profession isn't a single job but a collection of tasks, only one of which is legal writing. Their study from 2017 predicted how likely it might be for AI to impact employment for various of these tasks. The study also included data on the number of billable hours lawyers were invoicing, by task type.

Looking at billable time in firms with fewer than 1,000 lawyers, you find the expected spread by area, ranging from less than 1 percent for document management, to 14.5 percent for court appearances and preparation, to 27.0 percent for legal analysis and strategy. Legal writing clocked in at 17.7 percent.

For each task, Remus and Levy scored a projected impact of AI (now or in the near future) as "strong," "moderate," or "weak." The only task they found meriting "strong" was document review—not surprisingly, given how much this process is already automated. The kind of task where potential impact was seen as "weak" included fact investigation, advising clients, negotiation, other communications and interactions, and court appearances and preparation.

And legal writing. Summing all the categories where AI's prospects of displacing human lawyers were judged "weak," the total percent of the overall lawyering job was 55.7 percent. Bottom line: We still need lawyers, including for doing legal writing.[41]

Remus and Levy reasoned that legal writing can't easily be automated, since much of it "requires conceptual creativity and flexibility that computers do not currently exhibit." And: "The use of precedent, while second nature for a lawyer, is exceedingly difficult (and currently impossible) to model for a computer."[42] The critical word is "currently." In 2017 when their article was written, large language models had not yet revolutionized AI text generation. Given the ability of GPT-3 and its successors to amaze us, I'm reserving judgment.

What do American governmental forecasters say about prospects in the legal profession? The Bureau of Labor Statistics projects that during the 2020s, jobs for paralegals and legal assistants in the United States will grow 12 percent,[43] while for lawyers, the forecast is 9 percent.[44] The numbers feel reassuring, but it's not clear how much those doing the number crunching recognized the AI freight train barreling down the tracks.

What's more, as with journalism, AI isn't the only factor shaping the legal job market. As James Carville (Bill Clinton's 1992 campaign strategist) famously put it, "It's the economy, stupid." Law firms are businesses. They negotiate billable hours with major clients, are cautious about how many associates make partner, and farm out work to paralegals or overseas to trim costs. Perhaps there's a lesson from 2009—during the Great Recession—when some high-profile US firms paid newly hired first-year associates not to show up for a while.[45] Given the economy and budget constraints, there wasn't enough work to go around.

Divvying Up the Work

Increasing efficiency is a time-honored hallmark of progress. In the early eighteenth century, it took at least four months to travel by covered wagon between New York and California. Today, the flight's around six hours. You can even drive it in four or five days. No one's complaining the trek has been eased.

When it comes to legal services, affordability is a big factor. That goes for average citizens (many who continue to be priced out) but also for businesses large and small. Progressive use of AI-driven tools has sped up much of the legal work that used to require boatloads of human labor. Yet people are still necessary for meeting with clients and witnesses, non-document-based discovery, and for running the eDiscovery and legal research software. Unless a law firm is using the newest high-end AI, flesh-and-blood lawyers will continue to have jobs constructing arguments and drafting text. For now.

In one plausible scenario, substantial numbers of lawyers will morph into software managers and post-editors of drafts written by AI. An eerily parallel threat already looms for professionals in another field requiring writing expertise: translation.

Translator or Post-Editor?

The painting hangs on a gallery end wall in the Kunsthistoriches Museum. In June 2022, while in Vienna, I made a pilgrimage to see Pieter Bruegel the Elder's *Tower of Babel*, painted in 1563.

The King James Bible recounts in Genesis 11: 6–7 that the whole earth initially had a single language. Over time (after many begats), a group of Noah's descendants decided to build a new city and tower "whose top may reach unto heaven." God was not amused:

> And the Lord said, Behold, the people is one, and they have all one language; and this they begin to do: and now nothing will be restrained from them, which they have imagined to do.

His response was to sever communication:

> Go to, let us go down, and there confound their language, that they may not understand one another's speech.

If you're looking to help people "understand one another's speech," getting them to master the thousands of tongues spoken on earth today is a non-starter.

Someone needs to translate. Translation has long been a necessity for explorers and invaders, neighbors looking to trade, and missionaries spreading religion. Stealing a march on the enemy is another drive. As we recounted in Chapter 6, during the Cold War, machine translation of Russian into English was a major force behind funding AI research. Following initially rocky decades, enlisting computers to aid in translation became increasingly commonplace, from weather reports and operations manuals to the European Union's paperwork. Now that Google Translate, DeepL Translator, and similar tools are freely on tap, it's understandable to assume it's time to hand the whole job over to AI.

Not so fast. There's far more than meets the novice eye to transforming content, style, and context from one language into another. Just ask a skilled translator.[46]

Translatorese

Translators cope with the reality that languages are more than collections of words and combination rules. Rather, they're unique encodings of lived cultures and experiences. Think about the span of the color spectrum we call "red." Upon seeing that color, thousands of Americans used to fear Communists under the bed, while in France, minds may have turned to the Revolution's *tricolore* and *liberté, égalité, fraternité*. In China, associating red with good luck or happiness stretches much farther back. Same part of the color spectrum. Single words. But different culturally laden meanings.

It's rarely straightforward juggling differences between two languages. One tack has been resorting to what's been called "the third language" or "translatorese."[47] It's not actually a new language but a sort of halfway house between the source language (say, Papiamento) and the language into which you're translating (the target language—perhaps English).

Look up "translatorese" online, and you'll see the practice demonized as meaning poor translation. That's unfair. Expert translations oftentimes end up legitimately different from either of the two languages on the table. Translation scholars talk about a cluster of properties (sometimes called translation universals, resulting in translatorese) that characterize many translations, regardless of source and target languages.[48] These include

- *simplification:* meaning simplifying the message expressed, the language used, or both. An example is breaking up original long sentences into shorter ones.
- *explicitation:* meaning adding material not in the source text, such as background information. As a result, translations may be longer than originals.

- *normalization:* including choosing linguistic patterns characteristic of the target language you're translating into, not the source language you're translating from. Normalization might also show up as finishing sentences that were incomplete in the original.
- *leveling out:* meaning producing translations with less variation from one another than original texts in the source language. For instance, a group of translations might be more similar in sentence length or word choice than the same cluster of originals.

Translatorese is real, though demonstrating it empirically takes substantial effort. You need to analyze language at the granular level, such as counting the frequency of particular words and word classes (like articles or adverbs), along with maybe punctuation marks and types of verb forms. AI can help. Research has shown that computers can distinguish reasonably well between original texts (in this study, in Italian) and those translated (by humans) from other languages into Italian. In fact, when humans—including professional translators—were asked to identify originals versus translations, they weren't as successful as their digital brethren.[49]

Score one for the machines. But an obvious next question is whether machine translations are immune from translatorese. The answer seems to be no.[50] The problem stems from the way large language models work. What's frequent in the mass of data a model draws from tends to surface when you ask for new text. If you set AI to translate a document, it gravitates to words and grammatical structures appearing most frequently in the data on which the program is trained. Lexical and syntactic variety present in the source (original) language can end up washed out in the AI translation.

Computer Creep: AI and Professional Translation

If you're old enough, you remember transitioning from typewriters to writing on a computer. As the software improved, you might have ditched your print dictionary, since Microsoft Word or later a quick Google search offered up the basic information you needed. Fast-forward to the present, and now computers can edit what you write—and increasingly do the writing for you.

The translation profession has undergone similar progressive steps in using computer-based tools. Among the early ones were online dictionaries and optical character readers, converting into electronic files the printed texts you wanted translated. Then came more sophisticated systems, including programs letting you recycle material from prior translations.[51]

Labor-saving tools like these allow professional translators to harness computers in the service of human-based translation. Turn the tables now to machines doing full-blown translating, putting AI in the driver's seat. As AI programs keep improving, and as the market for translation continues to balloon, how many humans will we need in the translation business, and in what role?

"Enough" Versus "Good": Translation Job Prospects

We've talked about the difference between having enough jobs and having enough good ones. In the translation business, a disconnect between "enough" and "good" seems already underway.

The US Bureau of Labor Statistics paints a rosy forecast for jobseekers in the United States who can handle two languages. The projections are impressive, though keep in mind that the bureau's data combine interpretation (hearing one language and speaking another, as at the UN) and translation (where the output is written):

- employment as of 2020: 81,400
- projected 2030 employment: 100,700

That's a 24 percent growth rate, compared with an anticipated overall US job growth of 8 percent.[52]

Prime reasons for the predicted surge include the continuing rise in international business, mounting linguistic diversity in the United States, and ongoing military and national security needs. What's more, there's increased demand to translate not just traditional documents but online materials like websites and social media posts.

The profession should be riding high. Is it?

THE EXPLODING MACHINE TRANSLATION MARKET

Using technology for translation is big business. It's estimated there are more than 18,000 commercial players, bringing in over $56 billion annually. Companies come in all sizes, but among the heavyweights are TransPerfect, RWS, Language Solutions, Keyword Studies, and Lionbridge.[53] Only a small percentage of the work is now full-throated machine translation, though expansion looms large.[54]

AI-driven translation can be harnessed at many levels. At its simplest, make a beeline for Google Translate, DeepL Translator, or Microsoft Translator for do-it-yourself jobs. At the next level up, platforms like Google Cloud Translate or Amazon Translate will do the translating, charging with pay-as-you-go plans.[55] From there, you can hire companies for specialized tasks like translating websites (say, using Weglot) or more expansive projects, like translating the ongoing stream of documents needed for large-scale international business.

Especially in commercial contexts, there's more to translation than converting text from one language to another. A large chunk of today's commercial translation incorporates what's known as localization—tailoring the translation to a particular linguistic and cultural context. For starters, it means determining which variety of a language to use: Brazilian or European Portuguese, Québécois or French as recognized by l'Académie française. More nuance involves "translating" the tone likely to resonant with a local population, along with fine points such as knowing when to measure in kilos or pounds.

THE QUALITY ISSUE, OR NO MORE SOYBEANS

One lurking topic we've skirted so far is translation quality. Often a "good enough" translation is ample. Back in 1947, Warren Weaver had been willing to settle for "inelegant (but intelligible)" for translating scientific materials. But at times we need more, especially where the translation program isn't particularly adept with the source or target language. Take languages for which there are huge datasets that algorithms can draw from (especially English and Spanish, but also German and French) in doing machine translation. Their success rate is far higher than for languages like Arabic or Armenian, where there's very little training data.

These gaps can have real-world consequences.

A telling example involves hospital medicine, particularly in the ER. Patients with emergencies might speak any one of a multitude of languages. Even if hospitals can find human interpreters to mediate patient encounters (in person or through phone services), what happens when it's time to prepare discharge orders? They need to be written, but oftentimes translated. Google Translate might seem an efficient, cost-effective remedy.

If the patient speaks Spanish, you're in luck. Google Translate's English-to-Spanish accuracy level for medical information is over 90 percent. But when it comes to Farsi or Armenian, the success rate drops to 67 percent and 55 percent, respectively. Even for Chinese, where the translation dataset is large and accuracy generally good, there can be problems. Take these examples from a study of using Google Translate for ER discharge orders:

- English "You can take over-the-counter ibuprofen as needed for pain" became Armenian (back-translated into English) "You may take anti-tank missile as much as you need for pain."
- English "Your Coumadin level was too high today" morphed into Chinese (again, back-translated) "Your soybean level was too high today."[56]

Inaccuracies arising from raw AI translation might end up humorous or harmful. In either case, if resources permit, there's a remedy: Before the translation goes live, have a human do post-editing.

THE POST-EDITING BLUES

Invoking post-editing traces back to the earliest days of machine translation. We saw Yehoshua Bar-Hillel arguing for humans to be responsible for pre-editing, post-editing, or both for machine-processed text. These days, pre-editing is still in play, often to smooth over language that's likely to cause hiccups for AI translation algorithms.[57] But the real elephant in the room is post-editing: cleaning up after text has been run through the machine translation sausage machine.

Post-editing a machine translation (MTPE, as it's known) has become increasingly common. A human post-editor would spot that "Coumadin" doesn't translate into Chinese as "soybean," catch where punctuation or capitalization is inaccurate (not all languages follow the same systems), and adjust awkward grammar. Adaptive AI post-editing systems even learn from corrections humans make. In principle, post-editing, rather than letting humans translate from scratch, increases productivity and saves money. But it turns out that post-editing doesn't just do cleanup. It also shapes the resulting text.

Much as there's translatorese in both human and machine translation, there's evidence for "post-editese." Researchers compared human translations against both straight machine translation and (human) post-edits of machine translation. Not only did post-editese exist, but it was an exaggerated form of translatorese, since machine translation (with its own dose of translatorese) served as input to the post-editing.[58] The result may be technically correct, but it sometimes makes for boring reading—shades of some AI-generated news stories and, these days, essays produced by ChatGPT.

How do professional translators feel about post-editing? A 2019 international survey of more than 7,000 translators and interpreters is instructive. Among those surveyed, 89 percent said they preferred working on traditional (human) translation. While 35 percent did some work post-editing machine translation, only 3 percent preferred it. The remaining 8 percent favored editing human translations (the original form of post-editing).[59]

To interpret these numbers, it's helpful understanding the dynamics of the translation profession. Often it's a part-time freelance job, either by choice or because the economics make it hard to rely on translation for earning a living. But translating can also be a labor of love. When asked what they liked about the profession, 43 percent of those in the survey agreed it gave them a sense of purpose. No wonder respondents weren't big fans of post-editing a machine's work.

Before we leave post-editing, we should remind ourselves that not all translation jobs are created equal. When the task is boringly routine, humans understandably aren't enamored with doing it. Remember the Canadian translators we mentioned earlier who hated translating boilerplate weather reports time and again, and were happy to have TAUM-METEO do the scut work. As Lynne Bowker suggests,

> There is probably some kind of "sweet spot" where translators are happy to have [machine translation] systems deal with the dull texts (like weather reports) but would prefer to translate the more stimulating texts themselves (rather than post-edit them).[60]

The lion's share of written material being translated these days contains straightforward information: everything from contracts or governmental proceedings to websites or news reports. AI algorithms generally don't have to cope with metaphoric language like "a stitch in time saves nine" or "life's a journey." For these, humans are more up to the task.

It's hard envisioning a computer translating William Faulkner, much less James Joyce. Try this: Put "they were yung and easily freudened" (from *Finnegans Wake*) into Google Translate, ask for Russian, and then do a back-translation into English. Predictably, "yung" becomes "young"—obliterating Joyce's masterful veiled reference to Carl Jung.

Since the early days of machine translation, it was assumed that literature (fiction, but also well-crafted non-fiction) would never become grist for the computational mill. These days, that supposition is no longer valid. Translators could be losing their final toehold.

Literature: The Last Translation Frontier?

In the publishing business, there's sometimes debate over whose names go on the cover of a book that's been translated. Just the original author or also the translator? Maybe the translator doesn't particularly care, as when the job was essentially bread labor. Other times, the translator gets a cover byline and maybe writes an introduction. Too often, though, translators care but go insufficiently acknowledged. There are now campaigns afoot for including the translator's name on book covers, in reviews, and in marketing.[61]

Occasionally, the whole point of the publication is that it's a new translation. Take *Beowulf*. Since we don't know who wrote—or originally likely sang—the poem, there's little fight over whether the author gets sole billing.

More interesting is how many people (several dozen and counting) have wanted to have a go at translating that Old English into Modern. While many renditions of the poem are solidly serviceable, a few have made a splash, like Maria Dahvana Headley's 2020 feminist take on the tale. But it's Seamus Heaney's translation that turned the most heads, including winning the 1999 Whitbread Book of the Year Award. As the English poet Andrew Motion summed it up in the *Financial Times*, "[Heaney] has made a masterpiece out of a masterpiece."[62]

In its highest form, translation isn't a job but an art. One practiced by creative writers who begin by delving into the language, culture, times, even the mind of the original author. Gathering up these threads, translators draw upon their own writing talents to fashion works at once true to their source and birthing something new. Not all translations—even of nuanced literature—become their own creative works. Yet even for less memorable translations, those doing them still look to have a voice.

In the translation business, there's long been discussion of how much the translator's personal voice should come through. How much a scribe and how much an interpreter?[63] Translators (in fact, writers of all sorts) aren't the only intermediaries projecting personal voices. Think of voice actors recording audiobooks. Or take musicians. Beethoven devotees easily distinguish between David Oistrakh's and Anne-Sophie Mutter's renditions of the Violin Concerto.

What happens to a translator' voice and creativity when AI noses its way into literature?

There's an ingenious study comparing how Hans-Christian Oeser, a well-respected translator, fared when asked to post-edit the machine translation of a work he had translated (from English to German) two decades earlier. Since Oeser's translation style ("voice") had previously been analyzed, it was relatively straightforward comparing how much of this voice came through in his post-edited rendition versus in his original translation. In the post-edited version, Oeser's own characteristic translation voice was dampened.[64]

Professional literary translators haven't hesitated to share their feelings about post-editing. Here's some of what they had to say in one study:

> "[Post-editing] makes you a bit lazy. . . . You don't feel like changing too many things."

> "With [human translation] the reader reads your interpretation. With [machine translation] assistance the machine interpretation is still there."[65]

Plus: Given the choice, all six of those in the study preferred to translate the old-fashioned way. Among other reasons, they felt that machine translation with post-editing constrained their creativity and resulted in more boilerplate translations. One participant compared all-human translation to homemade food, while post-edited text was like pre-cooked dishes that "always taste the same."[66]

There's even research indicating that machine translations of literature are objectively less creative than translations humans do from scratch. In a pair of studies, Ana Guerberof Arenas and Antonio Toral assessed the creativity level of texts that had been translated entirely by humans, entirely by AI, and using machine translation plus human post-editing. Human reviewers served as judges. In both studies, the human translations were seen as most creative. Among other things, readers reported feeling more engaged with the narrative.[67] These findings jibe with observations by those who did the post-editing. As one translator put it,

> "In the post-editing phase, I felt that my creativity was limited, and I found it more difficult to think outside the box when I already had a translation provided. I felt a bit uncomfortable 'fixing' the text instead of giving my own translation."[68]

This translator's discomfort isn't unique to professionals tasked with post-editing translations generated by AI. Think about the millions of everyday writers relying on tools like Grammarly or Microsoft Editor, which ply us with suggestions on what we've just written. It can be uncomfortable sticking with our own version. Often it feels more reassuring to go along with whatever the grammar and style checker proposes. Sometimes the suggestions make sense, but other times they stifle our writing voice, our personal creativity.

Creativity. It's such an amorphous word, but inescapable in talking about writers. That cadre includes professionals like journalists, lawyers, and translators, but also everyday writers. We often tout creativity as a public cultural value. However, as we'll see in the next chapter, individuals who do the creating can also be enriched. Our foray into creativity will therefore probe *cui bono*—who stands to benefit—along with what happens when AI enters the ring as a contender.

NINE

The Creative Side of AI

The hamlet of Anchiano lies in the Tuscan countryside, nestled among stretches of vineyards and olive trees. I traveled there in 1969, seeking a small building that lay a three-kilometer walk from the nearby sleepy town where the bus had dropped me off. Reaching my destination, I knocked on the door of the farmhouse across the way. A middle-aged woman appeared, speaking no English—and I no Italian. But when I said "Leonardo," she fetched a large key and led us inside the edifice in which Leonardo da Vinci, illegitimate son of Ser Piero da Vinci and a household servant named Caterina, was born in 1452.

Besides me, my traveling companion, and the proprietress, not a soul in sight.

Returning decades later, the scene was unrecognizable. Tour buses disgorged streams of visitors to the state-of-the-art Museo Leonardiano in town. A shuttle bus was on offer to whisk you to Anchiano, where that once silent building now sports a projected reproduction of *The Last Supper.*

The personal lives of creative geniuses magnetically attract us. And we're willing to pay for proximity. At Kramgasse 49 in Bern, you're invited to ascend narrow steps to the third-floor apartment where Einstein lived when developing his theory of relativity (admission six Swiss francs). Vienna's Sigmund Freud Museum occupies the house where Freud lived and worked for forty-seven years. Perhaps you're intent on inspecting the storied couch on which the father of psychoanalysis treated patients. For that you'll need to visit Freud's London house (now a museum—admission fourteen British pounds) where he fled from the Nazis in 1938.

So many of us are fixated on Leonardo and Einstein and Freud. They epitomize our notion of creative people. By walking in giants' footsteps, maybe something of their genius will rub off. If we can't approach in person, we might make do with a poster of the Great One's likeness.

Who—and what—counts as creative? And where does the magic come from? Philosophers, psychologists, and now cognitive scientists continue weighing in on these puzzles. There's much talk these days about AI programs generating creative works—in music, in art, in writing. (In areas like science and mathematics, too, but we'll focus on the arts and humanities.) A timely question is whether, if you're a composer, a painter, or a poet, you should worry about competition.

To make sense of claims that AI can be creative, and to figure out whether we should care, it's reasonable to start by exploring what human creativity is, who has it, and how they got it.

The Human Side of Creativity

Picture Michelangelo's magnificent frescos adorning the Sistine Chapel. Gaze up to the ceiling, where God gives life to Adam, the pair's forefingers poised to touch. Whatever your religious predilections, we might metaphorically recast that image as including the prospects for human cognition, including creativity. A spark is lit, an idea begins percolating, a new work takes form.

Sometimes others notice.

What Counts as Creative?

"An act that produces *effective surprise*." That's what psychologist Jerome Bruner took to be "the hallmark of a creative enterprise."[1]

Surprise (the result of novelty) is a vital part of the creativity story. But there's more. The usual two-part definition is that creativity is an idea, act, fill in the blank that is novel *and* has value. Others must not only recognize the novelty but judge it useful or important. As a kid, I "created" the novel combination of sardines and chocolate syrup on rye bread (don't ask). Friends I invited to have a taste declined. No value in that enterprise. On the other hand, the Fluffernutter—made by combining Marshmallow Fluff with peanut butter—became a longstanding favorite, especially in New England. Value. Not as prized as Oysters Rockefeller, but valued nonetheless.

For big-league creativity flowing from the likes of Aristotle or Tolstoy, social value judgments are crucial in recognizing something (or someone) as having it. Psychologist Mihaly Csikszentmihalyi writes that the kind of creativity "that changes some aspect of the culture" is "never in the mind of a person."[2] Rather, it's a judgment rendered by gatekeepers of a cultural realm, such as critics, publishers, or panels awarding prizes.

Beyond novelty and value, there's a third leg on which creativity stands, and that's temporality. The psychologist Morris Stein argued that "The creative work is a novel work that is accepted as tenable or useful or satisfying by a group of people in some point in time."[3] In his lifetime, Vincent van Gogh was hardly celebrated as a paragon of creativity. Think of the furor created when works of avant-garde artists such as van Gogh were displayed at the 1913 Armory Show in New York.[4] Subsequent generations changed their minds. Even Shakespeare's reputation had its ups and downs.

Then there's creativity among lesser mortals.

Two Cs Good, Four Cs Better

On screen, he was invincible. But in 1964, actor John Wayne announced he had cancer. Looking to assure the public, he declared, "I licked the Big C."[5] That once unassuming third letter of the alphabet was embarking on a new semantic career.

In the 1970s, conversations about culture began distinguishing between "Big-C Culture" (encompassing literature, music, and the arts) and "little-c culture" (including beliefs and values).[6] By the 1980s, big and little were quantifying creativity: "'Big C' creativity is that which involves a big breakthrough innovation, while 'little c' creativity is innovative but has little impact."[7]

The 1990s saw an outpouring of research on creativity by philosophers and psychologists.[8] It's unclear who gets credit for the labels "Big C" and "little c" creativity, since the concepts were widely bandied about. For instance, Csikszentmihalyi wrote that "creativity with a capital C [is] the kind that changes some aspect of culture."[9] This contrasts with "small 'c' or personal creativity."[10]

Big C is creativity on a grand scale—the theory of relativity or *War and Peace*. Contrast this with more local productions that don't reshape our world, like your seven-year-old's violin recital or even a Nobel Prize–winning author whose works are now largely forgotten. Quick quiz: Try naming a work by Gerhart Hauptmann—1912 Nobel Prize in Literature—or Grazia Deledda (1926).

A two-way distinction is a good start, making room for creative efforts by billions of us not earning seats in the creativity stratosphere. The problem is, with only two options, we end up classifying too many people as engaging in little c creativity—placing a Suzuki Book 1 violin beginner on the same plane as Gil Shaham.

Seeking a remedy, psychologists James Kaufman and Ronald Beghetto introduced two more c's.[11] Here's the lineup:

- *mini c:* personal satisfaction derived from novel experiences, events, or activities (for instance, varying a standard peach cobbler recipe)
- *little c:* mini c that garners some recognition (maybe winning a blue ribbon at the county fair for that recipe variation)
- *Pro c:* professional creations that receive some recognition (say, J. K. Rowling's Harry Potter series)
- *Big C:* contributions for the ages that define the field, provide major benefit to humanity, alter the culture (the league of Shakespeare and, considering his impact, arguably Steve Jobs)

The literature on creativity runs the gamut from recounting genuine cultural shifts to highlighting personal accomplishments. Howard Gardner's *Creating Minds* invites us to view creativity through the Big C lens of Freud, Einstein, Picasso, Stravinsky, Eliot, Graham, and Gandhi.[12] Mihaly Csikszentmihalyi's *Creativity* is built around extensive interviews with ninety-one "exceptional" (aka creative) individuals, including sitar-player Ravi Shankar, politician Eugene McCarthy, linguist Thomas Sebeok, and philosopher Mortimer Adler.[13] Lots of Pro c.

Straddling the spectrum, journalist Matt Richtel writes in his book *Inspired* that

Creativity is . . . part of our more primitive physiology. It comes from the cellular level, part of our most essential survival machinery. We are creativity machines.[14]

Richtel's accounts of creative people sashay from rock stars to guitar instructors to army generals. Lots of mini c and little c, along with some Pro c.

Does It Matter Who Came First?

Return to the initial condition for creativity—that the idea or work be novel. But novel for whom?

It's widely recognized that in the late seventeenth century, Isaac Newton and Gottfried Wilhelm Leibniz each independently invented the calculus. Less known is that "infinite series"—an essential component of calculus—were recognized 250 years earlier in India, by the Kerala school of mathematics. Between the subsequent onslaught of European colonialism and the seminal texts being written in Malayalam (hardly an international *lingua franca*), the Kerala accomplishments remained largely unacknowledged until recently.[15]

If you're giving out prizes, it matters who got there first. In fact, supporters of Newton and Leibniz duked it out for pride of place. Leibniz was the first to publish, while the Newtonian camp accused Leibniz of plagiarism. But what's relevant for human culture is that the calculus (a Big C) was invented.

What about the rest of us? Suppose some unknown math whiz, unaware of the foundations of calculus, discovers them anew. Would that count as creativity?

Margaret Boden dealt with such possibilities by distinguishing between what she calls historical creativity (H-creative) and psychological creativity (P-creative). While the first is "novel with respect to *the whole of human history*," the second is "novel with respect to *the individual mind* which had the idea."[16] I'm not certain where Boden would place Newton's versus Leibniz's work on the calculus (perhaps a joint H-creative award, as with many Nobel prizes in the sciences or medicine). For sure, though, that hypothetical math whiz needs to settle for P-creative, since the cultural impact of calculus has long left the station.

Think ahead to AI. Might it ever qualify as H-creative? Earlier we mentioned the 2016 contest between DeepMind's program AlphaGo and international Go champion Lee Sedol. The much-vaunted thirty-seventh game move occurred in the second match, when AlphaGo did something either stupid or brilliant, a move neither Sedol nor any Go player had ever seen. After its thousands of training rounds, AlphaGo had developed its own playing style, leading to move thirty-seven, which clinched the win. Here's how one commentator described the feat:

> "[AlphaGo is] playing moves that are definitely not usual moves. They're not moves that would have a high percentage of moves in its database. So it's coming up with the moves on its own. . . . It's a creative move."[17]

Creative? At least by Bruner's definition of being surprising. The move also had obvious value, since it won AlphaGo the game. H-creative? Yes, by Boden's criterion. Big C? Hardly. No profound reshaping of human culture. Yet as AlphaGo's creator Demis Hassabis made clear, his sights were set on tackling far more pressing human problems—like figuring out protein folding—than winning at Go. We may need to wait years before deciding if programming models building on the likes of AlphaGo will join the medalist stand up there with calculus.

Can Human Creativity Be Measured?

It's been said that to a surgeon, everyone's pre-op. To a psychologist, all human behavior is potentially measurable. You just need the right test.

In his 1950 presidential address to the American Psychological Association, Joy Guilford argued for the importance of studying creativity scientifically. Presciently, one of his rationales involved potential threats from computers:

> We hear much these days about the remarkable new thinking machines. . . . [E]ventually about the only economic value of brains left would be in the creative thinking of which they [our brains] are capable.[18]

Psychologists went to work.

Guilford got the ball rolling by measuring what's known as divergent thinking—the ability to conjure up multiple answers to questions or solutions to problems. A standard example is, How many uses can you think of for a brick? By contrast, convergent thinking is homing in on a single answer or solution. The theory has been that creative people do more divergent thinking. Metrics such as the Torrance Tests of Creative Thinking built on this principle. Though not without its critics,[19] the divergent thinking argument retained popularity for half a century.

Once neuroimaging arrived in the late twentieth century, psychologists looking to track creativity latched on to the new technology. Maybe PET or MRI scans would reveal the creative brain in action.[20] Researchers have been amassing suggestive correlations, as well as pinpointing which parts of the brain light up during particular cognitive activity. For instance, PET scans reveal that the brain areas most active during random free association (presumably good for creative thinking) are the frontal, parietal, and temporal lobes.[21] There's also intriguing work surrounding the brain's so-called default network, a diffuse array of areas involved in thinking, remembering, and mind wandering. These areas show the most activity when people are least focused on the here and now. The hypothesis is that ability to daydream about the future, to let concrete thoughts slide by, is crucial for generating creative ideas.[22]

But before getting too excited that we're gazing upon the philosopher's stone of creativity, heed these words of neuroscientist Nancy Andreasen:

> It is obvious that there is a neural basis for ordinary creativity. . . . But are these the same properties that produce extraordinary creativity as well?[23]

Perhaps we can juice up mid-level creativity by practicing free association and intentional mind wandering. But don't set your sights on the next Leonardo emerging.

How Do People Become Creative?

Malvolio to Olivia in *Twelfth Night*: "Some are born great, some achieve greatness, and some have greatness thrust upon them." Is creativity like greatness? Maybe you're born with it, perhaps you toil to achieve it, or like winning the lottery, it's thrust upon you.

For thinking through the prospects of AI being creative, a reasonable first step is understanding potential sources of human creativity. A host of explanations have been proposed, with some debunked and others still up for grabs. Here are the highlights.

IQ

Maybe being smart helps make you creative. A century ago, people thought so, linking creativity with intelligence. These days, most say no, though with some codicils.

As we saw in Chapter 3, intelligence testing as we know it is the product of initial work in France by Alfred Binet plus refinements by Lewis Terman, a psychologist at Stanford in the early twentieth century. A modest man, Terman named the reformulated test Stanford-Binet, not Terman-Binet. The same Lewis Terman was also responsible for launching a decades-long study of the life trajectories of children whose IQs measured around 150. Did they end up more creative (measured by being recognized as writers, artists, scientists, and such) than kids with more average IQs (around 100)? No.[24]

But here's where the codicils come in. For starters, the measure of creativity Terman used corresponds to Kaufman and Beghetto's Pro (professional) c. Little c was presumably excluded, and no one made it to Big C.

Next, IQ tests like the Stanford Binet are at best ballpark indicators of intelligence. For decades, they (and most standardized tests) have been accused of bias. In addition, given Howard Gardner's theories of multiple intelligences (visual-spatial, logical-mathematical, verbal-linguistic, and so on), it's problematic assigning single IQ scores to people.[25] Picasso was an artistic marvel, though it's doubtful he could have tackled Fermat's last theorem.

Finally, while bigger-league creativity may not require qualifying for MENSA (the minimum Stanford Binet score is 132), some psychologists have proposed a "threshold theory." The argument is that a base level of intelligence is needed to be creative, but over a certain point (a Stanford Binet score of 120 is bandied about), all bets are off.[26]

GENES

Born creative? In 1869, Francis Galton—English polymath, cousin of Charles

Darwin, and eugenicist—argued as much in *Hereditary Genius*. By this logic, the accomplishments of so many Bachs and Brontës were hardly accidental. Arguments for and against the inheritance theory cover the map.[27] We find suggestive family pairings, but ample counterexamples. Paloma Picasso's jewelry is striking, but nothing in the league of *Guernica*.

ZEITGEIST

Maybe creativity is bolstered by the times in which people live. Nancy Andreasen, who's also a literary scholar, reminds us there are periods in history where the number of creative people of the Big C kind has been unusually large.[28] Think of Athens in the fifth and fourth centuries BCE, with Socrates, Plato, and Aristotle, not to mention Sophocles and Euripides. Think of Renaissance Florence, with Ghiberti, Leonardo, and Michelangelo. In the case of Athens, use of literacy, along with spirited discussion of what constitutes a well-run state (*polis*) and a life well lived, provided a fertile backdrop. In the Italian Renaissance, commissions by those with power—and money—surely helped.

But even then, the number rising to Big C level has been statistically miniscule. What's more, if you're alive in a humdrum era, you'll need to fall back on your own devices, beginning with personality and frame of mind.

PERSONALITY AND FRAME OF MIND

Perhaps the magic ingredient is personality. A flurry of work has focused on identifying psychological traits, positive and negative, that seem correlated with creativity.

Start with positives such as

- curiosity
- noticing things other people don't
- sensitivity
- making new analogies
- playfulness
- adventuresomeness
- persistence
- capacity for sustained hard work
- ability to handle uncertainty and ambiguity

Gregory Feist, a psychologist who writes about creativity and personality, put this last point well:

"It's a willingness to be confused and not understand and not know. . . . [Highly creative people] take pleasure in not understanding rather than withdrawing from it."[29]

But creativity researchers also mention traits that could portend trouble:

- easily bored
- reduced personal inhibitions
- doubts about likelihood of success
- vulnerability

Sometimes those behaviors are paired with psychological turbulence. Neurosis. Schizophrenia. Martin Luther suffered periods of depression. Virginia Woolf and Sylvia Plath killed themselves. So did van Gogh.

The idea that being mentally off-kilter is a typical fellow traveler with creativity traces back at least to Aristotle. As he (or, some argue, members of his school) wrote, "Those who become eminent in philosophy, politics, poetry, and the arts have all had tendencies toward melancholia."[30] In modern terms, they're sad or depressed. Maybe schizophrenic, perhaps suicidal.

Evidence associating creativity with mental issues is mixed. A 1920s study attempted to demonstrate that "genius" in Britain was associated with insanity.[31] In the United States, Nancy Andreasen interviewed thirty writers on the faculty of the famed Iowa Writers' Workshop (labeling them creative), alongside thirty matched controls whose professions weren't associated with (Pro c) creativity. Comparing their medical histories, she found 43 percent of the writers suffered from bipolar disorder (compared with 10 percent of the controls), and 80 percent were subject to mood disorders (among the controls, only 30 percent).[32] A more recent Swiss study argued as well for a correlation between creativity and mental illness.[33]

Assuming for the sake of argument that the correlations hold (and not everyone does), what do we conclude?[34] Correlation doesn't imply causation. Maybe vulnerability and sensitivity—traits often associated with creative people—help nudge some down a slippery psychic slope. Of course, it might be the other way around: that mental vulnerabilities potentially open a path to creativity. As Friedrich Nietzsche wrote in *Thus Spoke Zarathustra*, "One must still have chaos in oneself to be able to give birth to a dancing star."

Our accounting of human creativity—what counts as creative, how we measure it, how people become creative—provides metrics for judging works arising from AI programming labors. But before getting to AI, we'll need one more evaluative measure. And that's authenticity.

Real Dynel, Real Rembrandt: The Authenticity Question

In the 1960s, an ad executive named Jane Trahey came up with a powerful tagline for describing a new synthetic fur-like fiber manufactured by Union Carbide: "It's not fake anything. It's real Dynel." Reassuringly cloaked by the ad campaign, those sporting Dynel furs didn't have to pretend or take on animal rights activists railing against killing minks and sable, even rabbits, for their fur.

People care a lot about authenticity. Live flowers or artificial? Real crab or imitation? Handmade Persian rug or machine-made? Sometimes there's a huge price difference. Nowhere are questions of price, and value, greater than in the art world.

Take works attributed to Rembrandt van Rijn. Our admiration for them rises and falls with what the experts decree. Sometimes a painting once thought to be a Rembrandt is later judged a fake.[35] We also find the reverse: once seen as fake, later certified as genuine.[36] Plus we have toss-ups, where we're still not sure.[37]

Whatever the experts say, the paintings themselves don't change: It's our judgment of their worth that does. Money can also be at issue when authenticating the written word. A genuine signature of George Washington fetches tens of thousands of dollars. Of George who works at my local Whole Foods? Zip.

Then come literary works from which the community stands to benefit culturally. A good example is the play *Double Falsehood*. The eighteenth-century English playwright Lewis Theobald claimed the work was by Shakespeare. Most scholars demurred, concluding the play was actually Theobald's. Enter AI. Using machine learning, psychologists at the University of Texas at Austin created linguistic profiles of works by Shakespeare, Theobald, and John Fletcher, Shakespeare's sometime collaborator. A stylometric analysis indicated that the "entire play was consistently linked to Shakespeare with a high probability," with additional signs of Fletcher's hand.[38] "Authentic" enough to be included in the Arden Shakespeare series, though not seeing a spate of performances.

Of course, there's the even bigger Shakespeare question: Who was he anyway? A foil for Edward de Vere, 17th Earl of Oxford? Christopher Marlowe? Sir Francis Bacon? Really the man he claimed to be? What's relevant here is that whoever Shakespeare was, he was an authentic Big C human being. His life and experiences influenced his work, which, in turn, profoundly shaped our culture.

It's that living and lived process that AI lacks when it comes to creativity.

Process versus product. As humans judging creativity, we care about the act of creation—the context, the boredom, the hard work, the agony, the ecstasy—not just the finished result. Seen in this light, what does AI have to offer?

The AI Side of Creativity: Music and Art

Picture yourself back at the Sistine Chapel—sort of. Instead of Michelangelo portraying God giving life to Adam, the photographer Mike Agliolo conjured up *Creation of Robotic Adam*, in which the hand that God reaches for is part of a robotic arm. This time, let's envision humans (as creators of AI) infusing potential into computers and algorithms.

AI has been birthing works that are novel, even surprising, and potentially socially valued at a point in time. We'll begin with examples from obvious platforms for machine creativity: music and art. From there, we'll tackle AI as author. As we proceed, keep two questions in mind:

- Can humans distinguish whether a work was made by a human or was computer-generated?
- Do people care whether the creator was human or AI?

AI Does Bach and Beethoven

Johann Sebastian Bach was immensely prolific. His oeuvre includes countless chorales, preludes, fugues, and concerti, not to mention orchestral and keyboard works. Even for professional musicians, it can be hard keeping track of them all.

If you hear a Baroque-style piece but don't immediately recognize it, can you figure out if it was written by Bach or a computer? Back in the 1980s, composer David Cope's goal wasn't to fool listeners but to see if he could program in Bach's rules of composition and get a computer to generate new Bach-like works. He could and did, not just for Bach, but later for emulating the style of Mozart, Chopin, and other musical all-stars.[39] Cope dubbed his system EMI (Experiments in Musical Intelligence), also known as Emmy.

A reasonable question is whether Cope's algorithm-generated compositions could pass a musical Turing test. Live audiences confirmed that EMI could fool at least some of the people some of the time.[40] EMI even led Douglas Hofstadter (physicist, cognitive scientist, and opiner on AI) to rethink whether computers might be capable of producing creative music. In his 1979 book *Gödel, Escher, Bach*, Hofstadter had doubted whether AI would ever be able compose music that humans would find meaningful. Two decades later, after an EMI performance at Stanford, Hofstadter was less sure:

> "I find myself baffled and troubled by EMI. . . . The only comfort I could take at this point comes from realizing that EMI doesn't generate style on its own. It depends on mimicking prior composers."

But then Hofstadter continued:

> "[T]hat is still not all that much comfort. To what extent is music composed of 'riffs,' as jazz people say?"[41]

Musical greats have long drawn from the works of others, not to mention themselves. There's a reason a genuine Bach fugue we've never heard before sounds like Bach.

Cope's work has been a one-person enterprise. Others have undertaken team-based computer fabrications. The most audacious has been a score for Beethoven's Tenth Symphony.

Wasn't the Ninth his last? Yes, but.

Around 1817, Beethoven was commissioned by the Royal Philharmonic Society in London to compose his Ninth and Tenth symphonies. The Ninth premiered in 1824. Although Beethoven made some musical sketches for the Tenth, he never completed it, dying in 1827. A cadre of musicians, musicologists, and computer scientists asked themselves, If you started with those sketches, input Beethoven's other compositions, and harnessed contemporary AI algorithms, could you create a credible symphony approximating what Beethoven might have written? The goal was to have it ready for Beethoven's 250th birthday in 2020.[42] Create a symphony they did, though thanks to delays, it wasn't completed until fall 2021.

Not revealing the source, I put on the opening bars for my son, who plays violin. Immediately he pounced: "Fake Beethoven!" and refused to hear any more. If his judgment proves a bellwether for the broader public, Beethoven's Tenth doesn't meet the "social value" criterion for a work to be deemed creative. Following the symphony's premier in Bonn in October 2021, I haven't heard of orchestras scheduling performances. The issue of passing a musical Turing test doesn't arise. Unlike Bach's vast repertoire of shorter pieces, Beethoven's nine authentic symphonies are all recognizable.

Besides creation of artistic works "in the style of," what about productions—human or otherwise—that violate the rules? In many of his later works, Beethoven broke existing musical conventions of melody and harmony. And he was the first to combine instrumental and vocal music in a symphony (in his Ninth). There's a reason we call him a creative genius.

For their part, computers are well suited to generating works that violate convention. One computer scientist intrigued by such possibilities is Ahmed Elgammal, himself a key player in the Beethoven's Tenth project. As author Arthur I. Miller describes Elgammal's mission, it is

> to find a way for a machine to create new, original, and exciting artworks—not more of the same "in the style of" existing artworks, and not so way out as to be dismissed as bizarre, but artworks that stand comparison with works of the greatest contemporary artists.[43]

"Original," "exciting," but not "bizarre." If the new work really goes off the rails, we likely hesitate to call it creative. But judgments could change, just as they did for van Gogh's paintings.

But Is It Art?

Riffing on existing works or creating anew. Consider an art world equivalent of Beethoven's Tenth.

A project that launched in 2014 set out to see if, using a convolutional neural network, data scientists could create a portrait mistakable for a genuine Rembrandt. After selecting parameters based on typical features in the artist's oeuvre (Caucasian male with facial hair; between ages thirty and forty; wearing dark clothing, a white collar, and a hat; facing to the right), the programmers scanned in 346 paintings and then focused on 67 features, such as eyes and nose. Teaming up with experts in 3D printing, the group unveiled *The Next Rembrandt* eighteen months later.[44] I'm no historian of Dutch art, but online reproductions convince me I'd be fooled if the painting were hanging in Amsterdam's Rijksmuseum.

What distinguishes *The Next Rembrandt* from Beethoven's Tenth? Unlike the case with Beethoven, there really might be a "next Rembrandt," a work long hidden away and only now discovered and authenticated.

But back to the Rijksmuseum, whose most famous Rembrandt is arguably *The Night Watch* (more properly, at least according to the museum, called *The Militia Company of District II Under the Command of Captain Frans Banninck Cocq*). The original was completed in 1642. Some years later, when the painting was slated to hang in Amsterdam's town hall, the canvas wouldn't fit in the designated spot. The draconian solution was to chop off portions from all four sides. That's the version that's long been on display in the Rijksmuseum.

Fortuitously, a contemporary of Rembrandt had made a copy of the original before the butchery. Gerrit Lundens's reproduction didn't capture the master's style, but at least all the figures were there. Fast-forward 300 years to the age of neural networks. Robert Erdmann, senior scientist at the Rijksmuseum, used today's AI technology to recreate the missing panels, but this time capturing Rembrandt's own artistic style.[45]

Creative? Not in the sense of producing a new work. And not aimed at passing a Turing test. But yes, in demonstrating the power of AI to generate realistic art that has social value to viewers who can now behold the work as Rembrandt (almost) originally painted it.

Let's move on to more novel art, not looking to replicate patterns in someone else's body of work. A prime exhibit is *Portrait of Edmond Belamy*.

Sold by Christie's auction house in 2018, the portrait fetched a cool $432,500.[46] Not bad for a picture of someone who never existed and was generated by a computer algorithm. The efficient cause (to use Aristotle's term) was a Paris trio dubbing themselves Obvious. Using a generative adversarial network feeding on a data source of 15,000 actual portraits produced between the fourteenth and twentieth centuries, Obvious produced a series of fictional portraits of the imagined Belamy family, of which this was one. The resulting painting is somewhat blurred and pebbled, almost looking as if Belamy is under water.

Christie's had earlier estimated the portrait's value between $7,000 and $10,000. We'll assume that the deep pocket forking over nearly half a million dollars found the work in some way valuable. It remains to be seen if others—society—will.

The AI Side of Creativity: Writing

Chapter 8 focused on AI as author in professional realms like journalism, law, and translation. We highlighted the concern whether efficiency from AI-generated text threatens writers' financial security and personal job satisfaction. Practically, there are only so many news stories, so many legal briefs, and so many documents to translate. Our concerns in that chapter had more to do with the labor market than passing a Turing test or impacting culture.

The goal posts shift when asking whether writing done by AI merits the label "creative." With written works of this sort, there's no cap. Whether it's poetic forays by adolescents, attempts at the Great American Novel, or writing a new play, there's always room for more. And while authoring short stories or novels can be an honorable way to earn a living (ask Charles Dickens or Samuel Clemens), much of our written output that's at some level creative springs from emotional, not economic, motives.

Creative Writing Versus Writing That's Creative

Let's clarify what we're talking about when combining the words "creative" and "writing." Maybe you took an undergraduate creative writing course to develop your skills as a poet or short story writer. Perhaps you earned an MFA from a graduate program in creative writing, where you wrote and work-shopped your drafts under the tutelage of published authors. These programs generally focus on fiction or poetry, or maybe drama.

For sure, people write creatively in other genres. Take essays, beginning with Michel de Montaigne's *Essais*. There's artful and original biography (say, Sylvia Nasar's *A Beautiful Mind*) and history (Robert Fogel and Stanley Engerman's *Time on the Cross*), not to mention culture-changing volumes by Adam Smith and Max Weber, Jean Piaget and Sigmund Freud. But we need to pin down what kind of creativity we're talking about. Of ideas? No contest for the likes of Smith and Freud. Of facility with prose, in which case there's less agreement.

For our purposes, we'll basically restrict collocating "writing" and "creative" to what creative writing programs would likely recognize. You might add in shorter pieces like jokes and limericks. Researchers take all these as candidates when asking if AI can write creatively.

Time for some examples.

An AI Creative Writing Potpourri

Welcome to Expo 2020 in Dubai. Thanks to COVID-19, events were postponed a year, so the international extravaganza didn't open until October 2021. But it was worth the wait, especially to see the UK pavilion, designed by Es Devlin. The edifice stretched out from its base (resembling an elongated snout) and projected computer-generated poetry. Devlin built on her earlier AI experiments, this time harnessing GPT-2, trained on 5,000 poems. Every visitor was invited to contribute a word, with the newly generated poems projected in English and Arabic using LEDs.

Harken back to the first International Expo. London 1851. On display were new technologies that would reshape our lives and cultures, including Samuel Morse's telegraph and Charles Goodyear's vulcanized rubber. Devlin sees working with AI as a kindred cultural force: "Algorithms are among us. They are an ever-growing part of our culture."[47]

Move on to more conventional writing genres. Guess who wrote these lines:

"Yet in a circle pallid as it flow,
by this bright sun, that with his Light display,
roll'd from the sands, and half the buds of snow,
and calmly on him shall infold away"

Sounds a bit Shakespearean. The sonnet form, including scansion and rhyming patterns, seems right, as does the Elizabethan language, though readability and emotional appeal are a bit off. And no wonder. The words were produced by a program called Deep-speare, using a deep neural network and drawing on a digital corpus of about 2,700 sonnets available through Project Gutenberg.[48] Still, for a computer program written around 2018, the results are none too shabby.

What about AI-generated prose? Platforms like GPT-3 still tend to reveal their non-human origins when instructed to produce large amounts of text, sometimes repeating themselves or veering into weirdness. But like a moderated discussion group, extended written dialogue between an AI and a human can be coherent, sometimes even thought-provoking or eloquent. Take *Pharmako-AI*, a 148-page diary-style exchange created jointly by K Allado-McDowell and GPT-3. In reviewing the book, author Elvia Wilk wrote, "While reading, I . . . often forgot which author was speaking."[49]

Pharmako-AI wasn't the first natural-sounding feature-length algorithm-driven writing. One prior successful collaboration, between Hitoshi Matsubara and a computer, resulted in a short-form novel aptly named *The Day a Computer Writes a Novel*. Impressively, the novel made it through the first round of judging for the 2016 Nikkei Hoshi Shinichi Literary Award.[50] For the record: Of the 1,450 contest submissions that year, 11 were computer-generated. Perhaps the edge of a new literary wedge.

But are we comfortable labeling these sorts of writing "creative"? Let's put to work criteria we laid out for human creativity and see how AI's offspring fare.

How AI Creative Writing Compares

One place to start is with a Turing test: Can humans distinguish between AI and human-generated literary compositions? In a perhaps unsettling number of cases, the answer seems no.

Take the TEDx talk by Oscar Schwartz, co-inventor of a poetry generator and guessing game called Bot or Not. As his talk revealed, the audience judged a stanza by William Blake to be the work of a human poet, but concluded that Gertrude Stein's sprang from a computer.[51]

Matchups like this have become something of a nerdy game. For a number of years, Dartmouth's Neukom Institute for Computational Science ran an annual Turing Tests in the Creative Arts, in which contestants submitted AI-generated sonnets, limericks, stories, and the like, all judged against human works. The questions were whether evaluators could distinguish and which they liked better. Results were mixed.[52]

For Don Rockmore, the institute's director, the goal wasn't to ask if computers might replace humans as literary creators. Rather, it was to explore the nature of creation in each medium. As for the value of AI-generated works, Rockmore argues it's time to stop seeing acknowledgment of AI creation "as a kind of literary G.M.O tag" and instead recognize it "as an entirely new, and worthy, category of art."[53] In the same vein, Elvia Wilk asks, "Why do we obsessively measure AI's ability to write like a person? Might it be nonhuman and creative?"[54] Evaluate AI on its own terms, not ours. Not fake anything. Real Dynel.

Moving beyond Turing tests (and mindful of Rockmore's advice), how does AI creative composition stack up against yardsticks for human creativity?

NOVELTY, SOCIAL VALUE, A POINT IN TIME

As linguistic creatures, we understand each other because we share codes. By and large—though with different levels of sophistication, along with some crossed signals—speakers of a language operate with the same words, the same syntax, and the same sound system. When I ask you to open the door, you don't head for the window.

Novelty can be interjected in a host of ways, including making up words (Lewis Carroll's "slithy toves"), unexpected uses of grammar (the first time someone used "google" as a verb), or conjuring up metaphors, similes, or juxtapositions that don't match real-world expectations ("A cabbage walked into a bar"). Like humans, programs running on large language models draw upon the words and sentences others have used before them to create new written utterances.

The difference is that AI's supply of exemplars is much vaster than what's accessed by mere mortals. The result? We can expect AI-as-author to come up with novelties, including when trained on prior human linguistic innovations. How's this for fun: Researchers at Tel Aviv University used neural networks to expand vocabulary options in fictional languages like Klingon by modeling the style of those languages' lexicons.[55]

So AI authorship seems to pass the novelty test for creativity. Next up for consideration is social value. In the late 1990s, Margaret Boden addressed the issue of computer creativity and value:

> The ultimate vindication of AI-creativity would be a program that generated novel ideas which initially perplexed or even repelled us, but which was able to persuade us that they were indeed valuable. We are a very long way from that.[56]

More than twenty years on, it's not clear we're closing in on that goal. The purchaser of *Portrait of Edmond Belamy* and galleries displaying other art created by Obvious might think so, but the bulk of society isn't there.

Over time, will computer-generated works alter our perceptions of what's valuable? For comparison: Vincent van Gogh's way of seeing the world found its way into our cultural sensibilities (think of "Van Gogh: The Immersive Experience" or *Starry Night* splashed on scarves and tote bags), much as John Donne (panned by Ben Jonson and Samuel Johnson; later revived by T. S. Eliot) now dwells in our literary pantheon. Reputations of other human artists and writers have fallen by the wayside. Sorry, Gerhart Hauptmann, your Nobel Prize notwithstanding.

For AI, we'll need to wait and see. My own hunch is that we'll mostly come to value AI-generated literary works for their quirkiness, sometimes prodding humans to be more inventive in their own writing. It's possible that one day we'll see an AI novel winning the Booker Prize, but I'm not holding my breath.

LEVELS OF C

The first level (mini c) is easily dispensed with, since algorithms can't garner personal satisfaction from anything, including producing novel text. Little c and Pro c are different stories, since they're centered on a written product, not the producer's psyche. If an AI-generated poem can pass a Turing test, it's worthy of a little c designation. *The Day a Computer Writes a Novel* didn't win the Japanese competition, plus it had some human co-authorship. But it's conceivable that AI-generated works might garner lower-tier literary prizes. Who knows—maybe getting to Pro c. Maybe.

Can we envision AI creating Big C literary works? I strongly doubt it. Unquestionably, the development of artificial intelligence (and computer science more generally) are contributions for the ages. They've dramatically reshaped our lives. But when it comes to poetry and narrative prose, human readers are moved not only by words but by the historical, cultural, lived nature of their creator. Whoever he was, part of what made Shakespeare was that he was an Elizabethan. James Joyce was a twentieth-century Irishman. Reading their works, we also read their lives and times.

NOVEL TO WHOM? H-CREATIVE OR P-CREATIVE

Boden's notion of historical versus personal creativity isn't particularly applicable to AI's literary output. In principle, any new text from a large language model will be unique (historically creative), with the caveat that large language models sometimes spin out sequences of other people's words. But simply being unique doesn't assure a place in literary history.

GENESIS

A bit more promising are comparisons of human and AI sources of literary creativity. I say "a bit" because we can promptly rule out a string of options when it comes to AI. No default thinking (since there's no physical brain). IQ, genes, personality, and frame of mind don't apply, unless you're speaking of the programmer. Consciousness doesn't either. Recall Geoffrey Jefferson's position that it wasn't enough for a computer to write a sonnet or compose a concerto. Rather, before our agreeing that "machine equals brain," a machine would also need to have "thoughts and emotions" and "know that it had written" the creative work. AI remains a long way off from measuring up.

What about zeitgeist? Can we speak of a cultural climate that's fostering AI literary creativity? Given the hoopla—and commercial uptake—of tools built on the back of GPT-3 and its relatives, there's a public appetite for exploring the potential of AI as literary author. However, to date, we've seen no equivalent of an Elizabethan age nurturing Shakespeare and Marlowe, Jonson and, yes, Donne.

More applicable for literary AI is the idea of divergent thinking, along with ability to make novel word associations. Conjuring up alternative possibilities and making quirky matches are talents in which large language models can excel. An engaging example is the New Year's Resolution generator developed by Janelle Shane for her stint as Futurist in Residence at the Smithsonian Arts and Industries Building in Washington.[57] Using Davinci (a version of GPT-3), she seeded the program with offbeat sample resolutions. In response, Davinci offered up such gems as

"Eat my favorite book."

"Make broccoli the national currency and then paint it."

"Try to convince the dog next door that he is wearing a coat of moonlight."

"A coat of moonlight." Sounds like something a divergent-thinking human might have written. Shades of "Catch a falling star and put it in your pocket."

What ChatGPT Says About AI and Creativity

As I mentioned in the Prologue, OpenAI's ChatGPT was taking the world by storm just as I was completing this book. I couldn't resist asking what the bot had to say about creativity.

My prompt to ChatGPT: "Would you call GPT creative?" The first time I posed the question, here was the response:

"As a large language model trained by OpenAI, I am not capable of creative thought or artistic expression. I am a tool that can generate human-like text based on the input provided to me, but I do not possess the ability to create original works of art or literature."

Quite humble, I thought.

A few days later, I retried the same query. The answer this time was much longer and explicitly compared human creativity with what AI produces. Here's the relevant part:

> "GPT . . . is not capable of the kind of original, creative thinking that we typically associate with human creativity. This is because GPT is simply a tool that has been trained to mimic the patterns of human language, and it does not have the ability to think or reason for itself."

Great! Human thinking and reasoning still count for something. Yet if we're only looking at the output from AI and from humans, not the process of creation, it's not clear how we know what cognitive effort was invested.

Do We Care If AI Is Creative?

When new kids arrive on the block, it's only natural to size them up: New playmate? Potential rival? Much of the fuss over AI as a creative writer boils down to whether we stand to benefit from its potential or if it will eat our lunch. To put these alternatives in perspective, it helps to remind ourselves of AI's creative authoring strengths, but also why humans are motivated to write.

What AI as Author Can Do

Let's start with AI's contributions to creative writing. Here's a sampling of what AI can do on its own, as well as in tandem with humans.

CREATE NEW PRODUCTS

AI authoring tools bring forth would-be literary works that amuse, teach, even inspire. We've sampled a range of genres, but I'll add one more: storytelling. In Chapter 7, we talked about James Meehan's Tale-Spin and about explorations with hyperfiction. Another innovator in those early days was Mark Riedl, who has now logged two decades exploring what AI models can do for weaving tales.[58]

Are there limits to how successful AI can be as a creative author? I've already suggested that AI won't have the chops to achieve Big C writing, and even Pro c is generally a stretch. There are those who maintain that AI can never write literature successfully, while others are more optimistic.[59] What counts as creative literature is, to some extent, in the eye of the beholder. This isn't a battle we can settle here.

BOLSTER HUMAN CREATIVITY

The immediate benefit humans are most likely to derive from AI's creative writing prowess is boosting our own efforts. Tools like Sudowrite tout their ability to "Bust writer's block." Authors talk about AI writing programs spurring their own thinking, as well as offering possibilities for producing collaborative works. When we get to Chapter 11, we'll explore some options.

FOSTER BETTER UNDERSTANDING
OF HUMAN THINKING AND CREATIVITY

Margaret Boden asked, "How is it possible for people to think new thoughts?" Despite centuries of efforts, we still struggle to understand the workings of the human mind, including how it comes up with writing, art, or music we collectively find creative. One of Boden's arguments for pursuing the creative potential of computers has been to help puzzle out human creative thinking.[60]

Architects construct scaled models of buildings they plan to erect. Scientists rely on drosophila and mice to test drugs and medical procedures. Contemporary AI researchers rekindled earlier analogies between human neural connections and computer neural networks. Looking to AI for clues about what makes human writing valuable will, at worst, do no harm.

Why Creative Human Authorship Remains Important

AI creative writing poses little new threat to flesh-and-blood authors. You might not make a living from your poems, short stories, or novels (which has always been true), but you can still write them.

The real sticking point, as Joy Guilford suggested back in 1950, is that "thinking machines" challenge our sense of human uniqueness. People have long laid claim to language as an exclusive human property, though as we saw in the Prologue, non-human primates chipped away at that premise. The real threat we feel from AIs that can write decently, even creatively, is to our turf. Our self-definition.

The first several chapters of this book talked about what knowing how to write—and then writing and rewriting—can do for us as people. We vent, we make social connections, we struggle to come to know ourselves. Even in our graffiti, we assert our existence: "Kilroy was here." And sometimes we simply enjoy the writing process and personally revel in the product.

Several of the psychologists studying creativity have written about values that reach beyond the objective quality of what we create. James Kaufman argues that "a lifetime of mini- or little-c creativity is . . . associated with numerous personal benefits."[61] Among them are reducing stress, dealing with past negative challenges, affirming you have a story to tell. It's not accidental that the original subtitle of Mihaly Csikszentmihalyi's book *Creativity* was *Flow and the Psychology of Discovery and Invention*. Csikszentmihalyi's notion of flow (to oversimplify: being "in the zone") leads not just to creative works but to pleasure, a sense of well-being, happiness.

Bottom line: Don't let AI's prowess intimidate you as a writer. You have much to think about and much to say, regardless of prizes or whether tourists visit your birthplace. Plus, as we'll see in the next two chapters, AI can make for a cunning, often welcome partner.

PART IV

WHEN COMPUTERS
COLLABORATE

TEN

AI as Jeeves

One of humorist P. G. Wodehouse's most memorable characters was Jeeves, valet to the London layabout Bertie Wooster. Jeeves got stuff done and took initiative. So do a slew of AI programs, including for writing. Earlier we talked about AI-generated text in professional settings where humans generally don't claim credit. What about where AI has a hand, but the piece bears your name?

Sometimes AI's role is to tweak what you've already written. At others, AI produces the whole enchilada. Communication expert Jeff Hancock has a name for use of AI to do fix-up or drafting for us: artificial intelligence-mediated communication (AI-MC for short).[1] The moniker is a play on the concept of computer-mediated communication (CMC), which initially meant using computers as go-betweens for communicating between people: Think of email or instant messaging. (These days, CMC also enfolds digital devices like mobile phones and smart watches.) Hancock's AI-MC brings AI agents into the conversation. AI's potential jobs run the gamut from modifying or augmenting a human's message to generating brand-new text on a person's behalf. Taken together, largely what I'm calling AI as Jeeves.

Let's drop in on these AI programs at work, starting with editorial janitors.

Just the Basics: Corrections and Completions

In the Prologue, we introduced the idea of domesticating technology. A familiar example is spellcheck. The technology has become invisible. We take it for granted.

Spellcheck

We call it "spellcheck" but how do you spell it? Microsoft 365's Word seems happy with "spellcheck," "spell check," and "spell-check" (plus permutations with capital letters). On its support page, Microsoft talks about a "spelling checker," though all I hear people say is "spellcheck" (no "-er"). As for the spelling: Back in 1992, in its ads for Windows and MS DOS 5, Microsoft referred to Spellcheck. And so (sans capitalization) shall I.

The allure of a computer program cleaning up orthographic errors is understandably tantalizing. Researchers have been attacking the problem for more than sixty years.

Before the blossoming of personal computers, correction programs were envisioned for larger machines. At Stanford back in 1961, computer scientist Les Earnest created the first spellcheck program, which a decade later he put out on ARPANET.[2] Another effort was Warren Teitelman's 1966 MIT master's thesis, a program called PILOT, subtitled "A Step Toward Man–Computer Symbiosis."[3] The idea was for the computer code to collaborate with humans, who could save their energies for working on more difficult problems. Among Teitelman's proposals were an "undo" feature, a "do what I mean" function, and spellcheck.[4]

The 1970s and 80s witnessed a cascade of spellcheck software. In 1978, a cluster of linguists created programs in six languages for the IBM Displaywriter. By 1982, Henry Kučera at Brown University had produced spellcheck for DEC's VAX machines, to be followed by versions running on personal computers.

Spellcheck on PCs took hold, with versions landing in WordStar, WordPerfect, and Microsoft Word. These early systems were clunky and came as standalone software, though soon they were folded into the main word-processing programs. Initially, corrections weren't automatic. When a potential error was flagged, users had to authorize the change. Come 1993, Microsoft's spellcheck underwent a sea change with introduction of autocorrect. Now, you typed in a word whose spelling wasn't copacetic, and poof! It got corrected.

Maybe. Microsoft's first version of autocorrect relied on a list of common misspellings, such as "teh" for "the" or "saturday" for "Saturday." Later, autocorrect was tied to the contents of a dictionary.[5] Therein lay at least part of the rub.

Problem one: If a word wasn't in the program's dictionary, autocorrect offered up its nearest approximation. Legendary examples include how 2003 Word handled Barack Obama's name. "Barack" morphed into "Boatman," "Obama" into "Osama." A webmail version of Outlook suggested the president's first name was "Barracks."[6] You get the drift.

Problem two: Even if your intended word was in the dictionary, spellcheck might leave you in the lurch or misconstrue your intent. We've all been frustrated when homophones like "to," "two," and "too" don't get cleaned up. (Word still remains mum when I type "I have too left shoes.") Perhaps most notorious was "the Cupertino effect" that popped up in Word's 1997 edition. Because its spellcheck program only recognized the word "cooperation" when written with a hyphen (that is, "co-operation"), when you entered the unhyphenated version, it was autocorrected to "Cupertino."[7]

Mercifully, these kinds of bloopers have been diminishing as AI tools improve.

Writing on Mobile Phones

Correct spelling wasn't initially a concern on mobile phones. The big hurdle was inputting words in the first place.

Mobile phones got their start installed in cars. In fact, until 2020, the UK still had stores called Carphone Warehouse. The shift to personal mobility came in 1992, when the European consortium Groupe Spécial Mobile (GSM) launched its network. Though the system was designed for voice communication, a bit of bandwidth was left over, which the consortium made available for users to tap out brief messages on the keypad. This Short Message Service (SMS) appeared in 1993, originally for free. Much of the world knows texting as SMS.

Here was the challenge: You needed multiple taps to produce a letter—one tap on number 4 for a "g," two taps for an "h," and so forth. Punctuation was an even greater nightmare. Errors were abundant and messages were short, thanks to limitations on how many characters could be sent at a time (and for one price) and because using the system was so labor intensive.

A welcome reprieve came in the mid-1990s when the founders of Tegic Communications, Cliff Kushler and Martin King, invented T9 ("text on 9 keys"), which displayed a set of word choices after you entered a couple of letters.[8] Arrival of the iPhone in 2007 brought virtual keyboards, a new operating system, and the need for its own automated programs. Autocorrect for the iPhone was created by Apple software engineer Ken Kocienda.[9] QuickType (essentially autocomplete or predictive texting) on Apple phones arrived in 2014, giving you three options to choose from.

Problems solved? Not quite—no more than with kindred tools for computer word processing. Among the famous howlers begotten by autocorrect on mobile phones were "Your mom and I are going to Disney" morphing into "Your mom and I are going to divorce" and "Sorry about your fever" transformed to "Sorry about your feces."[10]

Yet consequences of automated word production go beyond hilarity, horror, or embarrassment. The AI in our phones may also be changing how we write. Philosopher Evan Selinger worries that autocorrect programs drive users into "personalized clichés." Analyzing the writing style in our past conversations, the algorithms tend to regenerate more of the same:

> [B]y encouraging us not to think too deeply about our words, predictive technology may subtly change how we interact with each other. As communication becomes less of an intentional act, we give others more algorithm and less of ourselves. . . . [A]utomation . . . can stop us thinking.[11]

Research on predictive texting supports Selinger's concerns. A Harvard study found that when we use predictive texting, our vocabulary becomes more constrained (more succinct—and less interesting) than when we come up with our own words.[12] In research I did with young adults, 21 percent reported their messages became simpler or shorter as a result of using predictive texting. More in Chapter 12 on that research.

Grammar and Style

Spelling and word prediction are but the iceberg's tip in writing. Choice of words and grammar matters, even more. Software developers have been building grammar tools for nearly as long as they've worked on spellcheck. Writer's Workbench was designed in the 1970s to run on Unix systems. Grammatik, debuting in 1981, ran on early PCs.

Meanwhile, the publisher Houghton Mifflin (already working with Henry Kučera on spellcheck programs) developed CorrecText, a stand-alone grammar checker.[13] Grammar and style advice arrived on Microsoft Word in 1992, when the company incorporated a grammar checking program derived from CorrecText. Over the next three decades, the programs evolved in scope and sophistication.

Did the programs work? That depends on whom you ask and what your writing goals are. Good writing takes more than following someone else's rules in lockstep. Can you begin a sentence with a conjunction? No!—English teachers drilled into my head. But style evolves. The same goes for when and where to use commas, and not all style sheets agree.

Then there's choice of wording. A few years back, I began worrying about effects of style checkers on word choice. At the time, I was reviewing essays written by students competing for prestigious awards like Rhodes, Marshall, and Fulbright. These applicants were among my university's most accomplished. Many were excellent writers. Why was Microsoft Word flagging so many words and phrases in their drafts?

Curious, I right-clicked on some of the items Word underlined, selected "Grammar," and up popped suggested edits.[14] Here are two examples of what I found:

Original Wording	*Microsoft Word Suggestion*
PTSD can be <u>exacerbated</u> due to cultural barriers	Consider using a simple word Suggestion: *worsened*
gain an insightful perspective on the challenges and pragmatic solutions <u>in the near future</u> and long term	Consider using concise language Suggestion: *soon*

The pattern was clear: Eschew long words or phrases, even though their use, stylistically, was in keeping with the tone of the essay.

As an inveterate experimenter, I more recently typed into Word the beginning of the US Declaration of Independence ("When in the course of human events"). I was informed that "in the course of" could be improved upon: "More concise language would be clearer for your reader." Word's suggestion was to replace the offending phrase with "during." More concise, yes, but neither grammatical nor meaningful. Thomas Jefferson, a skilled writer, would be horrified to see his document beginning with "When during human events."

There's a certain irony with style checkers counseling us to eschew longer words and always aim for concision. While teachers don't advise students to be verbose, they do encourage learning—and using—sophisticated and nuanced vocabulary. They're not alone. As we saw earlier, ETS's e-rater rewards using polysyllabic words. Talk about mixed messages.

Believing that like charity, clarity begins at home, I was curious to see why Word was balking at some of the sentences in the manuscript for this book. I admit that my writing style doesn't always have the directness of Hemingway, but I do try to be grammatical. Word instructed me on more than one occasion that I had run afoul of proper usage. When I wrote:

However we might define "good" writing, it's more than acing checklists.

Word scolded me for not putting a comma after "however." Sorry, Word. A comma doesn't belong there, since the adverb "however" is modifying "define," not the whole sentence.

To be fair, this wasn't a run-of-the-mill sentence, and I appreciate the programming challenge of getting all the syntactic possibilities handled accurately. As Edward Sapir cautioned, all grammars leak. My concern is that writers who are less certain of their command of English, including many learning the language, will follow Word's lead, ending up with grammatical pablum.

There's a disconnect between longstanding pedagogies for nurturing human writing skills and today's AI evaluation programs. This conflict isn't lost on linguists and composition teachers, who worry that automating metrics for spelling, grammar, style, and punctuation undercuts efforts to get students focused on content and personal voice.[15] If a grammar checker cleans up around the edges, we can be lulled into believing that somehow the real substance also passes muster. But if the software isn't assessing substance, don't hold your breath.

Anne Herrington and Charles Moran, two leading lights in the world of English composition, nailed the issue in a piece they wrote in 2012 focusing on ETS's Criterion. Like most grammar and style checkers, Criterion attends to the word and sentence level, not the holistic essay. As a result,

> it presents the revising task to come as one of moving through categories and eliminating errors, not of rethinking the argument or adapting to a particular rhetorical situation.[16]

More than a decade on, the problem remains.

Your Writing Tutor Is In: Teaching Moment or Free Ride?

When I think about software designed to assist in editing, I can't help asking who's benefiting. The software companies? Those genuinely attempting to improve their writing skills? Students wanting an easy out? Let's have a look at two of the big guns in the business, Grammarly and Microsoft, specifically the version of Word embedded in Office 365 (as of early 2023). Remember, please, that accuracy and functionality of these products continue to evolve and may no longer precisely match what existed when I wrote this chapter. That caveat goes both for Word, now that Microsoft is infusing GPT-4 into its programs, and for Grammarly, which is incorporating GPT-3.

Grammarly as Personal Tutor

Here's a question for you: What does plagiarism detection have to do with grammar tutoring? Answer: Very similar natural language processing tools underlie how both operate. The same, incidentally, goes for scoring essays and delivering grammatical advice, as we saw with ETS's e-rater doing double duty as Criterion.

The program known as Grammarly—with its 30 million active daily users—got its start in 2009, following a venture seven years earlier in the plagiarism detection business. Grammarly's founders explain:

> With our previous company, MyDropBox, we had built a product to help keep plagiarism out of students' writing. This led us to ask a serious underlying question: Why do people choose to plagiarize in the first place? Could it be that they were finding it difficult to communicate what they meant in their own voice?[17]

The new goal was to help students with grammar and spelling. Now, millions of non-students are also among the clientele.

As with much online software, there's the freemium version, providing edits to spelling, grammar, punctuation, and tone detection (things like confident, urgent, or respectful). Pay for premium, and additionally you get suggestions for word choice, options for formality level, sentence rewrites for clarity, tone adjustments, and plagiarism detection. To help Grammarly help you, writers can set goals by choosing audience, level of formality, area of writing (including business, email, or academic), and tone, along with purpose (for instance, to inform, describe, or convince).[18] As of now, Grammarly is only available in English.

Grammarly also has on offer opportunities not just for correcting but for learning. When an error is marked, there's the option of reading a grammatical explanation. I'd love to believe most users are thirsting for personal betterment, not simply looking for quick fixes. But I'm dubious. Ask yourself: When spellcheck corrects one of your misspellings (not typos but real misspellings), how often do you pause to say, "Let me memorize the correct version so I don't get it wrong in the future"? Why bother, since spellcheck will be there for you that next time.

If you want still more help, Grammarly has an "expert writing service" for those who "need extra confidence" that their "text is free of mistakes."[19] In other words, you can pay to have a human being edit your work. Prices vary with the level of services requested and the needed turnaround time.

Microsoft as Language Cop

Given the ubiquity of Microsoft Word, we're all familiar with its longstanding editing routines. Now there are additional AI-driven tools in Microsoft Editor, thanks to Microsoft's partnership with OpenAI. Among these are functions nudging writers to make their word choices less biased, less offensive, and more inclusive.

To see what I'm talking about, you may need to change some selections under "Preferences." Pass from "Spelling and Grammar" to "Grammar" to "Grammar & Refinements," finally landing on "Settings." Scrolling through the options, you'll likely find that many basic grammar and style items (all alphabetized) are prechecked. Cruise past the "W's," and next come additional suggestions (curiously, some unalphabetized) for issues such as jargon, passive voice, wordiness, and slang. Keep going, and you'll come upon the bias options: age, cultural, ethnic, gender, racial, sexual orientation, socioeconomic.[20]

You might well ask who decides what counts as bias. Even for some obvious candidates, does Microsoft Editor catch all offending instances? I went reconnoitering. Microsoft missed entirely several objectionable words I entered. Others were only flagged in the singular. Editor failed to snag some words I initially typed, but when I wrote more in the same vein, Microsoft went back to "correct" its slipup. (Presumably machine learning at work.) These are some highlights from my adventure:

Racial and Ethnic Terms	Flags both singular and plural	Derogatory terms for Spaniards (D-word), African Americans (N-word), and Vietnamese (G-word)
	Flags only singular	Derogatory term for Japanese (J-word)
	Doesn't flag at all	Derogatory terms for Jews (K-word and Y-word) and for Chinese (C-word)
Offensive Terms	*bitch, whore, slut*	Sometimes flagged, sometimes not, depending on rest of sentence
Inclusiveness	*mankind*	Recommendation to use a gender-neutral term like *humankind* or *humanity*

On the "mankind" issue: Microsoft Editor had no complaints about generic use of "man" (as in "What shall it profit a man") but objected to "mankind." Neil Armstrong's "One small step for man. One giant leap for mankind" upon landing on the moon in 1969 would be more gender inclusive but lose poetic luster—and historical accuracy—if updated to "for humankind" or "for humanity," as Editor suggested. Is the jeans brand 7 For All Mankind (with products for women, men, and kids) next on the chopping block? For now, it gets a Microsoft reprieve, since if "m" is capitalized, Editor stays mute.

And here's one that Microsoft flagged from my own manuscript. I had written:

Writing an AI program that could win against a Go master was a huge deal.

Microsoft didn't like the word "master," chastising me that "A gender-neutral term would be more inclusive." Its proposals were "expert," "head," or "primary." Let's try those out: "A Go expert"? I suspect Lee Sedol would find "expert" too milquetoast for characterizing his status. "A Go head"? Meaningless. "A Go primary"? The same. Pity the English language learner who conscientiously heeds Microsoft's advice, especially accepting either of the second two options.

Student-Based Writing Tutors

Beyond Microsoft and Grammarly's market penetration, other writing tutors keep springing up, including those specifically focused on students. One newish offering is ETS's Writing Mentor, a free Google Docs add-on.[21] Apparently targeting middle and high school students, the program incorporates a passel of tools found in e-rater and then Criterion.

Other initiatives have emerged from university research projects. Some aim at helping students with the basics of grammar and sentence mechanics like spelling and punctuation, while others are more conceptually sophisticated. Carnegie Mellon University's DocuScope project, begun in 1998 by David Kaufer and his colleagues, innovatively looked to guide students in identifying arguments in their writing.[22] Not to be outdone, at about the same time, ETS was studying use of NLP to identify arguments for scoring essays in the GMAT.[23]

Education or Evasion?

Writing well is hard work, and not just for students. Long past graduation, many of us have endured our share of embarrassment—a word misspelled or misused, awkward phrasing in a passage we thought we'd crafted carefully. My own worst woodshed moment came when an external reviewer had this to say about a sentence in the book manuscript I'd just finished:

> This is the worst-written sentence in the English language I have ever encountered.

Gulp. Perhaps digital writing tutors will eventually save us from ourselves. The question is, should they.

If our only automated Jeeves is leaving spellcheck on, does that count? (More on spelling in Chapter 12.) If grammar and style checkers merely offer suggestions, not legislate change the way autocorrect does, maybe using them isn't really different from looking things up in a grammar book, dictionary, or thesaurus. Perhaps you ask a friend to read over your draft. There are fair grounds for wondering if it matters whether a human or an AI algorithm is doing the reviewing.

Evidence—at least from Grammarly—suggests there are lots of satisfied customers. In winter 2011–2012, the company surveyed 392 university students who used their product. Among the findings:

- 70 percent reported increased confidence in their writing abilities.
- 93 percent reported Grammarly helped them save time on their writing.
- 99 percent reported Grammarly improved their writing grades.[24]

Yes, this was an in-house survey and yes, the data are more than a decade old. Yet I've no reason to assume a redo would yield real differences. Of course students felt more confident—the program told them where to make changes. Of course students saved time—they didn't need to undertake much (if any) proofreading or rewriting on their own. And of course their grades were higher. Teachers tend to mark down for the kinds of errors that Grammarly likely caught before the work was submitted.

What's less clear is whether students were actually learning. Daniel de Beer, a high school student in London, wondered if such tools "become a detrimental crutch":

> Quickly correcting the red line [through which Grammarly indicates an error] without even acknowledging why the word is incorrect does not make its users better writers; instead, it will make them rely too much on the app.

What's more,

Grammarly can remove students' artistic voice when writing. Rather than using their own unique style when writing, Grammarly can strip that away from students by suggesting severe changes to their work.[25]

On its website, Grammarly claims that 85 percent of premium users report the software has made them stronger writers. But de Beer ponders whether "Grammarly gives users false security . . . by simply accepting suggestions." Might it be, he asks, that users aren't really improving but are "simply being tricked into thinking they are better writers"?

Judging from the numbers of schools acquiring Grammarly site licenses, many college administrators are voting with their purchase orders. For those schools, the software has been domesticated into students' online academic lives, alongside Microsoft Office programs or statistical packages.

We also need to ask what teachers think. If you're overworked, don't relish making grammatical and stylistic corrections on student papers, or perhaps aren't a skilled writer yourself, the likes of Grammarly can feel like Monopoly's Get-Out-of-Jail-Free card. Presumably, instructors can then devote mentoring or assessment efforts to more conceptual issues. Sounds like the argument we heard earlier that with so much writing now being auto-generated, journalists can focus on investigation and in-depth stories—rather than losing their jobs.

Writing teachers' jobs probably aren't at stake, since students are typically advised to use both human and digital resources. More concerning is when digital feedback is simply wrong or when the software ends up stifling students' individual writing voices.[26]

Moving from education to the workplace, what about employers who count on their staff being able to write competently? While I can't speak for attitudes about employee reliance on grammar checkers, we do know that employers generally care that their recent college hires can write. As we saw earlier, the National Association of Colleges and Employers reported in 2022 that 73 percent of employers they surveyed judged writing skills to be important. A different study conducted for the Association of Colleges and Universities (AAC&U) reported that 90 percent of employers polled agreed that ability to communicate through writing was "very important" or "somewhat important."[27]

Do college graduates measure up? When the AAC&U survey asked if recent graduates were "well prepared" in particular skill areas, only 44 percent of employers said yes about communicating effectively through writing. Calling on high schools and colleges to remedy the problem hasn't worked.

But maybe that pipe dream is no longer a priority. If your employees' writing is being fed through Microsoft Word or Grammarly, perhaps that's good enough.

The issue is one of values shift. Pocket calculators undermined motivation for developing and retaining basic arithmetic skills. Word processing offered an alternative to legible handwriting. A lot of adults have made their peace with math amnesia and have given up on writing by hand. It's a reasonable guess that many students will do the same after graduation, if they haven't already.

Jeeves on Autopilot

Reliance on Jeeves as digital editor of our own work is one level of writing assistance. These days, we also have options for letting technology do full-fledged drafting. Conscripting personal ghostwriters is hardly new.

Complete Letter Writers, Greeting Cards, and Telegrams

Take what are called complete letter writers. They're books providing sample missives for all occasions, whether writing home to family or dunning a business associate. The genre became wildly popular by the eighteenth century among a newly burgeoning class of correspondents, both gentlemen and ladies. As novice letter writers, they were eager for guidance.[28]

Prefabricated messages would also be welcomed with spread of the telegraph. The technology debuted in 1844 to much fanfare, but for many decades, sending messages was expensive. Since telegrams were priced by the word, prudent composition was vital. Yet many people found it hard knowing what to write. Western Union to the rescue! The company began offering prewritten text "for those who needed help in finding the right words for the right occasion."[29]

Then there are greeting cards, which first appeared in the mid-1800s. As the greeting card business flourished in the next century, undergirded by ranks of back-office writers, all you needed to send your very best for birthdays and anniversaries and holidays was your signature and maybe a salutation.[30] You can also purchase blank greeting cards and compose your own messages. But in case you want suggestions on what to write, Hallmark Cards is ready with online advice.[31]

AI as Jeeves offers modern updates to these earlier writing helpmates. But unlike the case of those pre-printed greeting cards, now you get to claim authorship.

The Camel's Nose: Email and Sentence Rewrites

Time-saver or cop-out? That's the question I keep asking about email tools that offer up phrases to incorporate in a reply or that fill in text for new emails.

Best known among the email auto-generators are Gmail Smart Reply (introduced in 2015) and Smart Compose (launched in 2018). Using deep neural networks, the systems predict what your next words would likely be. With Smart Reply, you're given three choices (akin to predictive texting). With Smart Compose, the network proposes sentence completion. Here's an example, courtesy of Google researchers: If I type "Don't forget Taco Tuesday! I'll bring the ch," the email program fills in "ips and salsa."[32] Typical of today's neural networks, Gmail tools pick up on your writing style and, with time, offer suggestions increasingly aligned with email language you've produced on your own.

Google is hardly the only company offering to draft emails for us. New systems continue popping up. Who benefits? On the plus side, AI ghostwriting can save time, especially precious for those with hefty email loads. But ask yourself if this efficiency is always worth it, especially when emailing people you care about. One risk is not conveying your actual sentiments. Be forewarned that AI-generated email tends to sound more positive than many senders' own writing style. In fact, an early prototype of Gmail Smart Reply responded "I love you" to just about anything.[33]

Here are some questions we all need to roll around in our minds:

- Are these pre-formulations doing our thinking for us?
- Are they dumbing down our vocabulary?
- Are they homogenizing our voice?[34]

We've already seen these concerns surface for predictive texting, autocorrect, and grammar checkers. "Smart" email is no different.

Beyond tools for dispatching emails, AI-driven software now happily takes on whole sentences we initially draft and offers stylistic makeovers. Take, for instance, Wordtune, part of a larger transformer-driven suite from the company AI21.[35] Wordtune's mission is "to help you translate your ideas into writing by offering completely new ways to rewrite your sentences and express yourself more successfully." The Wordtune demo takes the sentence "This opportunity interests me" and pitches alternatives, adding first-person focus or more punch. If you're looking for a formal style, maybe opt for "I find this opportunity rather appealing." More casual? On the list of suggestions: "I dig this opportunity."

So efficient. You're spared expending energy in coming up with your own best wording. Business use cases of the sort we saw earlier with tools like Jasper are understandable. But how much do we want to reduce personal writing to advertising copy? Writing, and rewriting, support clarifying meaning not only to readers but to ourselves, a message we underscored in Chapter 2. Sentence rewrite software shrinks opportunity and motivation.

Because Wordtune runs on a transformer, all the sentences are presumably generated anew. The same goes for longer auto-generated text to which you might affix your name. It's with those longer texts that deep neural networks both shine and threaten incentives for human authorship.

Into the Tent: Longer Texts

Text generators typically work on one of two principles. The first is for people to seed some initial text, which the large language model then completes. GPT-3, Sudowrite (running on GPT-3), and InferKit (using GPT-2) work this way. Interaction with ChatGPT is a bit different, in that users pose a question or make a request (like "Write a 3,000-word essay on Viking invasions that a high school student would produce").

The second system produces the entire document for you, following basic information you input. An example is Article Forge, which (as of early 2023) would craft an article, blogpost, or essay of up to 1,500 words—in 60 seconds flat.[36] Users provide some core guidance (like intent and keywords), then specify desired length and language (with seven to choose from). Push that button, and out comes the finished piece. Just pay your monthly fee.

Marketing for tools like Article Forge suggests the intended users are businesses—essentially the same customer base as for Jasper and Copysmith, whose output likely doesn't carry a human byline. But nothing stops individuals from signing up, cranking out content, and calling it their own. So much for the act of writing being a form of self-discovery. AI has no self. And if it did, it's not ours.

A logical question is who owns content produced by text generators. We're back to the thorny issue of copyright on AI-generated works. Article Forge tells users that once they've generated a piece, they are "ready to use it wherever and however [they] wish." InferKit is more circumspect. While disavowing company rights in text that users produce, the site FAQ qualifies that InferKit grants license "to use it for any purpose (to the extent that we have that right)." I can see a lawyer hovering in the background.

What if students or professionals assert authorship of material spawned by AI? Even if humans haven't stolen another person's writing, that doesn't leave them in the clear.

AI as Vice Squad

Claiming ownership of language you haven't produced yourself is hardly new. Students in Harvard's English A did it with essay assignments in the late nineteenth century. For decades, college fraternity members did it with term papers. Melania Trump did it in her 2016 speech to the Republican National Convention.[37] The president of the University of South Carolina did it in a 2021 commencement address.[38]

They all borrowed others' words without attribution. The Harvard English A students paid someone else to do the writing. Those frat boys pulled papers from a communal bin. Melania Trump's speechwriter and the now–college president helped themselves to text from other people's speeches.

From Stolen Words to Contract Cheating

Plagiarism is filching someone else's words without acknowledgment. It's for good reason Thomas Mallon's classic book was called *Stolen Words*.[39] After all, a "plagiary" originally meant a theft (or the person who commits it), coming from the Latin word for kidnapper. Stealing another person's words can be tempting. Maybe you're out of time. Or you're lazy. Or you simply don't think you'll be nabbed. While it's hard to know how common plagiarism is (we can't tally what's not caught), reports we do have are worrisome.

Our best data on students come from self-admission. For years, business professor Donald McCabe studied student cheating in its many manifestations.[40] Between 2002 and 2005, McCabe collected responses from more than 71,000 undergraduates in the United States and Canada. Among his findings about shady conduct on written assignments:

- 38 percent admitted to paraphrasing or copying a few sentences from written materials without acknowledging where they came from.
- 36 percent admitted to paraphrasing or copying a few sentences from the internet without crediting the source.
- 8 percent admitted to turning in work copied from someone else.
- 7 percent admitted to turning in work done by someone else.

And these are just transgressions that students fessed up to. It was also early in the days of plagiarizing from the ever-growing cornucopia of online offerings, which remains ripe for pilfering.

Students aren't alone. Journals—scholarly and otherwise—are replete with cases.[41] In 2022, the vice chancellor at the University of North Carolina at Chapel Hill resigned when his plagiarism on a grant application was detected.[42]

Another method for claiming other people's words as your own is fee for service. Since 2006 the practice has sported a new name: contract cheating.[43] In common parlance, it's known as using a paper mill.

Contract cheating is more pervasive than you might imagine. Using self-reports from university students around the world between 2014 and 2018, Philip Newton found a whopping 15.7 percent admitting to paying others to write academic assignments for them.[44] These days, it seems Kenyans are doing a large share of the ghostwriting in English.[45]

Again, students aren't the only culprits when it comes to versions of contract cheating. International Publisher LLC (based in Moscow) arranges for a scholar's name to be added to a paper published in a reputable journal—for a fee, of course. Clients can choose their articles, which draw upon plagiarized materials originating in Russian and then translated into English. Between 2019 and 2021, the value of such co-authorship "slots" was about $6.5 million. These services are especially common in China.[46]

What's different these days is the potential for appropriating words produced not by a human but by an AI text generator. When ChatGPT bounded into our lives at the end of November 2022, students immediately began testing the waters.

Take students at Stanford University. The school newspaper, the *Stanford Daily*, conducted an informal poll the second week of January 2023, asking students whether they had used ChatGPT for their final assignments or exams the previous month. Of the 4,497 respondents, 17 percent said yes. For those who admitted leaning on ChatGPT,

- 59.2 percent used it for brainstorming, outlining, and forming ideas.
- 29.1 percent used it for help answering multiple-choice questions.
- 7.3 percent submitted written material from ChatGPT with their own edits.
- 5.5 percent submitted written materials from ChatGPT without edits.[47]

That last number translates into 247 students saying they handed in exactly what ChatGPT produced. Think about it. Only 4 percent of undergraduate applicants get into Stanford, suggesting those admitted are more than capable of doing their assignments and exams. While the poll was hardly scientific, the results should give us pause.

Considering the many tasks transformer-based programs like ChatGPT can take on—searching datasets for information, summarizing, doing translation, and coding, to name a few—the prospects are huge of bots being used in lieu of human effort for other academic endeavors. By early 2023, researchers in fields like science, law, and medicine were already testing the waters. And alarm bells began ringing.

Take the experiment to see if scientists could spot whether a research paper abstract was written by a human or ChatGPT. For ChatGPT's handiwork, human reviewers were only able to spot 68 percent of the abstracts as being AI-generated, incorrectly labeling 32 percent as written by humans. For the genuine abstracts, humans correctly identified 86 percent of them, but for the other 14 percent, the judges mistakenly attributed the work to ChatGPT.[48]

In the case of law, we've already seen how legal software can draw on huge datasets to generate legal writing. Perhaps it's no surprise that a tool like ChatGPT can do at least a middling job on law school exams or even bar exams. A study at the University of Minnesota Law School took actual law school exams containing essays and multiple-choice questions. Set to the task, ChatGPT performed, on average, at the same level as a C+ student. Not great, but passing.[49] There's also research indicating that GPT models can pass the evidence and torts sections in the multiple-choice component of the Uniform Bar Exam in the United States.[50]

Credentialing in other professions isn't exempt. A group of medical researchers had ChatGPT take the US Medical Licensing Exam. The bot performed at or near the passing threshold for all three parts of the exams.[51]

For now, would-be lawyers or physicians aren't using the likes of ChatGPT to take exams for them. And it's likely we'll find good uses for ChatGPT's skills in legal and medical education. However, we're at the very early stages of navigating our way through this brave new world, so it's too soon to know how the scale will tip between education and cheating.

To Catch a Thief

With so much appropriation of the written word, how do you catch cheating? Traditional methods included luck, familiarity with source materials, or hours of library gumshoeing. Sometimes the writing style gave away the culprit. Or you knew the person claiming authorship couldn't write that well.

For nabbing plagiarism, digital tools have been enlisted for some time. Searching corpora online is easier than working manually. Stylometric software can "fingerprint" a writing style, analyzing vocabulary choice, syntactic usage, and even punctuation patterns.[52] Beleaguered faculty suspecting student plagiarism have regularly turned to the internet to search for stolen words.

But these days, there's much higher-powered ammunition: AI software scrutinizing texts for plagiarism. The towering giant here is Turnitin.

The company we know as Turnitin dates back to 1998. An early goal of its four founders (then doctoral students at Berkeley) was to create an online peer-review system. That function, now called PeerMark, remains available in today's suite of options. However, with exploding use of the internet feeding escalation in unacknowledged online "borrowing," Turnitin shifted its focus to plagiarism detection.

For a detection engine to work, you need a vast reservoir of text, which the company has. As of 2022, their dataset contained 99.3 billion internet pages, 56,000 journals, and 89.4 million journal articles.[53] If it's published or online, Turnitin will likely find it.

But there's an additional source the company mines: student papers—1.8 billion and counting. This worldwide repository of prior submissions helps to combat the fraternity file gambit of submitting a paper someone previously turned in. What's more, the company can compare students' new assignments against papers they earlier wrote. If the styles don't match, Turnitin cries foul. Think of it as linguistic facial recognition.

Of course, with contract cheating and now tools like ChatGPT, Turnitin needs to look beyond its trough of existing student papers. Two weeks after ChatGPT launched, Turnitin mounted a blog post about meeting the AI writing challenge. A month later, the company posted a "sneak preview" of how the company was proceeding.[54]

Turnitin isn't alone. As of early 2023, the detection program generating the big buzz was GPTZero, written by Princeton senior Edward Tian.[55] Following on its heels was Stanford's DetectGPT and OpenAI's "AI classifier for indicating AI-written text."[56]

Educational buy-in for Turnitin is huge. According to a company blog post in January 2021, the software was used by 40 million students from 15,000 educational institutions in 140 countries.[57]

Students aren't the only ones whose work is being scrutinized. Turnitin's parent company, iParadigm, has turned its plagiary-detection power on the larger scholarly and professional world with a product called iThenticate.[58] Subscribers include a huge number of corporations and governmental organizations. It's also the tool of choice for scholarly journals. In fact, for authors submitting manuscripts, it's increasingly the first river to cross. Publishers like Elsevier or Taylor & Francis routinely run submissions through Crossref Similarity Check, a tool powered by iThenticate, before the papers go out for peer review. Another market for iThenticate is college admissions offices, looking to vet those all-important application essays.

Turnitin and iThenticate may be the most commonly used plagiarism tools, though they have competitors. Besides a range of stand-alone programs (such as HelioBLAST, Viper, or Copyscape), plagiarism checkers are incorporated into other products, including Grammarly. Text-generation programs like Article

Forge and Jasper do plagiarism sweeps by running their materials through Copyscape. Since the datasets these programs draw from contain millions of words—and sentences—other people have written, there's always the possibility an identical string of someone else's words could inadvertently surface.

But how do you spot contract cheating? This one's trickier, since the text is written anew. No searchable dataset. Turnitin can't help much, except to compare the new submission with the person's earlier writing style and presumed level of competence. Mediocre students don't suddenly craft polished, sophisticated papers. Yet don't underestimate the cunning of contract cheaters. Dave Tomar, who spent a decade as an academic ghostwriter for paper mills, explained that sometimes his clients requested intentionally flawed English or dumbed down vocabulary or syntax.[59]

And now there's automatic text generation. It's increasingly sophisticated, accessible, and skilled at mirroring writing styles. As we saw in the Prologue, Sudowrite (running on GPT-3) did a credible job of emulating the writing of Gay Talese. I'd still rather read Talese originals. But if I'm not already familiar with all his writings (think Beethoven's symphonies versus Bach's fugues), it's not clear I could tell the difference. If students in the future can feed in samples of their own writing and then use an AI text generator to create a new assignment in their style, will we know?

The Obsession with Plagiarism

After decades as a university faculty member (including, for several years, as convener-in-chief of plagiarism review cases), I've seen my share of student attempts at gaming writing assignments. And yet, now that I've been surveying digital software for catching plagiarism—among students and professionals—I sense something has changed.

For students, if their institution is one of those 15,000-and-counting using Turnitin, it can feel as if Big Brother really is watching. Play around on the company's site, and you'll find a plethora of tools—some for use by students (to pre-check their work for plagiarism, before submitting for grading) and some for "investigators" (meaning faculty or academic integrity boards). Among the weirder programs for investigators are "flags" of student attempts to fly under the Turnitin radar. One end run the software can unearth is substituting letters or symbols from another alphabet. Another is "hidden characters" put in the same color as the background.[60] The scofflaws' intention is to submit plagiarized text they have doctored so it gets past the Turnitin gatekeeper. Who knew students—or plagiarism trackers—could be so sneaky?

With new public access to AI text-generation tools like ChatGPT, what about fooling your professor into believing that you, not a bot, wrote that essay? Maybe not so hard. Take what the bot produced and doctor it a bit: Make a few grammatical mistakes. (ChatGPT's grammar is practically flawless.) Use less common words. (The AI algorithms generating text predict the next word by drawing on word combinations most frequent in its storehouse.) Throw in a couple of lines describing something personal, local, or timely that's not in the bot's data, like how many classified documents were eventually found in the homes or offices of US presidents or vice presidents. (ChatGPT's "knowledge" ended with 2021, and the bot has no internet access.)

Then there's professional scholarship. Doing plagiarism reviews before journal submissions are shipped out to readers reminds me of airport screening before boarding a plane. For sure, the deluge of scholarly plagiarism is unacceptable. But let's think through reasons for it. Publish-or-perish (or at least no salary raise) has driven an unchecked expansion in the number of journals published, so there's a better chance of finding somewhere to place your article. It's also fueled scholars' temptation to succumb to drastic measures to keep their publication rates up. The scholarship arms race now waged between universities needs to be stopped. Few people read most published scholarship, and the drive to keep churning it out pushes too many otherwise decent people off the path of righteousness.

The plagiarism challenge also reaches into the business and marketing world, where words (and ad lines) are prized for their commercial value, not for association with an author's name. I seriously doubt consumers would care if "It's not fake anything. It's real Dynel" were written by GPT-3 rather than Jane Trahey. However, since GPT-3 scrapes data from the web, there's the chance that "new" text might inadvertently replicate strings of words already out there. We need plagiarism checking to guard against copyright or trademark infringement.

And the rest of us? If you're asked to give a speech or write a grant application, credit your sources.

In looking at AI as personal writing Jeeves, we've hinted at ways in which the tools can function collaboratively rather than unilaterally. As we'll see in the next chapter, these days the AI world is abuzz with talk about "humans in the loop," meaning partnering with the technology rather than ceding it full control. Some in the AI business are even suggesting we rethink who's primary and who's second fiddle, and instead speak of "AI in the loop," where humans are indisputably running the show.

ELEVEN

Human–AI Symbiosis

It's Pleistocene times and you're stalking a mastodon. Chances are you can't take it down on your own. The assist might come from a fellow member of your tribe, though also from a piece of technology. Ironically for the beast, a good way to fell your prey is by hurling a sharpened mastodon bone at it.[1]

Humans have devised countless ways of getting a helping hand. We collaborate with people or technologies to improve efficiency or effectiveness, or to boost empowerment. A not-too-hidden advantage of most collaboration is saving time.

A Matter of Time

It's faster to move the contents of a house if two people team up. I cover more distance in the same time span if I bike or take a car rather than walk. The quest for cutting the time often drives invention. Trains are faster than horses. The telegraph was faster than the Pony Express or mail-bags-by-train.

Or take the original polygraph. Not the machine for helping detect liars but one for making an additional copy ("poly" plus "graph") of a handwritten document while you're penning the original. In 1803, Philadelphia inventor John Isaac Hawkins patented his "duplicating polygraph."[2] The machine so impressed Thomas Jefferson that he not only acquired multiple machines but declared the device "the finest invention of the present age."[3]

While Hawkins's polygraphy only created one copy, the notion of saving time in duplicating written text underlies the printing press. Scribal labor couldn't compete. In 1492—a bit less than forty years after Gutenberg's first use of moveable type in the West—Johannes Trithemius (the abbot of Sponheim) wrote to complain. Trithemius argued in *De Laude Scriptorum (In Praise of Scribes)* that the printing press made people lazy (by not "bothering with copying by hand").[4] Even further back, following invention of moveable type in China in the late ninth century, scholars objected that printing was sacrilegious and threatened their jobs as copyists.[5] At least on the latter point, we can all agree.

Collaboration in AI: New Name, Old Concept

Since Turing's time, a persistent question has been how much we're looking for intelligent machines to replace humans and how much we seek collaboration. Today, economists like Erik Brynjolfsson urge us to distinguish between automation (replacement) and augmentation (collaboration).[6] Brynjolfsson calls the automation model "the Turing Trap." He argues that the goal in AI shouldn't be building machines that match human intelligence (passing all manner of Turing tests) but programs giving human efforts a boost.

Think back to the late 1940s and early 1950s when Turing was writing about machine intelligence. While large computers existed, they weren't smart. The notion of a machine achieving human-level thinking was entirely theoretical. A more realistic bar was enlisting computer technology to automate labor. As we said earlier, the automation principle was central for the Allies in World War II, when the British Colossus was built to hasten codebreaking and the American ENIAC was designed to accelerate ballistics calculations. But elsewhere, automation could be deemed a social threat. Christopher Strachey projected computers would take over the work of clerks, both for arithmetical tasks and, eventually, for jobs involving written language.

Was having AI go it alone a realistic goal? Researchers working on early computer translation suggested no. Even now, for translation projects requiring precision or nuance, human pre-editing and especially post-editing remain part of a collaborative process.

In today's swirl of AI hopes and hype, there's much talk of prioritizing "humans in the loop"—acting jointly with AI, using AI to augment human intelligence rather than replace us. (The wording is generally "human [singular] in the loop," but I prefer the more inclusive plural.) Catchy though the phrase is, there's little new about the concept.

Human–Computer Interaction: An Earlier Model

Before there was talk of human–AI collaboration, there was the notion of "dialogue." The idea, emerging in the 1980s, was that computers and people needed to communicate with each other, a concept that came to be known as human–computer interaction (HCI).[7] If you want to harness the machines to get stuff done, humans and computers need to be able to converse.

Ben Shneiderman (the computer scientist who worked on hyperlinks) has long been the leading light of research on HCI. In 1987, he laid out "golden rules" for designing interfaces between humans and machines, such as striving for consistency and reducing (human) short-term memory load.[8]

More recently, work on human–computer interaction has sometimes been hitched to one of today's hot buzz phrases: human-centered AI. (More on that in a minute.) Familiar AI challenges like needing to root out bias or making AI's workings more transparent have been earmarked as areas where human-centered AI research can contribute to the broader human–computer interaction agenda.[9] Regardless of how we name the enterprise, what matters is that when talking about how computers work and what they're capable of, we need to include humans in the picture.

Looping in Humans

A loop is a closed unit. Preface the word "feedback," and you get a particular sort of symbiosis. Some part of the system's output can serve as input. Think of mechanical feedback loops. If the temperature rises, the furnace shuts off or the air conditioning kicks on. Or take economics. As share prices rise on the stock market, people buy more stock, which makes prices increase even more.

Now comes the role people might have "in the loop" with computers. One possibility is evaluating—or improving—program output, and then feeding results back to the computer. This is the sense typically invoked in discussing computer software. For instance, when we talk about "humans in the loop" for machine learning programs, we might have in mind joint efforts to increase the programs' accuracy, speed, or efficiency.[10]

But there's another, looser meaning of the phrase, more akin to the ordinary expression "keep me in the loop." Invoking these words doesn't necessarily mean we're asking to be part of evaluation or decision making that circles back to further action, though that's a possibility. We might just want to stay abreast of what's happening. Keep me informed. Keep me posted.

In AI contexts, calls for humans in the loop don't always refer to the same scenario. The words might indicate humans editing a program's output to improve its functioning. The meaning could be collaboration in a different sense, as when you feed GPT-3 some starter text and the program writes the rest of the paragraph. Or the phrase might imply something closer to "keep me in the loop," meaning that AI researchers should take their ultimate goal to be improving the lives of people, not creating intelligent machines that potentially replace us.

This human-centered approach is now woven into the fabric of a burgeoning cluster of AI research initiatives. To name a few: Stanford's Institute for Human-Centered Artificial Intelligence, UC Berkeley's Center for Human-Compatible Artificial Intelligence, and the University of Utrecht's Human-Centered Artificial Intelligence focus area. IBM boasts working on human-centered AI, and Ben Shneiderman has a new book, *Human-Centered AI*.[11]

These days, when it comes to working on AI, humans aren't just in the loop. They're often front and center.

Human–AI Teamwork

Think about the ways humans might team up with AI. The purpose might be for AI to assist humans in a task. Turn the tables, and human effort could be funneled into improving the way the AI does its job. A third option: human–AI co-creation.

AI Cognitive Assists

If you're looking to maximize your mental efforts, AI might help. In the words of Mira Murati, OpenAI's senior vice president of research and product, AI can enable "specialized professionals to focus on creativity and innovation rather than menial tasks."[12] The aspiration of harnessing computers to conserve human brain power for harder tasks goes back more than half a century. Recall Warren Teitelman's goal for his program PILOT: saving people's energies for tackling more difficult problems.

Another kind of assist is through interaction between AI and the user. Kevin Scott, chief technology officer at Microsoft, put it this way: AI "lets me get more mileage out of the brain I was born with."[13]

Today there are boundless examples of human–computer collaboration. We'll sample a trio: in chess, coding, and mental health.

HUMAN–AI COLLABORATION IN CHESS

Turing had predicted computers would probably play "very good chess." He was proven right, with the game becoming one of AI's early victories. In May 1997, IBM's Deep Blue bested Garry Kasparov, a chess grandmaster. In Kasparov's words, "Suddenly [Deep Blue] played like a god for one moment."[14]

Should human chess players pack up and go home? Kasparov said no. Instead, he turned the game from competition to collaboration, inventing what he called "advanced chess." Each side of the match is a team of human and computer.[15] For a time, it seemed that human–computer teams could beat stand-alone computers. As Kasparov wrote in 2010, in competitions, "Human strategic guidance combined with the tactical acuity of a computer was overwhelming."[16] But times change. Given today's deep neural networks and transformers, all bets may be off whether human–AI chess collaboration can still triumph over machines alone.

HUMAN–AI COLLABORATION IN CODING

OpenAI's launch of Codex was a big deal in the world of human–AI collaboration. Like GPT-3 (on which it's based), Codex starts with some human input and then predicts what comes next. But unlike GPT-3's usual text output, Codex serves up lines of computer code.

The notion of collaboration in coding is hardly new. The hacker culture of the 1960s embraced sharing code (human to human). Open source became a programming lifestyle, epitomized by Linus Torvalds's public release of his operating system Linux in 1991.[17] Commitment to sharing intellectual property, particularly in digital form, was epitomized in the establishment of Creative Commons in 2002 "to help address the tension" existing between creators' "ability to share digital works globally and copyright regulation."[18] In early 2022, Meta (aka Facebook) released the code for its large language model OPT (Open Pretrained Transformer), also making OPT freely available for non-commercial use.[19]

In today's programming world, the spirit of sharing is embodied in GitHub. Founded in 2008 (and later acquired by Microsoft), GitHub is a website where programmers can post and collaborate on code. (Fun fact: It was Linus Torvalds who had coined the word "Git" in context of a new collaborative program he was devising.[20]) GitHub has a huge usership. As of late 2021, more than 73 million programmers were participating, and many of their development projects are open source.

OpenAI's Codex and GitHub became a marriage made in heaven when, in 2021, they joined forces to create the platform known as Copilot. This time, instead of training GPT-3 on billions of words of text, the AI was trained on code, from GitHub and other online sources. As journalist Clive Thompson describes it, Copilot is "essentially autocomplete for software development."[21] Humans are in the loop, but Copilot does a goodly amount of the labor. What's more, the initial human input doesn't need to be code. It might be a natural language request like "Write a program that organizes all the donors in my database by zip code." The natural language capability is amazing but perhaps not surprising, given that GPT-3 is already a language wizard.

You might wonder whether Copilot only saves humans time or whether it also makes them better at programming. The question parallels what we asked in the last chapter about spellcheck and grammar check programs: Do they just clean up after us or make us better writers? You'll find believers on both sides. Yet for writing and coding alike, among the most grateful users are those with the fewest skills.

There are still bugs in Copilot (as with AI-as-author tools), so humans are smart to post-edit. For now, people retain a role in the coding loop. The program and humans are, literally, co-pilots. As with jobs in journalism, it's too soon to tell if employment for programmers could be imperiled.

HUMAN–AI COLLABORATION IN MENTAL HEALTH

The pandemic shone a harsh light on the continuing mental health struggles of so many adults and children. In 2020, it was estimated that 47.1 million people in the United States—19 percent of the population—had a mental health condition.[22] The numbers keep growing. Worldwide, there's a paucity of resources within sufferers' reach.

Could AI be of help? We've come far since Weizenbaum's ELIZA therapy program. But how far?

AI has engendered a flowering of mobile app chatbots designed to deliver mental health support that's both private and affordable. The programs have names like Woebot, Pacifica, Wysa, and MoodKit. Many are based on cognitive behavioral therapy (CBT), which is designed to help patients reframe their negative ways of thinking into more productive mindsets.[23] CBT has been recognized as an effective treatment, sometimes more successful than medication.

With the new apps, natural language processing tools replace the human therapist. There's evidence that AI-driven programs can work, at least some of the time. In the case of Woebot, a series of studies (mostly conducted at Stanford University School of Medicine) point to clear benefits for combatting substance abuse, reducing symptoms of depression, and managing postpartum mood changes.[24]

There's another way that AI and humans have been partnering to improve mental health treatment. This time humans remain the therapists, but AI is enlisted to enhance therapists' skills. Again, natural language processing plays a starring role. A mental health service in the UK called ieso has been using NLP to analyze conversations between therapists and patients, looking to pinpoint which kinds of language are associated with the strongest improvement for various disorders. These insights are then brought back to therapists, both those with years of experience and new trainees. One pragmatic goal is to make the time therapists and patients spend together more efficient, so more patients can be seen.[25]

Assisting AI

If AI can assist humans, what about humans helping AI? We're anthropomorphizing here, but the idea is using input from humans to improve AI performance—a classic feedback loop.

Anytime people are involved in the AI training process, you're activating that loop. In the early days of ImageNet, human judges were conscripted to sort through potential image candidates, drawn from the internet, for inclusion in the ImageNet dataset. Over time, as AI (powered by deep neural networks) became increasingly sophisticated, the programs required less and less human help.

Collaboration is now finding its way into the operation of transformers. In early 2022, OpenAI released InstructGPT, a refinement that became the default language model on the company's API (application programming interface, through which online applications communicate with each other).[26] OpenAI's strategy was shifting the way its transformer worked. While GPT-3 was trained to predict the next word in a text, InstructGPT was designed to respond to user requests: to use OpenAI's example, "Explain the moon landing to a six-year-old in a few sentences." The new model was keyed to respond with what users want to know, not just to churn out words.

In building InstructGPT, OpenAI went collaborative, inserting humans into the training process. Using the programming technique of reinforcement learning, humans "demonstrated" the kinds of responses that were desirable, enabling programmers to fine-tune the transformer. The goal was to help clean up GPT-3's act, given the ever-present risks of transformers spitting out untruths, bias, and bile. The process seems to be working. When output from InstructGPT is compared with that of GPT-3, InstructGPT is more truthful, makes up ("hallucinates") less often, and is less toxic. And the world of large language models continues evolving. OpenAI describes ChatGPT as a "sibling model to InstructGPT."[27]

Meanwhile, DeepMind (owned by Google/Alphabet) has been drawing on human feedback to improve Google search results. In September 2022, the company announced Sparrow, a chatbot built on their large language model called Chinchilla.[28] Sparrow's job is responding to human queries by doing online searches, but then giving actual answers rather than lists of hits. After all, the purpose of a chatbot is two-way dialogue. DeepMind's hope has been to cut down on the amount of misinformation and stereotyping for which online search results have been infamous. The fundamental motivation for the project is to improve the safety of using large language models, which now underlie online searches. You don't want someone drinking bleach just because a random online site said it cures hiccups.

Like InstructGPT, Sparrow is built on reinforcement learning. For the training, human participants were asked to choose among several answers to the same question. These preferences were then used to tweak results the chatbot might offer in future queries. What's more, like a good student, Sparrow was responsible for naming its sources (here, links to sites it used for constructing its answers).

Co-Creativity

Teaming up humans and AI has obvious mutual benefits when it comes to getting work done. Do these advantages also hold when the "work" is intended to be creative? Earlier, we talked about creative efforts where AI took center stage. What about when AI and humans collaborate?

Admittedly, it's sometimes hard drawing the line between solo and joint credit. Humans wrote the programs through which computers composed Bach fugues and painted *The Next Rembrandt*. But now let's rejigger the balance by looking at results from interaction happening during the generation process itself.

The guru of interactive creation is Ge Wang, a musician-*cum*-computer scientist-*cum*-designer at Stanford.[29] In Wang's words,

> the human-in-the-loop approach [to design] reframes an automation problem as a Human-Computer Interaction (HCI) design problem. In turn, we've broadened the question of "how do you build a smarter system?" to "how do we incorporate useful, meaningful human interaction into the system?"[30]

Wang contrasts this approach with what he calls reliance on a "Big Red Button," meaning AI technology (here, for creative design) that "reliably delivers the right answers while hiding the process that leads to them." In other words, inexplicable creative AI.

Wang argues that by bringing humans into the interactive design process, you reap multiple benefits:

- increasing transparency about how the work was created
- incorporating human judgments into the creation

- moving from searching for "perfect" AI algorithms to designing works that can iteratively and interactively be improved upon

As a musician, Wang has shown how AI and humans can join forces through his inventions like the Ocarina (which converts an iPhone into a flute-like instrument)[31] and the Stanford Laptop Orchestra.[32]

Examples of artistic collaborative work abound. One of them is paintings by the performance artist Sougwen Chung.[33] Chung paints alongside robots, which she refers to as her collaborators. Sometimes the robot arms respond to what she's just painted—and vice versa. She has also fed into the computer's memory a collection of her previous artwork and, more recently, patterns from surveillance video of pedestrians crossing streets in New York City, bringing the public into the collaboration. Chung and her robots co-create paintings before live audiences. Like Ge Wang, her goal isn't perfection but to see what human–AI cooperation might conjure up.

Finally, let's get to humans partnering with AI (or vice versa) in writing projects.

AI in the Writing Loop: From Outsourcing to Co-Creation

If you want AI's help with your writing, you have options. You might outsource the job entirely. Alternatively, get AI to kickstart your own work. Or, try co-creativity.

Outsourcing Writing Labor

Some of us enjoy writing. Others find it tedious or downright painful. Maybe we have writer's block. Perhaps we're lazy. Whatever the case, outsourcing production of strings of words has increasingly become the method of choice for including humans in the AI writing loop.

In earlier chapters, we looked at how contemporary AI can generate new text essentially out of whole cloth. But we also hinted at opportunities for a smidge of collaboration between user and software, including with business-oriented programs.

Think back on Copysmith's website tagline: "Content crafted by AI, perfected by humans." In its promotional material, Copysmith stresses human–AI partnership:

> Our goal at Copysmith isn't to replace humans with machines but to streamline content creation and delivery by enabling human–AI collaboration.

Yet tellingly, Copysmith goes on to make an analogy between its services and calculators:

> Even though mathematicians can live without them, the use of calculators drastically reduces the time it takes to solve equations. So, instead of spending say ten minutes to manually solve an equation, you can do that within ten seconds using a calculator.[34]

With calculators, humans input the numbers, and then the calculators do all the work. With article (or blog or ad) generators, humans enter a couple of parameters and potentially engage in some post-edits. But make no mistake: It's AI doing the writing.

Not all outsourcing is so full-throated. With spellcheck, autocomplete, and grammar programs, humans take the lead. but then AI kicks in. Whether AI's role is ultimately beneficial or not is a dilemma we take on in the next chapter.

Boosting Writing Efforts

More genuinely collaborative are AI writing tools that people use to jumpstart their writing. Think of jumpstarting a car battery. When the battery's dead, the engine won't turn over. In the world of humans and writing, the equivalent is writer's block or paucity of ideas. To give batteries or human brains the spark needed to get chugging, you harness an external assist—connection to a Good Samaritan's battery or an AI tool.

Sudowrite (the program enlisted to channel Gay Talese's style) offers this kind of jumpstart. Besides writing stand-alone text, the software presents itself as a "brainstorm buddy" to "bust writer's block."[35] Author Jennifer Lepp took Sudowrite up on the offer. Josh Dzieza has an insightful piece in *The Verge* on Lepp and text-generation programs like Sudowrite.[36] Lepp's story is instructive, especially given the surge in uptake of this kind of program by self-published authors.

Lepp makes good money as an indie author, distributing her books through Amazon's Kindle Direct Publishing. Her specialty is the paranormal cozy mystery. (Look it up. It's a real subgenre.) To keep the gravy train running, she sets herself a strict schedule for how many words she needs to write by when. Every nine weeks, Lepp comes out with a new novel. The pace was exhausting. To help ease the burden, she turned to Sudowrite.

Initially, Lepp largely used the program to come up with alternative wording and to write short descriptions of scenes or objects. Time and energy saved. Soon she found herself relying on Sudowrite to do more and more of the composing. Her production rate increased, but she realized something else was happening. She no longer felt immersed in her characters and plots. She no longer dreamt about them:

> "It didn't feel like mine anymore. It was very uncomfortable to look back over what I wrote and not really feel connected to the words or ideas."

Reading Lepp's words, I kept hearing in my head the comment a student in my research had made about predictive texting: "I feel like the message I sent is not mine."

Dzieza's article also includes an interview with Joanna Penn, another indie novelist. Penn shared her thinking about how tools like Sudowrite might be used in years to come. Quoting Dzieza,

> [Penn] foresees a future where writers are more akin to "creative directors," giving AI high-level instruction and refining its output. She imagines fine-tuning a model on her own work or entering into a consortium of other authors in her genre and licensing out their model to other writers.

Adolph Knipe's grammatizator, at last.

Besides generating text, Sudowrite has more tricks up its sleeve. One is offering editorial feedback on what you and Sudowrite have turned out. The tool is in keeping with a growing market for AI-driven programs that can analyze lengthy, even book-long manuscripts.

Say you've drafted a novel and want feedback before seeking a publisher. Traditionally, novelists have relied on friends, literary agents, writing groups, editors, or significant others for comments. If you don't have humans to call on, these days you might sign up for an AI program like Marlowe, which bills itself as a "self-editing tool."[37] In just fifteen minutes, you get an extensive report analyzing everything from narrative arc to pacing to word choice (too many clichés? repeated words or phrases?) to characters' personality traits to the usual spelling, punctuation, and offensive language alerts.

It's no accident that a prime mover behind Marlowe was Matthew Jockers, co-author along with Jodie Archer of *The Bestseller Code*.[38] Drawing on the kinds of forensic linguistic tools common in identifying authorship, Archer and Jockers set out to show how certain lexical choices, grammatical styles, and plot structures correlate with *New York Times* bestseller lists. If their model is credible, perhaps the real issue is that bestsellers have simply become too formulaic.

If you're not into novels, maybe you'd like to predict movie box office hits. Hollywood is already using AI for analyzing scripts to decide what motion pictures to make.[39] Marketing decisions made by Netflix? AI is hard at work behind the scenes.[40]

Writing Co-Creation

Beyond taking on labor outsourcing and giving assists, AI has also emerged as a more full-fledged writing partner. By the mid-2010s, a human–AI collaborative resulted in the musical *Beyond the Fence*, performed in a London theater in 2016.[41] We've already mentioned the Japanese novel *The Day a Computer Writes a Novel*, a remix between human and AI composition.

As we saw earlier, co-creative story writing dates back decades. For James Meehan's Tale-Spin, human users set the story parameters. In hyperfiction, readers had active roles in rearranging the parts and or choosing endings. But the degree of creativity and collaboration was limited. Technology has evolved and so have partnership options. Like Sougwen Chung's symbiotic painting with robots, computer scientists and authors are now exploring what active writing collaboration can look like. There are even songwriting contests for AI–human teams.[42]

One way of keeping a finger on the partnership pulse is checking out research presented at the International Conference on Computational Creativity (ICCC), an annual event of the Association for Computational Creativity.[43] To dip a toe into the ocean of options, here are two projects from the 2021 conference.

COLLABORATIVE STORYTELLING IN IMPROV THEATER

Live improvisational theater requires quick-witted and creative actors. For my money, best-in-class is the Improvised Shakespeare Company, historically based in Chicago.[44] A cast member invites the audience to propose a title for the evening's performance. Selecting one from those shouted out, the performer improvises a Shakespeare-style prologue. Soon, the rest of the troupe materializes on stage, and the wholly spontaneous play unfolds. Think of GPT-3 (the audience) priming the pump and then humans (the acting troupe) generating the rest.

What happens if you embed an AI into an improv troupe? Boyd Branch, Piotr Mirowski, and Kory Mathewson decided to find out.[45] The researchers teamed up GPT-3 with a professional group of improv actors to create scenes, live on stage. Unlike the Shakespeare improv, GPT-3 contributed lines throughout the narrative arc. In the experiment, a visual avatar "embodied" GPT-3, with a human narrator delivering GPT-3's lines to lend realism. Other technical wizardry ensured the AI suggestions were both relevant and not offensive. Surveyed afterwards, one of the human actors observed that "[the AI] helped the plot move forward, but without being too prescriptive," while another found GPT-3 "added a level of randomness and craziness different from the human brain."

INFLUENCE OF AUTOMATICALLY GENERATED
TEXT ON CREATIVE WRITING

We learn from examples. Sometimes they inspire us. It's often said that the best way to become a good writer is to read voraciously.

Much of the work on human–AI collaboration in writing entails co-creation. But what if humans drew upon AI-written output as examples for upping the creativity in their solo (human) writing? Would their writing now be more interesting than what they produced on their own? That's the question Melissa Roemmele took on.[46]

Using the idea of "inspiration through observation," Roemmele had both humans and GPT-2 create sentences out of lists of words. In one condition, the human authors and the AI produced their sentences independently. In the other, the humans observed what GPT-2 was generating at the same time they (the humans) were doing their own writing. The research question: Which human sentences were more interesting, defined as suggesting a story that people would want to read. A group of flesh-and-blood judges rated both sets of human sentences, concluding that the ones people created while looking over GPT-2's shoulder had a higher level of what Roemmele called "storiability." Modeling seemed to up the writers' game. Whether AI coaching can make humans more interesting writers in the long run remains to be seen.

Beyond these collaborations, there's one more I found particularly fascinating. In some ways, it's not as collaborative as the examples we've just been talking about. But it shines a light on how AI might help when words genuinely fail us. It's a true story, poignantly told by Vauhini Vara and GPT-3.[47]

Vara is an accomplished journalist and novelist, who's also intrigued with technology. Early in the life and times of GPT-3, she tried out the platform and became enthralled. What distinguishes her story is her decision to enlist GPT-3 in a task she had long avoided: writing about her sister's death from Ewing sarcoma, a rare form of bone cancer.

Vara's attempts began tentatively. She offered a brief sentence, to which GPT-3 responded with some bland ramblings. Vara tried again, adding more information—and personal feelings. The process continued for nine call-and-response sets, during which Vara wrote increasingly more openly:

as I tried to write more honestly, the AI seemed to be doing the same. It made sense, given that GPT-3 generates its own text based on the language it had been fed: Candor, apparently, begat candor.

As expected, GPT-3 produced some inconsistencies and falsehoods. But they were irrelevant to Vara's objective. GPT-3 enabled Vara to finally tell her own story by partnering with a non-judgmental fellow writer.

Whose Loop?

Human–computer interaction. Human-centered AI. Humans in the loop. Does it matter what we call human–machine collaboration? Linguists aren't the only ones caring about semantics. So do politicians and writers. "Incursion" and "assault" both accurately label an invasion, but the connotations are starkly different. The same goes for deciding to talk about "humans in the loop" or "AI in the loop."

For its fall 2022 conference, the Stanford's Institute for Human-Centered Artificial Intelligence (HAI) took as its theme "AI in the Loop: Humans in Charge." In the program description, the conference organizers wrote:

> Human-in-the-loop artificial intelligence refers to AI decision making processes where humans may provide feedback or confirmation. . . . [W]e hope to challenge [conference] participants to rethink this phrase and consider a future where humans remain at the center of all AI technologies. AI should effectively communicate and collaborate with people to augment their capabilities and make their lives better and more enjoyable. Humans are not simply "in-the-loop." Humans are in charge; AI is "in-the-loop."[48]

Back in the Prologue we talked about fears that AI might outsmart us and take over control. The new tack is to insist that humans remain at the helm, to have AI serve us and not vice versa. I'm reminded of those tripods Homer describes in the *Iliad*, scuttling about as they deliver food to the deities. Today's AI servants are infinitely smarter, but the goal is to keep them subservient. Partners, maybe, but junior partners.

As I think about giving priority to humans in the ways we design and employ AI, there's one clear area where we hold all the cards in deciding the place AI has in our lives. That's in choosing what role we want—or don't want—AI to play in our writing. In short, When is AI welcome?

TWELVE

Do We Always Welcome AI?

AI has proven incredibly powerful for authoring its own text, cleaning up what we write, and standing ready to collaborate. Increasingly, the tools are being taken for granted. We've talked about potential consequences for unquestioned reliance on AI's writing brawn, like plummeting motivation for learning foreign languages or for remembering spelling rules. Another likely victim is writing in our own voice, not marching lockstep with the machine.

What do today's everyday writers think about AI as a writing technology? You can't know if you don't ask.

Surveying Everyday Writers

Before I began work on AI and writing, I'd spent nearly a decade exploring differences between how we read in print versus on digital devices.[1] Psychologists and reading specialists have produced a myriad of experimental studies comparing things like comprehension for each type of reading, but I was interested in something different: What did readers have to say? On which medium did they feel they concentrated better? Multitasked more?

At the time, the move to reading digitally was galloping ahead. There was the convenience, plus typically eBooks were less expensive. Digital reading was becoming domesticated. You might assume most readers wholeheartedly endorsed the shift. Not so simple. One tidbit from my cross-national study of university students: 92 percent said they concentrated best when reading in print.

This time around, I set out to discover how much everyday writers welcomed the efficiencies of AI as personal writing Jeeves. While I was at it, I stirred in a couple more topics. Here's the list:

- spelling
- editing and proofreading
- software that writes for you
- handwriting
- impact of AI on writing-intensive jobs

Designing the Surveys

To explore what users thought about AI and writing, I ran two online surveys. Both were convenience samples, meaning that I took the participants available to me. Proper random samples (controlling for gender, age, education, and whatever else seems relevant) are a research gold standard. But convenience samples served my purpose, since I was looking for trends and insights, not level of statistical significance or oracular conclusions.

The first survey was in Europe, primary involving Italian doctoral students attending a summer program on digital humanities and digital communication at the University of Modena and Reggio Emilia (UNIMORE). The research was done in summer 2022, though I had previously tried out many of the questions with UNIMORE masters students the year before.[2] I ended up with 105 people taking the survey (about two-thirds male, as it turned out), mostly between ages twenty and thirty-five.

The second survey, in fall 2022, was of Americans. This time, I had 100 participants (60 percent female—typical of US convenience samples), with an average age of twenty-five. I used essentially the same questions in both surveys, with a couple of exceptions. For the US research, I dropped out a few earlier questions and added several others. Some questions were multiple choice, while others invited open-ended answers.

What did I find? I'll start with spelling results. But first a preamble.

Spelling

English spelling isn't fair. Unlike the more well-behaved orthographies for Italian or Finnish, where there's close correspondence between letters and how they're pronounced, English is a truant. Just think of "read" versus "read" versus "red." Or "laugh" versus "sleigh" (same final "gh," different pronunciations). Most times we can track down historical explanations for the troublemakers, including invasions, borrowings, or the vagaries of time. But that doesn't ease the pain of learning to spell.

As I mentioned earlier, the modern idea of standardizing English spelling didn't settle in until the early eighteenth century. Proliferation of dictionaries and spelling books in the late eighteenth and then the nineteenth centuries buoyed the status of spelling as a needed skill. Despite multiple attempts to reform English spelling, dictionary entries have barely budged.[3]

In America, the emphasis on proper spelling started early. School-based spelling bees were popping up by the mid-eighteenth century, with the first national contest staged in 1908.[4] Through much of the twentieth century, educators obsessed about spelling. There were weekly spelling lists. Teachers docked students a full grade for a single misspelled word. (My childhood memories remain raw.) Parents presented high school seniors with *Webster's Collegiate Dictionary* for graduation. No wonder millions of us breathed a collective sigh of relief at spellcheck's arrival.

The language you speak and write can shape your attitude towards spelling. So can culture. French is obviously used in France, but also in other countries. Half a dozen years back, when I was lecturing at the Catholic University of Louvain in Belgium's French-speaking city Louvain-la-Neuve, I chatted with some students about spelling. They surprised me by saying they tended to be careful in writing SMS's (aka text messages), making sure their spelling was correct, something my American students at the time usually didn't. As the Belgians explained, they didn't want to be seen as country bumpkins by French speakers in France.

Users' views on spelling might also be swayed by how complicated the system is. Because of its closer letter–sound correspondence, spelling is easier in Italian than in English. More than three fourths of my European cohort were native speakers of Italian. Might they be more likely than Americans to judge themselves good spellers and to believe learning to spell is important?

Does Spelling Matter?

In the age of spellcheck, there are still reasons to know how to spell. For starters, a boatload of research finds that children's spelling skills correlate with reading and writing ability.[5] The more you know about a word, including how to spell it, the easier time you have reading it and the more likely you are to use it in your writing.

Yet these days, many US schools spend precious little time on teaching spelling. Maybe it's because the 2010 Common Core State Standards largely sidestep spelling. Or maybe because getting students to spell correctly has long felt like a losing battle. As younger and younger students use word-processing programs with built-in spellcheck (along with predictive texting on their mobile phones), it's unclear what Americans will think about spelling education even a few years hence.

Judging Us by Our Spelling

The old saw has it, don't judge a book by its cover. But what about judging writers by their spelling? Before spellcheck became ubiquitous, assessing someone's spelling was easy: Give a test or read what the person has written. These days, unless the words are set down by hand, the second option is a no-go.

In some quarters, spelling still seems to matter. Look at teachers grading student essays. When evaluating written work that contains spelling errors, teachers are more likely to give lower marks to the content than if they read identical material without spelling mistakes.[6] Spelling and content are different kettles of fish, but as humans, it's all too easy to let spelling color our judgment about an essay's substance.

Then take employment scenarios. Do recruiters reading applications use spelling as a criterion for evaluating candidates? A study in France asked professional recruiters to review résumés and cover letters that varied in two ways: spelling errors and years of candidates' work experience. Spelling errors were as big a reason to reject applications as candidates' amount of experience. However, the spelling skills of the recruiters also mattered. (They were given spelling tests.) Those with strong skills were more likely to reject applications because of spelling errors than recruiters with low spelling scores. The study's authors reasoned that the poor spellers among the recruiters were less able to distinguish between applications with and without spelling errors.[7] Or maybe (my thought) those poor spellers empathized with applicants who made mistakes.

Keep in mind this study was done in France, where correct spelling likely matters more than in the United States. I suspect many American employers assume that when an employee is on the job, Microsoft Word will clean up aberrant spellings, like surgical nurses or residents doing mop-up after the surgeon finishes operating. What's more, those cover letters and résumés are now prepared on computers, with a personal digital Jeeves automatically running orthographic interference.

Spelling Survey Results

Now on to the surveys. My questions probed how participants judged their own spelling abilities, how much they used and trusted spellcheck, what impact they thought spellcheck had on their own skills, and how important they felt it was for children to learn to spell. The Europeans were asked about skills in their native language (for more than three out of four, it was Italian), while the US contingent were native speakers of English. Here are the highlights.

SPELLING SKILL IN YOUR NATIVE LANGUAGE

The Europeans were somewhat prouder of their spelling skills than the Americans, with 78 percent judging their skills "very good" compared with 65 percent of Americans. The difference isn't huge, and the survey only asked about user impressions. However, given that Italian orthography is simpler, it made intuitive sense that the scale tipped towards the mostly Italian Europeans.

USE OF SPELLCHECK WHEN YOU WRITE
ON A DIGITAL DEVICE

Spellcheck seemed largely domesticated to those in the survey. Close to half saw it as automatic, with a bit less using it "sometimes." Only a handful turned it off. Spellcheck could also serve as a kind of backstop. As one respondent wrote,

> "I always keep it on. because even if i am good with spellings but sometimes i make mistakes and it shows me my mistake. by that way i can correct my self and prevent future mistakes. "

TRUST SPELLCHECK TO PRODUCE THE RIGHT
CORRECTION AUTOMATICALLY

Spellcheck's accuracy was often questioned. Only around 7 percent said they trusted it entirely, with 58 percent trusting it "most of the time" and 28 percent saying "sometimes trust it." This AI writing tool may be domesticated, but it still generates healthy skepticism.

IMPACT OF SPELLCHECK ON OWN ABILITY
TO SPELL CORRECTLY

I'd been especially curious to see what users had to say on this question. My hunch had been that large numbers would say spellcheck made them worse spellers. I'll focus on the US responses, since it's spelling-in-America that I know most about.

The US data surprised me. While 21 percent felt spellcheck made them worse spellers, 42 percent believed the AI genie made them better at spelling. (The rest essentially said spellcheck had no impact on their own skills.) Instructions for the question explicitly asked about the impact of spellcheck on "your own ability to spell words correctly," implying users would learn to spell words that were corrected, then going forth to sin no more.

My gut feeling is some participants focused on their cleaned-up output, rather than on what they were capable of doing on their own. But since many US schools don't give a lot of spelling tests these days, and since we don't know how often spellcheck has been invoked for writing that students submit, it's hard to know.

IMPORTANCE OF TEACHING CHILDREN
TO SPELL CORRECTLY

Again, I was surprised: 80 percent of all participants judged it "very important" to teach children to spell. In fact, the American percentage (83 percent) was even a smidge higher than the European (78 percent). Given that spelling is deemphasized in many US school curricula, might the American responses reflect a "do as I say, not as I do" attitude? (I can't vouch for European practices.) Since spelling tests weren't included for study participants, we don't know how good the Americans' orthographic skills were. But my decades of reading student essays before modern spellcheck leave me skeptical.

Editing and Proofreading

Given today's digital writing tools like spellcheck, autocomplete, and predictive texting, plus punctuation guidance from grammar checkers, I wanted to tap into everyday writers' editing and proofreading habits. I was also curious about attitudes towards AI grammar and style programs more generally, so I included a question in both surveys.

EDITING AND PROOFREADING INFORMAL
EMAIL, TEXTING TO FRIENDS OR FAMILY

For informal email and texting, one third of the Europeans but almost half of the Americans said they took care in editing. Particularly in the United States, perhaps we're seeing what I might call the Facebook or Instagram effect. Beginning with the early days of social media, American young people have put great store in how they represent themselves online.[8] Maybe curating online presentation of self extends these days to informal emails and text messages.

EDITING AND PROOFREADING WRITING
FOR SCHOOL OR WORK

Regular editing and proofreading for school or professional writing was reported to be even more common: nearly 90 percent for both groups. Yet I can attest that at least among American college students, this presumed practice is often honored in the breach. Or maybe malefactors only enroll in my classes.

USING AI TECHNOLOGY TO CORRECT GRAMMAR AND PUNCTUATION

Like spelling, programs for correcting grammar and punctuation are now at our beck and call. My question was how heavily users were leaning on these programs in lieu of doing their own editing and proofreading. About 9 percent in my survey said it was wrong to rely on the technology. Roughly three fourths were open to collaboration, indicating they might use AI for suggestions but still make their own decisions.

But tellingly, 13 percent of the Europeans and 18 percent of the Americans said they were happy to let technology do editing and proofreading for them. I'd love to see research tracking how often young adults—and the rest of us—actually take or reject AI editing suggestions.

My next two questions, about Grammarly, were just on the American survey. (Again, the program is only available in English.) Of the 100 participants, 63 said they used Grammarly. And so the percentages for these two questions are calculated on a base of 63.

IMPACT OF GRAMMARLY ON OWN WRITING SKILLS

Just as I'd been curious about users' perceptions about whether spellcheck harmed or helped their orthographic skills, I wondered how those in the survey saw the impact of Grammarly on their writing skills: 27 percent said there was no effect, 8 percent felt it made them a worse writer, and a whopping 65 percent reported it made them a better writer.

Sounds as if tools like Grammarly are great personal grammar and style coaches. And maybe so. One participant wrote:

> "AI and other grammar correcting tools have come a long way, and are a great addition to the grammar lessons I learned in college, and high school."

But as with the question on whether spellcheck made you a better speller on your own, look at my exact wording for options on the questionnaire:

- "Grammarly has *made me a worse writer* because I rely on its corrections, knowing it will be there next time to correct the same issues."
- "Grammarly has *made me a better writer* because I learn from its suggested cor-

rections and don't make the same mistakes the next time."

Call me skeptical. Maybe students are more willing to learn from machines than from people. If so, more power to Grammarly. But I'd love to give grammar and punctuation tests to students on the items Grammarly corrected to see if its lessons really took. Even users sometimes recognized that the impact of Grammarly can be complicated:

> "Grammarly's effects on me as a writer are mixed, as its corrections help, but they also make it so I rely on some crutches in writing."

TRUST GRAMMARLY TO CATCH MISTAKES
AND NOT GIVE WRONG ADVICE

Most respondents seemed to recognize Grammarly can be fallible. While one out of ten said they trusted it all the time, three fourths trusted it most of the time, and the rest often didn't trust it. As with spellcheck, a "trust but verify" approach was commonly at play. One comment implied a love–hate relationship with the software:

> "I don't trust Grammarly but I do need to see its suggestions."

Software That Writes for You

Moving on from cleanup operations to creating new text, the next questions asked about predictive texting and using AI to generate essays. We'll start with predictive texting.

USE OF PREDICTIVE TEXTING

Roughly 30 percent across the board reported being happy using predictive texting. But then responses diverged between the Americans and Europeans. While only 9 percent of the Americans resented mistakes that predictive texting made, 31 percent of the Europeans did. And while 57 percent of the Americans said they'd rather write messages entirely themselves, only 29 percent of the Europeans did.

The Americans seemed much more likely to take predictive texting's fallibility in their stride, while voicing greater desire for control by writing their own messages. Don't get miffed, just do it yourself. Of course, sometimes there are trade-offs between effort and efficiency. As one American admitted about accepting whatever predictive texting came up with, "It's OK when I am feeling particularly lazy."

IMPACT OF PREDICTIVE TEXTING
ON YOUR TEXT MESSAGES

The two survey groups were strongly in sync on effects of predictive texting on their messages. More than 60 percent felt the technology had no effect, 11 percent said it made them write longer or more complex messages, and 21 percent reported that predictive texting led to their writing simpler or shorter messages.

But nestled in the participants' comments were indications of additional effects on content and their connection with it. Several worried that with predictive texting, the message was no longer what they would have written:

"I don't know . . . maybe it makes me a little too repetitive?"

Sounds like a large language model at work. And:

"Don't feel I wrote it."

Shades of Jennifer Lepp's complaint about using Sudowrite.

One remark from the US contingent was pointedly pragmatic:

"It wastes time because of the amount of time I have to erase the generated response."

This observation might help explain the Americans' preference for writing text messages themselves.

WOULD YOU USE AN AI PROGRAM
THAT CAN WRITE AN ESSAY FOR YOU?

Before talking about results, we need to remind ourselves when and where this question was asked. The data were all collected by mid-November 2022, before ChatGPT came on the scene. In the United States, there was already growing awareness of AI programs that could generate text, but for most people, this wasn't something they—or anyone they knew—had personal experience with. In Europe, familiarity (much less hands-on experience) with the technology was generally even lower.

A bit over 40 percent of both groups said they'd like to try out the technology for fun. Several commented that if they experimented with it, they still wanted to retain control:

"I would try it out and then edit the base text to make it more my style."

and

"It's tempting but I would rather check what an AI would write, then write my own. Like a writing buddy, rather than a secretary."

Augmentation. Not automation.

But then the groups diverged. Among the Europeans, 36 percent said they weren't interested in trying out text generation, while only 13 percent of the Americans declined. Either Americans were more adventuresome or (more likely) they had heard about large language models like GPT-3 and were eager to see for themselves how the programs worked.

My last question in this cluster was about cheating. Would they be tempted to submit an AI-generated essay as their own? For both groups, responses in the affirmative were in the single digits. We can only imagine what the numbers might have looked like if I asked the question several months later, following release of ChatGPT. The *Stanford Daily* survey we talked about in Chapter 10 offered but a first taste of how tempting tools like ChatGPT can be.

Handwriting

Why handwriting, you ask. For many, the skill is an endangered species, but not one meriting a defense team. When I ask today's students how they prepare written assignments, some report they can only think when their hands are at a keyboard, not when grasping a pen. They also moan about their atrocious penmanship. No surprise on either count: Use it or lose it. But a smattering of others tell me that writing by hand helps them work through what they want to say and how to say it, and to speak in their own voice.

It was the mid-2010s that the handwriting versus keyboarding issue started brewing in my mind, thanks to a collaboration with Sora Park, a communication professor at the University of Canberra.[9] Together we analyzed surveys from university students in Australia about their experiences writing on a mobile phone, a laptop, and (by hand) on paper.

While students praised the efficiency of writing on phones and laptops, Sora and I were struck by comments linking handwriting with cognition and emotions. Here's some of what they had to say about distraction:

"It's easier to get distracted [when using a laptop] . . . my mind doesn't register what I'm typing. When I'm writing [on paper], I have to constantly think if that makes sense."

and engagement:

"[with] handwriting you have to actually engage more. You have to concentrate on what you're actually writing, where typing, you can just blank out."

And then about feelings of personal connection:

"it's something I can touch, that I own. Whereas with the document that is saved on my computer, in the cloud, it doesn't really feel as real."

or

"Handwriting something to pen and paper is an extension of you. Because you physically can touch it, you can physically run your hands over the words, because there's indentation from the pen and the force that you've used on the paper."

Five years later, as I began mulling over the potential impact of AI on writing, I tried connecting the dots: Could writing with a digital device rather than by hand foreshadow AI dampening individual expression and how much thinking we do when writing? It was time to delve into the handwriting literature.

Commerce and Character

Knowing how to write well by hand is a time-honored skill. Nearly two thousand years ago, the Roman rhetorician Quintilian stressed the importance of cultivating good cursive handwriting. During the Middle Ages at the University of Padova, doctors were required either to write out their arguments legibly or dictate to a scribe.[10] A longstanding complaint about American physicians has been their illegible scrawl.

Handwriting later became a path to financial success. By the eighteenth and nineteenth centuries, commercial development led to a burgeoning need for people who could prepare invoices, receipts, and business correspondence. Writing masters and special schools set up shop to provide training. In the United States, rival approaches to penmanship emerged, one the brainchild of Platt Rogers Spencer and the other created by Austin Norman Palmer.

Handwriting wasn't only about money. Some viewed it as a window on the soul. Edouard Auguste Patrice Hocquart argued in 1812 that you could judge people's character by their handwriting. In the ensuing decades, handwriting was taken as a reliable indicator of everything from criminality to whether someone would make a good spouse or business partner.[11]

Times have changed. Physicians now dictate or type their notes. Business offices use word processing. And dating apps don't request handwriting samples. But that doesn't mean no one thinks about handwriting these days, including whether it's done by printing the letters ("manuscript" hand) or with cursive.

Culture and Cognition

If you have a child of primary school age, you'll recognize today's big hand-writing debate: Do you still teach cursive? In the United States, the picture is mixed. Thanks to adoption of the federal Common Core State Standards, since 2010 there's been no national requirement to include the skill in the lower school curriculum. Currently, twenty-one states mandate cursive be taught, though the level of instruction fluctuates.

The drumbeat against teaching cursive continues to grow louder, especially in America. Isn't printing enough, especially since written assignments have largely moved to digital keyboards? Attitudes towards cursive also have cultural overtones. In France, children begin with cursive as soon as they enter school. Learning to write means learning to write in cursive. In the United States, there's evidence of an association between teaching cursive and parental political or religious conservatism.[12]

You don't need to be French or conservative to value cursive writing. Your cursive hand is personal and, if you write well, has aesthetic value. For decades after the proliferation of typewriters, it was still good etiquette to write thank-you notes and condolence letters by hand, and yes, in cursive. These days, cursive is foreign territory to many. But if you'd like to send a cursive letter or greeting card, plenty of services will do the writing for you. Sometimes you even get the choice of human or robotic scribe.[13]

There's another part of the handwriting story, and that involves cognition. Research suggests that not just cursive but handwriting more generally aids reading and learning. The theoretical mantle enveloping the evidence is known as embodied cognition.[14]

The idea behind embodied cognition is that thinking and learning, reading and writing are mental activities embedded in a physical world. For instance, when we read, we not only process words on a page or screen, but we do it in a context: holding the book or tablet, sitting at a desk or sprawled out on the sofa, in a crowded subway car or alone under a tree. That physicality affects our mental processing.[15]

Writing is also embodied.[16] We do it sitting straight or hunched over. At a desk or on our lap. If you write by hand for long stretches, especially under time pressure—think of a three-hour essay exam—your hand often hurts. Those of us logging years of writing by hand still bear our "writer's bump," that callus on the inside of the first joint of the middle finger of the writing hand.

The aspect of writing embodiment we'll focus on is forming letters yourself rather than using a digital keyboard or keypad (earlier, a typewriter). Does this distinction translate into differences in what's happening in our brains and minds? In Chapter 1, we talked about the cognitive impact of literacy. Let's see how handwriting and typing might figure into the equation.

Handwriting and the Brain

Children first.

Psychologist Karen James and her colleagues have been using functional MRI scanners to explore connections between handwriting and brain activity in four- and five-year-old children who haven't yet learned to read or write. By "handwriting," what James means is drawing (freehand) a letter that's been presented to them. The children were also asked to reproduce the letter by tracing and by typing it. The kids then entered the scanner and were shown the three kinds of letters they'd produced. Different parts of the brain lit up when looking at letters created by handwriting, tracing, or typing. For handwriting, there was more brain activity in areas associated with adult reading and writing.[17]

Work by Virginia Berninger and her colleagues confirms that as children become literate, these sorts of distinctions continue. In studies of first, third, and fifth graders, the researchers found variation in brain patterns, depending on whether the students were writing in cursive, writing in print letters, or using a keyboard. What's more, when children wrote by hand, they generated more ideas than when typing.[18]

Further neurological evidence for handwriting's benefits comes from Norwegian research with adolescents and young adults.[19] High-density electroencephalography (which records electrical brain activity) was used to compare what was happening neurologically when people wrote in cursive, used a keyboard, or drew words. (There wasn't a separate condition for printing.) We know that specific types of brain activity are important for both memory and encoding new information. The investigators looked at differences in what the brain was up to when using alternative modes of letter production, rather than assessing memory itself.

With handwriting (here, cursive) and with drawing, there was more brain activity in areas important for memory and acquiring new information than when typing. Explaining these findings leads us back to embodied cognition. In the words of Audrey van der Meer, one of the study's authors,

> "The use of pen and paper gives the brain more 'hooks' to hang your memories on. . . . A lot of senses are activated by pressing the pen on paper, seeing the letters you write and hearing the sound you make while writing. These sense experiences create contact between different parts of the brain and open the brain up for learning."[20]

Recall the Australian student who talked about the physicality of handwriting.

Handwriting and the Mind

Brain studies aren't the only evidence linking handwriting with advantages for literacy and learning. Traditional experimental research adds confirmation.

Again, children first.

There's ample evidence that early writing skills in children correlate with emergent and subsequent reading ability.[21] As with the Karen James brain studies, conventional testing methods show that practicing with letter formation predicts later reading development.[22] In a study of children in grades four through seven, Zachary Alstad and his colleagues found that cursive writing (as opposed to printing or selecting letters on a keyboard) correlated with better spelling and composition skills.[23]

What about adults? Pam Mueller and Daniel Oppenheimer made a research splash in 2014 with their paper "The Pen Is Mightier Than the Keyboard."[24] University students were asked to take lecture notes, either using a laptop or writing by hand. When tested afterwards, those writing by hand showed more learning. The authors argued that with computers, students tend to record lecture information verbatim, as if taking dictation. By contrast, they're more apt to cast notes in their own words when using handwriting. Several replication studies yielded more mixed results.[25] But the ultimate question we need to be asking is this: Would we rather students show proficiency at parroting what some professor said or that they grapple with ideas, regardless of their scores on laboratory-style tests?

Handwriting Survey Results

A swath of research reveals real differences between handwriting and typing that most of today's digirati don't consider. But we should. Piggybacking on my earlier surveys of Australian students with Sora Park, I wondered what writers from other parts of the world thought about the effects of medium on their writing.

I asked participants in my new surveys four questions: what they liked most and liked least about writing by hand or with a digital keyboard. The answers were open-ended, meaning respondents could write anything they wished. After reading through all the answers, I came up with five broad categories for sorting the replies: practical, physical, cognitive, emotional/personal connection, and evaluative. The same categories proved a reasonable fit for all four questions.

WHAT IS THE *One* THING YOU *Like Most*
ABOUT WRITING BY HAND?

There was little surprise in responses about handwriting being *practical.* Comments showed appreciation for the control that users have—for instance,

"I can make diagrams and draw doodles."

Less predictable was the variety of answers relating to something *physical,* especially involving the senses. For example,

"I like feeling the paper and pen under my hands, being able to physically form words."

Especially rich were *cognitive* replies. People described the importance of handwriting for memory:

"I feel I remember better when I write by hand."

and for thinking:

"I like the commitment I build between the hand gesture and the thinking."

Particularly striking was the link between thinking and slowing down:

"I have time to think about what I am writing and this allows me to better elaborate my thoughts."

But now comes a dilemma: While some writers reported that handwriting helped slow down the brain and gave it time to think, we'll see in the coming sections that speed in writing is highly prized.

More cognitive advantages of handwriting, this time for its effect on engagement, concentration, or distraction:

"it feels less distracting vs using technology to write and being distracted by a million other things."

Then come links with creativity:

"it adds to a high level of creativity. The words just seem to flow better when you are writing by hand."

Shades of Mihaly Csikszentmihalyi's notions of flow and creativity.

Finally, I can't resist adding two responses from Italian graduate students in an earlier iteration of the survey:

"It leaves tracks in my mind."

"I can see what I'm thinking."

It's hard to imagine more eloquent images.

Another group of responses from the current survey involved *emotions or feelings of personal connection* when writing by hand. My favorite response:

> "The satisfaction of a whole page filled by handwriting, it feels like I climbed a mountain."

A cascade of comments were about handwriting giving a sense of personal connection:

> "It feels more personal and I am more connected to the writing."

plus

> "I enjoy looking at my handwriting because there is variance in the way the letters look as opposed to typing."

Finally, there was a cluster of *evaluative* responses, all talking about how real or authentic handwriting was:

> "It feels more real than writing on a computer, the words seem to have more meaning."

and

> "I feel that it's authentic."

I sat up at the words "real" and "authentic." In survey research I'd done on reading in print versus digitally, a number of students said what they liked most about reading in print was that it was "real reading." For at least some readers and writers, machine-assisted literacy tools feel, well, mechanical.

WHAT IS THE *One* THING YOU *Like Least* ABOUT WRITING BY HAND?

The biggest *practical* gripe about handwriting was speed:

> "Writing by hand takes a lot longer than typing."

Almost one fourth of all complaints about handwriting were that it was too slow.

But there were other concerns. Some talked about lack of digital tools for things like editing, spelling, or file storage. And then there came problems with what the finished product looked like. Sometimes it was messy:

"When I accidently smear the ink with my hand."

Worse still, people (including themselves) had poor penmanship:

"My handwriting is often illegible when I go back to read what I wrote."

Complaints about their own handwriting, including when writing quickly, were loudest among the Americans. And maybe no surprise, since handwriting isn't emphasized in most American schools.

When it came to *physical* issues, the biggest culprits were pain and fatigue:

"The strain on your hand after writing for awhile."

Americans were twice as likely to grumble about physical discomfort as Europeans (35 percent versus 16 percent of all objections to handwriting). I wonder if Americans are simply bigger complainers or if greater pain came from being out of practice.

There's nothing to report for the *cognitive* and the *emotional/personal connection* categories. But when it came to *evaluative* observations about what they didn't like when writing by hand, one person said:

"Sometimes I think it's a waste of time."

Or, as another simply put it,

"Everything."

WHAT IS THE *One* THING YOU *Like Most* ABOUT WRITING ON A FULL
DIGITAL KEYBOARD?

On the *practical* front, there's a lot to praise about digital writing. Front and center is speed, as in:

"You can just type fast and finish faster."

Of all the "like most" comments about writing with a digital keyboard, more than 40 percent were in praise of speed. It seems a lot of people are in a hurry.

Then come the usual round of suspects for other practical benefits of writing digitally, running the gamut from ease of correction to internet access to neatness:

"how neat and legible it looks."

On the *physical* front, several participants mentioned sound:

"The sound of keyboard."

As for *cognitive* issues, only one response came up:

> "Prefer physical computer keyboard because the space and distance between my fingers helps me think of what I want to write—the feel of the keys and the position is part of the thought drafting process."

The comment makes for an intriguing counterfoil to one respondent's earlier observation that what she liked most about writing by hand was "the commitment I build between the hand gesture and the thinking." Yet both responses exemplify the importance of embodied cognition.

And on *emotional/personal* connection and *evaluative* issues? Nothing.

WHAT IS THE *One* THING YOU *Like Least* ABOUT WRITING ON A FULL DIGITAL KEYBOARD?

A big *practical* complaint centered around typing. There was a lot of grumbling about making typographical errors and needing to adjust to different keyboards:

> "I mistype on the keyboard a lot."

> "Every keyboard is different and have to get used [to it]."

But then subtle differences between the Europeans and Americans peeked through. Several Europeans bemoaned their lack of touch-typing skills:

> "I can never remember where the keys are so I always have to look at the keyboard as I write."

None of the Americans did. (Overall, US students have been "keyboarding" longer than many European counterparts.) But what did keep surfacing in the US sample was blaming their typos on speed:

> "I make multiple mistakes when I type fast."

No surprise, given how many Americans had praised speed as what they liked most about writing digitally.

Also on the practical front were the kinds of grousing we'd expect about digital tools, including machine malfunctions:

"File loss and machine crashing."

Another complaint was about autocorrection:

"Sometimes spell check or grammar check keeps getting it wrong and you have to go back."

On the *physical* side, there was a medley of issues, such as fatigue or pain that came from working on a digital keyboard:

"My eyes get tired."

And being disturbed by sound coming from the machine:

"the sound is sometimes annoying."

—the opposite of those who enjoyed it.

But on to *cognitive* issues, where participants had much to say. They spoke about memory:

"Less retention."

about thinking:

"writing with a keyboard requires very little mental work while doing it. I do not have to put thought into what I'm writing because mistakes can be easily corrected."

and about engagement, concentration, or distraction:

"I am less focused compared to hand writing."

When it came to *emotion or personal connection*, there was a cornucopia of replies, including

"I feel detached from what I'm writing since it looks just like every other piece of text that people read online."

But my favorite was

"It's aloof."

We're back to Jennifer Lepp's discovery that after using Sudowrite to generate more and more of her text, "It didn't feel like mine anymore." The writer's personal ownership retreated.

Finally, there were *evaluative* judgments. Among them:

"It's less creative."

"There's no 'art' of writing."

and even

"I've lost my writing abilities."

From Handwriting to AI Jeeves

I've spent a lot of time talking about handwriting. There's a method to the madness. The hunch I've been following is that perspectives on the kind of writing stylus we wield—writing by hand or digital typing—might foreshadow attitudes towards AI as writing Jeeves.

Time to connect the dots.

Takeaways from AI as Jeeves Questions

As I sifted through what users had to say about AI's role in spelling, editing, and full-fledged writing, three main themes emerged:

- *Keep humans in control.* While everyday writers appreciate boosts from AI as Jeeves, they're clear about not wanting to give up control. Augment, don't replace. Trust, but verify. Save the last word for yourself.
- *Learn from the technology—maybe.* More people than I expected, especially in the United States, reported that AI tools like spellcheck and grammar programs improved their writing skills, not just providing a free lunch. I haven't lost my skepticism, but hope springs eternal that they're right.
- *Retain your own writing voice.* Preserving their personal writing voice, rather than passively accepting whatever predictive texting or grammar programs served up, was clearly important. Many of the survey results echoed what we heard in earlier chapters from Evan Selinger and Daniel de Beer about AI edging out the human writer's individuality.

Takeaways from Handwriting Questions

I've boiled down into three takeaways what people in the surveys said about handwriting, focusing on issues most relevant to use of AI writing tools:

- *Recognize trade-offs between efficiency and thinking.* Especially among the Americans—who tend to be typing speed demons—there was recognition that like oil and water, writing quickly and thinking don't generally mix.

- *Retain your individuality.* An ongoing drumbeat for handwriting was the individuality it affords. Your handwriting is uniquely yours, potentially expressing to others who you are.
- *Consider what makes writing feel more genuine.* Not everyone likes writing by hand. But some of those who do describe it as more "real" than digital typing. AI as Jeeves only works digitally. We need to ask whether writing that Jeeves has augmented—and to which we append our names—can feel genuine.

Connecting the Dots

Overlap between attitudes towards AI as Jeeves and towards handwriting shouldn't surprise us. For both undertakings, we're talking about writing. Bridging these two faces of writing, here are two broad recommendations:

- *Don't feel driven to wholesale adoption of new technology.* That goes for both AI as Jeeves and digital typing. Don't let yourself feel pushed around. Avoid blandness and sameness. And remember that writing is a way of thinking. Don't let the technology hamper a mind at work.
- *Retain control over what you write.* You decide—not the software—what your final version looks like. Don't let the technology undermine what you think, what you want to say, and how you say it.

Writing choices are and should be individual. All I suggest is keeping in mind what over 200 everyday writers had to say about their own experiences, choices, and rationales.

Before we leave the surveys, one more thing. My final research question was about AI and future job prospects for writers.

Impact of AI on Writing-Intensive Jobs

Since you've read Chapter 8, you know about potential consequence of AI as author for professions involving writing. I was curious whether young adults perceived such jobs to be at risk. The options I gave were journalists, lawyers, translators, and various traditional authoring categories (short story writers, novelists, essayists, poets, or playwrights). People could check multiple categories.

Jobs for journalists and especially translators were seen as most imperiled. Among Americans, half worried about journalists and almost three fourths about translators. Lawyers weren't perceived to be in as much trouble. Only a bit more than one fourth of respondents thought lawyers should be concerned.

When it came to poets and playwrights, fiction writers and essayists, there was moderate angst, especially among the Americans. However, now that ChatGPT and its competitors are on the loose, I strongly suspect the threat level needs to be raised.

Going Forward

Listening to young adults in these surveys helps us appreciate how nuanced—and sometimes contradictory—users' attitudes are about harnessing AI-driven technologies in their writing. A lesson learned is that everyday writers can appreciate the efficiencies of a technology, while simultaneously sensing it might eat away at their writing skills, thinking ability, or personal voice.

Contradictions are everywhere in our lives. Nuts are nutritious, but eating too many expands our waistline. Mobile phones are handy, but too often disturb our peace. The trick is reaching an equilibrium we're comfortable with, and that represents a choice, not a default. When it comes to writing, the balancing act means weighing the benefits of AI against where we believe human authorship matters.

CODA

Why Human Authorship Matters

What if the dream came true? Imagine a world where AI's current writing challenges have been solved. Where large language models (or their successors) don't churn out ugliness. Where using them is energy efficient. Where predictive texting, spellcheck, and grammar programs are infallible. Where AI can produce lengthy texts that are non-repetitive, stylistically interesting, factually accurate, and always on topic. Oh, and can generate text that's indistinguishable from what you might have written.

Where would this world leave us humans? While some of these accomplishments will take longer than others, the future is already knocking.

We began this book by looking at human writing—how it emerged, its connections with our minds and brains, and why we write and rewrite. After many pages and much discussion of AI research, it's time to reflect on what we've learned and to think about choices under our control.

As we weigh options, keep in mind potential blowback of getting what we wish for. Cultural lore—be it of King Midas in Greek mythology, the recurrent "three wishes" stories across European tales, or W. W. Jacobs's more modern "The Monkey's Paw"—reminds us that attractive prospects may bear unforeseen consequences. Some that glitters really is gold, but not all. Our job is to sort out for ourselves, in our own writing lives, which shiny objects go in which pot.

Being Human

He was only sixteen years old but astounded the chess world in February 2022 by beating five-time world champion Magnus Carlsen. Rameshbabu Praggnanandhaa (who also goes by Pragg) was the new Indian wunderkind, though Carlsen's skills should never be underestimated.[1]

DeepMind might well beat them both. So it's fair to ask why human chess players still bother. One fundamental reason is that playing chess makes you think. Winning may be edifying, but knowing how to strategize, to puzzle out how someone else approaches a problem, to learn from your mistakes, are precious skills in so much of life. Chess legend Garry Kasparov, now turned businessman, even wrote a book *How Life Imitates Chess*, tellingly subtitled *Making the Right Moves, from the Board to the Boardroom.*[2]

There's a reason our species is called "homo sapiens." The Latin *sapiens* means wise or capable of discerning. For that, you need to be able to think. Since the days of Turing and the Dartmouth Conference, the quest in AI has been to build computers and the programs running on them that could think. More recently, the goal has increasingly become to augment rather than replace human cognition. We need to figure out the right balance between machines and people. To launch that conversation, let me introduce some forgotten work of a television legend.

Before *Sesame Street*, there was coffee. In 1957, Wilkins Coffee—a local brand in Washington, DC—hired an unknown puppeteer to make spot television commercials. Growing up in the Washington area, I was privy to the antics of two of Jim Henson's Muppets, Wilkins and Wontkins.

Then came a project for Big Blue. In 1967, IBM hired Henson, who was still supporting himself by filming commercials. The resulting video short was "The Paperwork Explosion," an all-purpose advertisement touting the company's range of products that could simplify office work, from self-correcting typewriters to sophisticated dictation machines.[3] The film ended with a crescendo of voices proclaiming: "Machines should work. People should think." Let technology do the scut work. Save people for the stuff requiring human brains.

Now that machines are increasingly driven by artificial intelligence, it's getting harder to decide which work should be parceled out to technology and which best kept for people. We face this dilemma with AI and human writing: what to relinquish and what to keep for ourselves, in both our personal and professional lives.

Choices are individual. But to help in making them, I suggest building your own scorecard. Not a formal one, but staking out some reference points to guide your writing practices. Decisions need not be unilateral. They're yours, after all. Maybe, "OK, AI, draft my email replies, but I'm the arbiter for grammar and style." Lay out the authorial equivalents of your nuclear-free zones. But while you're at it, be honest in gauging time pressures, willpower, and sometimes laziness.

Questions to Consider

At the end of the Prologue, I posed eight questions the book was setting out to help answer. In constructing your scorecard, let's revisit those questions, drawing up what we've learned from the intervening chapters, along with some new food for thought.

1. What's Your Motivation for Writing?

Chapter 2 laid out an array of human motivations. It's time to reconsider those motivations in light of the human–AI division of labor.

QUOTIDIAN ACTS

Everyday writing pervades our lives: notes-to-self, letters, diaries, documents, emails, texting, online chat. The bulk of our writing is to record and communicate. When the medium is digital, AI as Jeeves has on tap an abundance of offerings, from autocomplete to bias warnings. Some of them edit our text automatically. Other assistance is opt in. A number of participants in my surveys were clearly making deliberate choices when to rely on Jeeves and when to ditch the advice. Many were adamant about having the last word.

WRITING AT OTHERS' BIDDING

A portion of our writing is at the direction of others: a required essay for a course we're taking, a news story assigned to a journalist. Increasingly, AI as Jeeves-on-autopilot can generate these pieces for us. The issue is becoming who gets to choose whether a human or AI does the writing. In professional contexts like journalism and translation, efficiency and the financial bottom line likely drive the decisions. Here, attribution of authorship is often less critical. But for those school essays, if students add their own bylines, it's called cheating.

TANGIBLE GAINS

If you write for a living or if publication enhances your career prospects, AI can be a handy resource, even when it's not working solo. Tools like Sudowrite offer to prod you past writer's block or, more proactively, to write whole passages for incorporating into your human efforts. We saw how indie authors capitalize on AI text generation to speed up book production, in the process enhancing sales. But collaboration can become a slippery slope, leaving writers to ponder how much of the resulting text—and its stylistic voice—is really theirs.

SHARING

AI as Jeeves-on-autopilot can shine when it comes to articles and even longer texts built on information sources. Remember Philip Parker's more than 200,000 auto-generated books, plus Beta Writer's *Lithium-Ion Batteries*? With large language models, it's not hard imagining AI whipping up pieces on everything from best recipes for leftover turkey to political takes on the 2020 US presidential election. (Your choice whether the slant should be left or right.)

But AI need not shoulder the whole burden. Much as the internet provides bountiful information that human writers might slot into their texts, natural language generation offers collaborative opportunities for offering up expertise or advice or crafting exposés. Humans make the call (at least for now) whether or not AI gets co-author billing.

LOOKING OUTWARD, LOOKING INWARD, PERSONAL RELEASE

I've coalesced these last three categories because it's here that human motivation to write is quintessential. It's where we harness the written word to formulate our thoughts and impart them to others. Looking outward, we reveal our ideas (typically to readers of literature) on what's wrong with our current world or how to make a better one. Looking inward, writing can be a personal vehicle for making sense of what's going on in our head. To reprise Flannery O'Connor, "I write because I don't know what I think until I read what I say."

And writing for personal release? I hardly recommend spray-painting graffiti or preparing manifestos justifying murder. But we also write diaries affording us space to be honest with ourselves, not to mention letters in which we're frank with others.

I'm not especially worried that people will be inviting AI in when it comes to these three motivations for writing. My concern is different. To write effectively, eloquently, or forcefully, we need to acquire writing skills and practice them. If we increasingly cede editing and text generation to AI, we need to ask ourselves how much ability and motivation we'll retain for the kind of writing that aims at self-knowledge and meaningful human connection.

2. Is AI a Threat to Human-Written Creativity?

It's clear that AI can conjure up stories, poems, and potentially novels that can pass for human productions. If humans had written them, we'd call them some version of creative (at least little c, maybe even Pro c). An obvious issue is whether AI's growing literary potential becomes a competitor with human creativity. For that challenge to materialize, we need to assume it's legitimate to bestow the word "creative" on AI's productions.

In the chapter on AI and creativity, I suggested that whether or not AI can be called creative is largely a matter of personal judgment. I was curious to compare my own take with that of everyday writers. And so I included an item about creativity on my European survey. (For reasons of brevity, I had to exclude the item from the US version.) The question was whether participants would call the results creative if an AI program wrote a poem or short story.

Of the responses, 13 percent said yes and 29 percent said no. Nearly all the rest hedged their bets with maybe. But a few weren't content with a yes-no-maybe-so answer, instead providing their own perspectives. One linked creativity to intentionality:

"I think that creativity needs intentionality and refinement not to be just the replication of other people's work."

while a second focused on emotions:

"It could potentially be considered creative in its form, but not in its content, cuz style can be replicated but emotions cannot."

Another talked about the role of humans in doing the programming:

"It can be called creative as a product of the programmers' own creativity in creating the AI, combined with the creativity of online resources the AI feeds on. I wouldn't say an AI program is creative per se."

There was also a comment on degree of originality:

"If the ai program fishes from a database of pre existing short stories and mashes them into one, then no. If the ai writes one ex novo then yes."

Of course, human works are also subject to this last kind of scrutiny.

Whatever label we settle on, I don't see creative writers having much to fear from AI. There's always more room at the table. You can perhaps be too rich and surely too thin. But you can't have too many short stories, novels, or poems. Plus, the primary beneficiaries of the creative act of writing are often the human writers themselves.

3. Which Writing Skills Are Worth Keeping?

We need to get one issue out of the way. Given how sophisticated today's speech recognition has become, some argue this technology will render much of everyday writing obsolete. We rely on spoken commands to Siri and Alexa. All manner of speech-to-text programs let us sidestep having to write out emails or even whole documents, if we choose. What's more, audiobooks and podcasts are justly popular forms of reading. That said, I don't see an avalanche of people abandoning their keyboards or their written books.

Let's assume human writers will be around for the foreseeable future. The decisions we need to make are about which skills are worth developing and maintaining, along with how much the physical side of writing matters.

SPELLING

Start where AI as writing Jeeves made its debut: spelling. Before getting to the pros and cons of using spellcheck, there's a more fundamental question: Does correct spelling (and knowing how to deliver it) still matter?

It's instructive to see what the English composition profession has to say. In 1988, Robert Connors and Andrea Lunsford undertook a study of the kinds of mistakes undergraduates made in their essays.[4] The largest number of errors were in spelling, by a landslide. Twenty years later, Andrea Lunsford, along with Karen Lunsford, reran the study.[5] This time around, spelling mistakes had dropped to eighteenth place.

Thank you, spellcheck. Spelling is no longer a standout problem on those computer-produced, spellchecked papers that students now submit. As a result, there's little for teachers of English composition (or the rest of us) to fuss over orthographically. (The exception, of course, is proper names, which spellcheck ignores.) At the same time, teachers know nothing about students' spelling abilities or how much (if any) effort poor or careless spellers may have expended to get things right.

Maybe knowing how to spell no longer matters. Yet if participants in my surveys are to be believed, four out of five assumed it was important for children to master spelling. A hefty number of those I surveyed also had confidence in their own skills.

What about attitudes towards spellcheck itself? Assume our "what if the dream came true" scenario, where spellcheck always gets things right, including figuring out homonyms like "to," "two," and "too." Few dispute that spellcheck has saved the bacon of many a writer. Because the tool has become domesticated, many of us don't realize it's an option we can accept or reject.

Case in point: It was only from my Italian students that I learned the program could be turned off.

A sizeable swath of those answering my questionnaires felt spellcheck made them better spellers (though particularly for the Americans, you'll remember my skepticism). Yet they voiced caveats. One concern was that AI as mop-up Jeeves erodes personal skills:

> "At some point if you depend on a predictive text [program] you're going to lose your spelling abilities."

Another was that AI tools more generally encourage sloth:

> "spellcheck and AI software . . . can . . . be used by people who want to take an easier way out."

What about the studies we talked about on cognitive—and, at least in France, potential employment—consequences of developing and maintaining spelling skills? You might say, I'm not French. Or that even if knowing how to spell was good for my developing brain when learning to read and write, I'm now an adult.

Your call. And your call as well whether you abandon the work entirely to spellcheck or at least try to learn from its corrections. I rely on spellcheck. I keep it turned on. I also know it's gnawing away at whatever spelling skills I once had. Whenever I need to write by hand, I face the music.

GRAMMAR AND STYLE

Unlike spelling, what counts as "good" grammar and style is often up for grabs. Should you pair a word like "group" or "crowd" with a singular or plural verb? It's your decision, depending on whether you're thinking of the assemblage as a single entity or a collection of individuals. Do you write "between you and me" or "between you and I"? Standard rules insist the first is correct, though the second reflects contemporary usage, perhaps including yours. Language continuously changes, but grammar books—and AI grammar checkers—can be slow to catch up.

Grammar also differs from spelling in that we acquire grammar in the process of learning to talk. Before we begin tackling spelling (typically through formal education), we already have a developed sense of how sentences are put together. We're also able to judge what's grammatical and what's not, at least most of the time.

When learning to write, we bring with us this grammatical knowledge. Education introduces more complex syntax and vocabulary, sometimes through teaching, sometimes through independent reading. Formal education also hammers into us grammatical rules ("between you and me": objective case after a preposition!). It's when these formal rules conflict with how we speak ("between you and I") that our English teachers or AI grammar checkers cry foul.

For spelling, you need to learn all the rules or, for words where pronunciation and orthography agreeably match up, deduce them. There's one set of rules for everyone writing American English. For other English-speaking countries like the UK and Canada, there are separate dictionaries reflecting national variants. But in each case, you have a single national standard.

With grammar, we have rules reflecting our speech and then rules drilled into us in school. "Remembering" the ones underlying speech is a non-issue. While most people can't explain what those rules are, speakers are aware when sentences follow or violate them. Not so for the rules we learn in school, particularly the ones that aren't part of our personal speech patterns. These are largely the rules up for grabs when we ask what elements of grammar and style are worth maintaining. Of course, there are also rules we never mastered, or perhaps never encountered, in the first place.

What are grammar checkers good for? First off, they're handy proofreaders. When I'm zipping along at the keyboard, I might accidentally type "The reasons was unclear." Had I gone back to proofread, presumably I'd have caught the error (plural "were" is needed). If grammar check offers to clean up number agreement for me, I haven't lost my grammar skills. I just relied on Jeeves to save me the editing effort.

Consider other scenarios. Suppose you never learned some of the rules of standard English usage, especially those differing from the way you naturally speak. Let's say you're a high school student who, along with a buddy, have created a mobile app for which you're hoping to get support from a school innovation fund. In your application, you write "Sam and me have written a terrific new app" because that's what you would normally say, reflecting your dialect of English. A grammar checker that adjusts your text to "Sam and I" will likely up your funding prospects. The software might not change the way you speak—or write—in the future, but sufficient unto the day.

Another group of users we need to think about are people who aren't fluent speakers of the language in which they're writing. Grammar checkers, particularly those offering explanations, are potentially valuable teaching tools. See what's wrong, read why, and don't repeat the error next time. The options are there, but it's up to individuals whether they follow through on steps two and especially three. For those who do, the issue becomes not keeping grammatical skills but acquiring them.

REWRITING

Writing—like reading—encourages us to reflect on words, our own or someone else's. Vladimir Nabokov famously declared, "One cannot read a book: one can only reread it." His dictum applies not just to fiction but, in principle, to other prose. And, by analogy, to writing. One step in writing is rewriting.

Ernest Hemingway is reputed to have said, "The first draft of anything is shit." Hemingway practiced what he preached. He's known for working through multiple iterations of his stories. In fact, it seems he drafted forty-seven different possible endings for *A Farewell to Arms*.[6]

Hemingway used to write his initial drafts by hand, after which he'd type them up and then edit by hand. Now, word processing has revolutionized the notion of drafts and rewriting. Unless someone strong-arms us to submit iterative drafts, we tend to tinker with just one version, one file. No one complains about the ease with which you can add, delete, or move around phrases or whole sections. But what's lost in today's editing process is the opportunity for taking measure of transformations between versions, not to mention a way of editing back to original wording and organization what you electronically axed yesterday. Yes, you could use Track Changes on iterative edits of your own writing and save each version. But who would?

The lack of a "wayback machine" when editing digitally isn't lost on some of today's young adults. One of my survey participants wrote that what she liked best about writing by hand on paper was

"being able to see what I wrote and make visible changes while I write, versus not seeing the changes that are made once you correct them on the computer."

I try to be a realist. While some of us who write professionally still print out and edit drafts by hand, my students rarely do. When I request they work through at least two drafts of an assignment before submitting it, I can hear the snickers. For the bulk of my students, it's one and done.

Learning to rewrite is a skill. But it's one that's increasingly difficult to gauge in others' writing. Word processing was the first technology to hide evidence of how much reworking an author may have done. More sophisticated AI writing tools are a second camouflage technology, though their effects are different. If I let loose a program like Grammarly and accept the changes it suggests, it can feel as if I've rewritten my initial draft. In truth, Grammarly did the rewrite, though at a superficial level.

HANDWRITING

You may well be weary of my talking about handwriting, especially given that most of us do so little of it. We use digital keyboards or keypads for typing documents, composing emails and texts, and for posting to social media. There are few if any bank checks to sign, since most of our financial transactions are done electronically. Even contracts are finalized online with programs like DocuSign. When we do need to sign by hand something like a plumber's bill, it's often with our fingernail on an iPad screen.

In the last chapter, I reviewed some of what psychologists have learned about the cognitive benefits of writing by hand. But I suspect those findings have less punch than what today's young adults say about handwriting being a vehicle for thought:

"It leaves tracks in my mind."

4. Can You AI-Proof Your Personal Writing Voice?

A nasty side effect of digital life is identity theft. Enticing targets are Social Security numbers, credit cards, bank accounts, and, these days, our voice and face. When it comes to theft and digital writing, there's obviously the plagiarism problem. But my concern here is something more subtle: letting AI software coax us to write in a particular way or unquestioningly acquiesce to its suggestions, in the process chipping away at our unique way of writing.

In American schools, there have long been complaints about "teaching to the test," particularly for standardized achievement batteries. What gets lost is the integrity of curricula that teachers themselves build and from which students would likely learn more. The same score-centered approach underlies strategies students were long coached to follow when writing ETS essay questions: Use lots of polysyllabic words. Follow the five-paragraph essay format. Originally, ETS human graders, and then e-rater software, were trained to look for these writing components.[7]

Hemingway surely knew a slew of polysyllabic words, but didn't feel impelled to always lace his writing with lexical mouthfuls. And on the five-paragraph essay—essentially an American invention from the late 1950s—it's just that.[8] An invention. Some compositions work well by devoting one paragraph to an introduction, another to your first point, another to your second point, another to your third, and then a concluding paragraph. But what if you only have one point—or have six—to make? The procrustean bed of the five-paragraph essay demands the essay be either stretched out (find more points) or chopped off (delete or consolidate) if you want a good score.[9]

If writing to the scoring instrument is one way of manipulating the words you choose to use, invoking AI as writing Jeeves is another. Only this time, the maneuvering comes when AI generates words or phrases to present as your own. AI fills in writing you begin (as with Gmail Smart Compose or predictive texting) or suggests replacements for your own word and grammar choices (as with Grammarly or Wordtune).

At various points in this book, we've illustrated the kinds of concerns writers have about text that's had an AI assist. In the professions, we've seen that auto-generated news stories tend to be more cookie-cutter-like than pieces written by humans. Translators tasked with post-editing machine translation speak of their creativity being squelched and it being hard to "think outside the box" when presented with work the computer has already done.

Not everyone's a journalist or translator, but all of us are everyday writers. It's in our day-to-day productions—with Microsoft Word or Grammarly or predictive texting programs perched on our shoulders—that our own distinct mode of writing is vulnerable. Writing is largely a solo activity and often a lonely one. That loneliness can engender uncertainty about whether we have anything worthwhile to say or have said it well. For less confident writers, whether or not they're fluent speakers of the language in which they're writing, AI Jeeves can feel reassuring.

The problem is knowing whether to trust it with your words. I'm reminded of all those medication ads on television that are obligated to spout the caveat "Don't take Magic Potion if you are allergic to any of its ingredients." How are you supposed to know if you're allergic until you take it? With suggestions from Word or Grammarly, if you're not a confident writer, how are you supposed to know whether to accept a particular piece of advice?

To illustrate my worries, take the message that popped up from Word when, as I was drafting this chapter, I wrote that Rameshbabu Praggnanandhaa was "the new Indian wunderkind." Word issued me an "Inclusiveness" flag, warning that "This language may imply bias against indigenous populations" and suggested I substitute "Indigenous" or "Native American." Yes, there are "indigenous" populations in Pragg's home country. But they're indigenous to India, and he doesn't belong to one of them.

I knew to ignore Word's counsel. From Pragg's Hindu name alone, not to mention the long tradition of playing chess in the country that invented the game, it was obvious to me what "Indian" meant. But writers for whom it wasn't self-evident might had ended up substituting "Native American," which would have been absurd.

What to do? The final arbiter needs to be you, and for good reason. As one person in my surveys said about the pitfalls of predictive texting,

"I know more about my native language than the software does."

Sometimes the challenge to your writing voice involves not accuracy or grammar but style. Think back to those essays drafted by students at American University who were applying for prestigious post-graduate awards. The student who had written "in the near future" chose a phrase that was stylistically paced, unlike Microsoft's recommendation of the more abrupt and bland "soon." The one who wrote "can be exacerbated" intentionally chose "exacerbated," not "worsened." I'm hoping these writers held their ground and ignored the machine.

It can take more user effort to review and accept suggestions from the likes of Word or Grammarly than to leave your original in peace. The issue here isn't one of efficiency. It's about weighing your confidence level, knowing when to accept a second opinion, and when to stand up for what you, not an algorithm, intend to say.

5. Is AI Redefining Authorship?

Glitches with grammar and style programs notwithstanding, today's AI tools do an impressive job of cleaning up prose we draft. When it comes to generating substantial text on their own, Adolph Knipe's dream has already largely come true. Among the remaining questions about AI as editor or author is what we decide to do with these success stories. Since I've spent my professional life in university education, I'll start there.

The problem boils down to this. Either now or in the near future, we may not be able to determine how much of their written assignments students have done themselves, leaving us struggling with how to evaluate their work. In an ideal world, there would be ongoing conversations between student and teacher about the piece, maybe including multiple drafts. But half a century in the halls of academe tells me that's largely a pipe dream.

AI isn't a unique challenge. Contract cheating and fraternity files paved the way. But with commercialization of programs running on large language models, the prospects for students accessing personal paper mills increase vastly. What's more, with refinement of programs that can mimic someone's writing style, one of the last bulwarks for detecting cheating ("There's no way Morgan could have written this") is crumbling.

I'm hardly the only person worrying this pedagogical challenge. In September and October 2022, there seemed to be a Great Awakening among US educators and journalists who write about them. Headlines proclaimed, "A.I. Is Making It Easier Than Ever for Students to Cheat" and asked, "Will Artificial Intelligence Kill College Writing?"[10] Some of the authors were extremely concerned. Others counseled teaching students how to collaborate with the technology. A few said not to worry (at least yet), since generative programs currently available to students weren't all that impressive, especially for essays calling for local knowledge that wasn't in the AI's dataset.

All this was before ChatGPT burst on the scene.

Since GPT-3 and its progeny are non-too-shabby as translators, it's hardly surprising ChatGPT also garnered attention in countries with dominant languages other than English. Here's what happened in Norway.[11]

On December 5—a scant week after ChatGPT launched—the Association for Norwegian Language Arts Education (essentially the union for teachers of Norwegian language and literature) sent a letter to the Norwegian parliament. The union's fear was that

> "in the long term [AI text generation] threatens the population's writing and reading skills, democracy and new development of ideas and knowledge."[12]

A cascade of discussion followed. Morten Irgens at Kristiania University College predicted that "This technology can clearly undermine the integrity of all education."[13] Siv Sørås Valand, general manager of the teachers' union, wrote that "it is the students' *writing skills* that are threatened by artificial intelligence." Valand argued it is through writing that

> we teach students to reason, structure, discuss, explore, be creative and critical, reflect, argue, analyze and interpret.[14]

For the Norwegians, the chief problem with generative AI appears to be that it undermines opportunities for students to use writing as a tool for thinking. For the Americans, the focus is more on how to stop cheating.

What to do? Advice from the Americans has focused on crafting assignments such that invocation of a large language model reveals itself. Essentially, design with the aim of stumping the machine. Police first; educate if there's room for it.

The Norwegian approach looks different, emphasizing writing as a learning process. Eirik Vassenden, a professor of Nordic literature at the University of Bergen, counsels avoiding assignments that "invite passive assembly of information" (which the likes of ChatGPT is good at) and instead stressing the process of "finding, organizing, and putting together observations and bits of information."[15] In the same vein, Valand urges distinguishing between the written product of textual interpretation (which AI can spin out) and "the student's practice in understanding and creating meaning in texts."[16] Education is the journey, not just the destination.

Some of the recommendations from educators bring nostalgic smiles. Irgens urges "more emphasis on oral participation in class, oral exams."[17] I was transported back to late-nineteenth-century Harvard University at the cusp of English A and Charles Eliot's switch from oral to written exams. Back then, having too many students to evaluate orally in class sealed the transition to written compositions. And the sheer efficiency of written exams seemed a no-brainer. Returning to oral metrics would address the "who wrote this" problem, but I don't envision reversion to orality happening at large scale.

The Norwegian teachers' union offered another vintage suggestion: having students "write by hand to a much more extensive extent," while acknowledging the idea wasn't practical.[18] Probably not. Though beyond the other virtues of handwriting that we've talked about, teachers would have far more assurance about who wrote what.

Lacking bright ideas of my own, I traveled to the belly of the beast and consulted ChatGPT. The question I posed was, "If chatbots can write student essays, what should composition teachers do?" ChatGPT's responses (I tried the query twice) were amazingly cogent—and lengthy. Here are two snippets from the first iteration, which centered on classroom techniques:

- "Focus more on teaching critical thinking skills and analysis, rather than just teaching students to write in a certain style or format."
- "Incorporate more collaborative and group work into the classroom, where students can work together to brainstorm ideas, share their writing, and provide feedback to each other."

And presumably do their own writing.

The bot's second go at the question began with some irrelevancies but then focused on the role of the teacher:

- "Chatbots are not capable of replacing the expertise and guidance of a trained composition teacher."
- "Composition teachers should continue to focus on teaching students how to conduct research, organize themselves clearly and effectively in writing."

Not much real help, other than suggesting teachers should keep their jobs.

Maybe the tech world will be part of the solution. In the Prologue, I whimsically suggested inserting digital watermarks into text that's AI-generated so we know its real provenance. OpenAI is working on just such a project.[19] Thinking back on AI's early connections with cryptography, it's ironic that OpenAI's approach has been embedding into AI-generated text a signal (the watermark) that can only be detected if you have the "key" to the code. Presumably, users (like schools or publishers or governmental organizations) would need to partner with OpenAI to access the code in order to give thumbs up or down on human versus AI authorship. But then, these organizations are already "partnering" with Turnitin.

A simpler sniff test already existed, thanks to work by OpenAI and several collaborators when the company was releasing GPT-2. The tool, publicly available from Hugging Face, was called GPT-2 Output Detector Demo.[20] You input a passage whose origin you wanted to verify, and the program returned a probability score, using a scale from "real" (human) to "fake" (AI). While the system was designed for an early large language model, it worked surprisingly well when I experimented with text ChatGPT had generated for me versus paragraphs I wrote in this chapter. I was relieved not to be deemed a bot. Be forewarned, though, that predictive accuracy declines with shorter passages, especially those written by AI.

Barely weeks after ChatGPT debuted, Edward Tian wrote GPTZero, a program for identifying AI authorship. As Tian freely admits, the tool is far from perfect, though it continues to evolve. And as we said in Chapter 10, other detection tools have followed.

As of February 2023, Tian's new move was to partner with the EdTech company K16 Solutions to embed GPTZero into the major learning management systems (LMSs) deployed in lower and higher education, like Canvas and Blackboard.[21] (A learning management system is software used as an online platform for academic courses.) The concept is a version of the Turnitin model, which sniffs out plagiarism by comparing new student papers against what those students have previously written (along with the billions of other works in the Turnitin dataset). With Tian's model, students submit written work through the LMS (a practice that's already quite common), and the papers are automatically run through GPTZero.

Shift over to the commercial world. Here authorship questions translate into who profits. If work you created—your intellectual property—is out there on the web, it becomes fodder for an AI model to cannibalize, and some other human user to profit from. Artists worry that people using an AI image generator can create a new work based on the original artist's distinctive style and then market the AI product as their own. To begin addressing this problem, Shutterstock (working in concert with OpenAI and its DALL-E 2) established a fund to compensate human creators who uploaded original art to Shutterstock that's now being used derivatively for AI-generated images.[22]

Artists aren't alone. Human translators are concerned that translations they've done and are available online are being accessed by machine translation programs for other people's projects, without royalties paid to the original translator. In the programming world, there's a lawsuit against GitHub Copilot (the product built on OpenAI's Codex and now licensed to Microsoft). It's unclear what rights, under copyright law, the originators of the code posted on GitHub might have when others reuse it.[23]

And speaking of copyright: To the extent modern authorship includes being able to copyright your work, we'll need more court cases before we can expect settled law—nationally and perhaps internationally—on who or what can hold rights to work generated by AI. While we're waiting for the law to catch up, I decided to consult ChatGPT for its take.

My question was, "Should it be possible for short stories written by GPT to be copyrighted?" In no time flat, the bot replied,

> "As a large language model trained by OpenAI, I am not capable of holding copyrights or owning any form of intellectual property. My primary function is to assist users in generating human-like text based on the input provided me."

Since large language models aren't human, ChatGPT was right in line with US law.

But being a careful scientist (or at least an inveterate experimenter), I wondered if the result was replicable. Large language models draw from vast datasets, so there's no guarantee that when they re-enter the data pool, they'll come up with the same answer. I posed my question a second time but was treated to a different response:

> "As a large language model trained by OpenAI, I do not have the ability to browse the internet or access information that is outside of my training data. I am not able to give you a definitive answer about whether short stories written by GPT can be copyrighted."

Did ChatGPT lose its nerve? Incidentally, that first sentence is something of a boilerplate, appearing as the opening of many ChatGPT answers.

I decided to throw the dice one more time. Now the bot was definitive, but with an opposite conclusion from its first try:

> "It is possible for short stories written by GPT to be copyrighted, just like any other original work of authorship. In order for a work to be protected by copyright, it must be original and fixed in a tangible form, such as being written down or recorded. If a short story written by GPT meets these criteria, then it would be eligible for copyright protection."

Try telling that to the US Copyright Office. Bots like ChatGPT can be intriguing tools to play with. Just don't believe everything you read.

There's one final issue that keeps sticking in my craw when it comes to authorship, and that's human honesty and trust. Lying is hardly a new fact of life, nor are attempts to ferret it out. But the internet and now AI language generation have led gatekeepers to see cheating as lurking behind every pillar and post. Plagiarism detection tools have multiplied like rabbits, and schools around the globe increasingly turn to programs like Turnitin. Scholarly journals and governmental organizations run written submissions through iThenticate. Even apps like Copysmith, which use large language models to generate "new" text, nonetheless do plagiarism checks.

As a scholar and author who's been writing and evaluating the work of others for decades, I feel the walls closing in. You must now pass through a plagiarism detector before being allowed to enter. I hardly condone plagiarism or other forms of cheating when it comes to writing. I understand the pressures (or lack of ethics) leading to these practices. Yet I grieve at transitioning into an authorial world in which trust between writer and reader has eroded so badly.

6. Does AI Threaten Professions Built on Writing Skills?

I'm no fortune teller or even a savvy bettor. In my defense, economists looking to forecast future job prospects for white-collar professions incorporating AI tools aren't always more successful at the game. We've seen the half-empty and half-full predictions, along with hedges involving the "near" versus "long run" future.

In the second part of 2022, a clutch of articles and reports argued human employment prospects weren't so endangered after all. There was Clive Thompson's story in *Wired* encouraging us to welcome AI for augmenting human abilities.[24] Farhad Manjoo's piece in the *New York Times* bore the reassuring title "In the Battle with Robots, Human Workers Are Winning."[25] Manjoo cited a report by Michael Handel, a research analyst at the US Bureau of Labor Statistics (BLS).[26] Drawing on BLS projections, along with additional literature, Handel proffered his forecasts about where a range of professions seemed to be heading in light of AI and automation.

Three of the professions on his list were the ones we've looked at: journalism, law, and translation.[27] Handel's conclusions essentially jibe with our discussion in Chapter 8:

- *In journalism*: Job numbers have been falling for decades, so the projected decline in news-related jobs between 2019 and 2029 isn't new news.
- *In law*: The BLS projection through 2029 is for modest increases in jobs for both lawyers and paralegals. As further corroboration, Handel cites the work of Dana Remus and Frank Levy, which we talked about earlier. You'll

remember that Remus and Levy emphasized that jobs in the legal profession involve a diversity of tasks, with some more endangered than others. When it came to legal writing, the authors hedged their predictions in terms of current AI capabilities, not what the future could bring.

- *In translation*: Handel reminds us that the number of jobs for translators and interpreters is anticipated to keep rising, thanks in large part to globalization. What he doesn't address is how many of these would likely be "good" jobs, in which professionals can meaningfully practice their craft rather than being relegated to the role of post-editor handmaiden.

For everyday writing, control over how much to rely on AI as Jeeves lies mainly in our own hands. Things are different in the business and professional worlds, where the long arm of capitalism is often the decider. No one sought to cripple the US economy by shipping so much manufacturing offshore in the name of increasing profits. But it happened. While individuals have little say on use of AI in the professions, at the very least we best keep our eye on the ball.

Looking to the future, hold two considerations in mind. The first involves quality: For which endeavors is AI's work up to human snuff and which not? Sometimes it's hard for non-professionals to tell the difference, as I'm reminded by those who are skilled in translation. In my European survey, one participant wrote,

> "the [job] threat to translators is MOSTLY due to non-translators not understanding how to judge the quality of AI translation."

Just because we have tools like Google Translate at our literal fingertips doesn't guarantee the accuracy or quality of what shows up. Sometimes we compromise on quality in the name of expediency or because that's what we can afford. But it behooves us to remember that, with translation, you often only get what you pay for.

The other issue is how we prepare ourselves for future work of any sort that includes high levels of augmentation—working alongside rather than being replaced by AI. As Stanford professor of radiology and biomedical informatics Curtis Langlotz put it,

> "Will A.I. replace radiologists" is "the wrong question." . . . "The right answer is: Radiologists who use A.I. will replace radiologists who don't."[28]

Our task will be finding a viable equilibrium between human and AI. Which brings us to the next question for our scorecard.

7. *Where Do You Draw the Line Between Collaboration and Handing over the Keys?*

Back in the day, a lot of math textbooks came with answers to the problems, parked at the back of the book. The same remains true today for many teach-yourself foreign language books. Are you the kind of person who figures out the answers and then checks them? Or do you peek? Skipping out on doing your own work first usually means not learning as much.

The challenge of AI as personal editor or authorial stand-in isn't that Jeeves will replace humans as writers. It's that it takes less effort to pass the reins than to do the work yourself. Getting help is one thing—like a pedal assist bike boosting you up that hill—but undermining your own skills and voice is another. It's all too easy to deceive ourselves about the wisdom of some choices we make. "That French cruller is only 100 calories" (as my then-dieting husband used to say), when it was surely north of 200. "I don't know what to write about. I'll let ChatGPT get me started." An AI brainstorming nudge is one thing. Letting your imagination snooze is another.

Back in the Prologue, we mentioned Stuart Russell's proposed defense against an AI takeover. When developing intelligent machines, build in enough uncertainty about goals so humans are needed to be the final arbiters of what people want done. One respondent in my surveys came up with a version of this scenario:

> "AI is convenient but it should never become so good that we rely on it 100%."

In essence, build in an Achilles' heel. Maybe we should leave some missteps in Word and Grammarly to keep humans on their toes.

Today's AI mantra is augment, not automate. The goal of human-centered AI is to improve human lives, not replace us. But often lurking in the background is the assumption that augmentation is done in the name of increased efficiency.

I'm reminded of the wealth of products bragging about their local origins but outsourced for manufacture. Check the back of your Apple devices, and you'll find in tiny letters "Designed by Apple in California. Assembled in China." In the shoe business, "Danish" ECCO started production in Bredebro, Denmark, but now has factories in Indonesia, Thailand, Slovakia, and yes, China. A few years ago, when on a trip to Copenhagen, I stopped in an ECCO store. The sandals I tried on weren't nearly as comfortable or well-made as a similar model I had purchased in the shop twenty years earlier. When I voiced my complaint, the sales associate wanly smiled and said, "We Danes no longer have control." Economic efficiency at work.

The line between augmentation and automation can become a slippery slope. The argument used to be that we should reserve for humans what they're best at. Things like working with people, handling unpredictable situations, being creative.[29] The problem with such advice is that AI continues to gain ground. It now offers mental health counseling, reads complex mammograms, and writes short stories. The boundaries of what AI can't do keep retreating.

Fei-Fei Li, co-director of Stanford's Institute for Human-Centered Artificial Intelligence, has been exploring what kinds of tasks people would be happy for robots to assume and which ones humans prefer to keep for themselves. On the list for handing over are things like cleaning the toilet. People wanted to hold in reserve activities like opening Christmas presents.[30] If robots are able to handle the delicate task of picking strawberries—and they now can, with 95 percent accuracy[31]—an AI could surely unwrap those presents. But we don't want it to.

As with toilets versus Christmas gifts, there's variation in the kinds of assistance writers may want from AI. We need to distinguish between "capable of" and "we want it to." Katy Ilonka Gero, a human–AI interaction researcher, has been exploring the difference by interviewing scores of writers. She asks,

> Which parts of writing are so tedious you'd be happy to see them go? Which parts bring you the inexplicable joy of creating something from nothing? And what is it about writing you hold most dear?[32]

Among the aspects writers wanted to keep for themselves was planning—things like working out plot lines and endings. Some of the writers Gero interviewed felt planning was part of what made writing a uniquely human enterprise. On the other hand, AI was welcomed when writers felt stuck about what the next word or sentence should be—a talent at which large language models excel. And if writers were looking to inject something unexpected, AI was at their service.

I was curious what ChatGPT had to say about human writing choices. When I asked my new friend about the broader effects of AI on human writing, here's part of what it wrote:

> "While some people may be concerned about the potential for AI to replace human writers, it is important to remember that AI is simply a tool that can be used to assist with the writing process. Ultimately, the impact of AI on writing will depend on how it is used and the choices that people make about how to incorporate it into their writing practices."

Not profound, but well said.

8. Will Disclosure Rules Help?

The incredible hype over ChatGPT was, in a way, curious. Fundamentals behind its programming weren't unique. (Google, DeepMind, and Meta have similar models.) What was novel about OpenAI's chatbot was its public launch. Millions of people could try it out themselves. Suddenly the core technology that techies already knew about was in open view. The media couldn't get enough of stories about the promises and threats of what, for most people, was a brand-new, revolutionary writing tool.

Much of the furor involved use of ChatGPT in education, where responses varied wildly: Some cried, "Ban the technology!" while others argued for embracing the bot's teaching potential. Since writing assignments are part of the curricular DNA of Western education, the demand for immediate action was understandable.

Yet students are hardly the only ones writing. We're all at the mercy of generative AI as author. In the writing professions, AI has already been hard at work for more than a decade. As everyday writers, the rest of us have long been using AI-driven editing tools. Commercial programs like Sudowrite, Jasper, and Wordtune—incorporating large language model technology—have already been on the market for anyone ponying up a credit card.

What's new is that we seem to have reached an inflection point. AI tools cranking out text are becoming domesticated. Maybe it's time for some rules of the road.

In the Prologue, we talked about Isaac Asimov's three laws of robotics, which defined how robots were allowed to behave. Frank Pasquale's "new laws of robotics" focused on the intersection between humans and machines, with dicta like "Robotic systems and AI should complement professions, not replace them" and "Robotic systems and AI should not counterfeit humanity."

Educators, professionals, and everyday users can't control what abilities Big Tech packs into the large language models it releases. But maybe we should try taking on counterfeiting.

In 2019, California adopted the "BOT bill" requiring disclosure when an automated program is used to incentivize commerce or influence voting.[33] Maybe a "disclosure" system would help address written "counterfeiting," here meaning taking credit for words actually generated by AI. In the publishing world, we already see cases of AI attribution: Beta Writer as author of *Lithium-Ion Batteries*; Tencent crediting Dreamwriter. Many news stories indicate where AI has written or co-written the article. Maybe school academic integrity codes, media outlets, law firms, and the rest could adopt guidelines mandating acknowledgment of when AI has written or contributed to a piece of writing that a human is putting out in the world.

For text entirely (or at least substantially) generated by AI, the system might be workable, at least in principle. But then comes the slippery slope: How much must be written by AI before requiring attribution? AI now pervades grammar and style programs (like Microsoft Editor and Grammarly). Programs like Sudowrite will only multiply. No one is suggesting you list Microsoft as co-author when you make use of spellcheck. But at what point should a novelist incorporating a paragraph produced by Sudowrite mention the software?

There's also the issue of whether attempts to include a large language model as co-author could backfire. When ChatGPT arrived in late 2022, a number of researchers began acknowledging its collaborative role by including it as a co-author. But several publishers cried foul, arguing that "AIs such as ChatGPT do not fulfil the criteria for a study author, because they cannot take responsibility for the content and integrity of scientific papers." Not surprisingly, other publishers maintained that AI's contribution needed to be acknowledged.[34] We're in unchartered waters here.

These questions aren't new. It's common for writers of all ilk to ask friends and colleagues to review a draft. Students incorporate rewording proposed by their teachers. If the input comes from humans, we need to decide when those assisting at least deserve credit in our acknowledgments, maybe even elevation to "contributor" or "co-author."

When credit for human contributions is due and we fail to give it, there's always the possibility those who helped us will find out. With AI, it's different. Algorithms don't have feelings and can't sue. Yes, some authenticity police might try looking for AI watermarks (assuming the company producing the program placed them there). And yes, stylometrics programs—or sharp-eyed teachers—can often spot if there's a discrepancy between the new text and the human's usual writing style.

But I'm doubtful that verification will work at scale. Beyond the logistical problems, we have no easy rules for deciding how much uncredited AI assistance is too much.

For My Own Scorecard: Parting Words

What we write is an expression of who we are. Countless writers are more eloquent and insightful than I can hope to be. But my words, even the misspelled ones, even the awkward sentences, flow from my own mind and lived experience. In filling out my personal scorecard, these things matter.

An AI program can manufacture a news story in a twinkling. ETS's software can grade student essays in a fraction of the time it takes me, maybe catching problems I miss. But when I write, it's my byline. And when I grade a paper, I'm reaching out to another human being.

The importance of that reach was forever seared in my brain by an experience early in my college career. At the time I was a sophomore, literally "wise fool," with an emphasis in this instance on the "fool" part. As a potential English major, I had enrolled in a course called "Literary Criticism from Plato to Dryden," taught by the poet J. V. Cunningham. Most of my classmates were seniors or graduate students, who actually belonged there.

I don't remember the topic for the first writing assignment, but do vividly recall agonizing as I worked on it. I was over my head. Cunningham, who suffered no fools, let me know he concurred. His lone comment, slashed across the first page of my paper, read:

This is a kindergartner's mishmash of a history of ideas. F.

He was, of course, right. After licking my wounds, I vowed I'd learn to analyze and to write. To this day, I'm immeasurably grateful that a skilled human reader didn't mince words with this neophyte.

No AI grammar or style tutor would have been as blunt and as effective.

ChatGPT or its descendants would have written a better paper. Maybe not especially insightful, though less of a historical mishmash. But the goal of the assignment wasn't to earn a respectable grade. It was to get me, a coming-to-be student of literature, to engage with authors from centuries past and to grapple with making sense of what they had written. In the process, I would hopefully take one more step towards thinking analytically and finding my own writing voice.

Human writing is a light sword for our minds and for connecting with fellow humans. It's on us to retain that sword's brightness, however efficient AI as writing Jeeves might be.

MAIN CHARACTERS

At the beginning of traditional books of plays and sometimes novels, you find a list of characters—a dramatis personae—to help guide you through the story about to unfold. I've taken the reverse tack by putting this listing at the end. My goal is to offer a brief, one-stop reference source for key acronyms and AI terms. I've also modernized the name. For "main," think *primary* (or, by whimsical association, even that dinosaur *mainframe computer*). And for "characters," yes, it's *players* (or, again, fancifully, *symbols we write with*). Ironically for a list of main characters, you won't find people in this one. But they're in the Index, as is the fuller array of terms used in the book.

A few words on what's here and what's not:

- *On the acronyms (alphabet soup)*: Most but not all involve AI. Where letter combinations look like acronyms but aren't (like ELIZA) or when most people have no clue what the letters stand for (like LaMDA), you'll find the entries under the definitions section.
- *For the definitions (all bite-sized)*: A handful of technical terms are only defined here, their explanations banished from the main text in the interest of streamlining. I've included a few items (like post-editing) that aren't restricted to use in AI. And I've omitted those we all know, like spellcheck and autocomplete. The same goes for decisions about names of AI companies: Everyone's familiar with Microsoft and Google (thus

237

not on my list), while fewer know about DeepMind or AI21 Labs (therefore included).

Alphabet Soup

ACE   Automatic Computing Engine

ACM   Association for Computing Machinery

AGI   artificial general intelligence

AI-MC   artificial intelligence-mediated communication

ALPAC   Automatic Language Processing Advisory Committee

API   application programming interface

ARPANET   Advanced Research Projects Agency Network

BABEL   Basic Automatic BS Essay Language Generator

BERT   bidirectional encoder representations from transformers

BLEU   BiLingual Evaluation Understudy

CBT   cognitive behavioral therapy

CCCC   Conference on College Composition and Communication

CERN   Conseil Européen pour la Recherche Nucléaire (European Council for Nuclear Research)

CMC   computer-mediated communication

DARPA   Defense Advanced Research Projects Agency

ETS   Educational Testing Service

fMRI   functional magnetic resonance imaging

GAN   generative adversarial network

GMAT   Graduate Management Admission Test

GPT   generative pretrained transformer

GPU   graphics processing unit

GRE   Graduate Record Examinations

HCI   human–computer interaction

HTTP   hypertext transfer protocol

LLM   large language model

LSTM	long short term memory neural network
MFA	master of fine arts
MLA	Modern Language Association
MRI	magnetic resonance imaging
MUD	multi-user dungeon (later called "multi-user dimension")
MUM	multitask unified model
NCTE	National Council of Teachers of English
NLP	natural language processing
NPL	National Physical Laboratory (in UK)
NSF	National Science Foundation (in United States)
OCR	optical character recognition
PEG	Project Essay Grade
PET	positron emission tomography
RNN	recurrent neural network
SAT	Scholastic Aptitude Test (no longer called an aptitude test, just "SAT")
SMS	Short Message Service
T9	text on 9 keys
TOEFL	Test of English as a Foreign Language

Bite-Sized Definitions of Key AI Terms and Names

AI21 Labs—Israeli company using own large language model as writing partner for humans.

alignment problem—Challenge of dealing with ethical and existential risks caused by AI decision-making.

Alphabet—Parent company of Google.

AlphaFold—DeepMind's program for deciphering protein folding.

AlphaGo—DeepMind's program that beat Lee Sedol at Go in 2016.

Analytical Engine—Charles Babbage's idea for a general-purpose computer.

Article Forge—Commercial company using own knowledge search engine for generating text like articles, blog posts, or essays.

artificial general intelligence (AGI)—Idea that a machine could simulate the full range of human intellectual activity, not just a single or limited number of tasks.

ASIMO—Humanoid robot at Tokyo's Miraikan Museum.

Automated Insights—Early commercial company using AI to write news stories from data.

Babel Fish—Name of both imaginary instant translator in Douglas Adams's *The Hitchhiker's Guide to the Galaxy* and actual translator available on Alta Vista, an early search engine.

backpropagation—Learning algorithm used for training feed-forward neural networks. Technique used in convolutional neural networks. See Rumelhart et al. 1986.

back-translation—After translating from the source language to the target language, retranslate back to the source language to compare with original text.

Bard—Chatbot introduced by Google in 2023, running on smaller version of LaMDA.

BERT—Google's early transformer. Important application was powering Google Search.

BlenderBot 3—Chatbot released by Meta in 2022, running on OPT-175B.

BLEU score—Yardstick for comparing success of written machine translation against benchmark translations.

Bombe—Electromechanical codebreaking device used during World War II at Bletchley Park.

ChatGPT—Chatbot released by OpenAI in November 2022. Technical name: GPT-3.5.

Codex—OpenAI's program for using natural language input to generate computer code. Through partnership with Microsoft and GitHub, was integrated into Copilot.

Cognitive Systems—Company founded by Roger Schank using natural language processing for business tasks.

Colossus—British computer built to aid in cryptoanalysis during World War II.

contract cheating—Hiring sometime to write a paper for you, and then claiming it as your own. Newer name for paper mills.

convolutional neural networks—Deep learning neural networks used for dealing with structured arrays of data. Applied to many AI tasks, including image classification and natural language processing.

Copilot—Program for using natural language input to generate computer code. Builds on OpenAI's Codex. Available through GitHub.

Copysmith—Commercial program using large language model (GPT-3) for business writing.

Criterion—ETS online writing tool available through schools. Based on e-rater.

DALL-E—OpenAI's initial model for generating graphic images from natural language input. Replaced by DALL-E 2. Competitors include Midjourney and Stable Diffusion.

Deep Blue—IBM's chess-playing program that beat Garry Kasparov in 1997.

deep learning—Machine learning technique using neural networks. Sometimes referred to as deep neural networks.

DeepMind—AI company co-founded by Demis Hassabis. Now owned by Alphabet.

deep neural networks—Approach to machine learning based on analogy with the human brain. Have multiple layers. Sometimes referred to as deep learning.

Difference Engine—Charles Babbage's idea for a special-purpose mechanical calculating machine.

ELIZA—Program developed in 1960s by Joseph Weizenbaum to mimic Rogerian psychotherapist.

ENIAC—Computer built during World War II at the University of Pennsylvania to do ballistics calculations.

Enigma machine—Cryptography machine developed by Germany and used extensively during World War II.

e-rater—Natural language processing tool for evaluating essay components of some ETS examinations.

expert systems—AI model popular in 1970s and 1980s for running inference engine on specialized knowledge base.

explainable AI—Concept of designing deep learning programs that reveal how the programs derived their results.

Ferranti Mark 1—Computer developed at Manchester University in 1951.

foundation model—New name given by Stanford HAI to large language models.

Galactica—Science-based large language model released by Meta in 2022 and quickly withdrawn.

generative adversarial network (GAN)—Deep learning model pitting two neural networks against each other to determine which makes more accurate predictions. See Goodfellow et al. 2014 for how GANs work and Shahriar 2021 for examples in visual art, music, and literary text.

generative AI—Use of artificial intelligence to produce new artifacts, including text, images, music, and computer code.

GitHub—Hosting platform for software. Now owned by Microsoft.

Gmail Smart Compose—Google program released in 2018 to autogenerate sentence completion in new emails.

Gmail Smart Reply—Google program released in 2015 to autogenerate suggestions for email replies.

GPT-3—Widely used large language model developed by OpenAI. GPT-4 appeared in March 2023.

GPTZero—Program created by Edward Tian for detecting when text was written by ChatGPT.

Grammarly—Widely used commercial program for editing user-produced text.

grammatical gender—Feature in many languages where nouns (and sometimes pronouns, articles, and adjectives) are grammatically masculine, feminine, or neuter. Example: German *die Brucke* is grammatically feminine.

human–computer interaction—Original terminology for describing interface between computers and humans using them.

humans in the loop—Contemporary term describing role of humans when using AI programs. More commonly termed "human [singular] in the loop."

hyperlink—Connection between digital locations, originally within a single document but now across the web.

hypertext fiction—Construction of stories by using hyperlinks to join together blocks of text.

ImageNet—Massive dataset of images developed by Fei-Fei Li and her colleagues.

InstructGPT—Large language model refinement by OpenAI, improving on earlier GPT-3 versions. ChatGPT is a "sibling" of InstructGPT.

iThenticate—Turnitin's plagiarism tool for professional contexts like scholarly journals and government.

Jasper—Commercial program using large language model (GPT-3) for business writing.

LaMDA—Large language model developed by Google. Smaller version drives Google's chatbot Bard.

large language model—Programming scheme using large dataset for predicting the next word in a sequence. Some examples: GPT-3 and LaMDA.

LexisNexis—Commercial legal and news research databases.

long short term memory neural network (LSTM)—Version of recurrent neural networks that can refer to sequences of data rather than only one data point.

machine learning—Model where computer programs can improve their performance ("learn") over time.

Memex—Vannevar Bush's imagined machine for linking documents representing all human knowledge.

Meta—Parent company of Facebook.

METAL Project—Machine translation project at the University of Texas at Austin.

Microsoft Editor—AI-powered tool within Microsoft Word (and other Microsoft programs) that provides editing functions. Introduced in 2020; main competitor is Grammarly.

Midjourney—Program for generating images from natural-language input. Similar technology used by DALL-E 2 and Stable Diffusion.

MUM—Transformer model currently powering Google Search, replacing BERT.

Narrative Science—Early commercial company using AI to write news stories from data.

natural gender—Real-world gender of nouns, such as "rams" (male) and "ewes" (female).

natural language generation—Aspect of natural language processing involved in producing new text, including completing human-generated text.

natural language processing (NLP)—Larger enterprise of using computers to generate and "understand" human language.

natural language understanding—Aspect of natural language processing involved in interpreting words and sentences. AI can simulate understanding of human language, but not understand it in a human sense.

neural network—In AI, a programming model based on analogy with human neural connections. Networks involving multiple layers are called deep neural networks.

OpenAI—San Francisco company creating GPT-3, DALL-E, Codex, ChatGPT, and GPT-4.

OPT-175B—Meta's open large language model. Used for chatbot BlenderBot 3.

perceptron—Single layer neural network.

post-editing—Humans editing text that a human or a computer has already translated.

reinforcement learning—Type of machine learning where training involves rewarding desired actions and rejecting undesirable ones. With InstructGPT and Sparrow, humans participated in training to improve answers generated.

RETRO—Language model designed by DeepMind to reduce energy demands.

Shakey—World's first AI-driven mobile robot.

SHRDLU—Early program by Terry Winograd using a robot hand to arrange blocks.

source language—Language that text is being translated from.

Sparrow—DeepMind's chatbot built on its large language model Chinchilla.

speech recognition—Use of AI to process spoken language for purposes like transcription into text, speech-to-speech translation, and interaction with virtual agents.

speech synthesis—Use of AI to convert written text into speech, such as reading email aloud.

Stable Diffusion—Program for generating images from natural language input. Similar technology used by DALL-E 2 and Midjourney.

Stanford HAI—Stanford University's Institute for Human-Centered Artificial Intelligence.

Sudowrite—Commercial text-generation program running on GPT-3. Used by everyday writers and fiction writers.

SYSTRAN—Machine translation system developed by Peter Toma, originally at Georgetown University.

Tale-Spin—Early story-generation program by James Meehan.

target language—Language that text is being translated into.

TAUM-METEO—Meteorological machine translation system developed at the University of Montreal.

transformer—Neural network architecture introduced in 2017. Basis for building large language models.

translatorese—Language adaptation that happens during the translation process.

Turnitin—Commercial plagiarism detector widely used in education.

uncanny valley—Masahiro Mori's image of the psychological effect when AI becomes too realistic.

Watson—IBM's natural language processing program seen on *Jeopardy!* Now used in science, business, and translation applications.

Wordtune—Program from AI21 Labs that offers sentence rewrites.

Writing Mentor—ETS online writing tutor for students, available as a Google Docs add-on app. Based on e-rater.

Wu Dao 2.0—Transformer model of the Beijing Academy of Artificial Intelligence.

XANADU—Ted Nelson's proposed system for a universal library, inspired by Vannevar Bush's Memex.

ACKNOWLEDGMENTS

Conventional protocol for organizing book acknowledgments dictates saving your spouse for last. You know the drill: Praise for your soulmate's moral support. For not complaining about missed meals and plans abandoned. All apply here. But this time, as I roll the credits, Nikhil Bhattacharya (my spouse) deserves top billing. *Who Wrote This?* wouldn't be here without him.

For decades, Nikhil seeded in me curiosity about computers and AI. In 1979, he coaxed me into buying an Apple II Plus, to be replaced five years later by one of the first Macintoshes. In the early 1980s, we commuted miles each week to attend courses on microcomputers, supplemented with trips to some of the first meetings of AAAI (initials now standing for Association for the Advancement of Artificial Intelligence). Then came a gamechanger: an AI conference run by the New York Academy of Sciences. The rostrum of speakers included an all-star cast of luminaries from computer science and philosophy. The icing on the cake was that, by chance, Nikhil and I shared a dinner table with Isaac Asimov.

Soon Nikhil was urging me to write a book about computer languages, from a linguist's perspective. The result was *Computer Languages: A Guide for the Perplexed*. Not being a computer scientist, I started out perplexed indeed. But my one-man cheering squad saw me across that finish line—and all the publishing finishing lines that followed.

Next up in acknowledgments is Felicia Eth, my literary agent. We've worked together for over thirty years, beginning with that book on computer languages. Felicia has known how to encourage and when to urge me out of my academic comfort zone, challenging me to take a stance about the issues at hand. My thanks, Felicia, for all your wise advice.

Then come those who have contributed to this particular book in ways large and small. My dear friend Marina Bondi, at the University of Modena and Reggio Emilia, welcomed me to Modena as a visiting professor and summer school lecturer. While there, I was able to try out my thinking about AI and language, plus had the opportunity to survey students about AI and writing. *Grazie mille*! Lynne Bowker, at the University of Ottawa, has been an invaluable guide as I learned about the intricate relationships, past and present, between AI and translation. (Special gratitude, Lynne, for answering my questions, lightning-fast, during Christmas week.) A trio of Canadian lawyers— John Laskin, Leslie McCallum, and Jesse Beatson— have graciously shared ideas (and references) about the law, writing, and AI. They helped ensure that legal discussions in the book were on solid ground.

A bevy of others have lent guidance, resources, or support of varying sorts. My appreciation (alphabetically) to Kumi Ishiyama, Natalia Lusin, Maria Mariani, Lisa Platnik, Hildegunn Støle, Leslie Wharton, and Ewa Witkowska. (You'll each know why.)

A huge measure of thanks to the loyal souls who read parts or all of the manuscript. Again, alphabetically: Lynne Bowker, Mary Findley, Natalia Kucirkova, Anne Mangen, Leslie McCallum, and Lonneke van der Plas. Your eagle eyes were priceless as I strove to get the facts right, clean up sloppy errors, and rethink passages that needed clarifying. My gratitude as well to the external reviewers whose suggestions were all constructive (and most of which I followed).

Choosing to publish with Stanford University Press was a kind of homecoming. From 1968–1972, I did my graduate work at what was then Stanford's Committee on Linguistics. I've returned to "the Farm" at least half a dozen times since then, including a stint as a visiting scholar at the Stanford Center for Advanced Study in the Behavioral Sciences. But publishing with Stanford was a first for me.

The welcome I received from the press was incredibly warm. Heartful thanks to my editor, Erica Wetter, and to associate editor Caroline McKusick for shepherding the book (and me). This gratitude extends to everyone orchestrating the review and publishing process. An especially loud shout-out to copyeditor Jennifer Gordon, who tactfully rooted out my many textual foibles.

Jennifer is living proof that AI programs cannot replace world-class human editors. What a pleasure it's been to be part of such a team.

And speaking of teams: Rebecca Basu, associate director of communications and media at American University, has been a stalwart (and ingenious) supporter and publicist for my research for many years. Rebecca, I owe you much more than lunch!

Finally, I acknowledge the legions of AI researchers, from Alan Turing up through creators of today's large language models, for driving us to think about how computers might turf out or complement human intellectual activity, including the skill and art of writing. *Who Wrote This?* is my modest contribution to collective attempts to understand the potential—for good or for ill—of today's wicked-smart writing machines.

NOTES

Prologue

1. Dahl 1996, p. 15.
2. M. Anderson 2022.
3. Vincent April 17, 2018.
4. Basu 2021.
5. Clark et al. 2021.
6. See Dou et al. 2022 for discussion of SCARECROW, an AI tool designed to flush out AI from human writing.
7. "What Grades Can AI Get in College?" n.d.
8. Thunström 2022. You can read the paper at GPT Generative Pretrained Transformer et al. 2022.
9. Gutman-Wei 2019.
10. Patterson and Linden 1981; Savage-Rumbaugh 1994.
11. R. Brown 1980.
12. Terrace 1979.
13. N. Chomsky 1959; Skinner 1957.
14. N. Chomsky 1966.
15. McCoy et al. 2021.
16. https://livestream.com/rutgersitv/chomsky/videos/100919931 (beginning at minute 50)
17. Quoted in Garfinkel n.d.
18. Knight 2022.
19. McKinney et al. 2020.
20. Barber 2021; Hie et al. 2021.
21. *Iliad*, Book 18.
22. The same Daedalus was credited with building the labyrinth in Crete and with fashioning wings for his ill-fated son Icarus.

251

23. Aristotle, *Politics*, Book I, Part IV.

24. Brynjolfsson and McAfee 2014; Levy and Marnane 2004; McAfee and Brynjolfsson 2017; D. Susskind 2020; Susskind and Susskind 2015.

25. Asimov 1981.

26. Pasquale 2020.

27. S. Russell 2019, p. 173.

28. Moncada 1983.

29. "Voters Turn Down Ban" 1983.

30. AI's advice may also reflect bias. See Christian 2020.

31. Strubell et al. 2019.

32. Heaven December 8, 2021.

33. For some alternative approaches, see Heaven May 3, 2022; Theron 2022; "Workshop on Foundation Models" 2021.

34. Quoted in Garber 2013.

35. https://googlefeud.com

36. https://www.wired.com/video/series/google-autocomplete-inverviews

37. https://www.studiosabia.com/wired-autocomplete-interview

38. Gibbs 2016.

39. Abid et al. 2021.

40. Ngo and Sakhaee 2022.

41. Bavarian Broadcasting n.d.

42. Lee and Lai 2021.

43. Hsu and Thompson 2023.

44. Heikkilä August 31, 2022.

45. European Union 2016, Article 39.

46. See Casey et al. 2019 for discussion of the challenge.

47. Vincent January 12, 2018.

48. Mac 2021.

49. Buolamwini and Gebru 2018. For more discussion of how AI algorithms perpetuate inequity, see Noble 2018. For DeepMind's analysis of challenges in detoxifying language models, see Welbl et al. 2021.

50. https://ai.google/principles/

51. Bender et al. 2021.

52. For a detailed account, see Simonite 2021.

53. Metz 2021.

54. See, for example, Broussard 2018.

55. Marcus 2022.

56. https://www.youtube.com/watch?v=PBdZi_JtV4c

57. For Marcus's ideas on how, see Marcus and Davis 2019.

58. Marshall 2021.

59. Silverstone and Hirsch 1992.

60. Baym 2010, pp. 45–49.

61. Ling 2012.

62. Wright n.d.

63. Mori 2012.

64. Gault 2022.

65. Neate 2021.

66. T. Adams 2010.
67. https://www.nextrembrandt.com
68. Klingemann 2020.
69. Zeitchik 2021.
70. Jefferson 1949, p. 1110.
71. Tiku 2022.
72. Gebru and Mitchell 2022.
73. US Food and Drug Administration n.d.

Chapter 1

1. "Gorham's Cave Complex" n.d.; "Neanderthals" n.d.
2. "Australia" 2021.
3. "How Sequoyah" 2020.
4. For a visual demonstration of the benefits of Hangul, see https://www.youtube.com/watch?v=MYT9VagKJQQ
5. "Year of China" n.d.
6. Mallery 1972.
7. "Cracking the Maya Code" n.d.
8. Bloomfield 1933, p. 21.
9. For example, R. Harris 2000.
10. N. Baron 1998, N. Baron 2008; Crystal 2001; a continuing skein of articles in the *Journal of Computer-Mediated Communication.*
11. Cressy 1980, pp. 178, 176.
12. *Waldorf Today* n.d.
13. C. Chomsky 1971, C. Chomsky 1979.
14. LaFranchi 1984; Martin and Friedberg 1986; Slavin 1991.
15. Plutarch *Aristides* 7.
16. Tsu 2022.
17. Cressy 1980, p. 117.
18. Messenger 2015.
19. "International Literacy Day 2021" 2021.
20. The script's predecessor, Linear A, was presumably used to write the Minoan language, about which we know precious little. Linear A remains undeciphered—at least in most people's judgment.
21. Coulmas 1989, pp. 164–165.
22. Goody and Watt 1963.
23. Biblical Archaeology Society 2020.
24. Halverson 1992.
25. Olson 1994, p. 242.
26. N. Baron 2000.
27. W. Harris 1989.
28. Greenfield and Bruner 1966.
29. Scribner and Cole 1981.
30. Costandi 2016.
31. Elbert et al. 1995; Peng and Park 2019.
32. Maguire et al. 2000.

33. Dehaene 2009; Dehaene et al. 2015.
34. Besides the ex-fighters, some housewives from similar backgrounds were included in the study.
35. Carreiras et al. 2009.
36. Dehaene et al. 2010.
37. Skeide et al. 2017.
38. Hutton et al. 2020a; Hutton et al. 2020b; Horowitz-Kraus and Hutton 2018.
39. Goldman 2021. Also see https://www.braingate.org/about-braingate/
40. C. Zimmer 2014.
41. Plato *Phaedrus* 275a–275b.

Chapter 2

1. Chadwick 1959.
2. Benson 1975.
3. Authors Guild n.d.
4. N. Baron 2000, pp. 48–53.
5. Minnis 1988, p. 12.
6. Minnis 1988, pp. 196–197, 199.
7. Feather 1994, p. 191.
8. British copyright protects "work that expresses an idea . . . but not the idea behind it" ("UK Copyright Law" 2021). The US Copyright Office spells out that while copyright covers "original works of authorship," it doesn't protect "facts, ideas, systems, or methods of operation, although it may protect the way these things are expressed" ("What Does Copyright Protect?" n.d.).
9. "UK Copyright Law" 2021; "Copyright Basics" n.d.
10. Slater 2014.
11. *Naruto v. Slater* 2016.
12. US Copyright Office 2014, §313.2.
13. Samuelson 1986, p. 1199.
14. US Constitution, Article 1, Section 8, Clause 8.
15. Bridy 2012, para. 51.
16. Grimmelmann 2016a; Grimmelmann 2016b.
17. "Summary of the Berne Convention" n.d.
18. Bridy 2016, p. 400, citing the New Zealand Copyright Act of 1994.
19. Zhou n.d.
20. For some examples, see https://lifearchitect.ai/books-by-ai/
21. Samuelson 2020.
22. Originally appearing in the *Chronicle of Higher Education* in 1976.
23. Lunsford et al. 2017, p. iii. Italics in the original.
24. Brogaard et al. 2018; C. Flaherty 2017.
25. In this section and the next, I draw heavily upon quotations compiled in *Aerogramme Writers' Studio* ("Why I Write" 2014). I've used my own judgment as to which sentiments belong in this section or the following one, but feel free to recategorize.
26. Nin 1974.

27. Z. Smith 2006.
28. Coelho 1996.
29. Green n.d.
30. Quoted in Flood 2009.
31. Zafón n.d.
32. Wiesel 1985.
33. Although the quotation is widely cited, I've been unable to locate its source.
34. See *Quote Investigator* n.d. for a chronology of instances.
35. These quotations, especially O'Connor's, commonly appear in print and online: *NPR* 2005. However, tracking down sources has proven challenging.
36. 1964 interview.
37. Dahl 1984.
38. "Chinese Dissident" 2001.
39. Liukkonen 2008.
40. Shepherd n.d.
41. Lahiri 2017, p. 18.
42. A. Flaherty 2004.
43. Crouse 2022.
44. NACE 2018.
45. NACE 2022.

Chapter 3

1. Swift 1991.
2. Scragg 1974.
3. Cited in Scragg 1974, p. 90.
4. Crystal 2006; Curzan 2014; Leonard 1929.
5. Crystal 2006, pp. 107–108.
6. Lindley Murray was an American but wrote his *English Grammar* after moving to England.
7. Abadi 2018.
8. Yates 1989.
9. Davies 1982, appendix, Table 1.
10. Eliot 1869a. *The Atlantic Monthly* has changed its name to *The Atlantic*.
11. Fithian 1950.
12. Eliot 1869b.
13. Diehl 1978.
14. Schiff n.d.
15. M. Mitchell n.d. a.
16. M. Mitchell n.d. b.
17. Myers 1996, p. 38.
18. Wozniak 1978, p. 8. Cited in Brereton 1995, p. 4.
19. Kennedy 1980.
20. Harvard University Archives Research Guides n.d., 1869–1870, p. 39.
21. "When Greek and Latin Ruled" 1914.

22. Harvard University Archives Research Guides n.d., 1869–1870, pp. 34–39.

23. E. Abbott 1876; Hill 1874. For lists of textbook requirements, see Harvard University Archives Research Guides n.d., 1874–1875, p. 44.

24. Brereton 1995, p. 34.

25. Briggs 1888; text reproduced in Brereton 1995, p. 60.

26. Harvard University Archives Research Guides n.d., 1884–1885, p. 74; 1885–1886, p. 42.

27. Brereton 1995, p. 11.

28. D. Russell 2002, p. 341 fn 38.

29. Reid 1959, p. 254.

30. C. Adams et al. 1897; text reproduced in Brereton 1995, p. 112.

31. See Payne 1895 for descriptions of writing programs at representative English departments; text reproduced in Brereton 1995, pp. 157–186.

32. Lounsbury 1911; text reproduced in Brereton 1995, p. 280.

33. Brereton 1995, p. 127.

34. Lounsbury 1911; text reproduced in Brereton 1995, pp. 282, 283.

35. We'll only be talking about grading prose assignments, not, say, homework in mathematics or computer science, where AI is making significant inroads; see Swafford 2021.

36. Brereton 1995, p. 18.

37. Brereton 1995, p. 22.

38. S. Brown et al. 1994.

39. Phelps 1912; text reproduced in Brereton 1995, p. 288.

40. Lounsbury 1911; cited in Brereton 1995, p. 270.

41. C. Adams et al. 1892; text reproduced in Brereton 1995, p. 76.

42. The history that follows draws upon Gallagher 2003.

43. For the history of standardized testing, including the role of James Conant, see N. Lehmann 1999.

44. Over time, ETS assumed responsibility for overseeing testing not just for college (SAT) and graduate school (GRE) admissions, but for earlier high school performance (PSAT), Advanced Placement Tests, English skills of non-native speakers (TOEFL), educational licensure (Praxis), and specialty college-level knowledge fields (CLEP). Plus, for lower education, ETS manages the National Assessment for Educational Progress (NAEP). Admissions testing for professional programs generally remains in the hands of organizations like the Law School Admission Council (LSAT) and the Association of American Medical Colleges (MCAT).

45. Much of this chronology is drawn from Jacobsen n.d. Also see Hartocollis et al. 2021.

46. College Board n.d.; Hartocollis et al. 2021.

47. Page 1966, p. 239.

48. Other companies have entered the computer-based essay evaluation business, such as the textbook publisher Pearson, with its Intelligent Essay Assessor.

49. ETS n.d. a.

50. Attali et al. 2010; Monaghan and Bridgeman 2005.

51. Besides a succession of US patents—all publicly available—you can find

papers delivered at computer conferences, along with two research handbooks, edited by ETS staff; see Shermis and Burstein 2013; Yan et al. 2020. For an ETS retrospective of fifty years of automated evaluation of writing, see Klebanov and Madnani 2020.

52. Kincaid et al. 1975.

53. Burstein et al. 2010; Klebanov et al. 2017.

54. ETS n.d. b.

55. CCCC 2004.

56. White 1969, p. 167.

57. Quoted in T. Smith 2018.

58. Powers et al. 2001.

59. Quoted in Winerip 2012.

60. Perelman 2020.

61. Cahill et al. 2018, p. 204.

62. Burstein et al. 2001; Burstein et al. 2004.

63. ETS Global n.d.

Chapter 4

1. M. Roberts 2019.

2. This history of the Enigma machine draws on Copeland 2004 and "History of the Enigma" n.d.

3. Copeland 2004, p. 228.

4. For a short demonstration of how the Enigma machine worked, see https://www.youtube.com/watch?v=DBn2J4xoNQ4

5. https://csenigma.pl/en/

6. Details about Turing's work at Bletchley Park, as well as content in the next section (on Turing and artificial intelligence), draw on Copeland 2004.

7. Alexander n.d.

8. For details on how the decoding process worked, see Copeland 2004, pp. 217–266.

9. Copeland 2004, p. 218.

10. Kindy 2022.

11. Turing 1937. The paper was delivered in 1936 (and referred to as a 1936 paper) but published in 1937.

12. The original manuscript is available on the National Physical Laboratory website. My references are to those page numbers.

13. Turing 1948, p. 107.

14. Turing 1948, p. 117.

15. Turing 1948, p. 127.

16. Turing 1950, p. 433.

17. Turing 1950, p. 434.

18. Turing 1951, in Copeland 2004, pp. 482, 483.

19. Turing 1951, in Copeland 2004, p. 485.

20. Turing et al. 1952, in Copeland 2004, p. 500.

21. Turing et al. 1952, in Copeland 2004, p. 502.

22. J. McCarthy 2006.

23. J. McCarthy 2006.

24. Moor 2006, pp. 88–89.

25. Navarria 2016.

26. This discussion of expert systems draws upon Russell and Norvig 2021.

27. "'Expert System' Picks Key Workers' Brains" 1989; Oravec 2014.

28. For more information on Sophia, developed by David Hanson, see https://www.hansonrobotics.com/sophia/ and https://www.youtube.com/watch?v=Sq36J9pNaEo

29. K. Johnson 2021.

30. https://guides.loc.gov/this-month-in-business-history/july/zip-code-introduced

31. Matan et al. 1991.

32. LeCun et al. 1998.

33. Li n.d.

34. https://www.image-net.org/about.php

35. Copeland 2004, p. 353.

36. Copeland 2004, pp. 562–563.

37. N. Chomsky 1993, p. 93. Cited in Copeland 2004, p. 565.

38. Michie 1986, p. 78. Cited in Copeland 2004, p. 562.

39. This chronology draws on Copeland 2004, pp. 356–358 and chap. 16.

40. Koch 2016.

41. Quoted in Heaven February 23, 2022.

42. The discussion of protein folding that follows draws primarily upon Callaway 2020 and Heaven February 23, 2022.

43. Quoted in Callaway 2020.

44. See Stanford Center for Research on Foundation Models: https://crfm.stanford.edu

45. For starters: A thorough textbook is Russell and Norvig 2021; for an entertaining, futuristic, but technologically grounded discussion, see Lee and Qiufan 2021.

Chapter 5

1. Sapir 1921, p. 39.

2. See Russell and Norvig 2021, pp. 24–25 for a concise overview of the transition.

3. Turing 1951, in Copeland 2004, p. 485.

4. Samuel 1959.

5. See "What Is a Neuron?" n.d. for a brief discussion of neurons; see Jabr 2012 on the word's origin.

6. Turing, writing in 1948, had assumed electrical circuits were like human nerves.

7. "New Navy Device Learns by Doing" 1958.

8. Minsky and Papert 1969.

9. This list draws upon the press release from the Association for Computing Machinery announcing the award: "Fathers of the Deep Learning Revolution Receive ACM A. M. Turing Award" 2019.

10. Chung 2019.

11. Vaswani et al. 2017.

12. Devlin et al. 2018.

13. In 2021, Google Search adopted a new transformer model, MUM (Multitask Unified Model), which was 1,000 times more powerful than BERT; see Nayak 2021.

14. Two billion more followed. By January 2023, negotiations were concluding for an additional $10 billion to integrate ChatGPT into Microsoft products; see Heikkilä January 17, 2023.

15. "Pope Ditches Latin as Official Language of Vatican Synod" 2014.

16. van Bezooijen 1995.

17. Lorenz 2021.

18. Baker and Gillick n.d.

19. Hao 2021.

20. Limbong 2021.

21. Jee 2022.

22. https://cloud.google.com/text-to-speech

23. Jia and Weiss 2019.

24. Crystal 2010.

25. Heaven March 29, 2022.

26. Ives and Mozur 2021.

27. Shah and Bender 2022.

28. Kim et al. 2021.

29. Potthast et al. 2020.

30. https://www.gov.scot/publications/scottish-governments-gaelic-language-plan-2022-2027/pages/4/

31. Disfluency repair software such as Microsoft's earlier TrueText has been available for nearly a decade. Updated models continue to be developed (see, for example, Lou and Johnson 2020).

Chapter 6

1. Bach 2018.

2. Hutchins 2002.

3. Letter incorporated in Weaver 1949.

4. Bowker 2012; Weaver 1964. I am grateful to Lynne Bowker for alerting me to this side of Weaver's interests.

5. Bar-Hillel 1951.

6. Walker 2015.

7. *Language and Machines* 1966. For a concise summary, see Hutchins 1996.

8. W. Lehmann n.d.

9. Slocum n.d.

10. https://www.systran.net/en/translate/

11. Gotti et al. 2014. See Bennett 1995 for a description of other applied projects through the early 1990s.

12. Thouin 1982, p. 43. I'm grateful to Lynne Bowker for alerting me to this human dimension.

13. P. Brown et al. 1988.

14. Bowker and Buitrago Ciro 2019, p. 42.

15. Cho et al. 2014; Kalchbrenner and Blunsom 2013.

16. See Wu et al. 2016 for technical details and Lewis-Kraus 2016 for an account in the *New York Times Magazine.*

17. Brynjolfsson et al. 2019.

18. While versions of the story appeared through the centuries in both literature and art, it's unclear how much is true; see Beard 2007, pp. 81ff.

19. Lynne Bowker, personal communication, December 19, 2022.

20. For an overview of gender bias in machine translation, see Savoldi et al. 2021.

21. Gender balances differ across countries; see Ramakrishnan et al. 2014.

22. https://www.aamc.org/news-insights/nation-s-physician-workforce-evolves-more-women-bit-older-and-toward-different-specialties; https://www.ncsbn.org/workforce.htm

23. M. Johnson 2020.

24. Boroditsky et al. 2003.

25. N. Baron 1981.

26. Weaver 1949.

27. See Boroditsky 2018 for a short overview of these issues.

28. https://cotoacademy.com/japanese-color-blue-green-aoi-midori-青い-みどり/ My thanks to Kumi Ishiyama for review of these language issues.

29. I am most grateful to Natalia Lusin and the Modern Language Association for making the 2022 data available to me before general release; see https://www.mla.org/Resources/Guidelines-and-Data/Reports-and-Professional-Guidelines/Teaching-Enrollments-and-Programs/Enrollments-in-Languages-Other-Than-English-in-United-States-Institutions-of-Higher-Education; https://apps.mla.org/flsurvey_search

30. Bar-Hillel 1960.

Chapter 7

1. Vincent April 10, 2019.

2. Cohen 2008.

3. Bosker 2013.

4. Baines 2017; Strachey 1954.

5. S. Roberts 2017.

6. "Listening to the Music of Turing's Computer" 2016.

7. Henrickson 2021.

8. Weizenbaum 1966.

9. Nelson 1980.

10. Bush 1945. *The Atlantic Monthly* has changed its name to *The Atlantic.*

11. Wolf 1995.

12. For more on the trajectory from Bush's Memex to the World Wide Web, see Barnet and Tofts 2013.

13. Montfort 2008.

14. Meehan 1977.

15. Wardrip-Fruin 2006.

16. Schank and Abelson 1977.

17. Landow 1992, p. 41.

18. Montfort 2008.

19. Coover 1992.

20. Coover 1993. See Mangen and van der Weel 2017 for a literary analysis of the problems with hypertext fiction.

21. S. Johnson 2013.

22. Advertisement in 1749 for the new *Quarterly Review*. Cited in Forster 2001, p. 171.

23. N. Baron 2015, pp. 45–56.

24. My account draws on Fyfe 2021.

25. Luhn 1958.

26. Luhn 1958, p. 160.

27. Springer et al. 1991.

28. Ruby 2023.

29. https://www.cmswire.com/customer-experience/gartner-names-content-marketing-leaders-appsflyer-names-svp-and-other-news/

30. Alkan n.d.

31. Nizinsky 2022.

Chapter 8

1. https://github.com/openai/dalle-2-preview/blob/main/system-card.md#econosumic

2. "Spurned Love Leads to Knitting Invention" 2014.

3. Conniff 2011.

4. D. Susskind 2020, p. 19.

5. Brynjolfsson and McAfee 2014.

6. Strachey 1954, p. 31.

7. Tyson and Zysman 2022.

8. Bommasani et al. 2021, p. 149.

9. Quoted in Terrell 2019.

10. Chalaby 1998.

11. Walker and Matsa September 20, 2021.

12. Shearer 2021.

13. Fassler 2012.

14. Colford 2014.

15. Eide 2019.

16. Clerwall 2014.

17. Thurman et al. 2017.

18. Quoted in Holmes 2016.

19. "Newspapers Fact Sheet" 2021.

20. Walker and Matsa May 21, 2021.

21. Edmonds 2022.

22. For instance, Diakopoulos 2019; Eldridge and Franklin 2019; Marconi 2020; Thurman et al. 2021.

23. Quoted in Fassler 2012.

24. Quoted in Colford 2014.

25. Quoted in Eide 2019.

26. Quoted in Carlson 2015, p. 421.

27. "Microsoft 'to Replace Journalists with Robots'" 2020.

28. Oremus 2021.

29. For an excellent source book on using AI in litigation, see Presser et al. 2021.

30. https://en.wikipedia.org/wiki/LexisNexis

31. https://lexmachina.com/legal-analytics/

32. https://www.lexisnexis.com/en-us/products/context.page

33. Moran 2020.

34. Heller et al. 2021, p. 116.

35. For more examples, see Swanburg 2021.

36. https://www.legalmation.com/platform-overview/

37. Wiggers November 23, 2022.

38. https://www.americanbar.org/content/dam/aba/administrative/market_research/2022-national-lawyer-population-survey.pdf

39. https://www.bls.gov/oes/current/oes232011.htm

40. R. Susskind 2017, p. 188.

41. Many others share the conviction that a strong need for human lawyers will remain. See, for example, Fagan 2022; Legg and Bell 2020; Markovic 2019; Pasquale 2018.

42. Remus and Levy 2017, pp. 519–520.

43. https://www.bls.gov/ooh/legal/paralegals-and-legal-assistants.htm

44. https://www.bls.gov/ooh/legal/lawyers.htm

45. Dickler 2009.

46. I'm most grateful to Lynne Bowker for her guidance regarding AI and translation.

47. Duff 1981; Gellerstam 1986.

48. M. Baker 1996.

49. Baroni and Bernardini 2006.

50. Vanmassenhove et al. 2021.

51. Bowker 2002.

52. https://www.bls.gov/ooh/media-and-communication/interpreters-and-translators.htm#tab-6

53. https://www.languagewire.com/en/blog/top-translation-companies

54. https://www.prnewswire.com/news-releases/machine-translation-market-to-value-usd-7-5-billion-by-2030--says-global-market-insights-inc-301563769.html

55. Lynne Bowker pointed out to me that while free translation programs retain your data and can reuse or repurpose it, paid platforms do not. What's more, it's possible to train paid platforms on corpora tailored to your translation area, such as law. Personal communication, December 19, 2022.

56. Wetsman 2021.

57. Bowker and Buitrago Ciro 2019.

58. Toral 2019.

59. Pielmeier and O'Mara 2020.

60. Lynne Bowker, personal communication, December 19, 2022.
61. Stewart 2021; Udagawa 2021.
62. Motion 1999.
63. Kenny and Winters 2020; Zhang 2016.
64. Kenny and Winters 2020.
65. Quoted in Moorkens et al. 2018.
66. Quoted in Moorkens et al. 2018.
67. Guerberof Arenas and Toral 2020, Guerberof Arenas and Toral 2022.
68. Quoted in Guerberof Arenas and Toral 2020.

Chapter 9

1. Bruner 1962, p. 18. Italics in the original.
2. Csikszentmihalyi 2013, p. 27.
3. Stein 1953, p. 311.
4. Vitale 2013.
5. Parkey 2021.
6. Merrotsy 2013.
7. Luckenback 1986, p. 9.
8. Boden 1991; Csikszentmihalyi 2013; Gardner 1993.
9. Csikszentmihalyi 2013, p. 7.
10. Csikszentmihalyi 1998, p. 81.
11. Kaufman and Beghetto 2009.
12. Gardner 1993.
13. Csikszentmihalyi 2013.
14. Richtel 2022, p.10.
15. "Calculus Created in India" 2007.
16. Boden 1991, p. 32. Italics in the original.
17. Quoted in Menick 2016.
18. Guilford 1950, p. 446.
19. Dietrich 2019.
20. For discussion of neurological bases for creativity, see Abraham 2018; Nalbantian and Matthews 2019.
21. Andreasen 2005, pp. 70 ff.
22. Zedelius and Schooler 2020.
23. Andreasen 2005, p. 74.
24. Andreasen 2005.
25. Gardner 1983.
26. Jauk et al. 2013.
27. Gardner 1983.
28. Andreasen 2005, pp. 127ff.
29. Cited in an interview, Richtel 2022, p. 233.
30. Aristotle *Problemata* XXX.1 953a10–14.
31. Ellis 1926.
32. Andreasen 2005, p. 95.
33. Kyaga 2015.
34. Grant 2018.

35. De Kamper and McGinn 2021.
36. Siegal 2015.
37. M. Brown 2020.
38. Boyd and Pennebaker 2015, p. 577.
39. T. Adams 2010.
40. du Sautoy 2019, pp. 200 ff.
41. Quoted in G. Johnson 1997.
42. For more details, see Elgammal 2021. For a video discussion and musical sample, see https://www.youtube.com/watch?v=kS6h1TKuOrw
43. Miller 2019, p. 113.
44. See https://www.nextrembrandt.com and Brinkhof 2021.
45. Brinkhof 2021.
46. "Is Artificial Intelligence Set to Become Art's Next Medium?" 2018.
47. Quoted in Ranjit 2021.
48. Lau et al. 2020.
49. Wilk 2021.
50. Jozuka 2016.
51. https://www.ted.com/talks/oscar_schwartz_can_a_computer_write_poetry
52. http://bregman.dartmouth.edu/turingtests/competition2018
53. Rockmore 2020.
54. Wilk 2021.
55. Zacharias et al. n.d.
56. Boden 1998, p. 355.
57. Shane 2021.
58. See Riedl 2021 for a tutorial on AI storytelling.
59. For some of the debate, see Fletcher and Larson 2022 versus Chun and Elkins 2022.
60. Boden 1991, p. 5.
61. J. Kaufman 2018, p. 740.

Chapter 10

1. Hancock et al. 2020.
2. Earnest 2012.
3. Teitelman 1966.
4. Engber 2014.
5. Engber 2014.
6. Wilson 2008.
7. B. Zimmer 2011.
8. Ganapati 2010.
9. Kocienda 2018.
10. B. Zimmer 2011.
11. Selinger 2015.
12. Arnold et al. 2020.
13. Dobrin 1990.
14. My experiment was in July 2020. As Word continues evolving, the same results might or might not appear.

15. Curzan 2014; McGee and Ericsson 2002.

16. Herrington and Moran 2012, p. 226.

17. Lytvyn 2021.

18. www.grammarly.com

19.https://support.grammarly.com/hc/en-us/articles/360029743831-Introducing-our-expert-writing-service

20. The attempts of both Microsoft Editor and Grammarly to eliminate bias and expand inclusivity have generated sharp public response. See, for example, D. Baron 2022; Onion 2022.

21. https://mentormywriting.org

22. https://www.cmu.edu/dietrich/english/research-and-publications/docuscope.html

23. Burstein et al. 1998; Klebanov et al. 2017.

24. https://www.grammarly.com/press/research/docs/grammarlystudentsurvey-121018133119-phpapp01.pdf

25. de Beer 2020.

26. See Mayne 2021 for discussion of both issues.

27. Finley 2021, p. 6; C. Flaherty 2021.

28. N. Baron 2002.

29. Lubrano 1997, p. 124.

30. See Shank 2004 on the history of greeting cards in the United States.

31. Berrong 2021.

32. Chen et al. 2019.

33. Corrado 2015.

34. A. McCarthy 2019.

35. https://www.wordtune.com

36. https://www.articleforge.com Article Forge runs on its own knowledge search engine.

37. Neely 2016.

38. N. Anderson 2021.

39. Mallon 1989.

40. McCabe 2005.

41. See, for example, Krokoscz 2021; Nordling 2018.

42. Mesa 2022.

43. Clarke and Lancaster 2006.

44. Newton 2018.

45. Kansara and Main 2021.

46. Abalkina 2021.

47. Cu and Hochman 2023.

48. Else 2023.

49. Choi et al. 2023.

50. Bommarito and Katz 2022.

51. Kung et al. 2022.

52. Chaski 2012.

53. https://marketing-tii-statamic-assets-us-west-2.s3-us-west-2.amazonaws.com/marketing/our-content-databases_brochure_us_0322.pdf

54.https://www.turnitin.com/blog/ai-writing-the-challenge-and-opportunity-in-front-of-education-now; https://www.turnitin.com/blog/sneak-preview-of-turnitins-ai-writing-and-chatgpt-detection-capability

55. Bowman 2023; https://gptzero.me

56. E. Mitchell et al. 2023; https://openai.com/blog/new-ai-classifier-for-indicating-ai-written-text/

57. Caren 2021.

58. https://www.turnitin.com/products/ithenticate

59. Tomar 2012.

60. https://help.turnitin.com/feedback-studio/flags.htm

Chapter 11

1. Switek 2011.

2. "Duplicating Polygraph" n.d.

3. https://www.monticello.org/site/research-and-collections/polygraph

4. Trithemius 1974.

5. Febvre and Martin 1976, p. 74.

6. Brynjolfsson 2022.

7. Card et al. 1983.

8. Shneiderman 1987.

9. Xu 2019.

10. Monarch 2021.

11. https://research.ibm.com/blog/what-is-human-centered-ai; Shneiderman 2022.

12. Murati 2022. Murati was writing here in context of the advantages of OpenAI's coding program Codex.

13. Scott 2022, p. 79.

14. Quoted in S. Levy 1997.

15. Thompson February 18, 2022.

16. Kasparov 2010.

17. https://linuxhint.com/history-of-linux/

18.https://certificates.creativecommons.org/cccertedu/chapter/1-1-the-story-of-creative-commons/

19. Heaven May 3, 2022.

20. H. Shah n.d.

21. Thompson March 15, 2022.

22.https://www.mhanational.org/number-people-reporting-anxiety-and-depression-nationwide-start-pandemic-hits-all-time-high

23. https://www.apa.org/ptsd-guideline/patients-and-families/cognitive-behavioral

24. https://woebothealth.com/img/2021/07/Woebot-Health-Research-Bibliography-July-2021-1.pdf

25. Jee and Heaven 2021; https://iesogroup.com

26. "Aligning Language Models to Follow Instructions" 2022.

27. https://openai.com/blog/chatgpt/

28. Heikkilä September 22, 2022.

29. For an introduction to Wang's thinking, see Wang 2019. The discussion that follows draws on Wang's overview.

30. Wang 2019.

31. https://ccrma.stanford.edu/~ge/ocarina/

32. https://slork.stanford.edu

33. S. Kaufman 2020. To view some of Chung's work, see her TED talk at https://www.ted.com/talks/sougwen_chung_why_i_draw_with_robots

34. https://copysmith.ai/jarvis-vs-copysmith/

35. https://www.sudowrite.com; https://gpt3demo.com/apps/sudowrite

36. Dzieza 2022.

37. https://authors.ai/marlowe/

38. Archer and Jockers 2016.

39. Rose 2020.

40. Fingas 2020.

41. Miller 2019, chap. 37.

42. Huang et al. 2020.

43. https://computationalcreativity.net

44. https://www.improvisedshakespeare.com

45. Branch et al. 2021.

46. Roemmele 2021.

47. Vara 2021.

48. https://hai.stanford.edu/events/2022-hai-fall-conference-ai-loop-humans-charge

Chapter 12

1. N. Baron 2015; N. Baron 2021.

2. My profound thanks to Marina Bondi, professor of English language and translation at UNIMORE, for all her help in facilitating my research.

3. For lively discussions of the history and future of English spelling, see Crystal 2012 and Horobin 2013.

4. Sealfon 2019; Riley 2022.

5. Ehri 2000; Hayes and Berninger 2014; Joshi et al. 2008.

6. Jansen et al. 2021.

7. Martin-Lacroux and Lacroux 2017.

8. N. Baron 2008, chap. 5.

9. Park and Baron 2018.

10. Saenger 1982, pp. 381, 386–387.

11. For details on the modern history of handwriting, see Thornton 1996.

12. Brick 2013.

13. J. Flaherty 2015.

14. Shapiro 2014.

15. Mangen and Schilhab 2012.

16. Mangen and Velay 2010.

17. James 2017.

18. Berninger et al. 2006.

19. Askvik et al. 2021.

20. Cited in an interview, Midling 2020.

21. R. Abbott et al. 2010; Berninger et al. 2002.
22. Hall et al. 2015; Longcamp et al. 2005.
23. Alstad et al. 2015.
24. Mueller and Oppenheimer 2014.
25. Morehead et al. 2019; Urry et al. 2021.

Coda

1. Holpuch 2022.
2. Kasparov 2007.
3. https://retrocomputingforum.com/t/machines-should-work-people-should-think-ibm-1967/1913
4. Connors and Lunsford 1988.
5. Lunsford and Lunsford 2008.
6. Temple 2012.
7. Regarding ETS's AI software for spotting thesis and conclusion statements—elements of the five-paragraph essay—see Burstein and Marcu 2003.
8. Tremmel 2011.
9. See Warner 2018 for a spirited critique of the five-paragraph essay.
10. D'Agostino 2022; Graham 2022; Peritz 2022; Schatten 2022.
11. My thanks to Anne Mangen for alerting me to the Norwegian story.
12. Quoted in Eriksen 2022.
13. Quoted in Eriksen 2022.
14. Valand 2022. Italics in the original.
15. Quoted in Eriksen 2022.
16. Valand 2022.
17. Quoted in Eriksen 2022.
18. Quoted in Eriksen 2022.
19. Heikkilä January 27, 2023; Wiggers December 10, 2022.
20. https://huggingface.co/openai-detector
21. https://gptzero.substack.com/p/gptzero-classrooms
22. Vincent October 25, 2022.
23. Krill 2022.
24. Thompson October 13, 2022.
25. Manjoo 2022.
26. Handel 2022.
27. Under "journalism," Handel's analysis included public relations specialists.
28. Quoted in Manjoo 2022.
29. Tegmark 2017, p. 121. Also see Roose 2021.
30. Hoffman 2022.
31. Evans 2022.
32. Gero 2022.
33. Diresta 2019.
34. Stokel-Walker 2023.

REFERENCES

Abadi, M. (March 26, 2018). "Americans and British People Spell Things Differently Largely Thanks to One Man with an Opinion." *Business Insider.* Available at https://www. businessinsider.com/spelling-american-vs-british-noah-webster-2018-3

Abalkina, A. (2021). "Publication and Collaboration Anomalies in Academic Papers Originating from a Paper Mill: Evidence from a Russia-Based Paper Mill." Available at https://arxiv.org/abs/2112.13322

Abbott, E. A. (1876). *How to Write Clearly: Rules and Exercises on English Composition.* Roberts Brothers. Available at https://www.google.com/books/ edition/How_to_Write_Clearly/NAZKAAAAIAAJ?hl=en&gbpv=1&pg=PA3&p rintsec=frontcover

Abbott, R. D., Berninger, V. W., and Fayol, M. (2010). "Longitudinal Relationships of Levels of Language in Writing and Between Writing and Reading in Grades 1 to 7." *Journal of Educational Psychology* 102(2): 281–298.

Abid, A., Farooqi, M., and Zou, J. (June 17, 2021). "Large Language Models Associate Muslims with Violence." *Nature Machine Intelligence* 3: 461–463. Available at https://www.nature.com/articles/s42256-021-00359-2

Abraham, A. (2018). *The Neuroscience of Creativity.* Cambridge University Press.

Adams, C. F., Godkin, E. L., and Nutter, G. R. (1897). "Report of the Committee on Composition and Rhetoric." In J. C. Brereton, ed. (1995), *The Origins of Composition Studies in the American Colleges, 1875–1925.* University of Pittsburgh Press, pp. 101–127.

Adams, C. F., Godkin, E. L., and Quincy, J. (1892). "Report of the Committee on Composition and Rhetoric." In J. C. Brereton, ed. (1995), *The Origins of Composition Studies in the American Colleges, 1875–1925.* University of Pittsburgh Press, pp. 73–100.

Adams, T. (July 10, 2010). "David Cope: 'You Pushed the Button and Out Came

Hundreds and Thousands of Sonatas.'" *Guardian*. Available at https://www.theguard-ian.com/technology/2010/jul/11/david-cope-computer-composer

Alexander, C. H. O'D. (n.d.). "Cryptographic History of Work on the German Naval Enigma." Typescript, pp. 19–20. Available at http://www.alanturing.net/turing_ar-chive/archive/b/b01/B01-022.html

"Aligning Language Models to Follow Instructions" (January 27, 2022). *OpenAI Blog*. Available at https://openai.com/blog/instruction-following/

Alkan, S. R. (n.d.). "The Copywriter of Tomorrow—How Companies Transform Text into a Revenue Driver Through a Copy Director." *AX Semantics*. Available at https://en.ax-semantics.com/blog/how-copy-directors-transform-text-into-a-turnover-driver/

Alstad, Z., et al. (2015). "Modes of Alphabet Letter Production During Middle Childhood and Adolescence: Interrelationships with Each Other and Other Writing Skills." *Journal of Writing Research* 6(3): 199–231. Available at https://www.ncbi.nlm.nih.gov/pmc/articles/PMC4433034/pdf/nihms-644747.pdf

Anderson, M. (December 9, 2022). "Preventing 'Hallucination' in GPT-3 and Other Complex Language Models." *Unite.AI*. Available at https://www.unite.ai/preventing-hallucination-in-gpt-3-and-other-complex-language-models/

Anderson, N. (May 14, 2021). "University of South Carolina President Resigns After Plagiarism Incident in Commencement Speech." *Washington Post*. Available at https://www.washingtonpost.com/education/2021/05/13/university-south-carolina-president-resigns-caslen/

Andreasen, N. C. (2005). *The Creating Brain*. Dana Press.

Archer, J., and Jockers, M. (2016). *The Bestseller Code: Anatomy of the Blockbuster Novel*. St. Martin's Press.

Arnold, K. C., Chauncey, K., and Gajos, K. Z. (2020). "Predictive Text Encourages Predictable Writing." *IUI '20*. Intelligent User Interfaces. Association for Computing Machinery. Available at https://www.eecs.harvard.edu/~kgajos/papers/2020/arnold20predictive.pdf

Asimov, I. (1981). "The Three Laws." *Compute* 18 (November): 18. Available at https://archive.org/details/1981-11-compute-magazine/page/n19/mode/1up?view=theater

Askvik, E. O., van der Weel, F. R., and van der Meer, A. L. H. (2021). "The Importance of Cursive Handwriting over Typing for Learning in the Classroom: A High-Density EEG Study of 12-Year-Old Children and Young Adults." *Frontiers in Psychology* 11, Article 1810. Available at https://www.frontiersin.org/articles/10.3389/fpsyg.2020.01810/full

Attali, Y., Bridgeman, B., and Trapani, C. (2010), "Performance of a Generic Approach in Automated Essay Scoring." *Journal of Technology, Learning, and Assessment* 10(3). Available at https://ejournals.bc.edu/index.php/jtla/article/view/1603/1455

"Australia: Oldest Rock Art is 17,300-Year-Old Kangaroo" (February 23, 2021). *BBC News*. Available at https://www.bbc.com/news/world-australia-56164484

Authors Guild (n.d.). "Who We Are." Available at https://www.authorsguild.org/who-we-are/

Bach, N. (August 8, 2018). "Facebook Apologizes for Algorithm Mishap That Threw Balloons and Confetti on Indonesia Earthquake Posts." *Fortune*.

Baines, S. (February 13, 2017). "Can You Code Love?" *Science and Industry Museum*. Manchester, UK. Available at https://blog.scienceandindustrymuseum.org.uk/can-you-code-love/

Baker, J., and Gillick, L. (n.d.). "Progress Report for DARPA SLS Program at Dragon Systems, Inc." Available at https://aclanthology.org/H91-1088.pdf

Baker, M. (1996). "Corpus-Based Translation Studies: The Challenges That Lie Ahead." In H. Somers, ed., *Terminology, LSP, and Translation: Studies in Language Engineering in Honour of Juan C. Sager*. John Benjamins, pp. 175–186.

Barber, G. (January 14, 2021). "Can an AI Predict the Language of Viral Mutation?" *Wired*. Available at https://www.wired.com/story/can-an-ai-predict-the-language-of-viral-mutation/

Bar-Hillel, Y. (1951). "The Present State of Research on Mechanical Translation." *American Documentation* 2(4): 229–237.

Bar-Hillel, Y. (1960). "The Present Status of Automatic Translation of Languages." *Advances in Computers* 1:91–163. Available at https://docplayer.net/167179-The-present-status-of-automatic-translation-of-languages.html

Barnet, B., and Tofts, D. (2013), "Too Dimensional: Literary and Technical Images of Potentiality in the History of Hypertext." In R. Siemens and S. Schreibman, eds., *A Companion to Digital Literary Studies*. Wiley-Blackwell, pp. 283–300.

Baron, D. (January 15, 2022). "Microsoft's Word Wokeness Checker Is Asleep on the Job." *The Web of Language*. Available at https://blogs.illinois.edu/view/25/520413787

Baron, N. S. (1981). *Speech, Writing, and Sign*. Indiana University Press.

Baron, N. S. (1998). "Letters by Phone or Speech by Other Means: The Linguistics of Email." *Language and Communication* 18: 133–170.

Baron, N. S. (2000). *Alphabet to Email: How Written English Evolved and Where It's Heading*. Routledge.

Baron, N. S. (2002). "Who Sets Email Style? Prescriptivism, Coping Strategies, and Democratizing Communication Access." *The Information Society* 18: 403–413.

Baron, N. S. (2008). *Always On: Language in an Online and Mobile World*. Oxford University Press.

Baron, N. S. (2015). *Words Onscreen: The Fate of Reading in a Digital World*. Oxford University Press.

Baron, N. S. (2021). *How We Read Now: Strategic Choices for Print, Screen, and Audio*. Oxford University Press.

Baroni, M., and Bernardini, S. (2006). "A New Approach to the Study of Translationese: Machine-Learning the Difference Between Original and Translated Text." *Literary and Linguistic Computing* 21(3): 259–274.

Barthes, R. (1970). *S/Z*. Editions du Seuil.

Barthes, R. (1977 [1967]). "Death of the Author." In *Image, Music, Text*, trans. S. Heath. Hill & Wang, pp. 142–148.

Basu, T. (December 16, 2021). "The Metaverse Has a Groping Problem Already." *MIT Technology Review*. Available at https://www.technologyreview.com/2021/12/16/1042516/the-metaverse-has-a-groping-problem/

Bavarian Broadcasting (n.d.). "Objective or Biased: On the Questionable Use of Artificial Intelligence for Job Applications." Available at https://interaktiv.br.de/ki-bewerbung/en/index.html

Baym, N. (2010). *Personal Connections in the Digital Age*. Polity.

Beard, M. (2007). *The Roman Triumph*. Harvard University Press.

Bender, E. M., et al. (2021). "On the Dangers of Stochastic Parrots: Can Language Models Be Too Big?" FAccT '21, March 3–10. Available at https://dl.acm.org/doi/pdf/10.1145/3442188.3445922

Bennett, W. S. (1995). "Machine Translation in North America." In E. F. K. Koerner and R. E. Asher, eds., *Concise History of the Language Sciences*. Pergamon, pp. 445–451.

Benson, E. (1975). "The Quipu: 'Written' Texts in Ancient Peru." *Princeton University Library Chronicle* 37: 11–23.

Berninger, V. W., et al. (2002). "Writing and Reading: Connections Between Language by Hand and Language by Eye." *Journal of Learning Disabilities* 35(1):39–56.

Berninger, V. W., et al. (2006). "Early Development of Language by Hand: Composing, Reading, Listening, and Speaking Connections; Three Letter-Writing Modes; and Fast Mapping in Spelling." *Developmental Neuropsychology* 29(1): 61–92.

Berrong, T. (March 19, 2021). "Sending Cards and Letters: Our Best Advice and Ideas." *Hallmark*. Available at https://ideas.hallmark.com/articles/card-ideas/ sending-cards-and-letters-our-best-advice-and-ideas/

Biblical Archaeology Society (2020). "Epistles: FAQ: Did Ancient Hebrew Have Vowels?" *Biblical Archaeology Review* 46(2). Available at https://www.baslibrary. org/biblical-archaeology-review/46/2/24

Bloomfield, L. (1933). *Language*. Holt, Rinehart & Winston.

Boden, M. A. (1991). *The Creative Mind: Myths and Mechanisms*. Basic.

Boden, M. A. (1998). "Creativity and Artificial Intelligence." *Artificial Intelligence* 103: 347–356.

Bommarito, M. J., and Katz, D. M. (December 31, 2022). "GPT Takes the Bar Exam." Available at https://papers.ssrn.com/sol3/papers.cfm?abstract_id=4314839

Bommasani, R., et al. (August 18, 2021). "On the Opportunities and Risks of Foundation Models." Stanford Institute for Human-Centered Artificial Intelligence, Center for Research on Foundation Models. Available at https://arxiv. org/pdf/2108.07258.pdf

Boroditsky, L. (May 2, 2018). "How Language Shapes the Way We Think." *TED Talk*. Available at https://www.youtube.com/watch?v=RKK7wGAYP6k

Boroditsky, L., Schmidt, L. A., and Phillips, W. (2003). "Sex, Syntax and Semantics." In D. Gentner and S. Goldin-Meadow, eds., *Language in Mind: Advances in the Study of Language and Thought*. MIT Press, pp. 61–79.

Bosker, B. (February 11, 2013). "Philip Parker's Trick for Authoring over 1 Million Books: Don't Write." *Huff Post*. Available at https://www.huffpost.com/entry/ philip-parker-books_n_2648820

Bowker, L. (2002). *Computer-Aided Translation Technology*. University of Ottawa Press.

Bowker, L. (2012). "Through the MT Looking Glass: Warren Weaver—Machine Translation Pioneer and Literary Translation Enthusiast." *Circuit* 116: 33–34.

Bowker, L., and Buitrago Ciro, J. (2019). *Machine Translation and Global Reach*. Emerald.

Bowman, E. (January 9, 2023). "A College Student Created an App That Can Tell Whether AI Wrote an Essay." *NPR*. Available at https://www.npr. org/2023/01/09/1147549845/gptzero-ai-chatgpt-edward-tian-plagiarism

Boyd, R. L., and Pennebaker, J. W. (2015). "Did Shakespeare Write *Double Falsehood*? Identifying Individuals by Creating Psychological Signatures with Text Analysis." *Psychological Science* 26(5): 570–582. Available at https://journals. sagepub.com/doi/abs/10.1177/0956797614566658

Branch, B., Mirowski, P., and Mathewson, K. (2021). "Collaborative Storytelling with Human Actors and AI Narrators." *Proceedings of the 12th International*

Conference on Computational Creativity, pp. 97–101. Available at https://arxiv. org/abs/2109.14728

Brereton, J. C., ed. (1995). *The Origins of Composition Studies in the American College, 1875–1925*. University of Pittsburgh Press.

Brick, M. (August 23, 2013). "Conservatives Are Very Upset That Kids These Days Can't Write in Cursive." *New York Magazine*. Available at https://nymag.com/ intelligencer/2013/08/conservatives-rally-to-defend-fancy-handwriting.html

Bridy, A. (2012). "Coding Creativity: Copyright and the Artificially Intelligent Author." *Stanford Technology Law Review* 5: 1–28.

Bridy, A. (2016). "The Evolution of Authorship: Work Made by Code." *Columbia Journal of Law and the Arts* 39(3): 395–401.

Briggs, L. B. R. (1888). "The Harvard Admission Examination in English," in *The Academy*. In J. C. Brereton, ed. (1995), *The Origins of Composition Studies in the American College, 1875–1925*. University of Pittsburgh Press, pp. 57–73.

Brinkhof, T. (August 23, 2021). "How to Paint Like Rembrandt, According to Artificial Intelligence." *Discover Magazine*. Available at https://www.discovermagazine.com/ technology/how-to-paint-like-rembrandt-according-to-artificial-intelligence

Brogaard, J., Engelberg, J., and Van Wesep, E. (2018). "Do Economists Swing for the Fences After Tenure?" *Journal of Economic Perspectives* 32(1): 179–194. Available at https://www.aeaweb.org/articles?id=10.1257/jep.32.1.179

Broussard, M. (2018). *Artificial Unintelligence: How Computers Misunderstand the World*. MIT Press.

Brown, M. (August 30, 2020). "'Fake' Rembrandt Came from Artist's Workshop and Is Possibly Genuine." *Guardian*. Available at https://www.theguardian. com/artanddesign/2020/aug/30/fake-rembrandt-came- from-artists-workshop-and-is-possibly-genuine-ashmolean-oxford

Brown, P., et al. (1988). "A Statistical Approach to Language Translation." *Proceedings of the 12th Conference on Computational Linguistics*, vol. 1, pp. 71–76.

Brown, R. (1980). "The First Sentences of Child and Chimpanzee." In T. A. Sebeok and J. Umiker-Sebeok, eds., *Speaking of Apes*. Topics in Contemporary Semiotics. Springer, pp. 85–101.

Brown, S. C., Meyer, P. R., and Enos, T. (1994). "Doctoral Programs in Rhetoric and Composition: A Catalog of the Profession." *Rhetoric Review* 12(2): 240–251.

Bruner, J. (1962). "The Condition of Creativity." In *On Knowing: Essays for the Left Hand*. Belknap, pp. 17–30.

Brynjolfsson, E. (2022). "The Turing Trap: The Promise and Peril of Human-Like Artificial Intelligence." *Daedalus* 151(2): 272–287.

Brynjolfsson, E., Hui, X., and Liu, M. (2019). "Does Machine Translation Affect International Trade? Evidence from a Large Digital Platform." *Management Science* 65(12): 5449–5460.

Brynjolfsson, E., and McAfee, A. (2014). *The Second Machine Age*. W. W. Norton.

Buolamwini, J., and Gebru, T. (2018). "Gender Shades: Intersectional Accuracy Disparities in Commercial Gender Classification." *Proceedings of Machine Learning Research* 81: 1–15.

Burstein, J., et al. (1998). "Computer Analysis of Essay Content for Automated Score Prediction: A Prototype Automated Scoring System for GMAT Analytical Writing Assessment Essays." *ETS Research Report Series*, pp. i–67. Available at https:// onlinelibrary.wiley.com/doi/abs/10.1002/j.2333-8504.1998.tb01764.x

Burstein, J., Chodorow, M., and Leacock, C. (2004). "Automated Essay Evaluation: The Criterion Online Writing Service." *AI Magazine* 25(3): 27–36. Available at https://ojs.aaai.org//index.php/aimagazine/article/view/1774

Burstein, J., Leacock, C., and Swartz, R. (2001). "Automated Evaluation of Essays and Short Answers." ETS Technologies, Inc. Available at https://citeseerx.ist.psu.edu/viewdoc/download?doi=10.1.1.58.6253&rep=rep1&type=pdf

Burstein, J., and Marcu, D. (2003). "A Machine Learning Approach for Identification of Thesis and Conclusion Statements in Student Essays." *Computers and the Humanities* 37: 455–467.

Burstein, J., Tetreault, J., and Andreyev, S. (2010). "Using Entity-Based Features to Model Coherence in Student Essays." In *Human Language Technologies: The 2010 Annual Conference of the North American Chapter of the Association for Computational Linguistics,* pp. 681–684. Available at https://aclanthology.org/N10-1099.pdf

Bush, V. (1945). "As We May Think." *The Atlantic* [*The Atlantic Monthly*] (July). Available at https://www.theatlantic.com/magazine/archive/1945/07/as-we-may-think/303881/

Cahill, A., Chodorow, M., and Flor, M. (2018). "Developing an e-rater Advisory to Detect Babel-Generated Essays." *Journal of Writing Analytics* 2: 203–224. Available at https://wac.colostate.edu/docs/jwa/vol2/cahill.pdf

"Calculus Created in India 250 Years Before Newton: Study" (August 14, 2007). *CBC News.* Available at https://www.cbc.ca/news/science/calculus-created-in-india-250-years-before-newton-study-1.632433

Callaway, E. (November 30, 2020). "'It Will Change Everything': DeepMind's AI Makes Gigantic Leap in Solving Protein Structures." *Nature* 588: 203–204. Available at https://www.nature.com/articles/d41586-020-03348-4

Card, S. K., Moran, T. P., and Newell, A. (1983). *The Psychology of Human–Computer Interaction.* Lawrence Erlbaum.

Caren, C. (January 21, 2021). "A New Path and Purpose for Turnitin." *Turnitin.* Available at https://www.turnitin.com blog/a-new-path-and-purpose-for-turnitin

Carlson, M. (2015). "The Robotic Reporter." *Digital Journalism* 3(3): 416–431.

Carreiras, M., et al. (2009). "An Anatomical Signature for Literacy." *Nature* 461 (October): 983–986.

Casey, B., Farhangi, A., and Vogl, R. (2019). "Rethinking Explainable Machines: The GDPR's 'Right to Explanation' Debate and the Rise of Algorithmic Audits in Enterprise." *Berkeley Technology Law Journal* 34: 143–188. Available at https://btlj.org/data/articles2019/34_1/04_Casey_Web.pdf

CCCC (2004). "Teaching, Learning, and Assessing Writing in Digital Environments." Conference on College Composition & Communication Committee on Teaching, Learning, and Assessing Writing in Digital Environments. Available at https://dtext.org/f14/505/readings/ncte-CCCC-digital-environments.pdf

Chadwick, J. (1959). "A Prehistoric Bureaucracy." *Diogenes* 26: 7–18.

Chalaby, J. K. (1998). *The Invention of Journalism.* St. Martin's Press.

Chaski, C. W. (2012). "Author Identification in the Forensic Setting." In P. M. Tiersma and L. M. Solon, eds., *Oxford Handbook of Language and Law.* Oxford University Press, pp. 489–503.

Chen, M. X., et al. (2019). "Gmail Smart Compose: Real-Time Assisted Writing." *KDD '19.* Knowledge Discovery and Data Mining. Association for Computing Machinery. Available at https://arxiv.org/abs/1906.00080

"Chinese Dissident, Winner of Nobel Literature Prize, Writes to Survive" (December 19, 2001). *Record-Courier.* Available at http://recordcourier.www.clients.ellington-cms.com/news/2001/dec/19/chinese-dissident-winner-of-nobel-literature-prize/

Cho, K., et al. (2014). "On the Properties of Neural Translation: Encoder–Decoder Approaches." *Eighth Workshop on Syntax, Semantics and Structure in Statistical Translation.* Association for Computational Linguistics, pp. 103–111. Available at https://arxiv.org/abs/1409.1259

Choi, J. H., et al. (January 25, 2023). "ChatGPT Goes to Law School." Available at https://papers.ssrn.com/sol3/papers.cfm?abstract_id=4335905

Chomsky, C. (1971). "Write First, Read Later." *Childhood Education* 47(6): 296–299.

Chomsky, C. (1979). "Approaching Reading Through Invented Spelling." In L. Resnick and P. Weaver, eds., *Theory and Practice of Early Reading,* vol. 2. Lawrence Erlbaum, pp. 43–65.

Chomsky, N. (1957). *Syntactic Structures.* Mouton.

Chomsky, N. (1959). "A Review of B. F. Skinner's *Verbal Behavior.*" *Language* 35(1): 26–58.

Chomsky, N. (1966). *Cartesian Linguistics.* Harper and Row.

Chomsky, N. (1993). *Language and Thought.* Moyer Bell.

Christian, B. (2020). *The Alignment Problem: Machine Learning and Human Values.* W. W. Norton.

Chun, J., and Elkins, K. (2022). "What the Rise of AI Means for Narrative Studies: A Response to 'Why Computers Will Never Read (or Write) Literature' by Angus Fletcher." *Narrative* 30(1): 104–113.

Chung, E. (March 27, 2019). "Canadian Researchers Who Taught AI to Learn Like Humans Win $1M Turing Award." *CBC News.* Available at https://www.cbc.ca/news/science/turing-award-ai-deep-learning-1.5070415

Clark, E., et al. (2021). "All That's 'Human' Is Not Gold: Evaluating Human Evaluation of Generated Text." In *Proceedings of the 59th Annual Meeting of the Association of Computational Linguistics and the 11th International Joint Conference on Natural Language Processing,* vol. 1: long papers, pp. 7282–7296. Available at https://arxiv.org/abs/2107.00061

Clarke, R., and Lancaster, T. (2006). "Eliminating the Successor to Plagiarism? Identifying the Usage of Contract Cheating Sites." *Proceedings of 2nd International Plagiarism Conference.* JISC Plagiarism Advisory Service, Newcastle, UK.

Clerwall, C. (2014). "Enter the Robot Journalist: Users' Perceptions of Automated Content." *Journalism Practice* 8(5): 519–531.

Coelho, P. (1996 [1994 in Portuguese]). *By the River Piedra I Sat and Wept.* Trans. Alan R. Clarke. Available at https://docs.google.com/viewer?a=v&pid=sites&srcid=ZGVmYXVsdGRvbWFpbnxsaWJJyY3NjfGd4OjVmMDg5MWU5YTllMDNiN2Y

Cohen, N. (April 14, 2008). "He Wrote 200,000 Books (But Computers Did Some of the Work)." *New York Times.* Available at https://www.nytimes.com/2008/04/14/business/media/14link.html

Colford, P. (June 30, 2014). "A Leap Forward in Quarterly Earnings Stories." *Blog AP.* Available at https://blog.ap.org/announcements/a-leap-forward-in-quarterly-earnings-stories

College Board (n.d.). "Chapter 10. About the SAT Writing and Language Test." SAT Suite of Assessments. Available at https://satsuite.collegeboard.org/media/pdf/official-sat-study-guide-about-writing-language-test.pdf

Conniff, R. (March 2011). "What the Luddites Really Fought Against." *Smithsonian*

Magazine. Available at https://www.smithsonianmag.com/history/ what-the-luddites-really-fought-against-264412/

Connors, R. and Lunsford, A. A. (1988). "Frequency of Formal Errors in Current College Writing, or Ma and Pa Kettle Do Research." *College Composition and Communication* 39(4): 395–409.

Coover, R. (June 21, 1992). "The End of Books." *New York Times Book Review*. Available at https://archive.nytimes.com/www.nytimes.com/books/98/09/27/ specials/coover-end.html?pagewanted=all

Coover, R. (August 29, 1993). "Hyperfiction: Novels for the Computer." *New York Times Book Review*. Available at https://archive.nytimes.com/www.nytimes.com/ books/98/09/27/specials/coover-hyperfiction.html?_r=4

Copeland, B. J., ed. (2004). *The Essential Turing*. Oxford University Press.

"Copyright Basics" (n.d.). *US Copyright Office*. Available at https://www.copyright. gov/circs/circo1.pdf

Corrado, G. (November 3, 2015). "Computer, Respond to This Email." *Google AI Blog*. Available at https://ai.googleblog.com/2015/11/computer-respond-to-this-email.html

Costandi, M. (2016). *Neuroplasticity*. MIT Press.

Coulmas, F. (1989). *Writing Systems of the World*. Blackwell.

"Cracking the Maya Code" (n.d.). *PBS Nova*. Available at https://www.pbs.org/wgbh/ nova/mayacode/time-nf.html

Cressy, D. (1980). *Literacy and the Social Order: Reading and Writing in Tudor and Stuart England*. Cambridge University Press.

Crouse, L. (January 28, 2022). "I Ditched My Smart Watch, and I Don't Regret It." *New York Times*. Available at https://www.nytimes.com/2022/ 01/28/opinion/smartwatch-health-body.html

Crystal, D. (2001). *Language and the Internet*. Cambridge University Press.

Crystal, D. (2006). *The Fight for English*. Oxford University Press.

Crystal, D. (2010). "Semantic Targeting: Past, Present, and Future." *Aslib Proceedings: New Information Perspectives* 62(4/5): 355–365.

Crystal, D. (2012). *Spell It Out*. St. Martin's Press.

Csikszentmihalyi, M. (1998). "Letters from the Field." *Roeper Review* 21(1): 80–81.

Csikszentmihalyi, M. (2013 [1997]). *Creativity: The Psychology of Discovery and Invention*. Harper Perennial Modern Classics.

Cu, M. A., and Hochman, S. (January 22, 2023). "Scores of Stanford Students Used ChatGPT on Final Exams, Survey Suggests." *Stanford Daily*. Available at https:// stanforddaily.com/2023/01/22/scores-of-stanford-students-used-chatgpt-on-final-exams-survey-suggests/

Curzan, A. (2014). *Fixing English: Prescriptivism and Language History*. Cambridge University Press.

D'Agostino, S. (October 26, 2022). "Machines Can Craft Essays. How Should Writing Be Taught Now?" *Inside Higher Ed*. Available at https://www.insidehighered.com/ news/2022/10/26/machines-can-craft-essays-how-should-writing-be-taught-now

Dahl, R. (1984). *Boy: Tales of Childhood*. Farrar, Straus, Giroux.

Dahl, R. (1996 [1953]). "The Great Automatic Grammatizator." In *The Great Automatic Grammatizator and Other Stories*. Viking, pp. 9–34.

Davies, M. W. (1982). *Woman's Place Is at the Typewriter: Office Work and Office Workers, 1870–1930*. Temple University Press.

de Beer, D. (November 3, 2020). "Grammarly Both Helps, Hinders Students." *The*

Standard. The American School in London. Available at https://standard.asl. org/16178/opinions/does-grammarly-help-or-hinder-students/

Dehaene, S. (2009). *Reading in the Brain.* Viking.

Dehaene, S., et al. (2010). "How Learning to Read Changes the Cortical Networks for Vision and Language." *Science* 330 (December): 1359–1364.

Dehaene, S., et al. (2015). "Illiterate to Literate: Behavioural and Cerebral Changes Induced by Reading Acquisition." *Nature Reviews Neuroscience* 16 (April): 234–244.

De Kamper, G., and McGinn, I. (May 21, 2021). "How We Proved a Rembrandt Painting Owned by the University of Pretoria Was a Fake." *Sunday Times.* Availableathttps://www.timeslive.co.za/news/sci-tech/2021-05-21-how-we-proved-a-rembrandt-painting-owned-by-the-university-of-pretoria-was-a-fake/

Devlin, J., et al. (2018). "BERT: Pre-Training of Deep Bidirectional Transformers for Language Understanding." Available at https://arxiv.org/abs/1810.04805

Diakopoulos, N. (2019). *Automating the News: How Algorithms Are Rewriting the Media.* Harvard University Press.

Dickler, J. (May 1, 2009). "Getting Paid Not to Work." *CNN Money.* Available at https://money.cnn.com/2009/04/30/news/economy/legal_deferrals/

Didion, J. (December 5, 1976). "Why I Write." *New York Times.* Available at https://www.nytimes.com/1976/12/05/archives/why-i-write-why-i-write.html

Diehl, C. (1978). *Americans and German Scholarship, 1770–1870.* Yale University Press.

Dietrich, A. (2019). "Types of Creativity." *Psychonomic Bulletin & Review* 26: 1–12.

Diresta, R. (July 24, 2019). "A New Law Makes Bots Identify Themselves." *Wired.* Available at https://www.wired.com/story/law-makes-bots-identify-themselves/

Dobrin, D. N. (1990). "A New Grammar Checker." *Computers and the Humanities* 24(1/2): 67–80.

Dou, Y., et al. (2022). "Is GPT-3 Text Indistinguishable from Human Text? SCARECROW: A Framework for Scrutinizing Machine Text." In *Proceedings of the 60th Meeting of the Association for Computational Linguistics,* vol. 1: long papers, pp. 7250–7274. Available at https://arxiv.org/abs/2107.01294

Duff, A. (1981). *The Third Language.* Pergamon.

"Duplicating Polygraph" (n.d.). NYU Department of Media, Culture, and Communication. Available at http://cultureandcommunication.org/deadmedia/index.php/Duplicating_Polygraph

du Sautoy, M. (2019). *The Creativity Code.* 4th Estate.

Dzieza, J. (July 20, 2022). "The Great Fiction of AI." *The Verge.* Available at https://www.theverge.com/c/23194235/ai-fiction-writing-amazon-kindle-sudowrite-jasper

Earnest, L. (November 26, 2012). "Oral History of Lester D. 'Les' Earnest." Interviewed by Dag Spicer. Computer History Museum. Available at https://archive.computerhistory.org/resources/access/text/2013/05/102746589-05-01-acc.pdf

Edmonds, R. (June 29, 2022). "An Updated Survey of US Newspapers Finds 360 More Have Closed Since 2019." *Poynter.* Available at https://www.poynter.org/business-work/2022/an-updated-survey-of-us-newspapers-finds-360-more-have-closed-since-2019/

Ehri, L. C. (2000). "Learning to Read and Learning to Spell: Two Sides of a Coin." *Topics in Language Disorders* 20(3): 19–36.

Eide, N. (May 16, 2019). "All About 'Bertie': Overhauling CMS Technology at

Forbes." *CIODIVE*. Available at https://www.ciodive.com/news/all-about-bertie-overhauling-cms-technology-at-forbes/554871/

Elbert, T., et al. (1995). "Increased Cortical Representation of the Fingers of the Left Hand in String Players." *Science* 270(5234): 305–307.

Eldridge, S., and Franklin, B., eds. (2019). *Routledge Handbook of Developments in Digital Journalism Studies*. Routledge.

Elgammal, A. (September 24, 2021). "How a Team of Musicologists and Computer Scientists Completed Beethoven's Unfinished 10th Symphony." *The Conversation*. Available at https://theconversation.com how-a-team-of -musicologists-and-computer-scientists-completed-beethovens-unfinished-10th-symphony-168160

Eliot, C. W. (1869a). "The New Education." *The Atlantic* [*The Atlantic Monthly*] (February). Available at https://www.theatlantic.com/magazine/archive/1869/02/the-new-education/309049/

Eliot, C. W. (1869b). Inaugural Address as President of Harvard College. Available at https://homepages.uc.edu/~martinj/Ideal%20University/5.%20%20The%20 19th%20Century%20American%20College/Eliot%20-%20Inauguration%20 Address%201869.pdf

Ellis, H. (1926). *A Study of British Genius*. Houghton Mifflin.

Else, H. (January 19, 2023). "Abstracts Written by ChatGPT Fool Scientists." *Nature* 613: 423. Available at https://www.nature.com/articles/d41586-023-00056-7

Engber, D. (June 6, 2014). "Who Made That Autocorrect?" *New York Times Magazine*. Available at https://www.nytimes.com/2014/06/08/magazine/who-made-that-autocorrect.html

Eriksen, D. (December 7, 2022). "Teachers Despair over New Artificial Intelligence." *NRK Culture*. Original Norwegian available at https://www.nrk.no/kultur/laerere-fortvilet-over-ny-kunstig-intelligens-1.16210580; English translation through Microsoft Translator.

ETS (n.d. a). "ETS Proficiency Profile: Optional Essay." Available at https://www.ets.org/proficiency-profile/about/test-content.html

ETS (n.d. b). "e-rater Scoring Engine." Available at https://www.ets.org/erater/how.html

ETS Global (n.d.). "Criterion." Available at https://www.etsglobal.org/fr/en/test-type-family/criterion

European Union (April 27, 2016). "Regulation (EU) 2016/679 of the European Parliament and of the Council: On the Protection of Natural Persons with Regard to the Processing of Personal Data and on the Free Movement of Such Data." Available at https://eur-lex.europa.eu/legal-content/EN/TXT/PDF/?uri=CELEX:32016R0679

Evans, C. (October 20, 2022). "'The Robot Is Doing the Job': Robots Help Pick Strawberries in California amid Drought, Labor Shortage." *CBS News*. Available at https://www.cbsnews.com/news/robots-pick-strawberries-california/

"'Expert System' Picks Key Workers' Brains" (November 7, 1989). *LA Times*. Available at https://www.latimes.com/archives/la-xpm-1989-11-07-fi-1112-story.html

Fagan, F. (2022). "Law's Computational Paradox." *Virginal Journal of Law and Technology* 26 (4). Available at https://static1.squarespace.com/static/5e793709295d 7b60295b2d29/t/63aa63a45c647b201f553c70/1672111013175/v26i4.Fagan.pdf

Fassler, J. (April 12, 2012). "Can the Computers at Narrative Science Replace Paid

Writers?" *The Atlantic*. Available at https://www.theatlantic.com/entertainment/archive/2012/04/can-the-computers-at-narrative-science-replace-paid-writers/255631/

"Fathers of the Deep Learning Revolution Receive ACM A. M. Turing Award" (March 27, 2019). *Association for Computing Machinery*. Available at https://www.acm.org/media-center/2019/march/turing-award-2018

Feather, J. (1994). *Publishing, Piracy, and Politics: A Historical Study of Copyright in Britain*. Mansell.

Febvre, L., and Martin, H.-J. (1976). *The Coming of the Book*. Trans. D. Gerard. NLB.

Fingas, J. (December 12, 2020). "Netflix Explains How It Uses AI to Sell You on a Show." *Engadget*. Available at https://www.engadget.com/netflix-explains-ai-for-show-marketing-201524601.html

Finley, A. (2021). *How College Contributes to Workforce Success*. Association of American Colleges and Universities, Hanover Research. Available at https://www.aacu.org/research/how-college-contributes-to-workforce-success

Fithian, D. F. (1950). *Charles W. Eliot's Contributions to Education*. PhD dissertation, University of Arizona. Available at https://repository.arizona.edu/bitstream/handle/10150/318982/AZU_TD_BOX3_E9791_1950_29pdf?sequence=1&isAllowed=y

Flaherty, A. (2004). *The Midnight Disease*. Houghton Mifflin.

Flaherty, C. (October 18, 2017). "Productivity: Age Is Just a Number." *Inside Higher Ed*. Available at https://www.insidehighered.com/news/2017/10/18/new-study-pushes-back-decades-studies-suggesting-scientific-productivity-peaks-early

Flaherty, C. (April 6, 2021). "What Employers Want." *Inside Higher Ed*. Available at https://www.insidehighered.com/news/2021/04/06/aacu-survey-finds-employers-want-candidates-liberal-arts-skills-cite-preparedness

Flaherty, J. (February 24, 2015). "Meet Bond, the Robot That Creates Handwritten Notes for You." *Wired*. Available at https://www.wired.com/2015/02/meet-bond-robot-creates-handwritten-notes/

Fletcher, A., and Larson, E. J. (January 25, 2022). "Optimizing Machines Is Perilous. Consider 'Creatively Adequate' AI." *Wired*. Available at https://www.wired.com/story/artificial-intelligence-data-future-optimization-antifragility/

Flood, A. (March 2, 2009). "Writing Is 'No Fun,' Says Tóibín." *Guardian*. Available at https://www.theguardian.com/books/2009/mar/02/colm-toibin-writing-pleasure

Forster, A. (2001). "Review Journals and the Reading Public." In I. Rivers, ed., *Books and Their Readers in Eighteenth-Century England: New Essays*. Leicester University Press, pp. 171–190.

Fyfe, A. (July 8, 2021). "Where Did the Practice of 'Abstracts' Come From?" *A History of Scientific Journals*. Available at https://arts.st-andrews.ac.uk/philosophicaltransactions/where-did-the-practice-of-abstracts-come-from/

Gallagher, C. J. (2003). "Reconciling a Tradition of Testing with a New Learning Paradigm." *Educational Psychology Review* 15(1): 83–99.

Galton, F. (1869). *Hereditary Genius*. Macmillan.

Ganapati, P. (September 23, 2010). "How T9 Predictive Text Input Changed Mobile Phones." *Wired*. Available at https://www.wired.com/2010/09/martin-king-t9-dies/

Garber, M. (August 23, 2013). "How Google's Autocomplete Was . . . Created/ Invented/Born." *The Atlantic*. Available at https://www.theatlantic.com/technol- ogy/archive/2013/08/how-googles-autocomplete-was-created-invented- born/278991/

Gardner, H. (1983). *Frames of Mind: The Theory of Multiple Intelligences*. Basic.

Gardner, H. (1993). *Creating Minds*. Basic.

Garfinkel, S. (n.d.). "Building 20: A Survey." Reflections on MIT's Building 20. Available at https://ic.media.mit.edu/projects/JBW/ARTICLES/SIMSONG.HTM

Gault, M. (August 31, 2022). "An AI-Generated Artwork Won First Place at a State Fair Fine Arts Competition, and Artists Are Pissed." *Motherboard*. Available at https://www.vice.com/en/article/bvmvqm/an-ai-generated-artwork- won-first-place-at-a-state-fair-fine-arts-competition-and-artists-are-pissed

Gebru, T., and Mitchell, M. (June 17, 2022). "We Warned Google That People Might Believe AI Was Sentient. Now It's Happening." *Washington Post*. Available at https://www.washingtonpost.com/opinions/2022/06/17/ google-ai-ethics-sentient-lemoine-warning/

Gellerstam, M. (1986). "Translationese in Swedish Novels Translated from English." *Scandinavian Symposium on Translation Theory*. CWK Gleerup, pp. 88–95.

Gero, K. I. (December 2, 2022). "AI Reveals the Most Human Parts of Writing." *Wired*. Available at https://www.wired.com/story/artificial-intelligence- writing-art/

Gibbs, S. (December 5, 2016). "Google Alters Search Autocomplete to Remove 'Are Jews Evil' Suggestion." *Guardian*. Available at https://www.theguardian.com/ technology/2016/dec/05/google-alters-search-autocomplete-remove- are-jews-evil-suggestion

Goldman, B. (May 12, 2021). "Software Turns 'Mental Handwriting' into On-Screen Words, Sentences." *Stanford Medicine News Center*. Available at https://med. stanford.edu/news/all-news/2021/05/software-turns-handwriting-thoughts-into- on-screen-text.html

Goodfellow, I. J., et al. (2014). "Generative Adversarial Nets." NIPS 14. *Proceedings of the 27th International Conference on Neural Information Processing Systems*, vol. 2, pp. 2672–2680. Available at https://arxiv.org/abs/1406.2661

Goody, J., and Watt, I. (1963). "The Consequences of Literacy." *Comparative Studies in Society and History* 5(3): 304–345.

"Gorham's Cave Complex" (n.d.). *UNESCO*. Available at https://whc.unesco.org/en/ list/1500/

Gotti, F., Langlais, P., and Lapalme, G. (2014). "Designing a Machine Translation System for Canadian Weather Warnings: A Case Study." *Natural Language Engineering* 20(3): 399–433.

GPT Generative Pretrained Transformer, Thunström, A. O., and Steingrimsson, S. (2022). "Can GPT-3 Write an Academic Paper on Itself, with Minimal Human Input?" *HAL Open Science*. Available at https://hal.archives-ouvertes.fr/hal- 03701250/document

Graham, S. S. (October 24, 2022). "AI-Generated Essays Are Nothing to Worry About." *Inside Higher Ed*. Available at https://www.insidehighered.com/ views/2022/10/24/ai-generated-essays-are-nothing-worry-about-opinion

Grant, D. (July 10, 2018). "The Problem with Studies Claiming Artists Have Higher Rates of Mental Illness." *Observer*. Available at https://observer. com/2018/07/psychiatrists-say-studies-linking-artists-and-mental- illness-are-flawed/

Green, J. (n.d.). Reading Guide, *Looking for Alaska*. Penguin Random House Canada. Available at https://www.penguinrandomhouse.ca/books/292717/looking-for-alaska-by-john-green/9780593109069/reading-guide

Greenfield, P., and Bruner, J. (1966). "Culture and Cognitive Growth." *Journal of Psychology* 1: 89–107.

Grimmelmann, J. (2016a). "Copyright for Literate Robots." *Iowa Law Review* 101: 657–681.

Grimmelmann, J. (2016b). "There's No Such Thing as a Computer-Authored Work—And It's a Good Thing, Too." *Columbia Journal of Law and the Arts* 39: 403–416.

Guerberof Arenas, A., and Toral, A. (2020). "The Impact of Post-Editing and Machine Translation on Creativity and Reading Experience." *Translation Spaces* 9(2): 255–282.

Guerberof Arenas, A., and Toral, A. (2022). "Creativity in Translation: Machine Translation as a Constraint for Literary Texts." *Translation Spaces* 11(2): 184–212.

Guilford, J. P. (1950). "Creativity." *American Psychologist* 5(9): 444–454.

Gutman-Wei, R. (December 12, 2019). "A 'Mic Drop' on a Theory of Language Evolution." *The Atlantic*. Available at https://www.theatlantic.com/science/archive/2019/12/when-did-ancient-humans-start-speak/603484/

Hall, A. H., et al. (2015). "Examining the Effects of Preschool Writing Instruction on Emergent Literacy Skills: A Systematic Review of the Literature." *Literacy Research and Instruction* 54: 115–134. Available at https://tigerprints.clemson.edu/cgi/viewcontent.cgi?article=1040&context=eugene_pubs

Halverson, J. (1992). "Goody and the Implosion of the Literacy Thesis." *Man* 27: 301–317.

Hancock, J., Naaman, M., and Levy, K. (2020). "AI-Mediated Communication: Definition, Research Agenda, and Ethical Considerations." *Journal of Computer-Mediated Communication* 25: 89–100. Available at https://academic.oup.com/jcmc/article/25/1/89/5714020

Handel, M. (July 2022). "Growth Trends for Selected Occupations Considered at Risk from Automation." *Monthly Labor Review*. US Bureau of Labor Statistics. Available at https://www.bls.gov/opub/mlr/2022/article/growth-trends-for-selected-occupations-considered-at-risk-from-automation.htm

Hao, K. (July 9, 2021). "AI Voice Actors Sound More Human Than Ever—and They're Ready to Hire." *MIT Technology Review*. Available at https://www.technologyreview.com/2021/07/09/1028140/ai-voice-actors-sound-human/

Harris, R. (2000). *Rethinking Writing*. Indiana University Press.

Harris, W. V. (1989). *Ancient Literacy*. Cambridge University Press.

Hartocollis, A., Taylor, K., and Saul, S. (January 19, 2021). "Retooling During Pandemic, the SAT Will Drop Essay and Subject Tests." *New York Times*. Available at https://www.nytimes.com/2021/01/19/us/sat-essay-subject-tests.html

Harvard University Archives Research Guides (n.d.). "Harvard Presidents Reports, 1826–1995." Available at https://guides.library.harvard.edu/c.php?g=638791&p=4471938

Havelock, E. (1963). *Preface to Plato*. Harvard University Press.

Hayes, J., and Berninger, V. (2014). "Cognitive Processes in Writing: A Framework." In B. Arfe, J. Dockrell, and V. Berninger, eds., *Writing Development in Children with Hearing Loss, Dyslexia, or Oral Language Problems*. Oxford University Press, pp. 3–15.

Heaven, W. D. (December 8, 2021). "DeepMind Says Its New Language Model Can Beat Others 25 Times Its Size." *MIT Technology Review*. Available at https://

www.technologyreview.com/2021/12/08/1041557/deepmind-language-model-beat-others-25-times-size-gpt-3-megatron/

Heaven, W. D. (February 23, 2022). "This Is the Reason Demis Hassabis Started DeepMind." *MIT Technology Review*. Available at https://www.technologyreview.com/2022/02/23/1045016/ai-deepmind-demis-hassabis-alphafold/

Heaven, W. D. (March 29, 2022). "Chatbots Could One Day Replace Search Engines. Here's Why That's a Terrible Idea." *MIT Technology Review*. Available at https://www.technologyreview.com/2022/03/29/1048439/chatbots-replace-search-engine-terrible-idea/

Heaven, W. D. (May 3, 2022). "Meta Has Built a Massive New Language AI—and It's Giving It Away for Free." *MIT Technology Review*. Available at https://www.technologyreview.com/2022/05/03/1051691/meta-ai-large-language-model-gpt3-ethics-huggingface-transparency/

Heikkilä, M. (August 31, 2022). "What Does GPT-3 'Know' About Me?" *MIT Technology Review*. Available at https://www.technologyreview.com/2022/08/31/1058800/what-does-gpt-3-know-about-me/

Heikkilä, M. (September 22, 2022). "DeepMind's New Chatbot Uses Google Searches Plus Humans to Give Better Answers." *MIT Technology Review*. Available at https://www.technologyreview.com/2022/09/22/1059922/deepminds-new-chatbot-uses-google-searches-plus-humans-to-give-better-answers/

Heikkilä, M. (January 17, 2023). "Here's How Microsoft Could Use ChatGPT." *MIT Technology Review*. Available at https://www.technologyreview.com/2023/01/17/1067014/heres-how-microsoft-could-use-chatgpt/

Heikkilä, M. (January 27, 2023). "A Watermark for Chatbots Can Spot Text Written by an AI." *MIT Technology Review*. Available at https://www.technologyreview.com/2023/01/27/1067338/a-watermark-for-chatbots-can-spot-text-written-by-an-ai/

Heller, J., Safdie, L., and Arrendondo, P. (2021). "AI in Legal Research." In N. Waisberg and H. Alexander, eds., *AI for Lawyers*. Wiley, pp. 107–118.

Henrickson, L. (April 4, 2021). "Constructing the Other Half of *The Policeman's Beard*." *Electronic Book Review*. Available at https://electronicbookreview.com/essay/constructing-the-other-half-of-the-policemans-beard/

Herrington, A., and Moran, C. (2012). "Writing to a Machine Is Not Writing at All." In N. Elliot and L. Perelman, eds., *Writing Assessment in the 21st Century: Essays in Honor of Edward M. White*. Hampton, pp. 219–232.

Hie, H., et al. (January 15, 2021). "Learning the Language of Viral Evolution and Escape." *Science*. Available at https://www.science.org/doi/10.1126/science.abd7331

Hill, A. S. (1874). *General Rules for Punctuation and for the Use of Capital Letters*. John Wilson & Son. Available at https://www.google.com/books/edition/General_Rules_for_Punctuation_and_for_th/CTkAAAAAYAAJ?hl=en&gbpv=1&pg=PA1&printsec=frontcover

"History of the Enigma" (n.d.). *Crypto Museum*. Available at https://www.cryptomuseum.com/crypto/enigma/hist.htm

Hoffman, R. (September 27, 2022). "AI's Human Factor." *Greylock*. Available at https://greylock.com/greymatter/ais-human-factor/

Hofstadter, D. (1979). *Gödel, Escher, Bach*. Basic.

Holmes, J. (April 3, 2016). "AI Is Already Making Inroads into Journalism but Could It Win a Pulitzer?" *Guardian*. Available at https://www.theguardian.com/media/2016/apr/03/artificla-intelligence-robot-reporter-pulitzer-prize

Holpuch, A. (February 23, 2022). "16-Year-Old Chess Prodigy Defeats World Champion Magnus Carlsen." *New York Times*. Available at https://www.nytimes.com/2022/02/23/arts/chess-magnus-carlsen-rameshbabu-praggnanandhaa.html

Horobin, S. (2013). *Does Spelling Matter?* Oxford University Press.

Horowitz-Kraus, T., and Hutton, J. S. (2018). "Brain Connectivity in Children Is Increased by the Time They Spend Reading Books and Decreased by the Length of Exposure to Screen-Based Media." *Acta Paediatrica* 107(4): 685–693.

"How Sequoyah, Who Did Not Read or Write, Created a Written Language for the Cherokee Nation from Scratch" (November 24, 2020). *PBS American Masters*. Available at https://www.pbs.org/wnet/americanmasters/blog/how-sequoyah-who-did-not-read-or-write-created-a-written-language-for-the-cherokee-nation-from-scratch/

Hsu, T., and Thompson, S. A. (February 8, 2023). "Disinformation Researchers Raise Alarms About A.I. Chatbots." *New York Times*. Available at https://www.nytimes.com/2023/02/08/technology/ai-chatbots-disinformation.html

Huang, C.-Z. A., et al. (2020). "AI Song Contest: Human–AI Co-Creation in Songwriting." *21st International Society for Music Information Retrieval Conference*. Available at https://arxiv.org/abs/2010.05388

Hutchins, J. (1996). "ALPAC: The (In)famous Report." *MT News International* 14: 9–12. Available at https://aclanthology.org/www.mt-archive.info/90/MTNI-1996-Hutchins.pdf

Hutchins, J. (2002). "Two Precursors of Machine Translation: Artsrouni and Trojanskij." Available at https://citeseerx.ist.psu.edu/viewdoc/download?doi=10.1.1.14.2564&rep=rep1&type=pdf

Hutton, J. S., et al. (2020a). "Associations Between Home Literacy Environment, Brain White Matter Integrity and Cognitive Abilities in Preschool-Age Children." *Acta Paediatrica* 109(7): 1376–1386.

Hutton, J. S., et al. (2020b). "Associations Between Screen-Based Media Use and Brain White Matter Integrity in Preschool-Aged Children." *JAMA Pediatrics* 174(1).

"International Literacy Day 2021: Literacy for a Human Centred Recovery: Narrowing the Digital Divide" (2021) *UNESCO*. Available at https://en.unesco.org/sites/default/files/ild-2021-fact-sheet.pdf

"Is Artificial Intelligence Set to Become Art's Next Medium?" (December 12, 2018). *Christie's*. Available at https://www.christies.com/features/a-collaboration-between-two-artists-one-human-one-a-machine-9332-1.aspx

Ives, M., and Mozur, P. (June 4, 2021). "India's 'Ugliest' Language? Google Had an Answer (and Drew a Backlash)." *New York Times*. Available at https://www.nytimes.com/2021/06/04/world/asia/google-india-language-kannada.html

Jabr, F. (May 14, 2012). "Know Your Neurons: The Discovery and Naming of the Neuron." *Scientific American*. Available at https://blogs.scientificamerican.com/brainwaves/know-your-neurons-the-discovery-and-naming-of-the-neuron/

Jacobsen, E. (n.d.). "A (Mostly) Brief History of the SAT and ACT Tests." Available at https://www.erikthered.com/tutor/sat-act-history.html

James, K. (2017). "The Importance of Handwriting Experience on the Development of the Literate Brain." *Current Directions in Psychological Science* 26(6): 502–508.

Jansen, T., et al. (2021). "Don't Just Judge the Spelling! The Influence of Spelling on Assessing Second-Language Student Essays." *Frontline Learning Research* 9(1): 44–65. Available at https://files.eric.ed.gov/fulltext/EJ1284840.pdf

Jauk, E., et al. (2013). "The Relationship Between Intelligence and Creativity: New Support for the Threshold Hypothesis by Means of Empirical Breakpoint Detection." *Intelligence* 41(4): 212–221.

Jee, C. (October 18, 2022). "Technology That Lets Us 'Speak' to Our Dead Relatives. Are We Ready?" *MIT Technology Review*. Available at https://www.technologyreview.com/2022/10/18/1061320/digital-clones-of-dead-people/

Jee, C., and Heaven, W. D. (December 6, 2021). "The Therapists Using AI to Make Therapy Better." *MIT Technology Review*. Available at https://www.technologyreview.com/2021/12/06/1041345/ai-nlp-mental-health-better-therapists-psychology-cbt/

Jefferson, G. (1949). "The Mind of Mechanical Man." Lister Oration for 1949. *British Medical Journal* 1: 1105–1110.

Jia, Y., and Weiss, R. (May 15, 2019). "Introducing Translatotron: An End-to-End Speech-to-Speech Translation Model." *Google AI Blog*. Available at https://ai.googleblog.com/2019/05/introducing-translatotron-end-to-end.html

Johnson, G. (November 11, 1997). "Undiscovered Bach? No, a Computer Wrote It." *New York Times*. Available at https://www.nytimes.com/1997/11/11/science/undiscovered-bach-no-a-computer-wrote-it.html

Johnson, K. (November 2, 2021). "Facebook Drops Facial Recognition to Tag People in Photos." *Wired*. Available at https://www.wired.com/story/facebook-drops-facial-recognition-tag-people-photos/

Johnson, M. (April 20, 2020). "A Scalable Approach to Reducing Gender Bias in Google Translate." *Google AI Blog*. Available at https://ai.googleblog.com/2020/04/a-scalable-approach-to-reducing-gender.html

Johnson, S. (April 16, 2013). "Why No One Clicked on the Great Hypertext Story," *Wired*. Available at https://www.wired.com/2013/04/hypertext/

Joshi, R. M., et al. (2008). "How Words Cast Their Spell: Spelling Is an Integral Part of Learning the Language, Not a Matter of Memorization." *American Educator* 32(4): 6–16. Available at https://www.aft.org/sites/default/files/periodicals/joshi.pdf

Jozuka, E. (March 24, 2016). "A Japanese AI Almost Won a Literary Prize." *Vice*. Available at https://www.vice.com/en/article/wnxnjn/a-japanese-ai-almost-won-a-literary-prize

Kalchbrenner, N., and Blunsom, P. (2013). "Recurrent Continuous Translation Models." In *Proceedings of the ACL Conference on Empirical Methods in Natural Language Processing*, pp. 1700–1709.

Kansara, R., and Main, E. (September 9, 2021). "The Kenyans Who Are Helping the World to Cheat." *BBC News*. Available at https://www.bbc.com/news/blogs-trending-58465189

Kasparov, G. (2007). *How Life Imitates Chess: Making the Right Moves, from the Board to the Boardroom*. Bloomsbury.

Kasparov, G. (February 11, 2010). "The Chess Master and the Computer" (review of Diego Rasskin-Gutman, *Chess Metaphors*, MIT Press). In *The New York Review of Books*. Available at https://www.nybooks.com/articles/2010/02/11/the-chess-master-and-the-computer/

Kaufman J. C. (2018). "Finding Meaning with Creativity in the Past, Present, and Future." *Perspectives on Psychological Science* 13(6): 734–749.

Kaufman, J. C., and Beghetto, R. A. (2009). "Beyond Big and Little: The Four C Model of Creativity." *Review of General Psychology* 13(1): 1–12.

Kaufman, S. L. (November 5, 2020). "Artist Sougwen Chung Wanted Collaborators. So She Designed and Built Her Own AI Robots." *Washington Post*. Available at https://www.washingtonpost.com/business/2020/11/05/ai-artificial-intelligence-art-sougwen-chung/

Kennedy, H. (1980). "The First Written Examinations at Harvard College." *American Mathematical Monthly* 87(6): 483–486.

Kenny, D., and Winters, M. (2020). "Machine Translation, Ethics and the Literary Translator's Voice." *Translation Spaces* 9(1): 123–149.

Kim, J., et al. (2021). "Which Linguist Invented the Lightbulb? Presupposition Verification for Question-Answering." *ACL 2021*. Available at https://arxiv.org/pdf/2101.00391.pdf

Kincaid, J. P., et al. (February 1975). "Derivation of New Readability Formulas: Automated Readability Index (Fog Count and Flesch Reading Ease Formula) for Navy Enlisted Personnel." *Research Branch Report 8-75*. Available at https://apps.dtic.mil/sti/pdfs/ADA006655.pdf

Kindy, D. (November 11, 2022). "Nazi Ciphers Were No Match for WWII Code-Breaking Heroine." *Washington Post*. Available at https://www.washingtonpost.com/history/2022/11/11/julia-parsons-woman-codebreaker-wwii/

Klebanov, B. B., Gyawali, B., and Song, Y. (2017). "Detecting Good Arguments in a Non-Topic-Specific Way: An Oxymoron?" In *Proceedings of the 55th Meeting of the Association for Computational Linguistics*, short papers, pp. 244–249.

Klebanov, B. B., and Madnani, N. (2020). "Automated Evaluation of Writing—50 Years and Counting." In *Proceedings of the 58th Meeting of the Association for Computational Linguistics*, pp. 7796–7810.

Klingemann, M. (July 18, 2020). "Another Attempt at a Longer Piece. An Imaginary Jerome K. Jerome Writes About Twitter." *Twitter* post. Available at https://twitter.com/quasimondo/status/1284509525500989445?lang=en

Knight, W. (December 7, 2022). "ChatGPT's Most Charming Trick Is Also Its Biggest Flaw." *Wired*. Available at https://www.wired.com/story/openai-chatgpts-most-charming-trick-hides-its-biggest-flaw/

Koch, C. (March 19, 2016). "How the Computer Beat the Go Master." *Scientific American*. Available at https://www.scientificamerican.com/article/how-the-computer-beat-the-go-master/

Kocienda, K. (September 4, 2018). "I Invented the iPhone's Autocorrect. Sorry About That, and You're Welcome." *Wired*. Available at https://www.wired.com/story/opinion-i-invented-autocorrect/

Krill, P. (November 10, 2022). "GitHub Faces Lawsuit over Copilot AI Coding Assistant." *InfoWorld*. Available at https://www.infoworld.com/article/3679748/github-faces-lawsuit-over-copilot-coding-tool.html

Krokoscz, M. (2021). "Plagiarism in Articles Published in Journals Indexed in the Scientific Periodicals Electronic Library (SPELL): A Comparative Analysis Between 2013 and 2018." *International Journal for Academic Integrity* 17(1). Available at https://edintegrity.biomedcentral.com/articles/10.1007/s40979-020-00063-5

Kung, T. H., et al. (December 21, 2022). "Performance of ChatGPT on USMLE: Potential for AI-Assisted Medical Education Using Large Language Models." Available at https://www.medrxiv.org/content/10.1101/2022.12.19.22283643v2.full

Kyaga, S. (2015). *Creativity and Mental Illness*. Palgrave Macmillan/Springer Nature.

LaFranchi, H. (April 27, 1984). "John Martin's 'Writing to Read': A New Way to Teach Reading." *Christian Science Monitor*. Available at https://www.csmonitor.com/1984/0427/042701.html

Lahiri, J. (2017). "Introduction" to Domenico Starnone, *Ties*. Trans. J. Lahiri. Europa Editions, pp. 11–19.

Landow, G. (1992). *Hypertext: The Convergence of Contemporary Critical Theory and Technology*. Johns Hopkins University Press.

Language and Machines: Computers in Translation and Linguistics (1966). Automatic Language Processing Advisory Committee, National Academy of Sciences. Available at https://nap.nationalacademies.org/resource/alpac_lm/ARC000005.pdf

Lau, J. H., et al. (April 30, 2020). "This AI Poet Mastered Rhythm, Rhyme, and Natural Language to Write Like Shakespeare." *IEEE Spectrum*. Available at https://spectrum.ieee.org/artificial-intelligence/machine-learning/this-ai-poet-mastered-rhythm-rhyme-and-natural-language-to-write-like-shakespeare

LeCun, Y., et al. (1998). "Gradient-Based Learning Applied to Document Recognition." *Proceedings of the IEEE* 86(11): 2278–2324.

Lee, K.-F., and Qiufan, C. (2021). *AI 2041: Ten Visions for Our Future*. Currency.

Lee, N. T., and Lai, S. (December 20, 2021). "Why New York City Is Cracking Down on AI in Hiring." *Brookings Education Blog Tech Tank*. Available at https://www.brookings.edu/blog/techtank/2021/12/20/why-new-york-city-is-cracking-down-on-ai-in-hiring/

Legg, M., and Bell, F. (2020). *Artificial Intelligence and the Legal Profession*. Hart.

Lehmann, N. (1999). *The Big Test: The Secret History of the American Meritocracy*. Farrar, Straus and Giroux.

Lehmann, W. P. (n.d.). "Machine Translation at Texas: The Early Years." Linguistics Research Center, University of Texas at Austin. Available at https://liberalarts.utexas.edu/lrc/about/history/machine-translation-at-texas/early-years.php

Leonard, S. (1929). *The Doctrine of Correctness in English Usage, 1700–1800*. Russell and Russell.

Levy, F., and Marnane, R. (2004). *The New Division of Labor*. Russell Sage Foundation.

Levy, S. (May 18, 1997). "Big Blue's Hand of God." *Newsweek*. Available at https://www.newsweek.com/big-blues-hand-god-173076

Lewis-Kraus, G. (December 14, 2016). "The Great A.I. Awakening." *New York Times Magazine*. Available at https://www.nytimes.com/2016/12/14/magazine/the-great-ai-awakening.html

Li, F.-F. (n.d.). "ImageNet: Crowdsourcing, Benchmarking, and Other Cool Things." Stanford University. Available at https://www.image-net.org/static_files/papers/ImageNet_2010.pdf

Limbong, A. (July 16, 2021). "AI Brought Anthony Bourdain's Voice Back to Life. Should It Have?" *NPR*. Available at https://www.npr.org/2021/07/16/1016838440/ai-brought-anthony-bourdains-voice-back-to-life-should-it-have

Ling, R. (2012). *Taken for Grantedness*. MIT Press.

"Listening to the Music of Turing's Computer" (October 1, 2016). *BBC News*. Available at https://www.bbc.com/news/magazine-37507707

Liukkonen, P. (2008). "James Fenimore Cooper (1789–1851)." Available at https://web.archive.org/web/20140823203150/http:/www.kirjasto.sci.fi/jfcooper.htm

Longcamp, M., Zerbato-Poudou, M.-T., and Velay, J.-L. (2005). "The Influence of Writing Practice on Letter Recognition in Preschool Children: A Comparison Between Handwriting and Typing." *Acta Psychologica* 119: 67–79.

Lorenz, T. (April 29, 2021). "What Is 'Cheugy'? You Know It When You See It." *New York Times*. Available at https://www.nytimes.com/2021/04/29/style/cheugy.html

Lou, P. J., and Johnson, M. (2020). "End-to-End Speech Recognition and Disfluency Removal." *Findings of the Association for Computational Linguistics*. EMNLP 2020, pp. 2051–2061. Available at https://arxiv.org/abs/2009.10298

Lounsbury, T. L. (1911). "Compulsory Composition in Colleges," in *Harper's Monthly* 123: 866–880. In J. C. Brereton, ed. (1995), *The Origins of Composition Studies in the American College, 1875–1925*. University of Pittsburgh Press, pp. 261–286.

Lubrano, A. (1997). *The Telegraph: How Technology Innovation Caused Social Change*. Routledge.

Luckenbach, T. A. (1986). "Encouraging 'little c' and 'Big C' Creativity." *Research Management* 29(2): 9–10.

Luhn, H. P. (1958). "The Automatic Creation of Literature Abstracts." *IBM Journal* (April): 159–165.

Lunsford, A., et al. (2017). *Everyone's an Author*, 2nd ed. W. W. Norton.

Lunsford, A. A., and Lunsford, K. J. (2008). "'Mistakes Are a Fact of Life': A National Comparative Study." *College Composition and Communication* 59(4): 781–806.

Lytvyn, M. (March 31, 2021). "A History of Innovation at Grammarly." *Grammarly Blog*. Available at https://www.grammarly.com/blog/grammarly-12-year-history/

Mac, R. (September 3, 2021). "Facebook Apologizes After A.I. Puts 'Primates' Label on Video of Black Men." *New York Times*. Available at https://www.nytimes.com/2021/09/03/technology/facebook-ai-race-primates.html

Maguire, E. A., et al. (2000). "Navigation-Related Structural Change in the Hippocampi of Taxi Drivers." *Proceedings of the National Academy of Sciences* 97(8): 4398–4403.

Mallery, G. (1972 [1893]). *Picture-Writing of the American Indians*. 2 vols. Dover.

Mallon, T. (1989). *Stolen Words*. Ticknor & Fields.

Mangen, A., and Schilhab, T. (2012). "An Embodied View of Reading: Theoretical Considerations, Empirical Findings, and Educational Implications." In S. Matre and A. Skaftun, eds., *Skriv! Les!* Akademika Forlag. Available at https://www.academia.edu/3850051/Mangen_A_and_Schilhab_T_2012_An_embodied_view_of_reading_Theoretical_considerations_empirical_findings_and_educational_implications

Mangen, A., and van der Weel, A. (2017). "Why Don't We Read Hypertext Novels? *Convergence* 23(2): 166–181.

Mangen, A., and Velay, J.-L. (2010). "Digitizing Literacy: Reflections on the Haptics of Writing." In M. H. Zadeh, ed., *Advances in Haptics*, pp. 385–401. Available at https://www.intechopen.com/chapters/9927

Manjoo, F. (October 7, 2022). "In the Battle with Robots, Human Workers Are Winning." *New York Times*. Available at https://www.nytimes.com/2022/10/07/opinion/machines-ai-employment.html

Marconi, F. (2020). *Newsmakers: Artificial Intelligence and the Future of Journalism*. Columbia University Press.

Marcus, G. (December 29, 2022). "The Dark Risk of Large Language Models." *Wired*. Available at https://www.wired.com/story/large-language-models-artificial-intelligence/

Marcus, G., and Davis, E. (2019). *Rebooting AI: Building AI We Can Trust*. Pantheon.

Markovic, M. (2019). "Rise of the Robot Lawyer?" *Arizona Law Review* 61(2): 325–350.

Marshall, M. (January 7, 2021). "Humans May Have Domesticated Dogs by Accident by Sharing Excess Meat." *New Scientist*. Available at https://www.newscientist.com/article/2264329-humans-may-have-domesticated-dogs-by-accident-by-sharing-excess-meat/

Martin, J. H., and Friedberg, A. (1986). *Writing to Read*. Warner.

Martin-Lacroux, C., and Lacroux, A. (2017). "Do Employers Forgive Applicants' Bad Spelling in Résumés?" *Business and Professional Communication Quarterly* 80(3): 321–335.

Matan, O., et al. (1991). "Reading Handwritten Digits: A Zip Code Recognition System." *AT&T 1991 Report*. Available at https://ieeexplore.ieee.org/document/144441

Mayne, D. (January 26, 2021). "Revisiting Grammarly: An Imperfect Tool for Final Editing." Writing Center, University of Wisconsin–Madison. Available at https://dept.writing.wisc.edu/blog/revisiting-grammarly/comment-page-1/

McAfee, A., and Brynjolfsson, E. (2017). *Machine, Platform, Crowd*. W. W. Norton.

McCabe, D. L. (2005). "Cheating Among College and University Students: A North American Perspective." *International Journal for Educational Integrity* 1(1). Available at https://ojs.unisa.edu.au/index.php/ijei/article/view/14

McCarthy, A. (August 12, 2019). "How 'Smart' Email Could Change the Way We Talk." *BBC Future*. Available at https://www.bbc.com/future/article/20190812-how-ai-powered-predictive-text-affects-your-brain

McCarthy, J. (2006). "The Dartmouth Workshop—As Planned and As It Happened." Available at http://www-formal.stanford.edu/jmc/slides/dartmouth/dartmouth/node1.html

McCarthy, J., et al. (August 31, 1955). "A Proposal for the Dartmouth Summer Research Project on Artificial Intelligence." Proposal to the Rockefeller Foundation. Available at http://www-formal.stanford.edu/jmc/history/dartmouth/dartmouth.html

McCoy, R. T., et al. (November 18, 2021). "How Much Do Language Models Copy from Their Training Data? Evaluating Linguistic Novelty in Text Generation Using RAVEN." Available at https://arxiv.org/pdf/2111.09509.pdf

McCulloch, W. S., and Pitts, W. (1943). "A Logical Calculus of the Ideas Immanent in Nervous Activity." *Bulletin of Mathematical Biophysics* 5: 115–133.

McGee, T., and Ericsson, P. (2002). "The Politics of the Program: MS Word as the Invisible Grammarian." *Computers and Composition* 19: 453–470.

McKinney, S. M., et al. (January 1, 2020). "International Evaluation of an AI System for Breast Cancer Screening." *Nature* 577: 89–94. Available at https://www.nature.com/articles/s41586-019-1799-6

Meehan, J. R. (1977). "Tale-Spin: An Interactive Program That Writes Stories." In *Proceedings of the 5th International Joint Conference on Artificial Intelligence*, vol. 1, pp. 91–98. Available at http://cs.uky.edu/~sgware/reading/papers/meehan-1977tale.pdf

Menick, J. (2016). "Move 37: Artificial Intelligence, Randomness, and Creativity." *Mousse Magazine* 55 + 53. Available at https://www.johnmenick.com/writing/move-37-alpha-go-deep-mind.html

Merrotsy, P. (2013). "A Note on Big-C Creativity and Little-c Creativity." *Creativity Research Journal* 25(4): 474–476.

Mesa, N. (March 11, 2022). "UNC Research Chief Admits to Plagiarism, Resigns."

TheScientist. Available at https://www.the-scientist.com/news-opinion/unc-research-chief-admits-to-plagiarism-resigns-69797

Messenger, R. (August 9, 2015). "The Wonderful World of Typewriters." *ozTypewriter.* Available at https://oztypewriter.blogspot.com/2015/08/street-scribes-in-istanbul.html

Metz, C. (February 19, 2021). "A Second Google A.I. Researcher Says the Company Fired Her." *New York Times.* Available at https://www.nytimes.com/2021/02/19/technology/google-ethical-artificial-intelligence-team.html

Michie, D. (1986). *On Machine Intelligence,* 2nd ed. Ellis Horwood.

"Microsoft 'to Replace Journalists with Robots'" (May 30, 2020). *BBC News.* Available at https://www.bbc.com/news/world-us-canada-52860247

Midling, A. S. (October 1, 2020). "Why Writing by Hand Makes Kids Smarter." *Norwegian SciTech News.* Available at https://norwegianscitechnews.com/2020/10/why-writing-by-hand-makes-kids-smarter/

Miller, A. I. (2019). *The Artist in the Machine.* MIT Press.

Minnis, A. J. (1988). *Medieval Theory of Authorship,* 2nd ed. University of Pennsylvania Press.

Minsky, M., and Papert, S. (1969). *Perceptrons.* MIT Press.

Mitchell, E., et al. (January 26, 2023). "DetectGPT: ZeroShot Machine-Generated Text Detection Using Probability Curvature." Available at https://arxiv.org/pdf/2301.11305v1.pdf

Mitchell, M. (n.d. a). "Curriculum." Excerpt from *Encyclopedia Brunoniana.* Available at https://www.brown.edu/Administration/News_Bureau/Databases/Encyclopedia/search.php?serial=C0780

Mitchell, M. (n.d. b). "Philermenian Society." Excerpt from *Encyclopedia Brunoniana.* Available at https://www.brown.edu/Administration/News_Bureau/Databases/Encyclopedia/search.php?serial=P0190

Monaghan, W., and Bridgeman, B. (April 2005). "E-rater as a Quality Control on Human Scores." *ETS R&D Connections.* Available at https://www.ets.org/Media/Research/pdf/RD_Connections2.pdf

Monarch, R. (M.) (2021). *Human-in-the-Loop Machine Learning.* Available at https://www.manning.com/books/human-in-the-loop-machine-learning#toc

Moncada, C. (December 15, 1983). "Takoma Park Votes Itself a Nuclear-Free Zone." *Washington Post.* Available at https://www.washingtonpost.com/archive/local/1983/12/15/takoma-park-votes-itself-a-nuclear-free-zone/e8664144-8055-47ac-8a4e-1925ce22b6e4/

Montfort, N. (2008), "Riddle Machines: The History and Nature of Interactive Fiction." In S. Schreibman and R. Siemens, eds., *A Companion to Digital Literacy Studies.* Blackwell, pp. 267–282.

Moor, J. (2006). "The Dartmouth College Artificial Intelligence Conference: The Next Fifty Years." *AI Magazine* 27(4): 87–91.

Moorkens, J., et al. (2018). "Translators' Perceptions of Literary Post-Editing Using Statistical and Neural Machine Translation." *Translation Spaces* 7(2): 240–262.

Moran, L. (February 25, 2020). "Casetext Launches Automated Brief-Writing Product." *ABA Journal.* Available at https://www.abajournal.com/news/article/casetext-launches-automated-brief-writing-product

Morehead, K., Dunlosky, J., and Rawson, K.A. (2019). "How Much Mightier Is the Pen Than the Keyboard for Note-Taking? A Replication and Extension of Mueller and Oppenheimer (2014)." *Educational Psychology Review* 31: 753–780.

Mori, M. (June 12, 2012). "The Uncanny Valley." *IEEE Spectrum*. Available at https://spectrum.ieee.org/the-uncanny-valley

Motion, A. (September 25, 1999). "Magnificent in Its Remoteness, Beowulf Is Also Shockingly Vivid." *Financial Times*.

Mueller, P. A., and Oppenheimer, D. M. (2014). "The Pen Is Mightier Than the Keyboard: Advantages of Longhand over Laptop Note Taking." *Psychological Science* 25(6): 1159–1168.

Murati, E. (2022). "Language & Coding Creativity." *Daedalus* 151(2): 156–167.

Myers, D. G. (1996). *The Elephants Teach: Creative Writing Since 1880*. Prentice-Hall.

NACE (December 12, 2018). "Employers Want to See These Attributes on Students' Resumes." National Association of Colleges and Employers.

NACE (February 15, 2022). "The Attributes Employers Want to See on College Students' Resumes." National Association of Colleges and Employers.

Nalbantian, S., and Matthews, P. M., eds. (2019). *Secrets of Creativity: What Neuroscience, the Arts, and Our Minds Reveal*. Oxford University Press.

Naruto v. Slater (2016). Order Granting Motions to Dismiss. Available at https://scholar.google.com/scholar_case?case=2028474831558505548&hl=en&as_sdt=6=scholarr

Navarria, G. (November 2, 2016). "How the Internet Was Born: From the ARPANET to the Internet." *The Conversation*. Available at https://theconversation.com/how-the-internet-was-born-from-the-arpanet-to-the-internet-68072

Nayak, P. (May 18, 2021). "MUM: A New AI Milestone for Understanding Information." *Google Blog*. Available at https://blog.google/products/search/introducing-mum/

"Neanderthals" (n.d.). *Gibralter National Museum*. Available at https://www.gibmuseum.gi/world-heritage/neanderthals

Neate, R. (December 15, 2021). "Sotheby's Sells Record $7.3bn of Art So Far in 2021." *Guardian*. Available at https://www.theguardian.com/artanddesign/2021/dec/15/sothebys-record-sales-art-2021-auction-house

Neely, B. (July 20, 2016). "Trump Speechwriter Accepts Responsibility for Using Michelle Obama's Words." *NPR*. Available at https://www.npr.org/2016/07/20/486758596/trump-speechwriter-accepts-responsibility-for-using-michelle-obamas-words

Nelson, T. (1980). *Literacy Machines*. Available at https://archive.org/details/literarymachinesoonels/page/n1/mode/2up

"New Navy Device Learns by Doing" (July 8, 1958). *New York Times*. Available at https://www.nytimes.com/1958/07/08/archives/new-navy-device-learns-by-doing-psychologist-shows-embryo-of.html

"Newspapers Fact Sheet" (June 29, 2021). *Pew Research Center*. Available at https://www.pewresearch.org/journalism/fact-sheet/newspapers/

Newton, P. M. (2018). "How Common Is Commercial Contract Cheating in Higher Education and Is It Increasing? A Systematic Review." *Frontiers in Education* 3, Article 67. Available at https://www.frontiersin.org/articles/10.3389/feduc.2018.00067/full

Ngo, H., and Sakhaee, E. (2022). "Chapter 3: Technical AI Ethics." In *Artificial Intelligence Index Report 2022*. Stanford University Institute for Human-Centered Artificial Intelligence. Available at https://aiindex.stanford.edu/wp-content/uploads/2022/03/2022-AI-Index-Report_Master.pdf

Nin, Anaïs. (1974). *The Diary of Anaïs Nin, Volume 5: 1947–1955*. Ed. and preface by Gunther Stuhlmann. Harcourt Brace Jovanovich.

Nizinsky, B. (2022). "AI Is Coming for Copywriters." *LinkedIn*. Available at https://www.linkedin.com/pulse/ai-coming-copywriters-brian-nizinsky

Noble, S. (2018). *Algorithms of Oppression: How Search Engines Reinforce Racism*. New York University Press.

Nordling, L. (November 16, 2018). "Widespread Plagiarism Detected in Many Medical Journals Based in Africa." *Nature*. Available at https://www.nature.com/articles/d41586-018-07462-2

NPR (September 30, 2005). "Joan Didion Survives 'The Year of Magical Thinking.'" Available at https://www.npr.org/transcripts/4866010

Olson, D. (1994). *The World on Paper: The Conceptual and Cognitive Implications of Writing and Reading*. Cambridge University Press.

Onion, R. (February 8, 2022). "Why Grammarly's New Suggestions for Writing About Slavery Were Always Going to Miss the Mark." *Slate*. Available at https://slate.com/technology/2022/02/grammarly-slavery-language-suggestions.html

Oravec, J. A. (2014). "Expert Systems and Knowledge-Based Engineering (1984–1991)." *International Journal of Designs for Living* 5(2): 66–75.

Oremus, W. (October 12, 2021). "Lawmakers' Latest Idea to Fix Facebook: Regulate the Algorithm." *Washington Post*. Available at https://www.washingtonpost.com/technology/2021/10/12/congress-regulate-facebook-algorithm/

Orwell, G. (1946). "Why I Write." *Gangrel* 4 (Summer).

Page, E. (1966). "The Imminence of Grading Essays by Computer." *The Phi Delta Kappan* 47(5): 238–243.

Park, S., and Baron, N. S. (2018). "Experiences of Writing on Smartphones, Laptops, and Paper." In J. Vincent and L. Haddon, eds., *Smartphone Cultures*. Routledge, pp. 150–162.

Parkey, K. (June 6, 2021). "John Wayne Coined the Term 'The Big C' While Doing Cancer Awareness Outreach." *Outsider*. Available at https://outsider.com/entertainment/john-wayne-coined-term-the-big-c-cancer-awareness/

Pasquale, F. (2018). "A Rule of Persons, Not Machines: The Limits of Legal Automation." Available at https://digitalcommons.law.umaryland.edu/cgi/viewcontent.cgi?article=2616&context=fac_pubs

Pasquale, F. (2020). *New Laws of Robotics*. Belknap.

Patterson, F., and Linden, E. (1981). *The Education of Koko*. Holt, Rinehart & Winston.

Payne, W. M., ed. (1895). *English in American Universities, by Professors in the English Departments of Twenty Representative Institutions*. D.C. Heath. Selections in J. C. Brereton, ed. (1995), *The Origins of Composition Studies in the American College, 1875–1925*. University of Pittsburgh Press, pp. 157–186.

Peng, J., and Park, W. (June 4, 2019). "The Remarkable 'Plasticity' of Musicians' Brains." *BBC*. Available at https://www.bbc.com/worklife/article/20190604-the-woman-who-feels-music-on-her-skin

Perelman, L. (2020). "The BABEL Generator and E-Rater: 21st Century Writing Constructs and Automated Essay Scoring (AES)." *Journal of Writing Assessment* 13(1). Available at https://escholarship.org/uc/item/263565cq

Peritz, A. (September 6, 2022). "A.I. Is Making It Easier Than Ever for Students to Cheat." *Slate*. Available at https://slate.com/technology/2022/09/ai-students-writing-cheating-sudowrite.html

Phelps, W. L. (1912). "English Composition" in *Teaching in School and College*.

Macmillan. In J. C. Brereton, ed. (1995), *The Origins of Composition Studies in the American College, 1875–1925*. University of Pittsburgh Press, pp. 287–291.

Pielmeier, H., and O'Mara, P. (January 2020). "The State of the Linguistic Supply Chain: Translators and Interpreters in 2020." *CSA Research*. Available at https://cdn2.hubspot.net/hubfs/4041721/Newsletter/The%20State%20of%20the%20Linguist%20Supply%20Chain%202020.pdf

"Pope Ditches Latin as Official Language of Vatican Synod" (October 6, 2014). *Reuters*. Available at https://www.reuters.com/article/us-pope-latin/pope-ditches-latin-as-official-language-of-vatican-synod-idUSKCN0HV10220141006

Potthast, M., Hagen, M., and Stein, B. (June 2020). "The Dilemma of the Direct Answer." *ACM SIGIR Forum* 54(1). Available at https://webis.de/downloads/publications/papers/potthast_2020j.pdf

Powers, D. E., et al. (2001). "Stumping e-Rater: Challenging the Validity of Automated Essay Scoring." *Computers in Human Behavior* 18(2): 103–134.

Presser, J., Beatson, J., and Chan, G., eds. (2021). *Litigating Artificial Intelligence*. Emond.

Quote Investigator (n.d.). "How Can I Know What I Think Till I See What I Say?" Available at https://quoteinvestigator.com/2019/12/11/know-say/

Ramakrishnan, A., Sambuco, D., and Jagsi, R. (2014). "Women's Participation in the Medical Profession: Insights from Experiences in Japan, Scandinavia, Russia, and Eastern Europe." *Journal of Women's Health* 23(11): 927–934.

Ranjit, J. (October 6, 2021). "UK Pavilion: A Poetic Expression Designed by Es Devlin at Dubai Expo 2020." *Parametric Architecture*. Available at https://parametric-architecture.com/uk-pavilion-a-poetic-expression-designed-by-es-devlin-at-dubai-expo-2020/

Reid, R. F. (1959). "The Boylston Professorship of Rhetoric and Oratory, 1806–1904: A Case Study in Changing Concepts of Rhetoric and Pedagogy." *Quarterly Journal of Speech* 45(3): 239–257.

Remus, D., and Levy, F. (2017). "Can Robots be Lawyers? Computers, Lawyers, and the Practice of Law." *Georgetown Journal of Legal Ethics* 30(3): 501–558.

Richtel, M. (2022). *Inspired*. Mariner.

Riedl, M. (January 4, 2021). "An Introduction to AI Story Generation." *Medium*. Available at https://mark-riedl.medium.com/an-introduction-to-ai-story-generation-7f99a450f615

Riley, M. (January 30, 2022). "The Scripps National Spelling Bee." *The Science Academic Stem Magnet*. Available at https://www.thescienceacademystemmagnet.org/2022/01/30/the-scripps-national-spelling-bee/

Roberts, M. S. (May 1, 2019). "Young Composer 'Solves' Elgar's Enigma—and It's Pretty Convincing." *Classic fM*. Available at https://www.classicfm.com/composers/elgar/news/young-composer-solves-enigma/

Roberts, S. (February 14, 2017). "Christopher Strachey's Nineteen-Fifties Love Machine." *New Yorker*. Available at https://www.newyorker.com/tech/annals-of-technology/christopher-stracheys-nineteen-fifties-love-machine

Rockmore, D. (January 7, 2020). "What Happens When Machines Learn to Write Poetry?" *New Yorker*. Available at https://www.newyorker.com/culture/annals-of-inquiry/the-mechanical-muse

Roemmele, M. (2021). "Inspiration Through Observation: Demonstrating the Influence of Automatically Generated Text on Creative Writing." In *Proceedings of* the 12th International Conference on Computational Creativity, pp. 52–61. Available at https://arxiv.org/abs/2107.04007

Roose, K. (2021). *Futureproof*. Random House.

Rose, S. (January 16, 2020). "'It's a War Between Technology and a Donkey'—How AI is Shaking Up Hollywood." *Guardian*. Available at https://www.theguardian. com/film/2020/jan/16/its-a-war-between-technology-and-a-donkey-how-ai-is-shaking-up-hollywood

Ruby, D. (March 9, 2023). "Jasper AI Review 2023." *DemandSage*. Available at https://www.demandsage.com/jasper-ai-review/

Rumelhart, D., Hinton, G., and Williams, R. (1986). "Learning Internal Representations by Error Propagation." In D. E. Rumelhart, J. L. McClelland, and PDP Research Group, eds., *Parallel Distributed Processing: Explorations in the Microstructure of Cognition, Vol. 1: Foundations*. MIT Press, pp. 318–362.

Russell, D. R. (2002 [1991]). *Writing in the Academic Disciplines*. Southern Illinois University Press.

Russell, S. (2019). *Human Compatible*. Penguin Random House.

Russell, S., and Norvig, P. (2021). *Artificial Intelligence: A Modern Approach*, 4th ed. Pearson Education.

Saenger, P. (1982). "Silent Reading: Its Impact on Late Medieval Script and Society." *Viator* 13: 367–414.

Samuel, A. L. (1959). "Some Studies in Machine Learning Using the Game of Checkers." *IBM Journal of Research and Development* 3(3): 210–229.

Samuelson, P. (1986). "Allocating Ownership Rights in Computer-Generated Works." *University of Pittsburgh Law Review* 47: 1185–1228.

Samuelson, P. (2020). "AI Authorship?" *Communications of the ACM* 63(7): 20–22.

Sapir, E. (1921). *Language*. Harcourt, Brace.

Savage-Rumbaugh, S. (1994). *Kanzi: The Ape on the Brink of the Human Mind*. Wiley.

Savoldi, B., et al. (2021). "Gender Bias in Machine Translation." *Transactions of the Association for Computational Linguistics* 9: 845–874. Available at https://arxiv. org/abs/2104.06001

Schank, R. C., and Abelson, R. P. (1977). *Scripts, Plans, Goals and Understanding: An Inquiry into Human Knowledge Structures*. Lawrence Erlbaum.

Schatten, J. (September 14, 2022). "Will Artificial Intelligence Kill College Writing?" *Chronicle of Higher Education*. Available at https://www.chronicle.com/article/will-artificial-intelligence-kill-college-writing

Schiff, J. (n.d.). "A Brief History of Yale." Yale University Library. Available at https:// guides.library.yale.edu/yalehistory

Scott, K. (2022). "I Do Not Think It Means What You Think It Means: Artificial Intelligence, Cognitive Work & Scale." *Daedalus* 151(2): 75–84.

Scragg, D. G. (1974). *A History of English Spelling*. Barnes and Noble.

Scribner, S., and M. Cole (1981). *The Psychology of Literacy*. Harvard University Press.

Sealfon, R. (May 2019). "The History of the Spelling Bee." *Smithsonian Magazine*. Available at https://www.smithsonianmag.com/arts-culture/history-spelling-bee-180971916/

Selinger, E. (January 15, 2015). "Will Autocomplete Make You Too Predictable?" *BBC Future*. Available at https://www.bbc.com/future/article/20150115-is-autocorrect-making-you-boring

Shah, C., and Bender, E. M. (2022). "Situating Search." CHIIR '22. Association for

Computing Machinery. Available at https://dl.acm.org/doi/pdf/10.1145/3498366.3505816

Shah, H. (n.d.). "How GitHub Democratized Coding, Built a $2 Billion Business, and Found a New Home at Microsoft." *Nira Blog*. Available at https://nira.com/github-history/

Shahriar, S. (2021). "GAN Computers Generate Arts? A Survey on Visual Arts, Music, and Literary Text Generation Using Generative Adversarial Network." Available at https://arxiv.org/abs/2108.03857v2

Shane, J. (December 30, 2021). "New Years Resolutions Generated by AI." *AI Weirdness*. Available at https://www.aiweirdness.com/new-years-resolutions-generated-by-ai/

Shank, B. (2004). *A Token of My Affection: Greeting Cards and American Business Culture*. Columbia University Press.

Shapiro, L., ed. (2014). *The Routledge Handbook of Embodied Cognition*. Routledge.

Shearer, E. (January 12, 2021). "More Than Eight-in-Ten Americans Get News from Digital Devices." *Pew Research Center*. Available at https://www.pewresearch.org/fact-tank/2021/01/12/more-than-eight-in-ten-americans-get-news-from-digital-devices/

Shepherd, R. (n.d.). "Why I Write." *Poets.org*. Available at https://poets.org/text/why-i-write

Shermis, M. D., and Burstein, J., eds. (2013). *Handbook of Automated Essay Evaluation*. Routledge.

Shneiderman, B. (1987). *Designing the User Interface: Strategies for Effective Human–Computer Interaction*. Addison-Wesley.

Shneiderman, B. (2022). *Human-Centered AI*. Oxford University Press.

Siegal, N. (June 9, 2015). "Disputed Painting Is Declared an Authentic Rembrandt After Decades." *New York Times*. Available at https://www.nytimes.com/2015/06/09/arts/international/lifting-doubt-over-a-rembrandt.html

Silverstone, R., and Hirsch, E., eds. (1992). *Consuming Technologies: Media and Information in Domestic Spaces*. Routledge.

Simonite, T. (June 8, 2021). "What Really Happened When Google Ousted Timnit Gebru." *Wired*. Available at https://www.wired.com/story/google-timnit-gebru-ai-what-really-happened/

Sinclair, U. (1906). *The Jungle*. Doubleday, Page.

Skeide, M., et al. (2017). "Learning to Read Alters Cortico-Subcortical Cross-Talk in the Visual System of Illiterates." *Sciences Advances* 3(5): 1–7.

Skinner, B. F. (1957). *Verbal Behavior*. Copley.

Slater, D. (2014). *Wildlife Personalities*. Blurb.

Slavin, R. E. (1991). "Reading Effects of IBM's 'Writing to Read' Program: A Review of Evaluations." *Educational Evaluation and Policy Analysis* 13(1): 1–11.

Slocum, J. (n.d.). "Machine Translation at Texas: The Later Years." Linguistics Research Center, University of Texas at Austin. Available at https://liberalarts.utexas.edu/lrc/about/history/machine-translation-at-texas/later-years.php

Smith, T. (June 30, 2018). "More States Opting to 'Robo-Grade' Student Essays by Computer." *NPR*. Transcript available at https://www.npr.org/transcripts/624373367?storyId=624373367?storyId=624373367

Smith, Z. (July 15, 2006). "On the Beginning." *Guardian*. Available at https://www.theguardian.com/books/2006/jul/15/zadiesmith

Springer, S., Buta, P., and Wolf, T. C. (1991). "Automatic Letter Composition for Customer Service." *Proceedings of the Third Conference on Innovative Applications of Artificial*

Intelligence. AAAI. Available at https://www.researchgate.net/publication/221016496_Automatic_Letter_Composition_for_Customer_Service

"Spurned Love Leads to Knitting Invention" (November 13, 2014). *BBC Home.* Nottingham. Available at https://www.bbc.co.uk/nottingham/content/articles/2009/07/20/william_lee_knitting_frame_feature.shtml

Stein, M. I. (1953). "Creativity and Culture." *Journal of Psychology* 36: 311–322.

Stewart, S. (October 15, 2021). "Translators Fight for Credit on Their Own Book Covers." *Publishers Weekly.* Available at https://www.publishersweekly.com/pw/by-topic/industry-news/publisher-news/article/87649-translators-fight-for-credit-on-their-own-book-covers.html

Stokel-Walker, C. (January 18, 2023). "ChatGPT Listed as Author on Research Papers: Many Scientists Disapprove." *Nature.* Available at https://www.nature.com/articles/d41586-023-00107-z

Strachey, C. (1954). "The 'Thinking' Machine." *Encounter* 3(4): 25–31.

Strubell, E., Ganesh, A., and McCallum, A. (2019). "Energy and Policy Considerations for Deep Learning in NLP." Available at https://arxiv.org/pdf/1906.02243.pdf

"Summary of the Berne Convention for the Protection of Literary and Artistic Works (1886)" (n.d.). *World Intellectual Property Organization.* Available at https://www.wipo.int/treaties/en/ip/berne/summary_berne.html

Susskind, D. (2020). *A World Without Work.* Metropolitan.

Susskind, R. (2017). *Tomorrow's Lawyers,* 2nd ed. Oxford University Press.

Susskind, R., and Susskind, D. (2015). *The Future of the Professions.* Oxford University Press.

Swafford, I. (July 27, 2021). "First-of-Its-Kind Stanford Machine Learning Tool Streamlines Student Feedback Process for Computer Science Professors." *Stanford News.* Available at https://news.stanford.edu/2021/07/27/ai-tool-streamlines-feedback-coding-homework/

Swanburg, C. (2021). "Research and Writing." In J. R. Presser, J. Beatson, and G. Chan, eds., *Litigating Artificial Intelligence.* Emond, pp. 505–524.

Swift, J. (1991 [1712]). "A Proposal for Correcting, Improving and Ascertaining the English Tongue." In T. Crowley, *Proper English? Readings in Language, History, and Cultural Identify.* Routledge, p. 37.

Switek, B. (2011). "Mastodon Fossil Throws Up Questions over 'Rapid' Extinction." *Nature.* Available at https://www.nature.com/articles/news.2011.606

Tegmark, M. (2017). *Life 3.0: Being Human in the Age of Artificial Intelligence.* Knopf.

Teitelman, W. (1966). *PILOT: A Step Toward Man–Computer Symbiosis.* MA thesis, Department of Mathematics, Massachusetts Institute of Technology. Available at https://apps.dtic.mil/sti/pdfs/AD0638446.pdf

Temple, E. (June 5, 2012). "A New Edition of 'A Farewell to Arms' Contains over 40 Alternate Endings." *Flavorwire.* Available at https://www.flavorwire.com/305974/a-new-edition-of-a-farewell-to-arms-contains-hemingways-40-alternate-endings

Terrace, H. (1979). *Nim.* Knopf.

Terrell, E. (January 17, 2019). "When a Quote Is Not (Exactly) a Quote: The Business of America Is Business Edition." *Library of Congress Blogs.* Available at https://blogs.loc.gov/inside_adams/2019/01/when-a-quote-is-not-exactly-a-quote-the-business-of-america-is-business-edition/

Theron, D. (July 28, 2022). "Getting Started with Bloom." *Towards Data Science.*

Available at https://towardsdatascience.com/getting-started-with-bloom-9e3295459b65

Thompson, C. (February 18, 2022). "What the History of AI Tells Us About Its Future." *MIT Technology Review.* Available at https://www.technologyreview.com/2022/02/18/1044709/ibm-deep-blue-ai-history/

Thompson, C. (March 15, 2022). "It's Like GPT-3 but for Code—Fun, Fast, and Full of Flaws." *Wired.* Available at https://www.wired.com/story/openai-copilot-autocomplete-for-code/

Thompson, C. (October 13, 2022). "AI Shouldn't Compete with Workers—It Should Supercharge Them." *Wired.* Available at https://www.wired.com/story/ai-shouldnt-compete-with-workers-it-should-supercharge-them-turing-trap/

Thornton, T. P. (1996). *Handwriting in America.* Yale University Press.

Thouin, B. (1982). "The METEO System." In V. Lawson, ed., *Practical Experience of Machine Translation.* North-Holland, pp. 39–44.

Thunström, A. O. (June 30, 2022). "We Asked GPT-3 to Write an Academic Paper About Itself—and Then We Tried to Get It Published." *Scientific American.* Available at https://www.scientificamerican.com/article/we-asked-gpt-3-to-write-an-academic-paper-about-itself-mdash-then-we-tried-to-get-it-published/

Thurman, N., Dörr, K., and Kunert, J. (2017). "When Reporters Get Hands-On with Robo-Writing." *Digital Journalism* 5(10): 1240–1259.

Thurman, N., Lewis, S. C., and Kunert, J., eds. (2021). *Algorithms, Automation, and News.* Routledge.

Tiku, N. (June 11, 2022). "The Google Engineer Who Thinks the Company's AI Has Come to Life." *Washington Post.* Available at https://www.washingtonpost.com/technology/2022/06/11/google-ai-lamda-blake-lemoine/

Tomar, D. (2012). *The Shadow Scholar.* Bloomsbury.

Toral, A. (2019). "Post-Editese: An Exacerbated Translationese." In *Proceedings of Machine Translation Summit XVII, Research Track*, pp. 273–281. Dublin, European Association for Machine Translation.

Tremmel, M. (2011). "What to Make of the Five-Paragraph Theme." *Teaching English in the Two-Year College* 39(1): 29–42.

Trithemius, J. (1974 [1492]). *In Praise of Scribes (De Laude Scriptorum).* Ed. K. Arnold, trans. R. Behrendt. Coronado.

Tsu, J. (2022). *Kingdom of Characters: The Language Revolution That Made China Modern.* Penguin Random House.

Turing, A. (1937). "On Computable Numbers, with an Application to the Entscheidungsproblem." *Proceedings of the London Mathematical Society* 42: 230–265.

Turing, A. (1948). "Intelligent Machinery." National Physical Laboratory. Typescript. Available at https://www.npl.co.uk/getattachment/about-us/History/Famous-faces/Alan-Turing/80916595-Intelligent-Machinery.pdf?lang=en-GB. Also in B. J. Copeland, ed. (2004), *The Essential Turing.* Oxford University Press, pp. 410–432.

Turing, A. (1950). "Computing Machinery and Intelligence." *Mind* 59(236): 433–460.

Turing, A. (May 15, 1951). "Can Digital Computers Think?" BBC Radio Program. Text available in B. J. Copeland, ed. (2004), *The Essential Turing.* Oxford University Press, pp. 482–486.

Turing, A., et al. (January 10, 1952). "Can Automatic Calculating Machines Be Said to Think?" BBC Radio Program. Text available in B. J. Copeland, ed. (2004), *The Essential Turing*. Oxford University Press, pp. 494–506.

Tyson, L. D., and Zysman, J. (2022). "Automation, AI & Work." *Daedalus* 151(2): 256–271.

Udagawa, A. F. (January 1, 2021). "New Year's Resolution: #Namethetranslator." *GLLI*. Available at https://glli-us.org/2021/01/01/new-years-resolution-nam ethetranslator/

"UK Copyright Law: Fact Sheet P-01" (2021). *UK Copyright Service*. Available at https://copyrightservice.co.uk/copyright/p01_uk_copyright_law

Urry, H. L., et al. (2021). "Don't Ditch the Laptop Just Yet: A Direct Replication of Mueller and Oppenheimer's (2014) Study 1 Plus Mini Meta-Analyses Across Similar Studies." *Psychological Science* 32(3): 326–339.

US Copyright Office (2014). *Compendium of US Copyright Office Practices*, 3rd ed. §313.2.

US Food and Drug Administration (n.d.). "When and Why Was FDA Formed?" Available at https://www.fda.gov/about-fda/fda-basics/when-and-why-was-fda-formed

Valand, S. S. (December 19, 2022). "Is It Now That the Living Writing Dies?" *Klassekampen*. Original Norwegian available at https://klassekampen.no/utgave/2022-12-19/debatt-er-det-na-den-levende-skriften-dor1/; English translation through Microsoft Translator.

van Bezooijen, R. (1995). "Sociocultural Aspects of Pitch Differences Between Japanese and Dutch Women." *Language and Speech* 38(3): 253–265.

Vanmassenhove, E., Shterionov, D., and Gwilliam, M. (2021). "Machine Translationese: Effects of Algorithmic Bias on Linguistic Complexity in Machine Translation." *Proceedings of the 16th Conference of the European Chapter of the Association for Computational Linguistics: Main Volume*. Available at https://aclanthology.org/2021.eacl-main.188/

Vara, V. (August 9, 2021). "Ghosts." *The Believer Magazine*. Available at https://www.thebeliever.net/ghosts

Vaswani, A., et al. (2017). "Attention Is All You Need." 31st Conference on Neural Information Processing Systems (NIPS 2017). Available at https://arxiv.org/abs/1706.03762

Vincent, J. (January 12, 2018). "Google 'Fixed' Its Racist Algorithm by Removing Gorillas from Its Image-Labeling Tech." *The Verge*. Available at https://www.theverge.com/2018/1/12/16882408/google-racist-gorillas-photo-recognition-algorithm-ai

Vincent, J. (April 17, 2018). "Watch Jordan Peele Use AI to Make Barack Obama Deliver a PSA About Fake News." *The Verge*. Available at https://www.theverge.com/tldr/2018/4/17/17247334/ai-fake-news-video-barack-obama-jordan-peele-buzzfeed

Vincent, J. (April 10, 2019). "The First AI-Generated Textbook Shows What Robot Writers Are Actually Good At." *The Verge*. Available at https://www.theverge.com/2019/4/10/18304558/ai-writing-academic-research-book-springer-nature-artificial-intelligence

Vincent, J. (October 25, 2022). "Shutterstock Will Start Selling AI-Generated Stock Imagery with Help from OpenAI." *The Verge*. Available at https://www.theverge.com/2022/10/25/23422359/shutterstock-ai-generated-art-openai-dall-e-partnership-contributors-fund-reimbursement

Vitale, T. (February 17, 2013). "'Amory Show' That Shocked America in 1913,

Celebrates 100." *NPR.* Available at https://www.npr.org/2013/02/17/17
2002686/armory-show-that-shocked-america-in-1913-celebrates-100

"Voters Turn Down Ban on Nuclear Arms Work in Massachusetts City." (November
12, 1983). *Washington Post.* Available at https://www.washingtonpost.com/
archive/politics/1983/11/12/voters-turn-down-ban-on-nuclear-arms-work-in-mas-
sachusetts-city/c6e9c205-782e-4dbe-8365-053ae3e46229/

Waldorf Today (n.d.). "7 Benefits of Waldorf's 'Writing to Read' Approach." From
Nelson Waldorf School. Available at https://www.waldorftoday.
com/2018/05/7-benefits-of-waldorfs-writing-to-read-approach/

Walker, M., and Matsa , K. E. (May 21, 2021). "A Third of Large U.S. Newspapers
Experienced Layoffs in 2020, More Than in 2019." *Pew Research Center.*
Available at https://www.pewresearch.org/fact-tank/2021/05/21/a-third-of-large-
u-s-newspapers-experienced-layoffs-in-2020-more-than-in-2019/

Walker, M., and Matsa, K. E. (September 20, 2021). "News Consumption Across
Social Media in 2021." *Pew Research Center.* Available at https://www.pewre-
search.org/journalism/2021/09/20/news-consumption-across-social-
media-in-2021/

Walker, P. R. (November 23, 2015). "The Trials and Triumphs of Leon Dostert '28."
Occidental College. Available at https://www.oxy.edu/magazine/issues/fall-2015/
trials-and-triumphs-leon-dostert-28

Wang, G. (October 20, 2019). "Humans in the Loop: The Design of Interactive AI
Systems." *Stanford University Human-Centered Artificial Intelligence.* Available
at https://hai.stanford.edu/news/humans-loop-design-interactive-ai-
systems

Wardrip-Fruin, N. (September 13, 2006). "The Story of Meehan's *Tale-Spin.*" *Grand
Text Auto.* Available at https://grandtextauto.soe.ucsc.edu/2006/09/13/the-story-of-
meehans-tale-spin/

Warner, J. (2018). *Why They Can't Write.* Johns Hopkins University Press.

Weaver, W. (1949). "Translation." Memorandum. Rockefeller Foundation. Available
at http://gunkelweb.com/coms493/texts/weaver_translation.pdf

Weaver, W. (1964). *Alice in Many Tongues.* University of Wisconsin Press.

Weizenbaum, J. (1966). "ELIZA—A Computer Program for the Study of Natural
Language Communication Between Men and Machines." *Communications of the
ACM* 9: 36–45.

Welbl, J., et al. (2021). "Challenges in Detoxifying Language Models." DeepMind.
Available at https://arxiv.org/pdf/2109.07445.pdf

Wetsman, N. (March 9, 2021). "Google Translate Still Isn't Good Enough for Medical
Instructions." *The Verge.* Available at https://www.theverge.
com/2021/3/9/22319225/google-translate-medical-instructions-unreliable

"What Does Copyright Protect?" (n.d.). *US Copyright Office.* Available at https://
www.copyright.gov/help/faq/faq-protect.html

"What Grades Can AI Get in College?" (n.d.). *EduRef.net.* Available at https://
best-universities.net/features/what-grades-can-ai-get-in-college/

"What Is a Neuron?" (n.d.). *Queensland Brain Institute.* University of Queensland,
Australia. Available at https://qbi.uq.edu.au/brain/brain-anatomy/what-neuron

"When Greek and Latin Ruled" (September 29, 1914). *Harvard Crimson.* Available at
https://www.thecrimson.com/article/1914/9/29/when-greek-and-latin-ruled
-pthe/

White, E. M. (1969). "Writing for Nobody." *College English* 31(2): 166–168.

"Why I Write: 23 Fascinating Quotes from Famous Authors" (March 27, 2014).

Aerogramme Writers' Studio. Available at https://www.aerogrammestudio.com/2014/03/27/why-i-write-23-quotes-famous-authors/

Wiesel, E. (April 14, 1985). "Why Would I Write: Making No Become Yes." *New York Times.* Available at https://www.nytimes.com/1985/04/14/books/why-would-i-write-making-no-become-yes.html

Wiggers, K. (November 23, 2022). "Harvey, Which Uses AI to Answer Legal Questions, Lands Cash from OpenAI." *TechCrunch.* Available at https://techcrunch.com/2022/11/23/harvey-which-uses-ai-to-answer-legal-questions-lands-cash-from-openai/

Wiggers, K. (December 10, 2022). "OpenAI's Attempts to Watermark AI Text Hit Limits." *TechCrunch.* Available at https://techcrunch.com/2022/12/10/openais-attempts-to-watermark-ai-text-hit-limits/

Wilk, E. (March 28, 2021). "What AI Can Teach Us About the Myth of Human Genius." *The Atlantic.* Available at https://www.theatlantic.com/culture/archive/2021/03/pharmako-ai-possibilities-machine-creativity/618435/

Wilson, C. (November 6, 2008). "Introducing President 'Barracks Boatman'—Updated." *Slate.* Available at https://slate.com/news-and-politics/2008/11/introducing-president-barracks-boatman-updated.html

Winerip, M. (April 22, 2012). "Facing a Robo-Grader? Just Keep Obfuscating Mellifluously." *New York Times.* Available at https://www.nytimes.com/2012/04/23/education/robo-readers-used-to-grade-test-essays.html

Wolf, G. (1995). "The Curse of Xanadu." *Wired.* Available at https://www.wired.com/1995/06/xanadu/

"Workshop on Foundation Models" (August 23–24, 2021). Stanford University Institute for Human-Centered Artificial Intelligence. Available at https://crfm.stanford.edu/workshop.html

Wozniak, J. M. (1978). *English Composition in Eastern Colleges, 1850–1940.* University Press of America.

Wright, L. (n.d.). "The History of Microsoft Word." *CORE.* Available at https://www.core.co.uk/blog/blog/history-microsoft-word

Wu, Y., et al. (2016). "Google's Neural Machine Translation System: Bridging the Gap Between Human and Machine Translation." Available at https://arxiv.org/abs/1609.08144

Xu, Wei (2019). "Toward Human-Centered AI: A Perspective from Human–Computer Interaction." *Interactions* 26(4): 42–46.

Yan, D., Rupp, A. A., and Foltz, P. W., eds. (2020). *Handbook of Automated Scoring: Theory into Practice.* Chapman and Hall/CRC.

Yates, J. (1989). *Control Through Communication.* Johns Hopkins University Press.

"Year of China: Introduction to Chinese Characters" (n.d.). *Brown University.* Available at https://www.brown.edu/about/administration/international-affairs/year-of-china/language-and-cultural-resources/introduction-chinese-characters/introduction-chinese-characters

Zacharias, T., Taklikar, A., and Giryes, R. (n.d.). "Extending the Vocabulary of Fictional Languages Using Neural Networks." Available at https://arxiv.org/pdf/2201.07288.pdf

Zafón, C. R. (n.d.). "Why I Write." *Carlos Ruiz Zafón.* Available at https://www.carlosruizzafon.co.uk/landing-page/carlos-ruiz-zafon/carlos-ruiz-zafon-why-i-write/

Zedelius, C. M., and Schooler, J. W. (2020). "Capturing the Dynamics of Creative

References

Daydreaming." In D. D. Preiss, D. Cosmelli, and J. C. Kaufman, eds., *Creativity and the Wandering Mind*. Academic, pp. 55–72.

Zeitchik, S. (November 26, 2021). "We Asked a Computer Program to Imitate Gay Talese's Writing. Then We Asked Talese What He Thought." *Washington Post*. Available at https://www.washingtonpost.com/technology/2021/11/26/sudowrite-gpt3-talese-imitate/

Zhang, Q.-x. (2016). "Translator's Voice in Translated Texts." *Journal of Literature and Art Studies* 6(2): 178–185. Available at http://www.davidpublisher.com/Public/uploads/Contribute/568c7f57043fe.pdf

Zhou, B. (n.d.). "Artificial Intelligence and Copyright Protection—Judicial Practice in Chinese Courts." Available at https://www.wipo.int/export/sites/www/about-ip/en/artificial_intelligence/conversation_ip_ai/pdf/ms_china_1_en.pdf

Zimmer, B. (January 13, 2011). "Auto(in)correct." *New Yok Times Magazine*. Available at https://www.nytimes.com/2011/01/16/magazine/16FOB-onlanguage-t.html

Zimmer, C. (June 20, 2014). "This Is Your Brain on Writing." *New York Times*. Available at https://www.nytimes.com/2014/06/19/science/researching-the-brain-of-writers.html

INDEX

abstracts: history of, 107–8; human
  vs. AI-generated, 173
ACE (Automated Computing Engine),
  53
AI (artificial intelligence). *See* bias in
  AI; Dartmouth Conference;
  disclosure of AI input; explainable
  AI; Turing
AI21 Labs, 71, 169
AI Roadmap, 57
AlexNet, 61
ALPAC (Automatic Language
  Processing Advisory Committee),
  85–86
alphabet, development of, 7–8
AlphaFold (DeepMind), 64
AlphaFold 2 (DeepMind), 64
AlphaGo (DeepMind), 62–63, 64,
  137
Analytical Engine, 52
Andreasen, Nancy, 138, 140, 141
Arabic writing, 7, 8. *See also* Semitic
  languages
Aristides the Just, 6
Aristotle, xii, xvi, 141, 146
ARPANET, 58, 59, 158
art generated by AI, 145–46; and

intellectual property rights, 227;
  social value of, 146. *See also*
  authenticity; *The Next
  Rembrandt*; *Portrait of Edmund
  Belamy*
Article Forge, 170
artificial general intelligence (AGI),
  xvii
artificial intelligence-mediated
  communication (AI-MC), 157
Asimov, Isaac, xvii, 233
authenticity, xxvi, 142–43, 234
author: etymology of word, 16–17;
  vs. writer, 15–16. *See also*
  copyright
autocomplete, xix-xx, 181
autocorrect, 158–60, 209
Automated Insights, 115–16, 117
automation, xvi, xxix, 43, 59, 112,
  113–14
automation vs. augmentation, 178,
  184, 200, 229, 231–32

BABEL (Basic Automatic BS Essay
  Language Generator), 44
Babel Fish, 88
Bach, Johann Sebastian, 143–144